Feminist International Relations

An Unfinished Journey

The impact of feminism on international relations in the past fifteen years has been enormous. In this book Christine Sylvester presents her own career as a journey within the larger journey that scholarly feminism has made in the field of International Relations.

The introductory section sets the context of the journey in International Relations as a field and in key works by Jean Elshtain, Cynthia Enloe, and Ann Tickner that helped carve out a distinctly feminist International Relations. Twelve of Sylvester's essays are then grouped in three sections. The first, "Sightings", features works that reveal the presence and effects of gender in international politics. Next, "Sitings" considers locations where gender can come into International Relations through innovative feminist methodologies. Finally, "Citings" considers a range of contemporary work in feminist International Relations and suggests where the scholarly journey needs to go in the future.

This unusual and wide-ranging book will both guide and challenge scholars and students of international relations theory, gender studies, and postcolonial studies.

CHRISTINE SYLVESTER is Professor of Women, Gender, Development at the Institute of Social Studies, The Hague, Netherlands. Her publications include *Producing Women and Progress in Zimbabwe: Narratives of Identity and Work from the 1980s* (2000), *Feminist Theory and International Relations in a Postmodern Era* (1994), and *Zimbabwe: The Terrain of Contradictory Development* (1991).

Feminist International Relations

CAMBRIDGE STUDIES IN INTERNATIONAL RELATIONS

Series list continues after index

Feminist International Relations

An Unfinished Journey

Christine Sylvester

Institute of Social Studies, The Hague

CAMBRIDGE
UNIVERSITY PRESS

PUBLISHED BY THE PRESS SYNDICATE OF THE UNIVERSITY OF CAMBRIDGE
The Pitt Building, Trumpington Street, Cambridge, United Kingdom

CAMBRIDGE UNIVERSITY PRESS
The Edinburgh Building, Cambridge CB2 2RU, UK
40 West 20th Street, New York, NY 10011-4211, USA
477 Williamstown Road, Port Melbourne, VIC 3207, Australia
Ruiz de Alarcón 13, 28014 Madrid, Spain
Dock House, The Waterfront, Cape Town 8001, South Africa

http://www.cambridge.org

© Christine Sylvester 2002

First published 2002

Printed in the United Kingdom at the University Press, Cambridge

Typeface Palatino 10/12.5 pt.   *System* LATEX 2$_\varepsilon$ [TB]

A catalogue record for this book is available from the British Library.

Library of Congress Cataloguing in Publication data

Sylvester, Christine, 1949–
Feminist international relations : an unfinished journey / Christine Sylvester.
p. cm. – (Cambridge studies in international relations ; 77)
Includes bibliographical references and index.
ISBN 0 521 79177 4 (hardback) ISBN 0 521 79627 X (paperback)
1. International relations – Philosophy.   2. Feminist theory.   I. Title.   II. Series.
JZ1253.2 .S95   2002
327.1′01 – dc21   2002025636

ISBN 0 521 79177 4 hardback
ISBN 0 521 79627 X paperback

To Karen Mingst

Contents

Contents

x

Acknowledgments

With fifteen years of work represented in this volume, there are many, many people to thank for their assistance and support – enough people to fill another book. The worry of leaving someone out has forced me into global and sweeping expressions of gratitude where I would wish to be more personal. One person I must mention is Professor Karen Mingst, my Ph.D. supervisor and until recently head of the University of Kentucky Department of Political Science. I was Karen's first Ph.D. student and I know I had her worried on more than one occasion as I journeyed toward an acceptable outcome. She and her colleagues were lovely and they were true to American political science. That I then went in a different direction after completing my degree, departing American IR/political science in practice, spirit, and lately in residence, does not signify, will never mean to me, that they were "wrong." I am proud of the training I received and call upon it often when formulating my own research puzzles and when addressing behavioralist critiques of post-positivist research. Karen imparted many words of wisdom that still resonate with me and which I pass on to my graduate students (e.g., "write at least three pages a day; always have something out under review; keep up your momentum"). How lucky I was to have a woman mentor at all – and Karen in particular – at a time of few women in political science!

Gettysburg College, where I worked in the first half of the 1980s, encouraged my determination to go to Southern Africa. If it were not for generous funding provided each summer for five years, I would probably not have become a Zimbabweanist – and I cannot imagine such a fate! Thanks as well to Nelson Moyo and the Economics Department of the University of Zimbabwe – and more recently, Rudo Gaidzanwa – for nurturing that interest along. As my work on feminist IR and on

Zimbabwean political economy began to intersect in the early 1990s, Northern Arizona University took up the position of generous financier. It funded summers in Zimbabwe and granted leave for senior associate memberships at St. Antony's College, Oxford University (1990 and 1995) and a senior visiting fellow post in the School of International Affairs at the University of Southern California (1991). Although I moved on from NAU, I never visit the USA without visiting my friends in Flagstaff.

The Australian National University supported my work in the mid- to late 1990s, through two visiting fellow appointments and then through a permanent position at the National Centre for Development Studies. Despite years of research on development issues in Zimbabwe, it took the unfaltering encouragement of Ron Duncan and Peter Larmour for me to add "development person" to a roster of other identities. Australia has influenced my life in many ways I did not anticipate when I first went to the ANU in 1994. It is there that I met my Swiss partner, Roland Bleiker, a man whose enthusiasm for my work and bright ideas for his own research enliven and enrich my life. Arizona is one homeplace and now Canberra and Brisbane form another.

The Netherlands is becoming yet a third home. I am now at the Institute of Social Studies in The Hague – four continents, several fields, and a few languages from my start at the University of Kentucky. ISS colleagues are a delight – supportive and kind – and the many pleasures of the Netherlands continue to unfold before me. The journey to Europe puts me closer now to a valued British and Nordic support network that includes Vivienne Jabri and Fiona Sampson in the UK, Erika Svedberg, Gion Koch, and Annica Kronsell in Sweden, and Osmo Apunen, Tarja Varynen, and Helena Rytovuori-Apunen in Finland.

In the category of special thanks for long-term support are my mother and my good friends Kevin Pyle and Karen Pugliesi. Also there are some key art people – Peter Garlake, Alyce Jordan, Helen Topliss, Barbara Murray, Derek Huggins, and Helen Lieros – whose sightings have changed my life and whose encouragement has helped put art into my work. Finally, my gratitude to Steve Smith and the six reviewers of this manuscript for Cambridge University Press, and to all the feminists who provide me with inspiration – Jean Bethke Elshtain, Cynthia Enloe, and Ann Tickner prime among them.

Part I
Introduction

1   Looking backwards and forwards at International Relations around feminism

For the academic field of International Relations (IR), the decade of the 1980s effectively opened with Hedley Bull's *The Anarchical Society: A Study of Order in World Politics* (1977) and/or with Kenneth Waltz's neorealist *Theory of International Politics* (1979) – depending on one's geographical and philosophical site in the field. The decade closed on a note that opened all of IR to radical departures from the general tenor (and tenure) of the Bull and Waltz tomes: it closed with Cynthia Enloe's *Bananas, Beaches, and Bases: Making Feminist Sense of International Relations* (1989). Elements of the new colors and tones washing into the field had been foreshadowed two years earlier in Jean Bethke Elshtain's *Women and War* (1987). The feminists were not the only challengers about (e.g., Ashley and Walker, 1990a; Der Derian and Shapiro, 1989), but they would turn into one of the most sustaining groups at IR's timbered doors.

Bull had presented the realist case for basing IR on the notion of an international society of sovereign states through which order is maintained and justice struggled over in world politics (see also Bull and Watson, 1986). Waltz had re-sited classical realist theory beyond the realm of states and society; he wrote about the systemic ordering principle of anarchy in international relations and its necessary spawns – rationality and self-help. In contrast to these key mainstream works of the decade, Enloe asked us everywhere to give up thinking that international relations consisted of peopleless states, abstract societies, static ordering principles, or even theories about them, and begin looking for the many people, places, and activities of everyday international politics. Locate those who make the world go round, she said, and cite them.

The decade's triad of society, system, and then (at the last moment) people turned on their heads the order of Waltz's earlier

3

levels-of-analysis notions in *Man, the State, and War* (1959), and Bull's (1969:26) assessment that a researcher pushing for science in IR was like a sex-deprived nun. Man as agent of international relations was out of most IR sights in Bull's and especially Waltz's books at the dawn of the 1980s. Enloe brought him back in as central to, and not to be lauded within, the inherited traditions of all IR. "He" reached between states and into society and system in power-laden and gender-enforcing ways. It may have been fashionable in the 1980s to block him out of the picture, but his marks and traces were everywhere. More, a secret was now out too: he was not alone in the power matrices of international politics.

There were many events of note in between those years and those books. The American field set its course around *Neorealism and its Critics* (Keohane, 1986), a compendium of arguments lined up for and against Waltz's move away from classical realism, for and against his scorn for the agency-oriented thinking of early Idealism. Its editor, Robert Keohane, was a sympathetic disputant in the argument. He was concerned that his preferred approach of neoliberal institutionalism, which sites circumstances of cooperation under anarchy, not be overruled; but he was also willing to admit that states were self-helping entities working under conditions of anarchy. Others who were brought into that dispute offered radical departures from the types of argument the field had hitherto heard; they intoned critical theory (Cox, 1986) and, most especially, postmodernism (Ashley, 1986). Those approaches, which Keohane called "reflectivist," would come to occupy a greater place in 1990s IR than might have been anticipated or desired by neorealists and other critics, who kept their arguments within pre-established epistemological boundaries as they debated.

Meanwhile, Elshtain veered off to argue in *Women and War* (1987) that what we hear of war comes to us as stories deeded by acceptable sources – acceptable in the sense of being associated with the Just Warriors entitled in most societies to engage in or own war. Certain other participants, deemed Beautiful Souls, are continuously disallowed war-telling by virtue of being assigned the homefront, where their protection becomes one reason men will go to war at all. Though the places in the drama seem set and the citations to authority in order, Elshtain taught us that the empirical and narrative realities of war are something different. Her treatment of a major activity of international relations put her work inside IR. Her insistence on sighting women within and around a main topic of the field, however, sited *Women and War* outside the central concerns of that American neorealist (versus . . .) moment. The IR inside

4

initially won: Elshtain was not part of the Keohane book, even though she had several IR-relevant writings preceding *Women and War* (e.g., 1985). No other woman of IR was included in that volume either. The outside, though, later folded inwards: a scant ten years on, Elshtain's book had received so many citations in IR literature that it could be considered part of the canon.

Across British IR, the decade of the 1980s was absorbed by ongoing work in the classical realist tradition, particularly around security, as well as overlapping areas of international society, normative theory, and international political economy. The English school of realism and society, spun, in part, off Bull's *Anarchical Society* (1977), also seemed to prevail for a while in Australia, where Bull began. This approach did not capture American IR's science-oriented audience. Even in the UK there was considerable talk during the 1980s of an inter-paradigm debate in which no single IR theory was seen to dominate the field. Rather, three paradigms were sighted as competitor streams of thinking: realism/neorealism; globalism/pluralism; and neo-Marxism/structuralism (Banks, 1985). The first two "paradigms" were common to US and British IR. Critical theory, sited within the third, neo-Marxist "paradigm," became the British contender for the more radical wing of IR. It poised itself against continental/North American postmodernism – against what John Baylis and Nick Rengger (1992:16) refer to as radical interpretivism. It made Habermasian efforts to complete the modern project by creating the social components of a post-Westphalian world (Hoffmann, 1987; Linklater, 1980, 1990); or it promoted Gramscian interpretations of hegemony and anti-hegemonic struggle (Cox, 1986).

During these same years of the middle to late 1980s, a few British women wrote IR, some radically and critically, some less so. The late Susan Strange (e.g., 1982, 1984), for instance, was a giantess of IR, making enormous contributions to international political economy. She did not engage in feminist research at all, but others did contribute to the establishment of a feminist IR tradition (e.g., *Millennium*, 1988; Grant and Newland, 1991). And in the early 1990s, Sandra Whitworth (1994), a Canadian trained in the UK, added a feminist voice to the British critical theory tradition, through her study of gender issues in international organizations. Today the feminist IR tradition flourishes in the UK among British and transplanted scholars, as the citations throughout this volume indicate.

British IR of all stripes has tended toward philosophical and historical methods, irrespective of the puzzles under consideration. In Britain, one sees them referred to as "classical" or "historical" (see Rengger, 1988), whereas North American behavioralists speak of "traditional" methods (e.g., Kaplan, 1969) carrying over from an era when the fledgling field of IR was concerned, on both sides of the Atlantic, with prescriptive theory and diplomatic history. In New World IR, physics became (and sometimes still is) the exemplary, though difficult to emulate, model of positivist research. Steve Smith (1996:17) argues that positivism, in fact, infused the entire field of IR, wherever located, owing to widespread belief in a "natural science methodology . . . tied to an empiricist episte-mology: together these result[ed] in a very restricted range of permis-sible ontological claims." And these restricted claims – which did not allow for the notion, for example, that epistemology might be secondary to ontology, emancipation might be a value guiding research on what is out there, or knowledge might best be seen as a powerful social practice rather than product of individual rationality – determined what could be studied by IR. In other words, they "determined what kinds of things existed in international relations" (Smith, 1996:11).

Positivism made its mark on the Anglo-American field of IR during the Cold War but was under challenge from the 1980s to early 1990s. IR's so-called Third Debate (Lapid, 1989) forced the canons of AmerEu-rocentric realism and positivism to defend the right to define vistas of international relations and set the epistemological tools required for analyzing them. New genres, such as postmodernism and feminism, clamored for IR to render an account of its knowledge and methods, arguing that the field could boast neither an impressive intellectual for-tune for its seventy or so years of existence nor a legacy of inclusiveness and justice. Critics often fingered positivism as the culprit and argued that only new projects of theorizing could set the field right. Thrown on the defensive, conventional IR discovered that the attackers could not be killed off by a few shots of the can(n)on or made to wither from lack of sympathy. American IR recoiled against Marxian world systems and critical theory, French-inspired radical interpretivism, historical so-ciological underminings of realist versions of the state, and a phalanx of differently sited feminists brandishing standpoint and postmodernist epistemologies. Some British conventionals outfitted themselves for bat-tle with postmodernism and armed even against "trendy" feminism (Coker, 1990). These were the sites of IR's philosophy and culture wars. In many ways, they remain so.

The field's big *faux pas* of the 1980s fed and helped inspire the many contestations. Few realists of any ilk would have argued that states

6

voluntarily go out of business and dismantle their territorial authorities. This the Soviet Union did. Few analysts imagined eerie slapstick moments in November 1989, when an Iron Curtain fell before an onslaught of Trabant-driving shopper-armies from the East. Few security experts would have anticipated that ethnic cleansing would soon be on the agenda in Europe, forty years after a major war and after an international tribunal had supposedly rooted it out. Fewer still might have imagined that rape would appear as a war-fighting strategy in a series of European wars conducted during the nuclear age; or that considerable diplomatic energy would soon go into wrangling over the military use of landmines.

The confluence of IR's theoretical weaknesses and a world seemingly out of order led two established figures in American IR nervously to admit in 1988 – even before the fall of the Soviet Empire – that:

> Many students of international relations, like the present authors, were once convinced that they were participants in a quest for theory which would, in time, unravel the arcane secrets of world politics. That quest would deepen our theoretical insights as we tested our ideas according to the canons of science. Knowledge and understanding would be gradual and cumulative, but, in the end, they might even enable us to overcome age-old scourges like war. In subsequent decades, we have witnessed changes in discourse in the field, the development of intriguing and ingenious methodologies, the creation of new forms of data, and the diffusion of American social science techniques throughout the world. Yet, our understanding of key phenomena is expanding only very modestly, if at all.   (Ferguson and Mansbach, 1988:3)

A touching and honest expression of malaise, a statement of this type was rare in mainstream IR circles, though appropriate to the times. Three years later, the same writers would revisit their anguish and admonish the field to rethink central concepts, cease endless debating aimed at determining a winning side, "venture beyond our field's familiar boundaries," and "tolerate the effrontery of others messing about in *our* intellectual territory" (Ferguson and Mansbach, 1991:383).

As the 1980s shaded further into the 1990s, some American and British academics drew closer around concerns of theory, ethics, and constitutive as opposed to explanatory approaches to research. Smith (1995:28) describes the English school, for example, as moving to ask "whether the meanings and interpretations of international society are constitutive of that society or are mere ciphers for structural forces," a question that gets at the issue of what we should be studying in IR. He asserts that this query has also turned up among American schools of realism in the post-Cold War period, as attention has been focused by some on clashes between cultures instead of between states (Huntington, 1993). Baylis and Rengger (1992:8) claim more broadly that there has been transcontinental overlap in two areas recently: around choice-theoretic frameworks in some cases and around various critical schools of thinking that challenge positivism.

The constructivism to which Smith alludes is, however, the new pivot point on both sides of the Atlantic, and of particular importance, along with rational choice frameworks, to American IR. The question underlying much constructivist work is how actors (agents), issue-areas, and structures of international relations are shaped or co-shaped by ideas, norms, rules, and values that are not, strictly speaking, rational (Burch and Denemark, 1997; Dessler, 1989; Finnemore, 1996; Wendt, 1995, 1999; Forum, 2000). Richard Price and Christian Reus-Smit (1998:263) argue pointedly that "[i]f the principal axis of debate during the 1980s lay between rationalists and early critical theorists, the major line of contestation now lies between rationalists and constructivists." To tender this argument, constructivism is made into an umbrella big enough to shelter postmodernist and some modernist contingents of IR (Price and Reus-Smit, 1998:267). From the perspective of constructivism's critics (e.g., Bleiker, 2000a; Campbell, 1996; George, 1994), however, there is no natural chumminess in such an enterprise. Critics argue that constructivism smuggles postmodernist thinking about the social construction of meaning, identity, and politics into positivist-inclined IR treatments of state and nonstate behaviors, in ways that kill off the partner. Constructivists respond that the critics have been so absorbed by metatheoretical concerns that they have offered the field no substantive research agenda. This has produced a void that is now filled by those who seek to address longstanding questions in the newer ways, and who find "answers that upon close analysis are often much more measured and persuasively defended than some of the claims that leapt out of the metatheoretical fire" (Price and Reus-Smit, 1998:271). The thrusts and ripostes persist into this millennial post-Third Debate era; only now there is even contestation about where the axes of shifting difference lie.

Enter feminism

It was during the destabilizing decade of the 1980s that feminists, our main focus of consideration here, began individual and collective journeys of self-aware identity, compensatory research, and climbs steeply uphill to recognition by the historical keepers of IR. We did not spring forth like Hobbes' famous mushrooms, with no parentage, no debts (Di Stefano, 1983). The contemporary international women's movement laid the political and epistemological groundwork in the 1960s; by the 1980s, feminists were numerous enough, confident enough, as well as sufficiently weathered, titled, and published to have women's studies programs in place, women and politics specialists on staff, and a stable of writings to consult – and internal debates to display (Sylvester, 1994a). Conferences and workshops introduced feminisms to mainstream IR audiences in London, Los Angeles, and Boston. By 1990 there was a Feminist Theory and Gender Studies (FTGS) section of the International Studies Association, followed by a similar section in the British International Studies Association. These organizations gave feminist scholars social and political visibility in the corridors of a field that Ann Tickner has often spoken of as lined mostly with "white men in ties." Indeed, Tickner carried forward the torch lit by Elshtain and Enloe with her important work on *Gender in International Relations: Feminist Perspectives on Achieving Global Security* (1992).

The volumes by Elshtain, Enloe, and Tickner offered sustained arguments about topics central to IR and revealed theoretical deficiencies across the field at large. No single-authored book emerging from any other country in the 1980s and 1990s would carry the intellectual stature and enduring importance to feminist IR of this trio. Most feminist IR writings of 1980–1993, while impressive, made contributions of a more confined scope, through articles, book chapters, edited volumes, or books focusing on somewhat narrower phenomena in the field than Elshtain, Enloe, and Tickner addressed (e.g., Cohn, 1987; Grant and Newland, 1991; Jaquette, 1982; *Millennium*, 1988; Peterson, 1992; Runyan and Peterson, 1991; Staudt, 1987; Stiehm, 1984). By contrast, in *Women and War* Elshtain took up the core IR topic of war while also discussing, in passing, what she called the dubious claims of IR knowledge. Tickner's *Gender in International Relations* also worked at the core to consider issues of security within a reappraisal of the realist tradition. Enloe became the great sighter of women in unexplored (because often unnoted) realms of the international and its relations. Her *Bananas, Beaches, and Bases* and Elshtain's and Tickner's two tomes, comprise work that the FTGS has deemed "eminent." In 1994, I contributed *Feminist Theory and International Relations in a Postmodern Era* (Sylvester, 1994a). It took on the field's formative debates to indicate what was missed, glossed over, or could not be fully submerged in discussions that ostensibly did not site women and gender in IR. Like the other three encapsulators of early feminist IR, it also drew attention to some of the modifications of IR theory that would arise if field lenses were trained (also) on excluded dynamics, such as decision making in feminist peace camps and processes of international political economy around Zimbabwean cooperatives.

There were various reactions to this first major wave of feminist IR. A few IR principals showed immediate interest. Keohane (1989a), for example, who had been Ann Tickner's Ph.D. supervisor, read early feminist IR work and sought to incorporate some of it into neoliberal institutionalism. Thomas Biersteker (1989) asked feminists to provide a distinctive construction of international security to contrast with a neorealist one. Richard Ashley and R.B.J. Walker (1990a) edited a special issue of *International Studies Quarterly* in which they named feminism as part of dissident IR and women as part of the margins the field shunned. Some readily referred to feminist IR writings when discussing new issues in the field (e.g., Brown, 1994; George, 1994; Goldstein, 1994; Halliday, 1988; Neufeld, 1995; Smith, 1992). Yet judging by the bibliographies framing many works, one could come away from IR texts of the time not realizing that feminism was around at all. Even among the interested parties, it has rarely been the case that sympathizers have adjusted their models or modes of approaching international relations to reflect lessons learned from feminist thinking. Citations often bunch feminists like daisies in a bouquet; it is correct to nod to them and then move on to name discipline-identified people and *their* new theoretical approaches (e.g., Linklater, 1992).

Tickner (1997) argues that there is a difficult relationship between feminist and conventional IR, owing to differences in ontological and epistemological approaches as well as differences in power. IR generally poses international relations in abstract and unitary terms, while feminists are mostly attuned to the social relations of the international, which I refer to as relations international. Feminists tend to see aspects of sociality – positive or negative in their outcomes for women and other groups in the international system – as the reality of international relations, just as neorealists see very little (and then often irritable) sociality in an anarchic state system. Feminists are also methodological innovators in the field, roundly preferring ethnographic approaches over hypothesis testing, and leaning on philosophical ancestors among feminist thinkers as well as the oft-cited men of political thought. Feminist research programs aim first to reveal places where gender and women are located in international relations and then to offer compensatory versions of theory and practice that are less partial and more just, while also highly central to feminist and/or IR knowledge.

To many conventional analysts within IR, feminism rings in the ears but is not an enterprise to be rung in as a full partner. Feminist IR has some power to command citation, but it sometimes does not receive proper credit for its ideas. To illustrate this point, consider Tickner's (1997:614) claim that "[a]lmost all feminists who write about international relations use gender in a social constructivist sense." Her position is close to the one offered by Smith (1995:27), who sees that "[m]ost of the work of postmodernists and critical theorists, and that of some feminists, fits into this broad category of constitutive theory." Constructivism, though, is routinely credited to Alexander Wendt (1987), Nicholas Onuf (1989), John Ruggie (1983), and Walter Carlsnaes (1992), and not to feminists. The possibility that some of those seen as (merely also) fitting the category may have helped introduce aspects of constructivism to IR, as is arguably the case with Elshtain's *Women and War* – which is about the social constitution of gender through ideas carried in war stories – is not mentioned, let alone explored. All-embracing constructivism, therefore, comes out as fathered, like most IR.

A similar situation confronts feminists interested in issues of culture and identity. A new body of work challenges the usual tendency in the field to make universalist statements about states, sovereignty, anarchy, foreign policy, politics, conflict, and so on (Chay, 1990; Goldstein and Keohane, 1993; Huntington, 1993; Klotz, 1995; Lapid and Kratochwil, 1996; Linklater, 1998; Walker, 1988). Some of it takes to heart postcolonial literatures that answer back to AmerEuropean histories of imperialism (e.g., Alker, 1992; Chan, 1993; Darby, 1997, 1998; Doty, 1996; Kothari, 1988); but since the postcolonial tradition of scholarship comes from Indian-based subaltern studies and the analysis of fiction written from many Third World perspectives, it has not yet made its mark on an IR concerned with heroic western topics (Sylvester, 1999c, 1999d). Similarly missing in much of the new IR culture literature is gender analysis. The work offers little of the feminist sense that men and women (as decision makers, culture objects/viewers/shapers, participants in transnational movements, citizens, and so on) often inhabit different cultures, idea-realms, and social positions within international relations (which is why they see things differently) and within their own nation-states (see Cohn, 1987; Enloe, 1989, 1993; McGlen and Sarkees, 1993; Sylvester, 1990, 1998a; Tickner, 1996). Culture and its accoutrements can thus turn up, at this late date in IR, as "innocently" ungendered – and sometimes ethnocentric.

Meanwhile, neoliberal institutionalism carries on about cooperative elements of the system without writing about failings of cooperation *vis-à-vis* women serving international relations from inside international institutions and regimes – though exactly these shortcomings were pointed out. The failure to respond to feminist arguments is not unusual in IR. In this case, Keohane (1998) claims he did his best to encourage feminists to join neoliberal institutionalism and received in turn only antipathy to his proposed alliance. It was not antipathy, exactly: I indicated the ways institutionalist cooperation and reciprocity parted company with feminist understandings of these processes (Sylvester, 1994a). Keohane did not respond. That there have been few if any feminists taking up his proposition says something about the commandeering attitude of IR *vis-à-vis* feminism. It also reveals reluctance in some quarters to embrace a mission that entails bringing feminist questions to IR rather than IR into feminism. The latter point needs clarification.

It is safe to say that all feminists involved with IR are appalled at the field for systematically excluding the theoretical and practical concerns that feminist theory raises to visibility. Some of us, though, do not seek to improve the flawed product line called IR so much as to take off in new directions altogether, because a marriage of feminist ways of thinking and doing research with IR's positivism appears doomed. We believe that a new international relations tradition is needed to accommodate and theorize people, places, authorities, and activities that IR does not sight or cite. IR would then become a site where feminist questions could be (also) asked about gender, sexuality, bodies, travel, difference, identity, voice, subjectivity, and patriarchy (see e.g., Harding, 1998; Weedon, 1999) in spaces of the world where social relations breach boundaries and spill out internationally. To find those places and work analytically within them, we "do" IR as transversal and liminal *vis-à-vis* philosophy, anthropology, literary and art theory, women's studies, cultural studies, postcolonial studies, history, psychoanalytic theory, and the like. Of course we have our differences: Enloe is a standpoint feminist and I incline toward postmodern feminism; Elshtain gracefully combines the two in *Women and War*. We have each been redoing international relations by doing something that carries IR echoes but is not embedded in IR frameworks. And, although our views on ontology, epistemology, scholarly style, and citational authority differ, these differences are small compared with those that set our thinking apart from most of IR.

Others among us assist IR to see that feminist theorizing and methods can bring missing vistas to the field's usual outlook. Tickner is a specialist in IR who recognizes its shortcomings and wants to infuse the field with feminist sensitivity. From a perch within, she presents feminist critiques of IR knowledge and practice and also seeks to strengthen IR so it can advance progressive agendas. The approach she takes is bolstered by Lara Stancich's (1998) argument that feminist IR is marginalized exactly because it is too keen to ground itself in feminist epistemologies and agendas and is therefore insufficiently attuned to IR, theoretically and practically.

At times there can be a fine line between feminist questions in IR and IR questions in feminism and other fields, and some of us have been known to go back and forth between the two. Yet there are research implications raised by work that brings feminism to IR relative to research that makes IR a subset of feminism. Posing a feminist question in IR maintains the authority and legitimacy of the father field, even as it seeks to help it wise up. Turning IR, in part at least, into a set of questions within feminism has the effect of "provincializing" much of IR *vis-à-vis* frameworks that foreground subaltern *and* world analyses (borrowed from Chakrabarty, 1992). Both approaches deal with issues we can associate with IR, such as war, peace, trade, cooperation, and international development. The departure points are there, though: those who work with feminist questions brought to IR allow that the field has contributed work that needs feminist enhancings and alterations; those who look at IR questions in feminism find the constitution of IR such that it cannot handle important feminist issues, such as rape as a war-fighting strategy.

In some sites of analysis, neither a feminist question in IR nor an IR question in feminism has been raised at all. Studies of international society are surprisingly silent on feminist thinking. I have yet to come across a sustained critique of Bull's *Anarchical Society* that raises questions about the salience of gender and/or women to his constructs of international sociality, to say nothing of an effort to move explicitly beyond Bull and into a feminist theoretical framework for international society. A special issue of *Millennium* entitled "Beyond International Society" (1992; see also Dunne, 1995) took up a variety of premises and problems of international society, but dropped the gender ball. Current

American rational choice research is not especially gender sensitive either. Feminist scholars rarely get into that fray, finding IR's preoccupations with rationality decidedly masculinist (Tickner, 1988), and game theory "the opposite of relational and the context dependent" (Fierke, 1999:405).

As well, despite laudable efforts in IR to revisit the history of the field with the tools of today, women, gender, and feminism still go missing. A panel at the International Studies Association meetings 2000 presented an impressive line-up of field historians (e.g., Tim Dunne, 1998; Brian Schmidt, 1998; Robert Vitale, 2000); but none among them so much as hinted at the possibility that women may have been *involved* in originary moments of "our" field, or that gender issues may have been *neglected* as the field's knowledge coalesced. Another panel showcased critical approaches to IR around another all-men cast of Steve Smith, Robert Cox, Rob Walker, Richard Ashley, and Yosef Lapid. Feminist IR analysis is critical in the broad sense of the term, and should have been represented on the broadly based panel. Smith mentioned the oversight; other panellists did not.

If we scan horizon lines, we can find more robust cases of feminist interest and actions outside the usual, and until now, dominant USA–UK orbit. In Australia, the department of IR at the Australian National University – the only field-specific department in the country –became devoted in the late 1990s to research on the Asia-Pacific region; thereafter it gave only passing attention to feminist IR. Scholars located elsewhere in Australia and around the ANU, however, continued to produce feminist IR/IR feminist work (e.g., Bleiker, 2000c; Pettman, 1996a; Sylvester, 1998a). Feminist IR/IR feminism is alive in Sweden (Aggestam et al., 1997), in pockets of Austria and Germany (Kreisky and Sauer, 1997; DVPW Kongress, 2000; *Femina Politica*, 2000), in the Netherlands (Ling, 2001; Marchand et al., 1998), at the University of Tampere in Finland, which publishes the journal *Kosmopolis*, and elsewhere. Along with the geographical spread of feminist research, there are signs of shifting focus within a diverse camp, from critiquing the mainstream of IR *en route* to other goals, to investigating various gendered phenomena within international politics. There are now feminist commentaries on globalization (Chin, 1998; Kofman and Youngs, 1996; Marchand and Runyan, 2000), royal marriage and European state formation (Saco, 1997), international policy formation and women's bodies (Bretherton, 1998; Buck et al., 1998; Neale, 1998), and the international sex trade (Moon, 1997; Pearson and Theobald, 1998; Pettman,

1996b; Tadiar, 1998) – as well as a continuing tradition of analysing masculinity in international relations (Carver et al., 1998; de Goede, 2000; Hooper, 2001; Zalewski and Parpart, 1998). Numerous textbooks introduce undergraduate students to feminist themes in IR (e.g., Peterson and Runyan, 1993; Pettman, 1996a; Steans, 1997; Tickner (1992) was designed as a textbook). One might say that the openings created by first-wave feminist IR have been enlarged, made pedagogically useful, and traversed in nuanced ways, albeit mostly by other feminists.

Feminist journeying

At the start of a new millennium, now nearly twenty years into feminist IR/IR feminism, I offer here an unfinished genealogy of an ongoing project. The first stop is at the three bedrock texts on which the subfield of feminist IR/IR feminist analysis built itself: Elshtain's *Women and War*, Enloe's *Bananas, Beaches, and Bases*, and Tickner's *Gender in International Relations*. Those revisitations, brief as they are, remind us – we of feminism, we of IR, we of both and also of overlapping fields – of the scope of the journey feminists undertook in the early days, and of the large questions of IR that have been made to defend themselves against the large questions introduced by feminist analysis. It is a moment of journeying worth contemplating, for these particular texts (each author has since gone on to other related projects) presented the field with enormous challenges and enormous possibilities. If we do not cast an eye backwards, partial vision, entrenched location, or citational myopia may hinder movement forwards. We may keep reinventing the wheel or we may forget about the wheel altogether, only to notice later that something has gone missing. So I pay attention to the progenitors in the introductory chapters and only then turn to my more particularistic and personal case of feminist journeying within a larger journey that has moments of resonance with the travels of Elshtain, Enloe, and Tickner.

All the discussions are set up around themes of vision, location, and reference. Drawing out the novel *sightings* of gender and women that one makes as part of the journey, I point to the ways we can anchor or *site* newly noticed subjects within international relations, feminism, and/or IR through a variety of stylistic and methodological innovations. I also call attention to the *citations* that feminists doing international relations rely on to make their cases and build authority in a field that still holds us at arm's length. The volume elucidates ways of seeing the shadowy presence of gender and of women in international relations, as well as the styles and methodologies by which such sightings have been brought to our attention. It follows one journey set in the context of others to reveal both the distinctive and the common perspectives of an early project that keeps us on our toes today.

That parallel, overlapping, and nonlinear genealogical journey I have undertaken in IR feminism is signposted through twelve of my essays and twelve genealogical introductions to them. The essays were written between 1985 and 2001 – although they are not ordered chronologically here – and roam widely in demonstrating the range of themes, methodologies, and research styles in the genre. Some essays echo or interweave personal with professional themes in the spirit of Elshtain's, Enloe's, and/or Tickner's biographical musings. Others move along more differentiated professional pathways. As a group the essays represent journeying within larger efforts to sight, site, and cite gender and women around international relations. As for the introductions to the essays, these provide a travelogue on how each essay came about: what I was thinking, seeing, and remembering at the time; why a puzzle compelled me to write; what books I was reading; and where I had to go to find "answers." Alone and cross-referenced with the early works of Elshtain, Enloe, and Tickner, the essays and introductions provide a sense of how feminist IR/IR feminism was developing coherence while also revealing wanderings by one sojourner around and beyond that project.

The structure of the volume reflects the sense that a genealogy of feminist IR/IR feminism requires both a reminder of the rise of a genre's main works and stories that break the apparent seamlessness of a project. Enloe (1989:196) claims that the personal is international in that "[t]o make sense of international politics we also have to read power backwards and forwards." To make sense of our work, by analogy, we should read the power of ideas back to those who personally inspire us and forwards to the ways that inspirational writings have powerfully spawned new aspects of personal biography and scholarship. Revealing the circumstances and thinking behind one's work feeds a single journey into others; whereas, when relations of the personal and international remain hidden, readers can imagine that a body of work just popped up, gathered steam, progressed in quantity and quality, and moved steadily into the citational stream of a field. In fact, fields and people in them move in all sorts of directions. Some, as I have heard James Der Derian say, scuttle sideways like crabs on a New England beach; others march off to the wilderness, and some follow the lead of others.

16

Offering essays on feminist IR/IR feminism, and making the stories behind them visible, should facilitate the reader's travel with one researcher who remembers the company of others while devising her own research program. Hopefully, the essays also enable us to picture links between a field often leery of feminism and feminist insistence on siting IR work in many places while also siting some of it in and around IR. The journey commences at the turn of the page.

2   Introducing Elshtain, Enloe, and Tickner: looking at key feminist efforts before journeying on

My journey through feminist IR/IR feminism moves alongside, ahead of, and behind the footsteps and voices of others. Before recalling aspects of the trip, those who marked out important pathways before me deserve to be sighted, sited, and cited. Nostalgia is not what pulls me to the early IR-relevant works of Jean Bethke Elshtain, Cynthia Enloe, and Ann Tickner; nor have these scholars produced research that is above criticism. Rather, these particular progenitors of the feminist IR tradition are lodestars because they developed methods of locating gender and the international around feminism, or women, men and gender around international relations (and IR); their work improved our visual acuity in IR and in feminism; and the citations they provided drew attention to everyday people of international relations and not just to the usual heroic or scholarly men. Works by these writers are also indisputable classics, which is to say they have sustained. Librettos, then, to their efforts.

Women and War

Jean Bethke Elshtain's *Women and War* (1987) is a bold rethink of conventional war traditions by an American political theorist who trained in IR but cut her teeth on feminism *cum* motherhood. Elshtain probes war by juxtaposing conventional and unconventional perspectives on what is done, said, and claimed in and around war. Hegel's Just Warriors/ Beautiful Souls dichotomy serves as the point of departure: western men are deemed fit to mastermind, conduct, and narrate wars, and western women are deemed too beautiful, soft, and motherly to be anything other than receivers of warrior tales. Elshtain crashes through this trope by showing us the women in war and the men who prefer not to be there, as well as revealing gender-related secrets about war studies celebrities. Many she cites are ordinary people. Some are fierce, others are modest, and many are at unexpected intersections of warrior–beauty sites. Throughout, Elshtain gives IR's contemporary research on war a pass, except to suggest that its approaches to this area of high politics can be ridiculous. Elshtain is also openly troubled by the feminisms of the 1960s and 1970s and lets us know where that stream of thinking is deficient. All the sightings are masterful, the style of presentation brilliant, the arguments trenchant, and the vision both bright and unaccountably myopic.

Not a soldier

Women and War sets up with two introductions to essays grouped around armed civic virtue and history's gender gap in war. The most innovative chapter in the book appears as the second of the two introductions, the one telling "Not-a-Soldier's Story: An Exemplary Tale." In it, Jean sights, sites, and cites herself as a war fighting-narrating child who turns into Jean Bethke – hobbled but warring as an adolescent – and then morphs into the battling mother-theorist Jean Bethke Elshtain. Her voyage to women and war flows with the grace of fine literature:

> Approaching stealthily, leapfrogging from behind a bush to the camouflage of a large, gnarled tree, trying not to stumble over her weapon or to fall and skin her knees, or worse, tear her dress, the determined, athletic eight-year-old prepares to surround her enemies – a curly-headed, befreckled, slim six-year-old and a plump, red-haired, three-year-old toddler. (p. 15)

One expects a passage like this in Kate Atkinson's fictional account of war-scarred childhood in *Behind the Scenes at the Museum* (1995), which won Whitbread Book of the Year (see chapter 14). The difference is not in writing quality but in the place myths of each. British wartime angst sets the backdrop of a little girl's tragedy in the Atkinson tale, whereas girls enacting a carefree Norman Rockwell scenario of 1950s Americana are at the center of the Elshtain passage. Young Jean is the boss of a game she shapes as she wants it to be: "You saw the movie. We both stand here and fight until one of us dies or gets hurt" (Elshtain, 1987:15). Jean then fights, and has fun doing so.

She borrows a "Block That Kick!" approach to her professional work (Elshtain, 1997:vii) from a mother who often showed "determination to make war, to fight when fighting seemed necessary"(p. 320). That fighting spirit wins out early in Elshtain's *Bildungsroman* and later through her influential writings and prestigious posts at Vanderbilt University and the University of Chicago. But in the early middle she is hurt. She, the hero (her word) of movie-mimicked stories of dusty cowboys and Indians, she a Jeanne d'Arc of Colorado, finds herself starring in a *noir* drama at the tender age of ten, year 1951: polio. Hospitalized and struggling against physical immobility, she finds she "had not relinquished my fascination with war, with combat, with tests of courage and loyalty. War promised a field of action more vital and serious than any other. War enlisted men in a common cause" (Elshtain, 1987:21). "War enlisted men," and Jean, gender-bending her way through childhood and adolescent hopes, says, wistfully: "My dreams of warrioring dashed, it still seemed possible I might recover sufficiently to be a war correspondent" (p. 20). Soldier men and a reporter woman animated an imaginary of war in which women no less than men could be intimately involved.

Elshtain moves on, episodically, to her years of motherhood. Or is it that she enters academia? Elshtain treats the two overlapping moments of her life as one set of influences on her war interests:

> By 1960 my childhood was over. I was a college student and the young mother of an infant (my first daughter), and my examination of war and fears of war and male/female identity more and more fell to one side or the other of a line that severed official, public *discourse* from unsystematic, private *understanding*. The public student of history and politics, inhabiting the sphere of official public/academic discourse, being taught the ways of the political world as the "realists" (Machiavelli, Hobbes, Bismarck, Clausewitz) understood it, and the private dreamer, mother, novel reader, and Beatles buff parted company.   (1987:31)

Journal writing softened the binary discomforts. It became the way Elshtain played with and won at education and motherhood without choosing between them. But that did not prevent her from asking: "Where was my voice? Was it a female voice, a mother's voice? Or that of a tough, no-nonsense expert, squeezing all possible sentimental nicety out of political thinking in order to bring politics and our discourse about politics into a more approximate mimetic relationship?" (p. 32). Although Elshtain says she could serve up the right IR "like a seasoned *realpolitiker*, impatient with expressions of fuzzy idealists who were ignorant of the ways of the world" (p. 32), she "hoped inchoately that I might one day put together mothering and political thinking rather than have to put aside the one in order to engage the other" (p. 32). Contradictions were everywhere and their resolution was something Elshtain deferred long enough to find countermeanings in those interstices. Kathy Ferguson (1993) would later suggest that keeping contradictions alive instead of working to resolve them prematurely is a feminist way of generating new knowledge.

Questioning the gender content of one's voice and life choices marks feminist thinkers from those who operate within academia with qualms of other ideological or methodological types. Choose motherhood and women can lose professional location and voice, finding themselves cited, favorably or unfavorably, mostly by family members. Choose a no-nonsense professional voice and risk losing the authority, pleasure, and understanding that come from sites of life left behind. Choose. One is meant to choose, Elshtain (1987:33) says, "between realist discourse and idealist principles, between strategic deterrence and civil disobedience, between the dominant image of the public man and the shaky vision of the private woman, her voice sounding strange and tortured as a public instrument . . ."

Her tale goes on to more babies – three by late 1963. No mention of the father of the children, of a husband or a partner or whoever it is whose help makes graduate training *cum* motherhood possible. Babies sprout from a myopic spot, where a homespun heroine, babes at breast, book in hand, and images of warriorhood stirring in the brain becomes a man-woman, Beautiful Soul-Just Warrior, self-contained conceivor. Elshtain warmly acknowledges her husband, Errol, in earlier and later volumes (1981:xvii, 1982; 1986; 1990), savvy in presenting him doing "occasional typing, Xeroxing, mailing, checking out and returning books . . ." (Elshtain, 1982: acknowledgments). In *Women and War*, husband is somewhere near home and wife is out with men who frequent IR's power centers – men such as Harry Truman, who did not think to "question whether one man should have the power to drop such a bomb on his own authority no matter what the situation" (Elshtain, 1987:39). Other male *copains* are exemplaries of civic virtue: Lincoln, one of Elshtain's childhood favorites, wins her adult respect because he can admit "I have not controlled events" (p. 251). That *Women and War* means to correct failures to see private influences in public spheres lends an irony to Elshtain's silence about the support at home that enables her to be a public figure. But then her point is that the private *is* a realm of sanctuary from public pressures, a place of conscience that can be brought to bear on public issues but is not itself public.

21

Elshtain enters public debate around feminism, a scene where the mother-theorist finds "an animus toward a maternal woman's voice as pronounced as that of any *realpolitiker* male from seminars in the past" (1987:40). Elshtain fights. In a 1979 essay for *The Nation*, she refuses the then-popular feminist slogan that "the personal is political," on the grounds that "if politics is power and power is everywhere, politics is in fact nowhere and a vision of public life as the touchstone of a revitalized ideal of citizenship is lost" (Elshtain, 1997:146). Elshtain wants to preserve the two spheres so that the private realm, where mothers and children dwell, can inform a civic ethos that does not rely on war for its legitimacy. She objects to the idea, then popular in radical feminist circles in particular, that the household is a site of male tyranny. She says in *Women and War* that radical feminism extols the female body as the site of goodness, and then has trouble dealing with pregnancy and childbearing that eventuate (at that time) only through cavorts with "bad" male bodies. Elshtain the mother is put off by this position and accuses radical feminism of exerting "a silencing effect over free and open debate on a whole range of issues ... even as it provides no alternative vision of a revitalized concept of 'citizenship'" (p. 149).

Elshtain expresses strong views but expects civil responses to her work. Instead, feminists accused her of every sin in the book, including labeling all feminism "radical," failing to acknowledge patriarchy, and refusing to see problems in the heterosexual family. At a twenty-year remove, I notice how dated the arguments on both sides sound, how well Elshtain fights, and how patently disinterested her critics truly were in citizenship issues as compared with now (e.g., Connolly, 1993; Curthoys, 1993; Jones, 1990, 1993). Elshtain is impatient with her critics and cleverer by a country mile than many of them. Yet her mental dexterity can be blinding: if the criticisms are ineloquently expressed, but do represent real worries, is it wise to fight so hard, to block so fiercely?

Elshtain's "exemplary" chapter is both a personal testimony and a public opening that helps us appreciate the concerns of feminists who were in proximity to IR in the 1980s. Visibility was a major concern. Women were not in the state- and system-centric works of IR because they were neither fighters nor leaders, except in unusual and exceptional and overlooked ways. Elshtain tells us (1981:301) that "[t]he activity of theory is, literally, about seeing. *Theorein*, the Greek word from which our own derives, meant to watch or to look at." Elshtain-theorist first sees herself in and around war, drawing an outline of herself there as an agentic person preoccupied by warriorism and its virtues and vices. She then sees how other identities add on over time and frame choices about which parts of oneself to highlight when talking about war (warrior, mother, student, current events analyst, feminist, citizen) and which to conceal (wife) in the private sphere of democratic society. The key, which is her argument against radical feminism, is "not to impose a prefabricated formula over diverse and paradoxical material" (Elshtain, 1987:xi). In the effort to avoid imposed theory, she and Sandra Harding (1986), who is writing her influential feminist treatise – *The Science Question in Feminism* – at the same time, strike a similar methodological note.

How rare it was in the middle 1980s for personal experience to beam out of scholarly research! How stunning when that experience was of a girl, woman, and mother, whose boundary-crossings put the wrong people into war. And how irrelevant Elshtain's exemplary chapter must have appeared to some in IR, who were undoubtedly accustomed to minding the fact/value dichotomy by providing only scant and impersonal information on issues behind a study. Positivism held the line between scholarly objectivity and the "personal biases" that could appear in novels, poetry, and art. Elshtain, an outlaw from positivism's rules, posed "filiations of childhood narrative" (1987:25) as data, along with journal excerpts, interpretations of popular films, and "sometimes pained, more often ironic, commentaries on the complexities of identity and knowledge, of being a mother and becoming a political theorist" (p. 25). The result is a methodologically innovative feminist ethnography of war.

To war fields

The remainder of *Women and War*, which is most of it, examines experiences with and reports of war and peace other than her own. In the section on armed civic virtue, Elshtain cites and discusses stories rehearsed by students of IR: the Greek citizen army arrayed; Sparta prepared; the casts of Homer's *Iliad* and Plato's *Republic*; Machiavelli and Rousseau, whose ideal republics are plump with armed civic virtue. Hegel celebrates the nation at war and Marx and Engels struggle. There are new, war-enabling sightings too. Mrs. Clausewitz curtsies into view as the person responsible for publishing Karl von Clausewitz's monumental *On War*. Her words of preface to the work, which are reproduced only in some editions (e.g., Clausewitz [Howard and Paret, eds. and trans.], 1984), tell of how Karl had half-joked to his wife: "*You* shall publish it" (Elshtain, 1987:79). She does so, all the while wrestling to "overcome the timidity which makes it so difficult for a woman to appear before the reading public even in the most subordinate manner" (p. 79). Self-demeaning words rescue a woman from near extinction in the war enterprise and have us pondering *On War* as a woman's work to some degree – who knows how many changes a "she" made to the text?

Elshtain then decries IR for fitting a tradition of armed civic culture that automatically excludes such wives. By turns funny and savage, she aims her verbal guns at the confidence of "those whose point of view long ago won the war," those who no longer have to make sure themselves that all "alternatives are evaluated *from the standpoint of realism*" (p. 87). We learn she studied under Kenneth Waltz in his Brandeis days and that she has no intention of mocking him (p. 87, note), though IR is worthy of parody: "Encumbered with lifeless jargon, systems and subsystem dominance, spirals of misperception, decision-making analysis, bipolar, multipolar, intervening variables, dependence, interdependence, cost-effectiveness, IR specialists in the post-Second World War era began to speak exclusively to, or 'at,' one another or to their counterparts in government service" (p. 89). She lashes out at the masculinism of this dissociative citadel, the foolishness of its computer simulations, the presumption that "politics can be reduced to questions of security, conflict management, and damage control" (p. 89) – that politics can even be controlled. She spits out epithets: IR's war discourse is "professionalized." It is "dubious." Then she takes the would-be mighty down through a simple citation: "The man, and the woman, 'in the street' often knows how fragile it all is, how vulnerable we all are" (p. 91). With this, Elshtain gives most of IR, especially scientific realism, the boot and moves on.

Subsequent sites of armed civic virtue are places and traditions where women make sense of war and do not merely suffer it or stand by a warrior man out of duty. We see Southern Civil War mothers and wives resisting Union forces, able to "partake of received notions of glory, honor, nobility, civic virtue" (p. 102); some women follow men to battle to rescue the wounded or take on clandestine military missions. During World War I British warrior wannabes, like one Rose Macaulay, rhapsodize that men "have the luck, out there in blood and muck" (p. 112). American suffragettes come out for war. Women war correspondents find activities at the front impressive. These fringe warriors can be "empowered in and through the discourse of armed civic virtue to become an *author* of deeds – deeds of sacrifice, of nobility in and through suffering, of courage in the face of adversity, of firmness in *her*, and not just her polity's 'right'" (p. 93, emphasis in original). Some of them, that is, can cite war from experience.

Christianity, handled in turn, offers phases of resistance to war and doctrines for it that enable women either to make sense of suffering or to disarm warrior civic virtue. Elshtain notes that in the beginning, "[t]he model for Christian love, *agape*, was the mother's unconditional love for her child, marking a feminization of Christian ideals of fellowship and community" (p. 126). Women were loving, nonviolent, beautiful. That they were also martyred with men in Roman times means women were accorded public agency by the state. Augustine gave them some rights; he opposed "deformed codes of virtuous conduct for Roman women" (p. 129), such as those that demanded of a woman raped during wartime that she kill herself to preserve family honor. As Christian stories carried on, men warred against Christians and Christians against "heathens."

War and women in the Middle Ages: some women held fiefdoms (at least initially), some were hunters or worked in trade guilds, and others handled animals. Women, however, could not train as knights. Christine de Pizan's *The Book of the City of Ladies* chronicles the rectitude, reason, and justice that rendered women unable to engage in wars and other nasty deeds. Luther then bans images of women saints from churches, thereby drastically reducing the symbolic power of motherly virtue and peace in the public sphere of Christianity. Elshtain says Luther "prepares the way for the political theology that underlies the emergence of the nation-state" (p. 136), by "masculinizing theology" and promoting "secular male dominance" (p. 143). "Women," once a site of hope for humanity, becomes an identity sequestered in privatized zones.

But some women do not know their place and leave the private feminized hearth for sites of war or violence. Elshtain calls this shorter section, "Life Givers/Life Takers." New England colonial women slaughter imprisoned Native Americans in acts of violence that shock sensibilities. A woman held by indigenous Canadians manages, with her nurse and a teenage boy, to slay ten captors; her violence is perpetually cited through a public monument. Elshtain explains the discrepancy: male violence has been channeled through the institution of war and its various rules of conduct. Women, with no comparable institution – by virtue of the constructions of peacefulness built around them – seem out of control when they engage in violence, unless the act mirrors imagined male valor. The Just Warrior is also confounded when some men refuse assigned war and become conscientious objectors or deserters. Like ferocious women, they can appear odd and askance.

And then the crescendo that closes history's gender gap: Elshtain has us contemplate an ontological turnaround in the Just Warrior/Beautiful Soul dichotomy. The ideal-typical warrior, she argues, crosses the meaning terrain to that of a good mother. Good soldiers sacrifice for country and good mothers sacrifice for their children, both feeling guilty about whether they have done their duties well enough. Men under fire plead with god, as do women in labor; but then both remember those respective experiences in nostalgic and sentimental ways. On it goes until we are asked to recognize a common condition of exclusion that underscores both the differences and the similarities between mothers and soliders: "[w]omen are excluded from war talk; men, from baby talk" (p. 225). Elshtain has maintained the tensions long enough and countermeanings now creep out: "Perhaps we are not strangers after all," Elshtain whispers (p. 225).

Elshtain, who will later call herself a moral realist (1998a:448), has positioned herself in *Women and War* for a postmodern feminist climax beyond war and peace. She does not want any more "ahistorical abstractions; unreflective celebrations" (Elshtain, 1987:240). Instead, we must face the fascinations of war that seize hold of men and women and claim for civic action "war's generative powers without its destructiveness" (p. 231). She especially seeks "a *way of being in the world* that promotes civic identity and connection, even – at times, especially – if the form it takes is to reject the politics of the day or many of its central features. I have in mind the complex filiations of *private conscience* brought to bear on public lives and actions, offering tragic recognitions of necessary, even insoluble, conflicts, and, consequently, of limits to understanding and deed doing alike" (pp. 247–248, emphasis in original). She has in mind crossovers that illuminate good soldier/good mother storylines as places of distancing irony.

With these nonabsolutes in mind, we can move away from a patriotic preoccupation with power and interests to a chastened ethos that "refuses to see *all* right and good on one side only" (p. 257, emphasis in original). Like Lincoln, we realize that we can only work with events politically through public debate and "inner dialogue with one's own 'others'" (p. 258). "The dream I am dreaming as I end these reflections is not one of solemn deed doers," insists Elshtain, "but of zestful act takers, experimenting with new possibilities playfully but from a deep seriousness of purpose" (p. 258). Elshtain has taken her arguments to a place that is moderate but transformed, allowing the private to influence the public and enabling new possibilities to emerge through work and play, rather than through unmediated illusion or historical allusion. It is a fine *tour de force* in which she lets us see women's stories blocked and "female participatory capability" (Elshtain, 1981:348) mobilized for "a transformed vision of the political community" (p. 348).

Elshtain, though, does not delve into the issue of what constitutes war. War is armed civic action. Virtue or vice, it is a phenomenon of guns and bombs and theories/stories/texts supporting them. This is a myopia. There can be pieces of war in peace and pieces of peace in wartime – dirty little wars of words and deeds can hide in good families and hate wars can systematically target women, gays, blacks, Jews, fellow students, or gangs on the other side of town – all in peacetime. Warlike acts are common in a gun-crazed, civically armed United States at peace. So are wars against drugs and battles with the environment. Meanwhile, "comfort women" of all sorts provide bodily peace to a variety of would-be warriors (Enloe, 1989; Moon, 1997). Yet in *Women and War*, Elshtain (unlike Enloe in *Bananas*) does not see peacetime politics as part of war dynamics. By staying with a realist sense of war, even while revealing realism's larger research limitations, Elshtain accepts a pregiven ontological take on this site of women and questions mainly the epistemology surrounding the ontology.

Three other myopias concern me. From an international perspective, where is the rest of the world in all this American fiddling beyond war and peace? Does Elshtain's discussion feed the prevalent sense abroad that IR academics in the USA cannot see beyond themselves, even when they try to formulate a politics that is beyond such certitude – because they are not good at sighting and citing everyday others? Could it be a power move for Americans to accept Elshtain's (1987:258) invitation to "take unilateral initiatives" in this area? Even in her later work, she keeps an eye on the ways Americans could improve their national civic life and thereafter reorient their perspectives on others (Elshtain, 1998b).

And which Americans? From a sociological point of view, where does private conscience fit into Elshtain's thinking when it is expressed through families differently constituted than those she sights and sites in *Women and War*? What if they revolve around marriages of the same sex or childless unions? What if the arrangements are temporary or occur in sequence? In her earliest work, she seems reluctant to probe the parameters of family, noting in *Public Man/Private Woman* (1981:322, emphasis in original), and only in a footnote, that "I recognize that there is no such thing as 'the family' but that there are multiple variations on this theme. Nevertheless, in discussing the imperatives that must be infused within *any* familial form in order for it to serve the humanizing functions I explicate it is more economical simply to speak of 'the family.' " After *Women and War*, her position is clearer and most controversial:

> To be sure, families in modernity coexist with those who live another way, whether heterosexual and homosexual unions that are by choice or by definition childless; communalists who diminish individual parental authority in favor of the preeminence of the group; and so on. *But the recognition and acceptance of plural possibilities does not mean each alternative is equal to every other with reference to specific social goods* . . . The intergenerational family remains central and critical in nurturing recognitions of human frailty, morality, and finitude and in inculcating moral limits and constraints. (Elshtain, 1990:60)

Her view here lacks the distancing irony to see that families of other sorts work daily with all the issues she enumerates. For her, good soldiers-good mothers come out good citizens in good families of a certain type. Yet if the good soldier bears a strong resemblance to the good mother, there may be grave problems with soldiering, with mothering, and maybe even with their family enthusiasms (Sylvester, 1993d:38). Soldiering and mothering may be bound up in a tragedy of social role expectations rather than a liberty of identity. And what of good fathers? Where *are* the fathers?

Finally, permeating all, do not issues of power strongly affect the seep of private conscience on to public civic actions? If some women do not have a convenient vehicle for stepping out of self-effacement – such as Mr. Clausewitz's text to publish – will they be able to enter the public arena? The tragedy for many women is that they are already (too) chastened. Jane Flax (1990:233) asks us how to "assure that everyone has a chance to speak . . . that each voice counts equally . . . how to effect a transition from the present in which many voices cannot speak, are necessarily excluded, or are not heard to a more pluralist one . . . how to compensate for the political consequences of an unequal distribution and control of resources." These conundrums are not broached in *Women and War*.

Elshtain today is an engaged public intellectual at a time when many people who populate academic departments of IR, women's studies, and the like often eschew public debate. She still writes in what she terms "the heat of the battle" (Elshtain, 1997:vii), while advocating "a form of political reason that enables us to avoid equally unacceptable extremes" (p. 320). In her view, both her writing and the positions she takes exercise the Arendtian "faculty of action" (p. 258), the narrative voice of citizenship. Elshtain strives for a more complex form of communication than repetitions of popular slogans ever allow, a way of sighting issues of importance without consigning them to rigid and extreme sites of thought and action. Ultimately, she wants to avoid narratives of closure for "perspectives that, more modestly and sure-footedly, give us insight, even insistencies robustly defended" (Elshtain, 1993:101–102; 1997:96). Yet she does not always maintain her own standards of openness and balance. Her work thus remains highly controversial, modern, postmodern, old-fashioned, ahead of the pack, behind, destabilizing, embarrassing in parts, and very partial. It is with those partialities and myopias in mind that others have entered the fray of feminist IR/IR feminism, myself included.

Bananas, Beaches, and Bases

This second feminist IR classic, by Cynthia Enloe, is a multivalent conversation with and about women and power in the world. Traveling to and beyond war sites, it tells stories about various (de)feats of women, and it does so with citational reference to such unsung IR heroines as Carmen Miranda, Pocahontas, and chambermaids in a Jamaican hotel. Enloe magnificently insists on pushing realist IR to see "how *much* power it takes to maintain the international political system in its present form" (Enloe, 1989:3, emphasis in original), as a landscape "peopled only by men, mostly elite men" (p. 1). She is not especially interested in IR beyond contemplating its power. The refrain running through Enloe's work is: "Where are the women?" (p. 133) – not in IR *per se* but in the world IR purports to study.

Enloe is known for cleverly titling her feminist works and *Bananas, Beaches, and Bases: Making Feminist Sense of International Relations* is no exception: the title alludes to traded commodities and to military compounds, but it also suggests that beaches are to be made sense of in international relations. Getting down to business expeditiously, she lets us know in a short preface that *Bananas* will expose "how relations between governments depend not only on capital and weaponry, but also on the control of women as symbols, consumers, workers and emotional comforters" (p. xi). Women working within the masculine landscape of international politics absorb her, as does the notion of women consuming other women's work. In eight site-specific chapters, Enloe endeavors to display the power dimensions of gendered militarism, work, and consumption that IR neglects to sight in international relations.

Within *Bananas* are echoes of Elshtain. Looking back at *Women and War*, one catches the whiff of *Bananas*. Mutual resonances are not surprising, for the two writers are peers. Both attended graduate school in political science during the momentous 1960s; each became a lively and original writer with interest in everyday circumstances of everyday women; each is also especially fascinated by war and aspects of the military. But there are also differences. Elshtain hails from a town of 185 souls, whereas Enloe was born a New Yorker a few years earlier. Elshtain attended humble Colorado State University, while Enloe went to posh Connecticut College (then for women only). Each hopped coasts for graduate training – Elshtain went east to Brandeis and Enloe journeyed west to Berkeley. There were few women in academic political science at the time they earned their Ph.D.s, which means the material they imbibed in their training, and the sage words they heard from podiums, were mostly by men about men and the world men supposedly created. Both admit to having been "taken in" by early disciplinary training to some degree. Elshtain moved through it quickly towards political theory and an IR informed by the women's and anti-war movements of the time. Enloe persevered for years with what she characterizes as "a young comparative politics discipline . . . Southeast Asia was just beginning to loom on American academics' intellectual horizon" (Enloe, 1993:228). Her research world was initially womenless, until she too moved, more slowly but then with great enthusiasm, toward feminist study.

That Enloe's journey to women took added time is ironic given that she lives a life that rattles Elshtain's family values. Enloe has a woman partner. Even now, she does not present this aspect of personal experience as a launching pad for her IR feminism; nor does she cite it along the way. There is no exemplary tale of sexual identity in any of her books. Enloe and Elshtain both leave some self-referential citations at home, such that Elshtain steps forward as a feminist mother in *Women and War* but is reticent about her identity as wife, and Enloe presents herself as a feminist seeker but says nothing about her lesbian identity. A fighter for women, Enloe is not particularly concerned to make her personal life an emblem of the good and the bold the way Elshtain does.

Nationalism, ethnicity, and the military – and then women

Enloe has been a *very* prolific book writer, with tomes on ethnic politics (e.g., Enloe, 1970, 1973, 1980a), Southeast Asia (Enloe, 1970, 1981), development (Enloe, 1973), and police–military relations (e.g., Enloe, 1980a, 1980b). Nationalism was on her mind for a long time: "how, when, why, and with what effects people in any country developed a distinctly national consciousness with effective national institutions to match" (Enloe, 1993:229). That interest brought her to identity politics, understood then mostly in ethnic and racial terms. A book-length treatment of the politics of pollution (Enloe, 1975) was a weigh station *en route* to work on ethnicity and the military in developing countries.

We are so accustomed to Enloe's vibrant and eager feminist spirit that it can be disconcerting to peruse her early nonfeminist writings. Through the Berkeley years, she said she hardly "noticed that the word *woman* scarcely ever crossed the lips of political science lecturers" (Enloe, 1993:228). And on her lips? In the preface to *Ethnic Conflict and Political Development* (1973:xiii), she worries that Malaysian readers might not recognize their country in her study and consoles herself with this thought: "[i]magining an audience can paralyze a writer, but it can also keep him on the straight and narrow." Him? Just as surprising, as late as her co-authored *Diversity and Development in Southeast Asia* (Pauker, Golay, and Enloe, 1977), Enloe offers no index references to women, gender, or feminism at all.

From 1980 on, Enloe begins to regard women as an identity group imbued with research-relevant politics. There is the odd mention in *Ethnic Soldiers* (1980a), but *Does Khaki Become You? The Militarization of Women's Lives* (1983) makes the breakthrough of putting identity and the military together with women. Enloe is inspired to do so in what we now think of as a characteristically feminist way: by a fragment of autobiography that brings the "women point" home to her. Like Elshtain, Elshtain like her, a mother enters the picture:

> It was a warm June afternoon, so my mother and I took our glasses of ice tea out on her porch. We also carried several of my mother's diaries. I wanted to know more about what her days had been like during the second world war, those years when my father had been in the Army Air Corps and she had been left to manage the household and my brother and me. My mother began keeping a diary in 1923 when she was a teenager in California and she hadn't missed a day since then . . . this was the first time I had ever imagined that I could learn a lot about militarisation from those small leather-bound books. (p. ix)

Well into her career by the time she writes this, Enloe is discovering that her mother's life has citational relevance to the high politics of military relations. She says, "[s]o much of military history and defence spending is written as though women didn't exist, as though the Second World War (or the Falklands war or the Vietnam war) depended solely on men in war rooms and in the trenches, as though my mother didn't need to be mentioned at all" (p. ix). In *Khaki*, Enloe declares: "More than perhaps any other writing projects I have set out upon, this book has been affected by daily interactions with the women whose experiences I have been trying to understand" (p. x). Sighting and then listening to average women becomes her new research approach and, judging by the work that follows, it is a *raison d'être* that leads to ever further sightings, sitings, and citings at the margins of IR.

Enloe announces in the first chapter of *Khaki* that the identity politics informing her study of the military and women's lives is feminist, entitling one section "Why Should a Feminist Study the Military?" She does not elaborate the content of her feminism, though, at any point in the book. She evokes women's groups opposing British militarism, Australian women inserting women into the annual ANZAC remembrances of 1982, and women in Boston linking sexual harassment with militarism. It intrigues her that "[s]o many women's relationships to their military and to their own soldiers were wrapped in memories, myths, aspirations, fears, and confusions" (p. xiv). She finds it eye-opening that "abstract military doctrines such as 'mutually assured destruction' or . . . 'low intensity conflict' rely on concepts such as motherhood and homemaking" (p. xiv). Her feminism sights women and makes men visible as men involved in masculine politics throughout international relations. But there is nary a word on feminism's many debates.

Enloe's evocation, rather than discussion, of feminism also characterizes *Bananas, Beaches, and Bases*, her leap into IR. Appearing more than a decade after she became a professor at Clark University, and two decades after she finished a Ph.D. in comparative politics, this work weaves a generic feminism around high and low IR politics topics. Enloe can sound like a constructivist sometimes, commenting that "[a]s one learns to look at this world through feminist eyes, one learns to ask whether anything that passes for inevitable, inherent, 'traditional' or biological has in fact been *made*" (Enloe, 1989:3, emphasis in original). Yet she is after the women in international politics, and for her women (like feminism, perhaps) are self-evident: you know one when you see one. There is no ironic pause to see how gender can ring ambiguous identity bells, with good mothers sliding into good soldiers. For Enloe, we can find women doing work in international relations that neither gets credited to them nor advances their interests.

Happy hunting

Women and War begins with memories and Enloe commences *Bananas* in a similarly unconventional way: "I began this book thinking about Pocahontas and ended it mulling over the life of Carmen Miranda" (p. xi). Enloe dryly adds: "These women were not the sorts of international actors I had been taught to take seriously when trying to make sense of world affairs" (p. xi). Miranda symbolizes campaigns to link women with international trade in commodities. Pocahontas might be thought of as an early version of the woman about the military base, who marries an officer and goes abroad. Pocahontas and Miranda accompany Enloe and all the women of *Bananas* on their particular journeys. These are odd companions for IR but precisely the travelers one wants along on a feminist odyssey.

Marie von Clausewitz's flashier counterpart early in *Bananas* is Fawn Hall, secretary to Oliver North, Mr. Iran/Contragate, 1987. Enloe sights this blonde beauty keeping and shredding the secrets of her egomaniacal boss as a high-powered government investigation closes in. With her few months of fame as a pro-Contra lovely – only slightly stretching Andy Warhol's estimate of celebrity time in the late twentieth century – "Fawn Hall is meant to represent the feminine side of High Politics of the 1980s: worldly, stylish, exciting, sexy" (p. 8). Enloe helps us see that Hall's work for a power man in contemporary Washington is as important as Marie von Clausewitz's unheralded editing of a war book in an earlier time. Enloe's point is this: "if we made concepts such as 'wife', 'mother', 'sexy broad' central to our investigations, we might find that the Iran/Contra affair and international politics generally looked different" (p. 11). And the world could, thereby, be resited and remade (p. 17).

Setting off from these stage-setting remarks, Enloe goes hunting in earnest for unacknowledged women in international politics. Her first stop is the beach. There the worldly women tourists and conference go-ers pick through postcards, looking for ones that capture just the right *je ne sais quoi*. Enloe thinks a feminist-minded tourist will (twirl the display away from women's naked, sandy buttocks, away from the topless shots and exotic hula dancers) choose cards depicting local women working at everyday tasks, such as fishing or harvesting. These quaint jobs snap well and enable a feminist abroad to convey correct sight to those at home. Meanwhile, down the street, behind the hotel district, set off from the lapping waves, women may be jammed together on a plastics or electronics shopfloor. Sex workers are out on the streets and in the smoky bars of foreign men. Such images will be too exotic for the middle-class woman traveler to ponder, click, or buy. Ditto the chambermaids changing the hotel bed sheets: quaint but prosaic – and not site-specific enough. Here's the real snapshot then: women out traveling the world – once was that men went abroad and women stayed home – make work for other women *and* usually fail to appreciate the ways local women figure into the images in the postcards.

This is Enloe's lead-in to stories about other women leaving home in a spirit of wander and liberation. Vita Sackville-West dresses as a young man and goes off to Paris after World War I with her woman lover. Women join the military with or without disguise. A woman signs on for the US Army Nursing Corps during the Vietnam War and prepares by going shopping: "It was January and we would go to all the 'cruise' shops looking for light-weight clothing. I wanted everyone to think I was going on a cruise" (p. 22). Enloe goes back too to the often wealthy "lady adventurers" of the Victorian era, who set off to the colonies for their fun. Such women challenged the assumption that exploration was a masculine activity (like soldiering), but some among them opposed suffrage and wished to be seen as gender exceptional. The artifacts brought home became part of natural history displays and world's fair mappings of western progress (also Coombes, 1994). Western women could not yet vote but could measure their material condition against that of foreign women powerfully made to look primitive.

Enloe (1989:44) then returns to one of the oldest sites in her research repertory – nationalism. This time she wants the reader to see that "[b]ecoming a nationalist requires a man to resist the foreigner's use and abuse of his women." Nationalism rarely if ever takes women's experiences as the point of departure, the rallying cry. Indeed, Enloe bluntly states that "nationalism typically has sprung from masculinized memory, masculinized humiliation and masculinized hope" (p. 44). Colonialism too sprang from masculinized dreams of power and adventure: like Elshtain, Enloe looks at Hollywood films as culture markers of the past and present, and notices the ways they showcase white women colonists and relegate local women to an unnarrativized background (think of *Out of Africa*). She has us revisit Muslim women and the veil, pressing us to think of a piece of male attire that stirs as much comment ("Sikh men in India and Britain have had to fight for the right to wear their turbans ... yet one doesn't see Sikh women acting as the chief proponents or enforcers of this male ethnic practice" (pp. 53–54)).

34

Militarized nationalist movements of the twentieth century draw her particular feminist ire, perhaps because she examined nationalism for so long and did not see this aspect. Presaging what has come to be, Enloe tells us that "[t]he militarization of Afghanistan [by the Soviet Union] has proved disastrous for women" (p. 57). She has in mind the bombings they suffered; today we think of the prohibitions on women that accompany the restoration of power to nationalist fundamentalists. Masculine "tradition" also became stronger during the *intifada*, Enloe argues, because "[t]he more imminent and coercive the threat posed by an outside power – a foreign force or the local government's police – the more successful men in the community are likely to be in persuading women to keep quiet, to swallow their grievances and their analyses" (p. 56).

Military bases now loom into Enloe's view around women in the shadows of realism. Although Elshtain too has stopped in this vicinity to notice women recruits and warfighters, Enloe adds to the scene the symbiotic relations of NATO soldiers and the sex workers arranged to preserve men's morale. In effect, local women protect the spirit of men who are meant to be protecting them with overseas military power. Race–gender issues emerge in cross-cultural dating on the bases. Soldiers' wives are pitted against or seen as extensions of local sex workers in a context where military training equates women with a destructive softness. Wives of officers, removed from the ordinary wives on a base, serve in hostessing capacities even though they are inhospitably isolated from reward and position in the military and in the study of international politics. These are the women Enloe wants to include in the topic of women and war.

In *Bananas*, she eliminates one of Elshtain's concerns from sight: men. There are no such progenitors of IR in her book, no Marx or Hegel or Clausewitz named and considered. The absence of men-centered stories (except for Mr. Thomas Cook, who masterminds women's international tourism at the turn of the twentieth century) means that, unlike Elshtain, Enloe is not concerned in this book to show that men have had it rough too, that both sides have been trapped in gendered narratives that refuse to allow the good soldier to be the good mother. Here Enloe puts most problems at the feet of patriarchy – a term Elshtain uses less often, reminding her, as it does, of radical feminism. We cheer Enloe's forthrightness; and I also squirm, knowing that more systematic, less anecdotal research is required before we can say, as she does, that "[t]he very structure of international tourism *needs* patriarchy to survive" (p. 41).

In a welcome departure from Elshtain's approach, though, Enloe locates overseas women within international politics. Elshtain is the chastened American patriot, whose eyes often look inward at western civilization and at US responsibilities within it. Enloe is rarely in the USA throughout *Bananas*; she writes it in Britain with sources from Africa, Samoa, and the Native American cultures that were on Elshtain's backdoor as she grew up in Colorado (but that figure into *Women and War* only as tropes). Enloe is also keen for us to see local women's organizations, such as Thai groups working with women in the international sex-tourism industry. Elshtain, burned by US feminist organizations, can seem defensive in speaking of women's groups.

Enloe world-travels on to the international politics of the banana, a political economy trip that has no counterpart in Elshtain's work. In signature form, Enloe personalizes the abstract:

> When she appeared on screen, the tempo quickened. Dressed in her outrageous costumes, topped by hats featuring bananas and other tropical fruits, Carmen Miranda sang and danced her way to Hollywood stardom. While she was best known for her feisty comic performances, she also played a part in a serious political drama: the realignment of American power in the Western hemisphere. Carmen Miranda's movies helped make Latin America safe for American banana companies . . .   (p. 124)

This is vintage Enloe – vintage feminist Enloe, that is. Revisiting a bit of diplomatic history that few in IR now cite, she places a showbusiness "bombshell" into Franklin Roosevelt's wranglings to win Latin American markets through a "Good Neighbor" policy. She shows us what was involved in the early days of marketing – a woman paraded around Hollywood and Broadway with exported bananas on her head.

In one especially useful section of the book, Enloe explains that "[t]he banana has a gendered history" (p. 127). Once bananas landed on affluent Boston dining tables in the 1870s, banana growing, buying, and selling were shaped around masculine and feminine concerns. Plantations were and still are run and worked by men and sustained by the women who service the workers as mothers, wives, and sex objects. Customers, by contrast, have been overseas women appealed to through marketing campaigns that bond women in consumption sites to those in the producer sites. Thus Miranda. Thus also United Fruit's Chiquita Banana, a singing half-banana, half-woman cartoon figure associated with one brand – as if there could be much difference between bananas of export quality. Over the years, the Chiquita cartoon has transmogrified into a simpler logo sticker that women shoppers in the USA and elsewhere can still see as a symbol of quality rather than as the outcome of marketing finesse.

Bananas are also grown by private cultivators, most of whom, Enloe writes, are women. This factor has implications for land policy. Enloe cautions: "If land reform is implemented without a critical examination of *which* small farmers will receive the precious land title, land reform can serve to perpetuate patriarchal inequities in the countryside" (p. 144). The one effective answer, she thinks, is for women to develop an analysis of their plight and organize independently of other worker organizations to publicize it, as has an organization called RICE in the Philippines. Watch out, she also wisely cautions, for the militarization of bananas: "In the Philippines, as in Honduras and Colombia, union activists have been assassinated by troops loyal to a government that sees multinational agribusiness as good for the economy" (p. 147).

Warmed to the topic of international business, Enloe takes us to the garment industry in the USA and abroad, an area well known for its armies of female workers. Here she spotlights Benetton (before it develops its controversial Colors of the World marketing strategy) as one of many clothing producers that contract work to low-paid household producers. Women find the work attractive because they can be mothers at home and workers in the economy. Husbands approve of the arrangements too, seeing in them a shield for "their" women against urban temptations. Sweat shops, staffed by illegal immigrants from Asia and Mexico, also set up in Los Angeles and New York, where the producer is a woman doing what many companies think is an extension of housework. This is a different type of public/private filiation than Elshtain discusses. Here, women are victims, but Enloe also shows cases of their involvement in efforts to bring justice to the workplace against the backdrop of "[a] leaner, more competitive world" (p. 174).

We are home again – with our Filipina nanny tending the children. Working women have few childcare options in countries where facilities are expensive and gender customs militate against men sharing childcare duties. Mothers feel guilty about paying another mother with children to clean the mess and so set their sights on being exemplary employers. Enloe says they "try to hire only nannies without children ... try to include domestic workers in their decisions about holidays and moving house" (p. 179); some try to turn the cleaning lady into a friend. "International debt politics has helped create the incentives for many women to emigrate [for such work], while at the same time it has made governments dependent on the money those women send home to their families" (p. 184). This can be a recipe for abuse and exploitation, and Enloe chronicles several incidents in which Filipina or Sri Lankan women have been imprisoned in houses of overseas Middle Eastern employers, or made to work overlong hours because they are illegal or at risk of visa nonrenewal. In sites of the private conscience that Elshtain admires, Enloe sights some women with no civic rights, or only limited ones.

At the end of *Bananas, Beaches, and Bases*, Enloe reminds readers that the feminist slogan Elshtain dislikes – the personal is political – "is like a palindrome, one of those phrases that can be read backwards as well as forwards" (p. 195). She turns it so we can see – not another slogan substituting for complex analysis, as Elshtain might think, but how the political is personal as international politics enters the lives of women. There is power in the personal and power in the political. One should read forwards and backwards around both sites, bearing in mind that the political exists internationally and not just at one's own doorstep. Hers is a call for a pro-woman spirit in a global era.

If Elshtain blocks kicks, Enloe is comfortable taking first strikes. She tirelessly points out the women and worries more about them throughout *Bananas* than about men in international relations. She outlines women's images with dark paint so they appear clearly in the landscapes. Like Elshtain, though, Enloe is more concerned to find and engage women inside/outside their allocated ontological spaces than she is to fit women into a field that has historically studied international relations without them. Enloe uses realist IR power slogans against themselves and Elshtain dismisses the behavioralist apparatus of IR out of hand. Concerned in their different ways with bringing international relations to feminism, both writers decide that IR's usual knowledge contains little of value in the study of women, gender, and topics such as war and bananas.

Given Enloe's explicit interest in making feminist sense of it all, however, it is surprising that she does not delve into feminist strategies for tackling the power issues she presents. Radical feminists think of the world as structured around gender relations of patriarchy that can be dismantled through strategic moves such as separatism. Enloe talks of patriarchy but not of the merits or demerits of a strategy such as this. Postmodern feminisms take apart named structures to reveal the strategic activities that both sustain and also dismantle monolithic blocks of power. Enloe engages in revealings and then misses much of the dismantling capability of alternative power. Pulled along by her marvelous big screen images, we respond viscerally to claims that "[i]t has taken power to keep women out of their countries' diplomatic corps and out of the upper reaches of the World Bank" (p. 198). In fact, we need to ask more questions about the dynamics of that power. Whereas Elshtain's war narratives leave us contemplating new forms of civic virtue, Enloe's narratives of women have us nodding knowingly while embarrassed at lapses of our vision; we are then thrown on to our own resources to fathom how (monolithic) patriarchy might be undone.

After *Bananas* Enloe reconsiders women's militarized sites in a post-Cold War era. Her *The Morning After* (1993), anecdotal in style like *Bananas*, depicts the Cold War as a monolith of militarism, which still bears down on women everywhere in mostly unfortunate ways. Less stylistically smooth than *Bananas*, it does show substantive concern with men as victims as well as perpetrators of militarism. Her latest book on the intricate maneuvers involved in militarizing women is even more attuned to theorizing masculine power (as keeping women with similar interests separate from and opposed to each other) (Enloe, 2000a). Throughout all these works, Enloe can write enchantingly, and with her own agenda in mind, thus avoiding head-on collisions with IR and its traditions. That she avoids feminist specificity too – and sometimes generalizes too exuberantly from a few sources – means that her work is not quite as challenging as it could be. None the less, her visual acuity is admirable; it is certainly a quality I have emulated as I try to cast eyes on women and gender in hidden relations of the international.

Enloe has also called IR to attention in an inimitable way, and in the spirit of the anecdotes peppering her writings, I offer one about her. In 1994, Cynthia and I sat in the audience of a conference celebrating the seventy-fifth anniversary of the founding of the first IR department in the world, at the University of Wales, Aberystwyth. We were the only outside women asked to present our ideas at the conference, and neither of us had yet had our turn to do so, feminist issues and women being down the agenda relative to realism, world systems, and international political economy. After listening to yet another great man of IR audaciously repeat the virtues of his own work, Cynthia put up her hand and asked, earnestly: "When was the last time you were surprised?" The speaker at the podium blinked several times and muttered that he did not understand the relevance of the question. An embarrassed silence came over the audience. I whispered to Cynthia that this might not be the right crowd for her question. She nodded. And then we watched as every succeeding speaker delayed launching into his remarks until he had addressed her question! Each wanted the audience to know that he had been surprised by new things in the world or by anomalies in what seemed to be normal IR. "When were you last surprised?" emerged as an unofficial theme of the conference. Cynthia had found a way to refocus us once again (see Enloe, 2000b).

Gender in International Relations

J. Ann Tickner is a contemporary of Elshtain and Enloe. She too can remember something of the tumult of World War II, as well as the days when attending graduate school was a mostly-male affair – "one of only three female graduate students in my year in Yale University's International Relations Program in the early 1960s" (Tickner, 1992:ix–x). Elshtain's and Enloe's early formative experiences were in the United States. Tickner is British by birth and lived with her family in London until she was an adolescent. Her diplomat father was then assigned to the United Nations in New York and Tickner subsequently made her home in the USA. She earned a Masters degree from Yale in 1961 and married fellow student Hayward Alker, who would become a "big man" of IR. She told me many years later that she did not then envisage doing a Ph.D. and becoming a professional; nor did it strike her as odd to think that way. Her views changed fifteen years later when, with three daughters nearly grown, her husband at MIT, a family home in Brookline, Massachusetts, and a summer retreat on Block Island, Tickner returned to Brandeis University for her Ph.D. Kenneth Waltz had taught Elshtain there but had since departed for Berkeley. Robert Keohane, newly arrived after a stint at Swarthmore, became Ann's mentor.

Although Tickner shares an age cohort with Elshtain and Enloe, in her professional life she is a contemporary of those who began IR careers a decade to fifteen years later. Tickner finished her doctorate in the mid-1980s rather than the late 1960s, and thereafter took a teaching-heavy position at Holy Cross University. Her list of publications is shorter than Eshtain's and Enloe's, and it is fair to say that she has less prominence in political science at large. Well regarded within IR circles, Tickner has been a Vice President of the International Studies Association, a frequent speaker in academic circles, and recipient of a Ford Foundation grant for a major conference on gender and IR. She is now a member of the International Relations Department at the University of Southern California, as is her husband.

Tickner's first book, *Self-Reliance Versus Power Politics* (1987), was her Ph.D. dissertation. Reminiscent of Enloe's early interest in development and nation-building, it sites concerns with the USA and India within IR's North–South framework. And, like Enloe's early pieces, *Self-Reliance* seems a detour *en route* to a feminist calling. Tickner's second book, *Gender in International Relations* (1992), is resoundingly feminist and also has had more impact within IR. The same can be said of her article evaluating the legacy of Hans Morgenthau's realism from feminist perspectives (Tickner, 1988) and new works that assess the marginalization of feminist scholarship in IR (Tickner, 1997) and its analytic achievements (Tickner, 2001).

Tickner has said that when she returned to university at a point she refers to as "late in life," people often remarked on how nice it was that she was getting more education: she could help her husband with his research! Not suprisingly, the first sentence of *Gender in International Relations* laments the paucity of women in IR and the few writings by women in IR's stable of works. Tickner finds a dearth of women in policy-making too, particularly in security circles, and discovers that remarks posed to those who do enter such fields are like those she received upon undertaking a Ph.D. The message is that good women do not aspire to do good men's work in international politics. Tickner explains the lopsided gender demographics of IR in precisely these terms: an entire field assumes men and gender hierarchy and writes them into its canons and offices as the norm. This pattern of scholarship, practice, and seeing the world would change, she asserts, "if the central realities of women's day-to-day lives were included" (Tickner, 1992:xi). Indeed, this is the theme of her book.

Gender uses IR in an agenda-setting manner, constructing its points around IR's realist, liberal, and Marxist texts. Unlike Enloe, Tickner does not dwell on locations of everyday women in international politics *per se*, and unlike Elshtain, she cites few women in war. What we find here is not a host of women's voices but mostly Tickner's voice of analytic reason bringing feminist questions to important issues of IR.

Gender, women, and feminism

Tickner argues that gender insinuates into international relations along the lines Elshtain suggests in *Women and War*, that is, through realms of (just) masculinity and (beautiful) femininity. Offering the usual locations and meanings of gender, she presents "women" as a gender group that is made to exist apart from the subject matter of an IR and an international relations that are dominated by men and their concerns. Despite the gender separation, she argues that women are often under threat by the field's projections of masculine experience as human experience. Whether people enact gender identity in the ways Tickner assumes is not something *Gender* probes. We have seen that Elshtain and Enloe also evade the issue of defining "women" and "men," though the former reveals activities that trick the gendered texts and practices of war, and the latter sees women's typical experiences being manipulated and sold as nimble fingers or banana-strutting stage acts. Tickner is the most accepting of women as a commonplace around which there would be little reason to pose an identity problematic.

Perhaps for that reason, she seems comfortable throughout *Gender* with standpoint feminism, which she says is "an engaged vision of the world opposed and superior to dominant ways of thinking" (quoting Ruddick in Tickner 1992:16). In most versions, feminist standpoint is the vision of women mediated by feminism. Tickner's *Gender* – like *Women and War* and *Bananas* – predates some research that queries the commonplaces of gender identity (e.g., Bordo, 1993; Butler, 1993; Braidotti with Butler, 1994; Grosz, 1994). Since her book came out in 1992, though, it does postdate writings that were shifting attention from solving women's problems to problematizing the concept and apparatus of women-naming, women-acting, and women-expecting (Braidotti, 1989; Butler, 1990; Riley, 1988). Such references are absent from Tickner's slim text. As she once told me, *Gender* is meant to be an accessible, preliminary feminist cut through IR for undergraduates.

Tickner is more explicit than Enloe, though, in identifying multiple streams of feminist thinking, mentioning by name liberal, Marxist, radical, socialist, and postmodern feminisms. She is more interested than Elshtain was in *Women and War* in showing how various feminist lights can reveal womanly shapes and forms a field implicitly denies. To Tickner, feminism in all its permutations can alert us to the ways "women are affected by global politics or the workings of the world economy" (Tickner 1992:14) and raise questions about how "hierarchical gender relations are interrelated with other forms of domination" (p. 14).

That the job of *Gender* is to introduce, remind, evoke, prick, and summarize the ways that feminist interventions can change how we see international relations, means that it leaves much of the feminist countryside untouched. But, like tornado gales weaving narrrowly through a prairie, it impressively evokes much using few words tied to a restricted mission. With mere gestures to feminist standpoint thinking, Tickner cues the naïve reader to realms of analysis we might sight were we to look at international relations through the eyes of disenfranchised observers. For example, she revisits IR's usual levels of analysis – man, the state, and war – and spins a discussion that binds masculinity *in* our lives *to* every level of international analysis. Bettering Elshtain, she sites male violence both in families and in international settings. She sees preparations for war as state security processes that link with threats against women who step out of secured places at home during peacetime. A common penchant to lionize warriors corresponds in her view to the low social regard noncombatant women perennially receive. And the gesture of assigning concern with peace to women actually enables us see women's absence from the warring institutions of international politics.

Tickner's main point is that when one dons feminist lenses, the preoccupations behind American IR's security writings can seem magnified beyond reason. And then there is the question of alternative understandings of the few plausible concepts that remain in IR. Power, for example, is something Tickner (1992:65) finds feminists associating with "mutual enablement rather than domination," although to reach this preferred approach, Tickner must neglect those feminist streams that might take a different tack. Suffice to say that Tickner's strengths in this book lie in rendering IR accountable for its slights to people we commonly, unproblematically call women and broadening its usual concepts.

Becoming economically secure

Tickner calls for the elimination of gender hierarchies as a way of achieving global security. This is a strong call to a field that has had disillusions with realism, idealism, neorealism, and behavioral methodologies but has barely taken note of gender long enough to be disillusioned with gender hierarchies. Focusing almost exclusively on American IR, Tickner sketches canonical positions on security in realism, international political economy, and international environmental studies, and indicates where aspects of the canon have been challenged within the IR tradition. Her punchline each time is that the field and its usual challengers do not and cannot go far enough to consider women and gender in ways that feminist analysis requires and international security demands.

Tickner's discussion of global economic security is especially tren-chant. She reminds readers of the many moods of economic security over time – mercantile, liberal, on a gold standard, seeking a New International Economic Order. She comes to rest canonically at the three ideologies of international political economy devised by Robert Gilpin (1987): liberalism, economic nationalism, and Marxism. But she does not rest well in their company once she begins asking "whether and how gender has circumscribed each model's understanding of the workings of the world economy" (Tickner, 1992:70).

Tickner accuses economic liberalism of projecting economic gain as the main and universal human passion, and of lodging this passion in isolated individuals who pursue self-interested utilities. Notwithstand-ing the stark ethnocentrism behind such assumptions, there is also a sticking point, she says, of community and cooperation: both emerge in liberal economic ways of thinking as conditions to be explained rather than assumptions on which to build. Feminists, contrastingly, often take sociality and interdependence as usual conditions of life; they presume that people occupy sites outside the mainstream of economic decision making when they nurse a child or tend an elder parent. Moreover, mar-kets extolled by liberal economists affect men's and women's securities differently, as numerous labor or development feminists have pointed out. As Tickner (p. 78) puts this, an economic model of security "based on instrumentally rational market behavior does not capture all the eco-nomic activities of women" – unless, I might add, it turns every moment of life into a context for rational choice.

Economic nationalism draws Tickner's measured ire in a different way. Here, the state is the main actor and not the individual. States strive for economic self-sufficiency and to protect their economic inter-ests. They induce conflict with other states – and insecurity – along the way, in acts that recall realist certainties about power pursuits and neo-realist worries about survival. But what is that unitary state? Or, more along Tickner's lines of query, who is it and whose interests does the state "protect?" Again Tickner has us asking about beneficiaries and losers under a particular construction of reality that has become commonplace in international political economy. She maintains, quite standpoint sim-ply, that if "women have been peripheral to the institutions of state power and are less economically rewarded than men, the validity of the unitary actor assumption must be examined from the perspective of gender" (p. 83). Exactly why are women clustered and rendered in-secure at the lower ends of economic nationalist states? Why assume

44

the Prisoner's Dilemma under economic nationalism, when there is evidence that it is mostly western men who prefer the games of skill that PD assumes? Tickner is one of the first to ask feminist questions in IR that, although briefly raised, cut to the bone of international political economy thinking.

Marxist approaches do not escape her attention either. Marxism receives kudos for introducing the notion that knowledge is not disinterested, not unself-serving, not universal across economic sites. Yet it also annoyingly departs women and their usual economic sites and activities for those of male producers. Marxisms most often neglect to site the reproductive roles of women within an economic framework, which means unpaid work in the household or informal economy is sited outside class history, outside amelioration. In international relations, these Marxist strengths and weaknesses recur in dependency theory, although Tickner says little about related world systems work in the early 1990s on gender (Wallerstein, 1991).

Tickner ends up placing the bulk of responsibility for male-biased assumptions across international political economy at the doorstep of usual understandings of rationality. She wants us to start with a differently defined individual, one who is rationally connected, interdependent, and whose daily activities often revolve around reproduction. Although this redefined individual poses its own binary barriers – Am I a woman if I don't define myself this way? – Tickner (the mother) takes her argument to the point of asserting, rather awkwardly compared with Elshtain, that "[w]ere childbearing and child rearing seen as more valued activities, also rational from the perspective of reproduction, it could help to reduce the excessive focus on the efficiency of an ever-expanding production of commodities, a focus whose utility in a world of shrinking resources, vast inequalities, and increasing environmental damage is becoming questionable" (Tickner, 1992:92). She also calls for a breakdown of barriers between public and private sites and contents of work, by which she means, in effect, that the work women usually do in the home should be taken into account in public economic statistics. She does not suggest that the lawn-mowing and house-maintaining activities of many suburban men be treated likewise, and it is unclear whether this liberal extension of the argument would be part of her feminism in IR standpoint.

The final case Tickner examines takes us to a topic area that has been marginalized in canonical IR – ecological security. This is arguably her most interesting discussion. Reminding us that ecology refers to "the study of life forms 'at home' " (p. 98), she points out that this is the realm that comes closest, in use of language and metaphors, to womanly concerns. It is also an issue area that challenges realist versions of international relations by calling attention to often ethereally unsightable (and at other times unsightly) consequences of state security actions. Ecological problems defy national boundaries and require collective action to resolve; neither characteristic fits "well with the power-seeking, instrumental behavior of states" (p. 97). And yet natural resources and national power are often put together by IR's realists. IR feminists, who, one might assume, would be most interested in this "home" issue, have sometimes been unnerved by a topic that draws unflattering links between women and nature and, on the other side, asserts that nature is essential to national power.

Tickner points out changes in attitudes toward nature over time. Medieval England granted animals rights and had them appearing as witnesses in court cases. Renaissance Europeans placed emphasis on human abilities, and then Enlightenment philosophy took this point to the extreme of degrading women within those abilities by associating them with nature's recalcitrant qualities. Nature had to be tamed, mastered, and managed during the industrial revolution, the way women had to be stopped if they showed signs of independent power. "Wastelands" abroad were there for the taking. Geopolitical notions of competition for global resources justified the insecuring of others so as to secure one's own state. Anarchy as a concept in IR was not far behind the state of nature thinking that made all spaces open to self-help efforts.

Tickner takes the view that western civilization's subjugation of women relates to its hierarchical constructions of power and agency, with men and men's public creations valued as pinnacles. She wants to transcend this distorted wisdom rather than seek to work within its contours. She notes cases in which women, who are poorly represented in national and international institutions, often work at local levels to redress ecological damage and to reclaim a cultural sagacity that has been debased by modern society. This is the type of movement Tickner would like to see at the global level, and concedes that "[a]s long as metaphors such as 'global housekeeping' associate ecological security with the devalued realm of women, it will not become an issue of priority on the foreign policy agendas of states or in the mainstream discipline of international relations" (p. 125).

Tickner ends *Gender* by drawing us back to her main point: "attempts to alleviate these military, economic, and ecological insecurities cannot be completely successful until the hierarchical social relations, including gender relations, intrinsic to each of these domains are recognized and substantially altered" (p. 128). American IR – and Tickner is speaking almost exclusively outside the British tradition – has dithered around these issues. It pulls between canonical ideas and challenging streams of thinking without addressing what Tickner sees as the key issue: there is no recourse to security where there are unjust social relations. At the same time, because Tickner is thinking globally, it is unclear how the problem can be resolved – and she wants to see gender inequities resolved.

Tickner suggests that the field of IR replace its dominant warrior image with a mediator image. Her sketches encourage us to dream of the moment after "hierarchical social relations, including gender relations, that have been hidden by realism's frequently depersonalized discourse," the moment "we begin to construct a language of national security that speaks out of the multiple experiences of both women and men" (p. 66). With little room in the book for discussions of complex feminist disagreements and determined canonical resistances – the stuff of politics – the dreams may dangle precariously, like hot air balloons buffeted by strong winds. Missing in Tickner are robust notions of how we are to get down to the places where she wants us to be.

Tickner's recent work retains some interests from *Gender* and expands into human rights, global order, democratic participation, and issues of identity for IR. In one place she picks up the idea popular in the UK that society is the hot spot of the future, which means identity is the variable to telescope, not anarchy or power in the old realist sense. While these notions are new to American IR, she reminds us that they are not new to feminists, who have shown consistent concern with understanding the ways that gender identity affects the world IR sees and women's opportunities within it. She talks about impediments or misunderstandings that still stand in the way of effective feminist and IR conversations (Tickner, 1997, 2001), concerned that we stay transdisciplinary, critical, and connected to a field that needs to resite and re-cite itself. Disappointed so far, she is also willing to keep trying to bring feminist IR into official IR, a mission Elshtain and Enloe have traveled away from. If anyone can prevail at that task it is Tickner; she is the one who cracked the *International Studies Quarterly* with her 1997 feminist IR

piece – a good ten years after feminist IR started its journey. To her I am
indebted for confronting the partial and mistaken logics of IR directly –
something that Elshtain and Enloe do not do – and unwaveringly.

Echoes in the chambers

The purposes of Part I have been twofold: to help the reader remember the contexts in which feminist IR/IR feminism arose and grew
roots; and to showcase leading first-wave feminist writings about IR.
We remember the dislocations and excitements of the 1980s here, the
American and British currents, the third debate, the hunkering down
and rising up of an IR grappling with what Tickner refers to generally
as new thinking. We also revisit key sites on the way to sighting and
citing aspects of the new we now associate with feminist thinking.

Elshtain looms as the mother–family philosopher, the witty and lucid
expositor of people who enter realms of war but whose experiences are
not always recounted in war stories. We meet through her the problem of the western patriot, who cannot stop glorifying, rehearsing, and
warring. We contemplate his and her chastening, as the wisdom of private conscience that Elshtain encourages seeps and oozes into forbidden
spaces of the public. We wonder and we worry about good mothers and
good soldiers, about families that do not fit the bill, and about sex worker
women not given voice in Elshtain's war narratives.

We journey on. Enloe has surprises – Indian princesses, dancing fruit
hats, liberated women tourists burdening Third World women with
their fun, diplomatic wives minding the business of nations from behind
kitchen pots, and domestic servants traveling the world for a little in-
come. It is all there in Enloe: the world comes to us through vivid pictures, unexpected citations, lively sitings. We see women everywhere;
what power-feminist sense we are making of them is a stumble in her
work, but one we are (too) happy to pick ourselves up from and move on.

Tickner has us look squarely at IR as a professional American field
that has bought heartily into the language and tribal customs of social
science and warriorhood. It is too full of power, rationality, insecurity,
autonomy, and vigilance to see, let alone cite, the ways of the world
feminists notice. Tickner wants to integrate feminist perspectives into IR
as a first step on the road to a new international relations that transcends
gender altogether. She provides readers with numerous opportunities
to see extant gendered aspects and to conceptualize alternative starting
points that make more sense. Hers is a leaner and more textbook-type

approach, and if it is wobbly on the variegations of gender, women, and feminism, it is strong on picking up IR's pomposities.

Despite differences, these first-wave writers of feminist IR have much in common. They are, first of all, concerned to explain, with varying degrees of candor, why they are blaspheming IR by insisting that someone important is missing from its knowledge. In doing so, they work from autobiography, with Elshtain attaining a level of virtuosity. The first-wavers are also, as a second point, interested in asking the key question Enloe explicitly raises: where are the women? Enloe and Tickner, in particular, lose no sleep over whether women exist as they are customarily portrayed. They are, to some degree, users or borrowers of the feminist standpoint tradition, which operates from the assumption that women are tangible, real, legitimate, or meaningful in identity, site, and/or word. Elshtain's stories slip and slide so much around gender assignments that she ends up in something of a postmodernist camp at the end of the day. Enloe infuses her concern about women with issues of power and how much it takes to make gender work the way it does in the world. Tickner takes us through sites of security studies as IR sees them and then as various feminist scholars depict them. Hers is a story of how knowledge becomes a trope for those who rehearse it in certain ways, a barricade, ultimately, against sight – and against reasonable argument.

Feminist IR/IR feminism is innovatively ethnographic while also showing sympathy with methodological traditionalism. Elshtain directly appeals to historical texts and philosophical arguments in *Women and War*. Tickner does this too with respect to the texts of IR and feminism. Enloe has a mixed style with mixed methods, now ethnographic, now historical, then using anecdotes and commonsense arguments. Neither she nor Elshtain strives to conform to social science writing styles entirely, and in Elshtain's case, this produces work that is more eloquent than most; indeed she seems to take to her keyboard like a novelist who cannot hold wit *cum* moral intensity within the confines of her words. Enloe is the insightful, quirky, world-travel writer who also wanders the earth constantly – now in Istanbul, now in Mexico City, now peering out from a feminist postcard in red hi-top sneakers. None among these writers presents statistics in order to make the point. All are way beyond and underwhelmed by positivism.

Finally, each in her own way tells us why IR has let her down. Elshtain is disappointed by the narrowness of stories bolstering the field, the thinness of the civic virtue that figures around IR. Enloe cannot understand how IR has got away with posing power as a central concept and then pulling back from the gender implications of power in its own discourses. Tickner is the student of IR who cannot take the masculine aura of the field any longer and hopes to transform it beyond recognition by tackling its problems head on.

The essays that follow these impressive acts form a self-genealogy within the first-wave genealogy represented by Elshtain, Enloe, and Tickner. Through pieces written across a period of fifteen years, a personal and professional odyssey emerges; for, as I suspect others would agree, feminist IR is an autobiographically driven quest that takes one to places unanticipated when beginning. My journey has been to the feminist questions in IR and IR questions in feminism – and then some. I have tried the elixirs of IR; departed standard IR for Zimbabwe, feminism, postcolonial and development studies, imaginative literature and art; and have generally endeavored to push the margins of feminist and IR intellectual risk. Along the way, I have tried and tried to unclog my stuffed mind, unblind my eyes, unsite myself, and cite themes of some import in the world. The paths I have taken have not been linear, and thus within each part that follows the chapters can be read in any order. I have taken my own turns – for good or ill – but have never been alone. Throughout, Elshtain, Enloe, and Tickner and other feminists have whispered in my ear, given me ideas, made me cross, and made me think. Whether the journey alongside and sometimes away from them has been worthy, the reader will have to judge.

Part II
Sightings

3   Handmaids' tales of Washington power: the abject and the real Kennedy White House

We commence at a moment and place of international relations that Elshtain, Enloe, and Tickner did not address. The setting is the early 1960s White House. John Kennedy is president; Jacqueline Kennedy graces the covers of fashion magazines; Marilyn Monroe is hot; and missiles in Cuba press on US and international nerves. The missiles are real enough, but the White House principals live at odds with their Madison Avenue smiles, relying on scores of unseen handlers to polish images and keep secrets. "Handmaids' Tales" weaves those years and those people around feminist theory, feminist fiction, and feminist international relations of the 1990s.

"Handmaids' Tales" is the rejigged title of Margaret Atwood's novel *The Handmaid's Tale* (1985). Set in the near future, the novel portrays a traumatized, depopulated western society obsessed with women's bodies – not as visual stimulants as today, but as machines for desperate procreation. A handmaid is what radical feminists used to call a "breeder," but with a twist: she is forced by society leaders to limit her life to themes of childbearing. Handmaids must wear billowing red garments that simultaneously signal their status as potentially fertile females, hide those bodies from public view, and restrain the sight and movement of the wearers. They are Madonnas of survival, and they are feared, resented, and envied. Intertile commanders of society minister to them sexually in private acts watched over by wary, infertile commanders' wives. The rest of the time handmaids "rest," like Carmen Mirandas immobilized by bittersweet fruits piled too high.

Atwood's handmaids are disarmed feminists recast as good sexual soldiers and good mothers in waiting. Their privacy is a public filiation. Indeed, it is instructive to think of Elshtain (1987) and Atwood writing at about the same time of different spheres of privacy spilling into new notions of citizenship and civic patriotism. In the society Atwood creates, Elshtain's arguments about the wisdom of private conscience for society lead to nasty outcomes – perverse, chilling, and narratively closed for women. We are aghast. Yet regard the White House past and present and see those who contribute to the survival of politicians; they only get public attention for their work if the president is shamed. We are not aghast enough, I would say, by norms of Washington power that sweep men-empowering handmaids into invisible or darkened corners.

"Handmaids' Tales" lets me conjoin memories and imaginative literatures to IR question(s) in postmodern feminism. Alongside my reading of Atwood, I take in Judith Butler's (1993) ideas on performativity, Julia Kristeva's (1982) sense of the abject, Rosi Braidotti's (with Butler, 1994) insistence on sexual difference as a marker of feminism (and not just gender, as feminist theorists in North America have preferred), and Elizabeth Grosz's (1994) and Susan Bordo's (1993) words on bodies that seep and ooze. These writers are part of a wave of feminist theorizing that came after *Women and War* and *Bananas*, and around the time of *Gender in International Relations*.

"Handmaids" also reflects childhood memories of Kennedy and wrapped-up white, middle-class USA in the early 1960s. An impressionable ten when John Kennedy took office, I was at the beginning of a quest to work out the sense of politics. Against the backdrop of the first presidential election I could comprehend, I asked family members and teachers to explain the differences between Republicans and Democrats. Everybody stumbled around that one, talking about bankers versus people, and conservatives here and liberals there. Kennedy's inaugural address was simpler, more poetic, and more concise. This young Connecticut Yankee gazed on that other New Englander as the best thing since the transistor. Somewhat later, huddled with friends in the schoolyard, I listened to reports of missiles in Cuba with a sense of excitement and expectation, confident that the talent in this White House was too great for another state to better. And so it seemed to be.

I later learned IR versions of the missile tale starting with the Graham Allison scenarios. Still enthralled, I devoted the first undergraduate class I taught as a graduate student in political science to explicating his views on Kennedy's decision-making context. Well after any retelling could possibly strike a note of immediacy in student hearts, I carried on. But now look: Allison and the Cuban missile crisis – and the glamorous Kennedy – come out differently in "Handmaids' Tales." A new set of actors slips on to the stage for a bow.

There are other interests served by this piece. At fifteen, I hauled an enormous collected works of William Shakespeare up a tree in my backyard, where I spent the summer reading amongst branches and leaves that sheltered me from intrusive family agendas (and gave me wicked poison ivy). Earlier, I had volunteered at the children's branch of the local town library, shelving books and reading them in nearly equal numbers. Books were important to me and I still read fiction with the sense that my life depends on it. My IR feminist writing increasingly relies on imaginative literatures for textures and places, triumphs and worries, economies and politics that IR does not provide. Like visual art – another intrusion from the past that creeps into my present work – novels keep my feminist eyes open and IR questions in feminism easy to imagine. I introduce fiction with feminist IR here and then come back to it throughout the ensuing feminist journey; it is, in effect, my research counterpart to the films, diaries, postcards, and classrooms that have intrigued Elshtain, Enloe, and Tickner.

$$* \quad * \quad *$$

Richard Reeves has added seven hundred and ninety-eight pages to the reams of scholarship, histrionics, and sex in John F. Kennedy's White House. In his *President Kennedy: Profile of Power* we are presented with another narrative of what the thirty-fifth president of the United States "did at crucial points of his three years in power" (Reeves, 1993:18). This account, though, is different than its key predecessors, the author claims, because it was written from newly available records and from interviews with witnesses to the dailiness of Kennedy's White House.[1]

"Dailiness" conjures images of women as well as of men, of bodily functions and caretaking, of private moments in and out of public eyes. In this regard, the start of the book is promising: Reeves draws our attention to the existence of "men and women of White House courts" (p. 13). But a glance at the references shows that the narrative is based on new interviews or previously recorded conversations with

---

This part of the chapter is reprinted by permission of Sage Publications Ltd. from *Body and Society*, 4, 3, 1998.
[1] Reeves's concern for the daily workings of the Kennedy White House, and his conclusions about disorder therein, set this political biography apart from earlier ones by Schlesinger (1965) and Sorensen (1966). Reeves's tome draws on those sources and on Parmet (1984), Galbraith (1969), Bradlee (1975), and Fay (1966).

eighty-three people who have men's names (p. 664). Indeed, Reeves merely tips his hat to the women around the president in cloying bursts of now-let's-see-Jack-with-the-ladies: we find only nine women's names in the list of those interviewed or listened in on. To Reeves, and to Kennedy as reconstructed by him, "women" are reiteratively and citationally outside the main events of a singular Washington story. Like Margaret Atwood's fictional handmaids from Gilead, whose stories appear in her novel *The Handmaid's Tale* (1985), White House women grease the machines of power with faces hooded, protected from the glare of recognition, publicity, and agency.

The people and practices Reeves documents in the Kennedy White House, and the ways he documents them, compose an exemplary text about bodies in high places. It is a story of people missing from power scenes, of ghosts sighted fleetingly, perhaps, in the background of important events. Such bodies, to use Judith Butler's (1993:243n) terms, are abject; they are "cast off, away or out ... within the terms of sociality." They are sent to "those 'unlivable' and 'uninhabitable' zones of social life which are nevertheless densely populated by those who do not enjoy the status of the subject" (p. 3). In the company of abject handmaids, visible politicos can be "casual to a fault tonight. Jacket off, elbows on the table" (Atwood, 1985:237); because power from the uninhabitable zone is, at best, "restrained, off to the side, at the edge of your vision, present on some horizon of it" (Lyotard, 1991:20–21). It can be casually ignored, left uncited.

Yet, as Julia Kristeva (1982:2) points out – and as Atwood's fictive handmaids illustrate rather well – "from its place of banishment, the abject does not cease challenging its master." Bodies whose work makes citations to Washington decision-makers possible have the capacity to circumscribe the assignment of abjected "sex" through never-successfully-contained power leaks. Handmaids ooze power with, around, or over those they loyally attend. They do so through their decisional capacities as recorders and machine operators, fetchers of reports, and deciders of where to seat whom or what to shred from the main story. Their access to resources is real, their location "off to the side" an opportunity as well as a liability.

This essay asks us to consider abject handmaids as fixtures of Washington power past and present. It suggests some of the tasks such people and statuses have in uninhabitable zones. It also glimpses the ways that power from abjection can "disturb identity, system, order," can "not respect borders, positions, rules," and can be "in-between, the ambiguous, the composite" (Kristeva, 1982:4). In short, we see how handmaids may "extend the frameworks which attempt to contain them" (Grosz 1994:xi).

The discussion begins in feminist debates about bodies and sex and the performances, margins of nonbelonging, and fluidities that enable handmaids to enter realms of power. We then follow a variety of could-be handmaids to the backlots and the front offices of the Kennedy White House. Occasionally it is necessary to move forward in time so the issues discussed are not seen as in the past, finished; or there is lateral movement to differentiate the Washington handmaid from someone who could be thought to be one or who escaped being one. Our Washington tale moves on from there to the days of missiles in Cuba. In discussions of one of the seminal moments of Kennedy's years in office, we find that handmaids make important appearances at the margins of the story as Reeves recounts it. They are completely abjected, though, in Graham Allison's (1969, 1971) study of crisis decision making. The feint that obscures women participants from Allison's view (and Reeves does not take them quite seriously either) is so convincing that one might imagine Washington as an especially closed system of masculine privilege at times of national emergency.

Throughout a corrective tale, handmaids from houses in Gilead that Atwood made famous seep through fiction to "real" places, situations, and bodies of "sex" and decision making in Washington. In the absence of sufficient citations by Reeves to White House women in policy circles and around missiles, the Gilead handmaids help us see how official power is beholden to activities of those made abject by it. Such circuitous tracings combine feminist theory, international relations, and fiction to find the real Washington decision making, and the uncited bodies that matter, in power capitals. Atwood (1985:289) urges us on: "find out and tell us." "Find out what?" I say. I feel rather than see the slight turning of her head. "Anything you can" (p. 289).

Feminists consider bodies, sex, gender, power

The first terrain of finding takes us to expectations people generally bring to certain types of bodies, particularly those of "women." This is the turf of feminism: feminist theorists have continuously sought to apprehend the links between bodies, sex, gender, and power. Their explorations have produced debates around the extent to which "woman" is a powerful site of authentic meaning, identity, and bodily experience relative to being a socially constituted subject status that conforms or not to the power of assigned identity.[2] Recent discussions of these points by Judith Butler, Rosi Braidotti, and Elizabeth Grosz help us see how a particular type of body – a "handmaid" – emerges at the fulcrum of arguments about bodies enacting and evading the sex and gender expectations that surround them.[3]

Butler (1993) argues that the distinction often made between sex as relatively fixed body biology and gender as the social meanings and practices associated with biological differences offers no direct access to "sex." That is, "sex" is absorbed by gender as something "retroactively installed at a prelinguistic site" (p. 5). "Sex" matters, says Butler, and it matters as a norm, an expectation, a performance that has power as "part of a regulatory practice that produces the bodies it governs" (p. 1). Normed performances of "sex" exert strong conformist power for bodies and for gender. None the less, performed "sex" results in bodies that we can think of neither as entirely fictional nor fixed facts. Bodies, Butler (p. 2) argues, "never quite comply with the norms by which their materialization is impelled." That is, the imperative norm of "sex" enacts what it names, but not always convincingly. Butler (p. 188) explains:

> this imperative, this injunction, requires and institutes a "constitutive outside" – the unspeakable, the unviable, the nonnarrativizable that secures and, hence, fails to secure the very borders of materiality. The normative power of performativity – its power to establish what qualifies as "being" – works not only through reiteration, but through exclusion as well. And in the case of bodies, those exclusions haunt signification as its abject borders or as that which is strictly foreclosed: the unlivable, the nonnarrativizable, the traumatic.

Braidotti does not agree with Butler's emphasis on the performativity of "sex." She would "re-connect the feminine to the bodily sexed reality of the female, refusing the separation of the empirical from the symbolic, or of the material from the discursive, or of sex from gender" (Braidotti, 1989:93). This reconnection centers on complex issues of sexual difference. She argues that the dominance of men over women, for example,

---

[2] One thinks of the very different approaches to women and "women" in Daly (1978) and Lerner (1986) versus Riley (1988) and Trinh (1989).
[3] See discussion of this debate in Butler (1994) and Ferguson (1993). Also, Moore (1995), Bordo (1993), Grosz (1994), and Gatens (1996).

has to do with a phallic expectation of abstract virility. Through it, holders of the Phallus are able to lose the body and gain "entitlement to transcendence and subjectivity" (1994 with Butter: 38), a powerful form of masculinity. Women, lacking the symbolic Phallus, are "over-embodied and therefore consigned to immanence" (p. 38), a less esteemed set of processes. In Braidotti's account, we can see inscriptions of sexual difference that are not physical, material, or performative. They are, rather, empirical and symbolic sex and gender processes that are difficult to dislodge. Women's excentricity from the phallic system, their "margin of nonbelonging" (p. 39), offers a point of power in counter-memories of what has been denied to the feminine. Braidotti: "one's imaginary relations to one's real life conditions, including one's history, social conditions, and gender relations, become material for political and other types of analysis" (p. 42).

In between Butler's and Braidotti's positions lies that of Grosz (1994) and the construction of women that Atwood's (1985) fiction reveals, laments, warns of in *The Handmaid's Tale*. Grosz takes a sexual difference position that is similar to Braidotti's but less phallic in its references. She argues that "[o]ur conceptions of reality, knowledge, truth, politics, ethics, and aesthetics are all effects of sexually specific – and thus far in our history usually male – bodies, and are all thus implicated in the power structures which feminists have described as patriarchal, the structures which govern relations between the sexes" (Grosz, 1994:ix). Braidotti speaks about possibilities of multiplicity within the sexual difference that is "women," and Grosz too draws sexual difference as a mobile or volatile concept "able to insinuate itself into regions where it should have no place, to make itself, if not invisible, then at least unrecognizable in its influences and effects" (p. ix). Her sense of how volatility occurs, though, is a bit different than Braidotti's: "woman" insinuates through a mode of inscription in which she appears as a seepage. "Woman" has as much corporeal solidity as "man" and "men" have fluid seepages like "women." But "insofar as they are women, they are represented and live themselves as seepage, liquidity . . . liquidities that men seem to want to cast out of their own self-representations" (p. 203).

By this logic, the culturally marked seepages that are "women" can flow from Braidotti's margin of nonbelonging, and from the margin of abjection encrusted in Butler's notion of performative "sex," into places "if not invisible, then at least unrecognisable in influences and effects." That "woman" is not supposed to transgress margins, even though she is inscribed in a way that enables her to do so, is clear in Kristeva's discussion of what happens to secretions, seepages, and unstopped-up flows: they become excrement. Some excrement is cast off, as "the danger to identity that comes from without," and some as the "danger issuing from within the identity . . . [that] threatens . . . the identity of each sex in the face of sexual difference" (Kristeva, 1982:71). In any event, says Grosz (1994:207): "The (social and psychical) goal is to establish as great a separation as possible from the excremental, to get rid of it quickly, to clear up after the mess"; some excrement, however, "cannot be escaped, or fled from . . ."

One seepage "that threatens the identity of each sex in the face of sexual difference" is menstrual blood. This excrement is usually kept out of view and memory in power places in Washington; but Atwood's fictional handmaids help us find it at the center of power concerns. In Gilead, all handmaids are of childbearing age and capacity in a society where femininity has been culturally reconnected in a most essentialist way to the bodily experience of maternity. Handmaids are made to dress in menstrual red so everyone can see the symbols of their sexually inscribed excrement. At the same time, those "sexed" bodies are made nearly to immaterialize behind the large oozing-red garments, a "sex act" that other citizens of Gilead – the Commanders, Commanders' Wives, Jezebels, Guardians, Eyes, Marthas, and the like – do not experience. The body abjection that handmaidenly costuming suggests, the nonnarrativizable that secures a border of maternity, ends up fictionalized through the agency and visibility handmaids are accorded in species survival. Those who ooze blood have *the* power of procreation for a dwindling society in which "[t]here is no such thing as a sterile man anymore, not officially. There are only women who are fruitful and women who are barren, that's the law" (Atwood, 1985:79).

Other fruitful "sex acts" include stereotypical women's work: "There's a rug on the floor, oval, of braided rags. This is the kind of touch they like: folk art, archaic, made by women, in their spare time, from things that have no further use" (p. 9). But the key "sex act" for handmaids in Gilead is physical sex, and they perform it publicly, humiliatingly, as absolutely body-tied persons "without a shape or name" (p. 3). Commanders ritualistically do "sex" with them, seeping body fluids in the process; but these men perform for maternity very badly. "He" is usually the one who cannot fertilize the handmaid, and her shapeless body indicates that this is so – month after month. Some handmaids come to sense through this iterated experience that power in Gilead is less zero-sum than performatively tied to celebrations of power-men who depend on the bodies they abject: "Occasionally I try to put myself in his position. I do this as a tactic, to guess in advance how he may be moved to behave towards me. It's difficult for me to believe I have power over him, of any sort, but I do; although it's of an equivocal kind" (p. 272).

In fact, we find power lessons in all this fiction: handmaidenly drips on to capital power-people are made to appear to disappear, to appear to be unspeakable, in order for seemingly undripping bodies of cited citizens to materialize performing their more powerful "sex." Yet it is all a *trompe-l'oeil*. Throughout the process of materialization, handmaids seem to be the ones who "don't sit on chairs, but kneel"(p. 351). It is surely the case that for handmaids it's "hard to look up, hard to get the full view, of the sky, of anything" (p. 40). None the less, we find that their anticipated power performance "haunts signification as its abject borders" through "sex acts" that can put handmaids in full pregnant view of all or, through their flat bellies, suggest insufficiencies in the phallic right to transcend bodily inadequacies.

Siting feminist debates in a perspective that includes the "fictional" handmaids Atwood creates produces useful cross-fertilizations of vision, location, and reference. We see compelled social performances in Gilead that resonate with Butler's general notions of "sex" as performed expectations that do not entirely work as premised nor render "women" as abject as they look. Gilead assigns women stereotypical "sex acts" that enable power-men to occupy that sphere of bodily transcendence that Braidotti finds characteristic of phallic expectation: if a handmaid does not fall pregnant, the problem lies with her not him; she has not gotten the job done. And seepages of power from handmaidenly quarters fall in line with what Grosz and Kristeva identify as transgressive leakages beyond assignment that serve as at least equivocal forms of power from the abject zone. Given our elaborate academic costumes, rules, and habits of thought, it takes a combination of texts to begin to find multiple ironic manifestations, influences, and effects of handmaidenly power in capital places.

Who is minding the corpo-real White House?

In high policy circles in Washington, we find another realm of expectations about which bodies may have power. Particularly in circles dealing with international politics, bodies seem compelled to be materially, symbolically, and culturally male. Ann Tickner (1992:1) writes that "in 1987, women constituted less than 5 percent of the senior Foreign Service ranks." She also testifies that this small number culturally "reinforces the belief, widely held in the United States and throughout the world by both men and women, that military and foreign policy are arenas of policy-making least appropriate for women" (p. 3). Even those men's bodies that are in view can be constituted as performing abstractly as virile "decision-makers," as if the cultural and symbolic identities in a body-transcending construct could impersonally disguise the usual bodies of decision. Allison (1969, 1971), a key progenitor of decision making literature in the field of International Relations, depicts Washington foreign policy decision-makers as rational pulsating brains detached from other body parts, as bureaucratic men who "differ concerning what must be done [and t]he differences matter" (1969:707), or, between those poles, as creatures of organizations whose roles both make and disguise (men's) bodies experienced in them.

Certain material bodies are certainly absent from our view of Washington politics. Lacking canonical recognition, they are compelled, in effect, to be outside the cultural meaning of a place and its dynamics. Such bodies come to work, are asked to do innumerable tasks, but are not credited fully, publicly and in academic texts with making contributions of the magnitude of those whose corporeality is assumed to have power. None the less, the language gives it all away: jokes about secretaries, wives, mistresses; gossip passed on by power brokers; worries and legal brouhaha when Monica Lewinskys and Paula Joneses implicate a Washington power-body in sexual improprieties.[4] All of these seeped words suggest the threatening power of bodies that work at mean jobs in Washington.

A breezy example of that power appears in Reeves's rendition of Kennedy's electoral triumph in 1959: "Kennedy had celebrated victory in his house at Hyannis Port with a joke about his wife and Toni Bradlee, the wife of a friend, Ben Bradlee, the Washington bureau chief of *Newsweek* magazine. Both women were pregnant. 'Okay, girls, you can take out the pillows now. We won'" (Reeves, 1993:24)! Beyond the zone of canonical recognition, adult "girls" become "sex"-linked pregnant wives, whose body experiences make a man's cultural image but

[4] I am referring in the last example to scandals that enveloped Bill Clinton's administration after several women suggested that illicit presidential sex was taking place in the White House, had occurred in and near the Governor's Mansion in Arkansas, and was apt to pop up in other venues.

whose power is deemed performative, decorous, soft, removable – like a pillow.

Minders who are not handmaids

Having sighted Washington terrains where handmaids tread, it is important to point out that not every woman in and around Washington men can be termed a handmaid. Atwood's typology of roles in fictional Gilead provides useful signposts for finding the handmaids among the myriad others.

Presidential *Wives* are not, strictly speaking, handmaids. They are the power behind the throne, we like to say. They are hidden and not-hidden, showcased and bound within a glass showcase. Abjected and not quite abject, people such as Jacqueline Kennedy are boundary-walkers, who are partly in a husband's shadow and partly able to put many in shadows they themselves cast. Their power – in Washington as in Gilead, where Atwood's handmaids shuffle amidst Commander's Wives – comes from legal intimacy with the body of the president. A presidential wife is not really the power behind the throne; she is the throne of "sex" starchily materialized into a body-beacon of high culture that hides her privileged access to the president's (hidden) body fluids, his viscosity. Presidents as men do not have viscosity. They are not supposed to leak and flow – even though their excretions make for first families and other sexual events. The knower of the secret – that the president secretes – is cast off from official power and usually does little to disturb carefully cultivated presidential identity, performance, and order, although exceptions come to mind: Hillary Clinton splintered the glass showcase when she stepped forward to defend her husband's alleged "sex acts" with women other than her. Still, a presidential wife is recognized mainly because she is with him, whether supporting and defending his activities, setting fashion in pink pillbox hats, or undertaking projects of her own. Not handmaids quite, wives are semi-abjected by cultural mediations that stop up the knowledge-power flows of First Lady (Bodies).[5]

Other bodies can share a wife's space, access to presidential body fluids, and semi-abjected status, and also not be handmaids. Reeves tells us that "Marilyn Monroe was trouble. She was telling people in Hollywood of an affair with the president ..." (Reeves, 1993:315).

---

[5] Mrs. von Clausewitz comes to mind. See Elshtain (1987). Hillary Clinton may have also broken this mold by gaining public office in New York while her husband was US president.

Monroe was a power person in her own independent right. She was scripted to abject that power – to disidentify with it – during alleged moments when she was a *Jezebel* to the president of the United States. She and others like her become "trouble" because they materialize an excess of "sex" in the White House and misidentify their body power with Washington power. Their sex flows threaten to disturb pristine presidential identity, the cultural system of family values surrounding his institution, and the control and order associated with a high culture of fluidless propriety.

Jezebels can be publicly recognized for their boundary blurring practices, their degradations, contaminations – both admired and scorned for their transgressions: "Certainly I am not dismayed by these women, not shocked by them. I recognize them as truants. The official creed denies them, denies their very existence, yet here they are" (Atwood, 1985:306). The key point is that Jezebels do their "sex acts" where they are not socially sanctioned to do them. By contrast, Jackie Kennedy, who is officially where she is supposed to be, may do her "sex acts" as sex – keeping it all appropriately robed, unspeakable.

Another semi-abjected near-handmaid in Washington is the body that has proper symbolic sex for power but is not marked by other Commanders as sufficiently enculturated: "Arthur Schlesinger had sat in a corner throughout the meeting, too junior to vote on small surrogate wars. To many of the others, the professor's status was measured by the fact that his office was in the East Wing of the White House. 'With the women,' Rusk noted" (Reeves, 1993:82). "With the women," to put it esoterically, means being outside "the Cartesian fantasy of the philosopher's transcendence of the concrete locatedness of the body (and so of its perspectival limitations) in order to achieve the God's-eye view, the 'view from nowhere'" (Bordo, 1993:39). It is, more simply, to perform "sex" wrongly, to violate body boundaries. Yet, whereas handmaids that are "sexed" female "have learned to see the world in gasps" (Atwood, 1985:40), Schlesingers may leave the abjected sex behind, in the past, to become Cartesian subjects grasping policy. Very simply, they may stop being *Guardians* to Commanders, and cross beyond the symbolic oozing line associated with women, because, ultimately, they have the cultural right to transcend the body. "If they are able to gain enough power and live to be old enough, [they can be] allotted a Handmaid of their own" (pp. 29–30).

There is also a category of semi-abjection for women within the public glare of power: "women" in foreign policy circles – a performance of power that lacks a certain credibility, does not really pass out of an incorrect materialization of "sex, " an incorrect body experience irrespective of the body ambiguities all around Washington. These women are so rare that we have to move forward from Kennedy's time in order to cite one telling secrets about power blockages in the White House:

> I have heard it said that one top White House person, opposing my appointment to a higher-level job at one point, said, "at the end of the day when people sit around with their feet up, she just isn't one of the boys." That wasn't said in my presence, obviously, so it's hearsay, but it's hearsay from very close sources.
>
> (Jeanne Kirkpatrick in McGlen and Sarkees, 1993:58)

> I was offered an embassy in the spring of 1977 and I said "yes." I went home and thought about it, talked with a friend of mine and got angry after the discussions. My whole career had been bounced around on the edges, Philippines, Palermo. I wasn't ever in the middle of anything except for my one little NATO job. Palermo was an island, Manila was an island, the Bahamas were islands, and here they were, about to send me to another island.
>
> (Rozanne Ridgway in McGlen and Sarkees, 1993:172)

The wrong material, symbolic, and cultural "sex." Still, these insiders are appointed, recognized, cited by colleagues, and interviewed. They are not handmaids. More likely, they are like Gilead's *Aunts*: "They also serve who only stand and wait, said Aunt Lydia. She made us memorize it" (Atwood, 1985:25).

The final category before coming to handmaids is peopled (lightly) with those who don the manner of a powerhouse man and the clothes of some 1960s stereotype of a matron in order to pass into official power. These women are at the apex of "sex" and politics. We move ahead again and laterally for a good sighting: Margaret Thatcher in a period costume. Safe was s/he on both sides of "sex." Her "sex" became unrepresentable as "she" defied any sense one might have that "she" could not possibly last long in office, in power. "She" was not really the truth of sex – even when her hair climbed up to a feminine extreme, lightened to a metallic glow, and sensible suits gave away the legs "men" so rarely are compelled to show in public office. With her female cues and blistering politics, her sex was homeless, misidentified, disidentified – a movement of the boundaries of body. "She" made it into the glare of publicity. "She" turned a nearly abjected status – women in politics – into a subjecthood.[6] She shared terrain with young Schlesingers who can eventually make it to the top, in that her power was commanding, convincing, expected, and recognized despite her bad materialization of "sex." Once she passed, though, "she" did little for people who identified as women, because "she" admitted no closure on her-Self and arrogantly seemed to disidentify with those who did. Indeed, "[p]erhaps [s/]he is an *Eye*" (Atwood, 1985:24, emphasis added) who, upon attaining legal power, foils the transgressive ambitions of others.

Sighting the handmaids

Handmaids are different than any of this. We find them in the abject zone rather than at an apex or semi-abjected place. They are culturally constituted as the product of necessity rather than agency. Their body work is required for certain bodies of power to exist at all; none the less, that power of necessity, in and of itself, is not deemed important to politics. Their job descriptions are lacking. Their training is lacking. Their "sex" too is lacking. Handmaids are where they are because "it is like *that*: I am sexed" (Braidotti, 1989:101, emphasis in original). Culturally sexed female by others, whether or not this body status makes sense, handmaids are compelled into being as workaday secretaries and confidantes, valets, chauffeurs, administrative assistants, and para-everythings.

All of this "sex act" assignation occurs in Washington irrespective of corporeality (unlike in Gilead) because, as Grosz (1994:206) suggests: "Bodily differences, marked and given psychical and cultural significance, are of course not restricted to the particular bodily regions in which they originate: they seep ... outside of and beyond the body, forming a kind of zone of contamination." Handmaid is a zone of contamination, of womanhood seeped out to others who perform all the work that is excrement in Washington. It is a reproductive category in which babies are not the praised end product; rather, what is reproduced is the formal power of someone else: "her" blood – menstrual or otherwise – flows into his veins.

Butler (1993:13) claims that the "norm of sex takes hold to the extent that it is 'cited' as such a norm, but it also derives its power through

[6] Nancy Hirschmann (1992:19) writes about the US context: "women who succeed in public office are the exceptions to the rule ... women have an anomalous place in politics, not a usual one, and certainly, according to party organizations as well as the electorate, not a welcome one." Also see Carroll (1985).

the citations that it compels." Handmaids do not compel citations to their bodies or their "sex" or their work. They seem to work within "sex" convincingly, despite the incompleteness, perhaps the contrariness, of their apparition – despite their seepage. They do not appear to misidentify or disidentify with abjectness, to disagree with the rules of the game, to suffer the *ressentiment* that Friedrich Nietzsche (1969:230) associated with "[a]nger, pathological vulnerability, impotent lust for revenge, thirst for revenge, poison-mixing in any sense ..."[7] Rather, handmaids are constituted as sites of fatalism, "tenaciously clinging for years to all but intolerable situations, places, apartments, and society, merely because they happened to be given by accident; it was better than changing them, than *feeling* that they could be changed – than rebelling against them" (p. 231, emphasis in original).

Handmaids of all materialized and symbolic sexes and subjectivities rarely perform culturally and symbolically convincing body-boundary power crossings. Undoubtedly they have "multiple registers of existence ... [which may be] lived in resistance to competing notions of one's allegiance or self-identification" (Alarcón 1990:365–366). These identifications may encompass racial, sexual, gender, generational, ethnic, and linguistic components of difference as sites of resistance to a compelled "sex." But handmaids are not constituted as leaking out of their positions and, therefore, are *not seen as* seeking citations to power through body-mind-expertise, through an agentic will to (conventional Washington) power. Such an unruly "unthought would have to make your machines uncomfortable," to borrow a phrase from Jean-Francois Lyotard (1991:20), and these are not unruly bodies, not unreliable or frail bodies. They are loyal and strong. Reeves discovers a certain disorder in the Kennedy White House, but it is not theirs; it is (unthinkably) his.[8] Meanwhile, "I'm sitting in the Commander's office, across from him at his desk, in the client position ..." Atwood's (1985:237) handmaid continues her thought in a power-insinuating direction: " ... as if I'm a bank customer negotiating a hefty loan." There is a contamination of assignment here, a mixed behavioral/symbolic performance,

---

[7] One outcome of *ressentiment* can be the bitter abject hero, who crosses over from an anger that is couched in social compassion, from "ready to wear motley ... [to] the well-dressed courtier ... he is willing to thunder against the court's degeneracy, but only in the hope of being invited to share in its delights." See discussion in Bernstein (1992:30 and *passim*).

[8] Reeves (1993:18) writes: "The Kennedy I found certainly did not know what he was doing at the beginning, and in some ways never changed at all, particularly in a certain love for chaos, the kind that kept other men off-balance."

a job well done which spills out of its container into a forbidden yet logical arena of implied power. The power of the abject zone is the contamination it seeps but rarely announces. Those who are not culturally authorized to exercise control and authority disrupt body orders by the power, laughably overlooked, that comes from performing assigned tasks well. They can insert words into a paragraph, into a decision, as an instance of what we call "proof-reading" or "editing." They can shred decisions on which pages lie the words of state. The power of the handmaid is about judiciously placed and timed – decided – phone calls. It is about deciding power-seating arrangements. It is about myriad insertions into pre-programmed scripts, insertions that do not command recognition and citation and, therefore, cannot possibly be "trouble," be power.

Handmaids make up part of the "real" as Butler (1993:192) understands it: "always that which any account of 'reality' fails to include."[9] They often leak into regions where they should have no place – sometimes invisibly into places of forbidden power beyond restricted "sex" – because so much power depends on them:

> Kennedy came downstairs to his office with his usual run of morning memos for Evelyn Lincoln ... For McGeorge Bundy, he had another complaint about the State Department. "I want a report ... I asked Secretary Rusk about this, on whose idea it was for me to send the letters to the MidEast Arab leaders."   (Reeves, 1993:189)

> On May 5, Kennedy was at another meeting of the National Security Council. Those around the big table in the Cabinet Room ... were now talking about the possibility of a Communist takeover of British Guiana, a small colony on the north coast of South America, when Evelyn Lincoln, the President's secretary, walked in and whispered to him.   (p. 117)

> Of Mrs. Lincoln, his secretary, the President said that if he called to inform her that he had just cut off Jackie's head and wanted to get rid of it, the devoted secretary would appear immediately with a hatbox of appropriate size.   (p. 104)

The Lincoln handmaid is cited by Reeves only as a creature Kennedy compels; but her body is given unfettered access to the resources of

---

[9] For discussions of the Lacanian real, see Botting (1995) and Zizek (1989). Also Lacan (1977). I put the term in inverted commas to draw attention to the meaning Butler gives the real as opposed to that which Reeves and Allison suggest we interpret as real in Kennedy's Washington.

Washington power and decision – reports, meetings, minutes, and hat-boxes. Decisions are made through her conveyance, through her interpretations. "She" is "a leaking, uncontrollable, seeping liquid ... a formlessness that engulfs all form," beyond the domains of control (Grosz, 1994:203). In this "seeping" is the body ambiguity and equivocal power of abjection. Everyone needs you; you are there; but you are not there behind your garments of "sex."

Handmaids in the corridors of official power, presidential power, foreign policy decision making: undead specters invented to creep about, to be useful, to be right hands of those who may openly stand in the political light of day with two-fisted power. Outside the parameters of well-established foreign policy history (time) and textual space, handmaids are homeless within the usually noted practices and accounts of international relations (Sylvester, 1998b). Few analysts of Washington try to grasp their importance, because handmaids seem to be "Dutch milkmaids on a wallpaper frieze, like a shelf full of period-costume ceramic salt and pepper shakers, like a flotilla of swans or anything that repeats itself with at least minimum grace and without variation" (Atwood, 1985:275). But if a grasping is tried, that which is "real" about handmaids semi-abjects the real stories we rehearse about Washington decision-makers. Power thereby becomes ironically elusive, sloppy, and undecidable.

Kennedy's difficult decisions

> ... we still had our bodies. That was our fantasy.   (Atwood, 1985:4)

When Kennedy was inaugurated, the Golda Meirs and Margaret Thatchers had not yet ascended the thrones of power as models of "escape" from abjection. The early 1960s had "carbon paper, stencils, mimeographs, vacuum tubes, and flashbulbs" (Reeves, 1993:14). It was the time when a "presidency was recorded by stenographers and typists; secretaries listened in and took notes during telephone calls" (p. 14). Those secretaries were mostly women who "learned to whisper almost without a sound" (Atwood, 1985:4). But there were others: in one case, a racially marked male handmaid was given as a payment for political favors: "Thomas, a fifty-five-year-old Negro, had been a gift from Arthur Krock, who repaid past debts to Joseph Kennedy by sending his own valet to take care of Joe's son when he came to Washington" (Reeves,

1993:314). These were the early days of the Civil Rights movement, a movement Reeves describes Kennedy earnestly seeking to avoid rather than engage.[10]

These were also the days just before the international women's movement would burst on the scene, first with Betty Friedan's 1963 bestseller *The Feminine Mystique,* and then, in the mid- to late 1960s, with various feminist marches on Washington. The Commander's Wife was still compelled (as she is to this day in the USA) to be a body-bound helpmate to the president: "What do you want to do, Mrs. Kennedy?" Ambassador Duke had begun. "As little as possible," she said. "I'm a mother. I'm a wife" (Reeves, 1993:154). "She" was given bodily grievances, such as "headaches and continuing bouts of depression after the birth of John F. Kennedy, Jr, in late November 1960" (pp. 146–147). Her power is recognized by Reeves, in part, as the expected manipulations of a fairer sex that will ultimately perform proper "sex" for her man:

> "This is another one Mrs. Kennedy should do," Salinger told the President one morning in the Oval Office. A delegation of Girl Scouts was coming to the Rose Garden . . .
>
> "Just give me a minute," said the President. "I'll straighten this out."
> He was gone for fifteen minutes, but came back smiling.
> "Mrs. Kennedy is going to do it," he said. "Set it up."
> "How did you do it?" Salinger asked. Mrs. Kennedy was not an easy woman.
> "It cost me," Kennedy answered. "Bet you won't guess what it is."
> "A new dress?" the press secretary asked.
> "No," Kennedy said. "Worse than that: two symphonies."   (p. 476)

(As for that other "sex" in Kennedy's White House, Reeves is ever gentlemanly with the president. He buries most references to the bodies Kennedy sexed – "I got into the blonde last night" (p. 707n) – in a lengthy footnote.)

---

[10] Reeves (1993:465) points out that "[a]t the Lincoln Birthday dinners across the country on the nights of February 12 and 13 [1963], leaders of the party of Lincoln – the party which had retained the voting loyalty of Negroes from the end of the Civil War to the New Deal of Franklin D. Roosevelt – were attacking the President for his cool civil rights record." It seems that "Kennedy was most concerned about domestic racial troubles as a foreign policy problem. He didn't want to see the problems give the country a bad name abroad." Father Theodore Hesburgh, the US Civil Rights Commission appointee of 1961, "understood immediately not only that Kennedy thought civil rights was peripheral but that he intended to keep it that way if he could, at least until after he was up for reelection in 1964" (p. 60).

Reeves's text gives the sense of the daily order, positions, trade-offs, and rules in John Kennedy's Washington. So also, Allison's studies of decision making during the Cuban missile crisis have given us frameworks that affect our perceptions of who constructed foreign policy through which bodies in those Kennedy years. We know that foreign policy was at the center of Washington attention in a harsh Cold War time and that the Cuban missile crisis was at the apex of Kennedy's Cold War skills. There are many things, however, we do not know – have not yet found out – because there has yet to be a body/sex/gender/power analysis of the modes of decision making Allison reconstructed from events of those thirteen days. Without an effort to find handmaids in the Kennedy White House, Allison's models continue to have undeniable seminality despite critiques of them from a variety of angles (e.g., Bender and Hammond, 1992; Ferguson and Mansbach, 1988).[11] Embedded assumptions, therefore, about who made such foreign policy decisions in what bodies and performances and places, persist.

To see the possibilities for contamination that would disturb bodies, positions, and rules – to find efforts to keep power from the abjected zone blocked up in those days of missiles – it is useful to consider Allison's scientifically conceived models in some detail and against the backdrop of Reeves's reconstruction of the non-scientific everyday in the Kennedy White House. Atwood's handmaids follow us to days of missiles, and yet a change in tone occasionally seeps into this particular part of the finding exercise. Foreign policy decision making, after all, is no laughing matter: "Once we had the transcription in hand – and we had to go over it several times, owing to the difficulties posed by accent, obscure referents, and archaisms – we had to make some decision as to the nature of the material we had thus so laboriously acquired. Several possibilities confronted us" (Atwood, 1985:383).[12]

Rational decision making

His first stop was usually the desk of his secretary, Evelyn Lincoln, where he dictated a short list of things-to-do, which she distributed, in turn, to his staff and Cabinet members . . .   (Reeves, 1993:65)

[11] Declassified documents have also cast the "facts" Allison drew upon for his models in a new light. See, for example, Lebow and Stein (1994), Thompson (1992), Hilsman (1996), and White (1996).
[12] "Historical Notes on *The Handmaid's Tale*" (Atwood's epilogue).

Evelyn Lincoln. Identification: caricature of the quintessential hand-maid. This phantom of the abject warrants a mention here and there in the Reeves biography of Kennedy less because she is a body that matters than because her handmaidenly presence was a foil for the figure of a president who said "his White House organization would look like a wheel with many spokes and himself at what he called 'the vital center'" (p. 19). Lincoln was a modest, "if not invisible at least unrecognizable in influences and effects," sub-spoke in the wheel. Kennedy was the mastermind, the rational leader of the band of mostly "men" – and that "woman," whose body was central and yet never counted.

If we are to believe Allison's rationalist reconstruction of the days of decision surrounding the discovery of missiles in Cuba, the spokes of the wheel acted in concert – at least in terms of the common methodology followed. The rational policy scenario, Allison's (1969:693) "standard frame of reference," presents decision making in a Washington crisis as a cool and calculated process that involves computer-like brains attached to no bodily needs, no prior histories, no social dysfunction, and no distractions. Nothing mars the exercise of reason – not intrigue, distrust, neurosis, inefficiency, sabotage, alcoholism, parental responsibilities, lust, or illness. There is no source of seepage of any kind here. For every possible course of action, the brains consider "one set of perceived options, and a single estimate of the consequences that follow from each alternative" (p. 694). Once available information is collected, the most cost-effective alternative is the rational choice.

The constituted absence of anything that would contaminate rational thought means that there are none of the concerns with bounded rationality that we see in later literatures on decision making. This neglect of the uncontrollable does not matter for the analysis at hand: later work on conditions of constrained rationality inherits the Allisonian freedom from the contamination of "sex." Safe they all are with numbing "decision-makers," "individuals," or simply with "they" (e.g., Keohane, 1984; Levy, 1992; Parker, 1993; Simon, 1982). As well, no secretaries figure directly into early or latter-day rational models, because those models slavishly replicate a conventional wisdom in which "women have been defined on the side of the body and men on the side of the mind" (Grosz, 1994:203).

There are, however, "consumers" in the shadows, at least of Allison's tale. The rational decision-making model, he tells us, "is an analogue of the theory of the rational entrepreneur which has been developed extensively in economic theories of the firm and the consumer" (Allison, 1969:694n). The rational entrepreneur makes calculated choices about what to buy and what to by-pass using information on quality, prices, design, and so on. Presumably, the consumer is similarly inclined, as another sturdy, abstract, and disembodied brain that calculates. Yet feminist analyst Maria Mies (1986:106) has argued that "consumers" are likely to be empirically and culturally constituted bodies that are chained (sometimes most gladly) to a regulatory sexual regime called "housewifized women":

> The creation of housework and the housewife as an agent of consumption became a very important strategy in the late nineteenth and early twentieth centuries. By that time not only had the household been discovered as an important market for a whole range of new gadgets and items, but also scientific home-management had become a new ideology for the further domestication of women. Not only was the housewife called on to reduce the power costs, she was also mobilized to use her energies to create new needs.

The rational decision-making model appropriates and reverses "woman consumer." It misidentifies it in a way that causes "women" to enfold into "buyers" armed with the calculating attributes that, though "womanly" in abjected household practice, are discursively denied "women" in the public sphere (Thiele, 1986). By extension of the logic, a handmaid in the office of power is the consumer of dictated "lists of things-to-do," who reduces the costs of the office in a way that reminds us of a housewife. "She," however, performs these "sex acts" in the absence of intimate familiarity (usually) with the viscosity of the Commander. "She" is not a Wife; nor is she, in her capacity as non-sex-giving consumer, usually a Jezebel. A handmaid to rational decisional processes, rather, uses her culturally determined gaggle of office "gadgets and items" to reduce power costs in the professional arena. Her energies may certainly create new needs too.

We do not get to find out how Evelyn Lincoln and her cohorts may have trimmed costs here and proved entrepreneurial and energetic there during the days of missiles. Allison performs a magic trick of abjection with consumers. Presto: before our eyes consumers become the talking heads of decision-makers in foreign policy. These are the people who count, while rational handmaid-consumers become mere traces of power as allusion. Owing to such corpo-real sleights of logic, we might say that a rational fiction emerges.

73

Another fiction: there is not one semi-abjected she-body among the Executive Committee members deliberating about missiles in Cuba. This suggests, on the one hand, that the rational model applies not only to certain symbolic, culturally mediated bodies but to certain materialized bodies as well: men. On the other hand, because the model is constructed under the rubric of decisional science, one is meant to think that presences and absences of bodies do not really matter at all to rational decision making, that decisional processes are not really a matter of "sex" or "gender." Rational decision making is modeled neutral, compellingly bodiless. Yet the rational scenario is based, at least in part, on an appropriation/reversal of the existence and spheres of certain consumer bodies; anon, male nonbodies overrun it. Evelyn Lincoln, handmaid *par excellence*, was not seen to be seeping key "sex acts" into the Executive Committee; yet there can be little doubt that the work she was called upon to do "reduced the power costs" of the Committee. Indeed, one could go further and argue that the Executive Committee could only appear to be all male in composition and power because Evelyn and others were placed, and compelled to perform their "sex," on that "margin of nonbelonging" of which Braidotti speaks.

The strategic calculations of the rational model, the exclusions of some bodies through silence and sleights, call to mind Donna Haraway's (1989) discussion in *Primate Visions* of certain evolutionists who have made reason the ultimate trait of survival-oriented organisms.[13] To them, all organisms are "strategists in a vast game whose stakes are reproductive fitness, i.e., staying in the game as long as possible" (p. 327). In fact, though, organisms cannot really reproduce themselves in order to stay in the game, because the gene "issue from the self is always (an)other" (p. 352). They reproduce themselves only in the context of social relationships in which norms of reproduction are reiteratively cited. Armed with biologically driven arguments about natural (as opposed to social) reproductive reasoning as the preserver of the species, however, the evolutionists' world of theory and the world itself become unified around "exercises in military-like strategies" (p. 327). So also in the rational decision-making model there is no Evelyn Lincoln reproducing social relations of power. There are only impersonal strategies.

Allison (1971:28) claims that deeply ingrained strategic thinking has something to do with "a simple extension of the pervasive everyday assumption that what human beings do is at least 'intendedly rational,' an

---

[13] In illustrating her argument, Haraway focuses on the work of Tooby and DeVore (1987).

74

assumption fundamental to most understanding of human behavior."
Is not the law of reason like the law of "sex," in that both are "repeatedly
fortified and idealized as the law only to the extent that [they are] reiterated as the law, produced as the law, the anterior and inapproximable
ideal, by the very citations [they are] said to command" (Butler, 1993:14)?
The "law" suggests, through a strategic silence, that handmaids do not
partake of rational decision making. Absences of natural reproductive
reasoning in power society are given "lists of things-to-do"; "intended
rationality," thereby, becomes a bodily experience denied those who
"woman" the office, those who really "keep us in the game as long
as possible." Handmaids are not organisms despite also-reproductive
bodies. They are odd.

Allison (1971:28–29) sums up grandly: "[w]hat rationality adds to
the concept of purpose is *consistency*: consistency among goals and objectives relative to a particular action; consistency in the application
of principles in order to select the optimal alternative." Consistency
among those who understand this public/private regulatory regime.
Consistency of some principles as against principles people with statuses positioned elsewhere might question. Consistencies such as these
suggest why handmaids cannot be accommodated within rational models. A handmaid has one foot in the public referential realm of policy
processes and another in some uncited margin of the office "with the
women" – from whence s/he may merely visit and assist the realm of
true significance. Consigned to the abject, s/he can venture forth and
whisper but may not seep into the assumptions and practices of decision. Sometimes, as in Arthur Schlesinger's case, it is possible for certain bodies to materialize, powerfully, from the abject realm; but Evelyn
Lincoln is consistent as . . . who?

Rational decision-making models are chockablock with references to
"sex." To Allison (p. 1) "[t]he Cuban missile crisis was a seminal event."
Evelyn Lincoln, however, was not a seminality. That was not her cultural "sex," her compelled experience, her symbolic realm, albeit she
may have been familiar with the body fluids of seminality. She was a
whisper, a consumer, a secretary, but not a seminality. We do not know
exactly what she did during the Cuban missile crisis. Maybe we will
never know. The larger point is that she was Kennedy's "first stop"
of the day. Everyday corpo-reality seeped and "distributed" to insiders
from a place inside the real that was a "constitutive outside." Handmaid
Lincoln has become a nonnarrativizable, unspeakable portion of the
Cuban missile crisis story, her possible mis- and disidentifications

with handmaidenly "sex," her power-loyal identifications with it during those thirteen days, unsighted, unsited, and uncited.[14] In her absence, the crisis itself, therefore, must be said to be undecided. And given the equivocal nature of handmaid power, it may be ultimately undecidable.

Organizational decision making

> The two young Guardians salute us, raising three fingers to the rims of their berets. Such tokens are accorded to us. They are supposed to show respect because of the nature of our service. (Atwood, 1985:28)

Allison (1971:3–4) warns that the rational decision-making model is flawed even though it so readily comes to mind when "[p]rofessional analysts of foreign affairs (as well as ordinary laymen) think about problems of foreign and military policy." It is flawed primarily because it implies that monoliths such as the state perform large actions for large reasons that demand unified thinking. To Allison, "monoliths are black boxes covering various gears and levers in a highly differentiated decisionmaking structure" (pp. 5–6). It is more telling, in his eyes, to ask who operates those images of modernity and its machines? Who writes and manipulates the rules of reiterative machine practice?

These very good questions, which could lead us to the realm of abjection and semi-abjection, are answered promisingly: "large acts result from innumerable and often conflicting actions by individuals at various levels of bureaucratic organizations in the service of a variety of only partially compatible conceptions of national goals, organizational goals, and political objectives" (p. 6). Despite a sense that organizationally bound, rule-governed "individuals" are bodiless, this model seems to come close to the zones of abjection, to the "sex" of those "in the service of," close to those who operate office machines. But the realm of independent judgment that is implied by "partially compatible conceptions" is quickly and monumentally disciplined. Individuals are attached to agencies rather than agency. Agencies have particularistic missions, sets of priorities in advancing those missions, and independent information bases that reflect their own standard operating procedures:

---

[14] There is one interesting recent sighting of Lincoln in Seymour Hersh's *The Dark Side of Camelot* (1998:409): a suggestion that she took some White House tapes concerning the Cuban missile crisis home with her.

"We can go to the washroom if we put our hands up, though there's a limit to how many times a day, they mark it down on a chart" (Atwood, 1985:92). The organization is the backdrop against which "individuals" caught up in larger-than-life machinery must disidentify with some and identify with others in order to perform prescribed roles.

A secretary to the organizational man may be a cog in the wheels of service, but to what degree is "she" molded by organizational affiliation? Would the handmaid Evelyn Lincoln really bear a hatbox of appropriate size to Kennedy so that he, arbiter of his executive agency, could neatly dispose of a decapitated Jackie? Or is this a misidentified, wishful-grisly projection of surreptitious organizational sex-bonding, sex-norming, on to the handmaid Lincoln? Put differently, is it the case that people constituted as handmaids become one with the machinery of agencies, such that their "sex" merges with, oozes and seeps into an organizational role? Or is "role" a body-specific site that is presented in the organizational decision-making model as a "sexless" fiction?

Here, we come up against the ironies of the feminist model of ooze. Following from Grosz, men are not constituted as, do not themselves live as, flow and seep. They can easily take on an organizational role by transcending their (secretly seeping) bodies to become subjects in a zone others like themselves inhabit. "Women" tend to be abjected in such organizations, as the testimony of recent foreign policy women demonstrates. Yet some can flow into organizational missions from positions at those margins of excentricity. Moving forward again in time from the Kennedy years, we see Fawn Hall, loyal handmaid in the service of Oliver North's version of Ronald Reagan's foreign policy. When the media glimpsed Fawn Hall's face – when her handmaid's hood was taken off – it saw her decorously, as the good-looking blonde, the excess of sex around North. All her secretarial shredding of documents became seen as "sex acts" for beloved men (North and her Contra lover). In effect, we made Hall flow and seep in ways that denied her any simple organizational role.[15]

Consider Jacqueline Kennedy again. Reeves constitutes her as an embodied Kennedy-aura prop and manipulator. Surely, though, she was

---

[15] Cynthia Enloe (1989:9) devotes several pages of her *Bananas, Beaches, and Bases: Making Feminist Sense of International Politics* to the case of Fawn Hall within a "clerical labor force that has made the complex communications, money transfers and arms shipments possible."

something of an organizational insider, someone on the Kennedy team, albeit perhaps a bit headless in Jack's mind, a bit "difficult." Reeves's inside sources on the Cuban missile crisis do depict a body materializing at points as a locus of seepage that subverts the role of presidential trim one like her is assigned:

> It was not until eight o'clock on Monday night, while the President was having dinner . . . with his disabled father – Mrs. Kennedy was on a four-week holiday in Italy, providing the press of the world with lively pictures that the President thought were hurting him politically – when the photographic interpreters finally concluded that they were looking at pictures of eight ballistic missile launch pads under construction in a remote area in the west of Cuba. (Reeves, 1993:368)

> After lunch, [Kennedy] invited UN Ambassador Adlai Stevenson to come upstairs. He was showing Stevenson the aerial photographs when his wife walked into the sitting room. Jacqueline Kennedy liked Stevenson as much as her husband disliked him, so there was some cheek-kissing before she left. (p. 374)

One yearns to know more about Jackie's disagreements and disagreeable moments, her identifications and disidentifications within the organization, her excesses. But Reeves rushes on to stories about notables of correct "sex," such as the Joint Chiefs of Staff. Only once in a while, and then only in an informal aside, do we read about a Mrs.' leaks of anti-role within the service.

Similarly, only occasionally do we glimpse a situation in which a textually abjected, outside handmaid is cited for putting her finger on the pulse of Washington better than a notable, somewhat inside, carrier of correct "sex" and role:

> At the Alsops, Kennedy and Bohlen paced at the back of the garden . . . Susan Mary Alsop watched them – and watched her roast lamb turning browner and drier. At the table, the President took over, asking the male guests . . . variations on this question: "Historically, how have the Russians reacted to great pressure? When their backs were against the wall?"
> "Sitting next to Jack tonight was like sitting next to the engine of a powerful automobile," Mrs. Alsop told her [syndicated columnist] husband after everyone had left. "He was enjoying himself greatly in some way I don't understand. Something is going on. Didn't you feel it?"
> "What are you talking about?" he said. (p. 377)

Indeed, Susan Mary Alsop, President Kennedy, and other guests were dining together as precipitating, but still quiet, events of the Cuban missile crisis unfolded. "She" was meant to "live in the blank white spaces at the edges of [her husband's] print" (Atwood, 1985:74). But she haunted signification by performing, in this case, "above him, looking down; he is shrinking" (pp. 377–378).

Allison's presentation of the organizational decision-making model emphasizes "routines" and "outputs" rather than feelings that something is going on. Moreover, all the organizations that matter in his analysis are large – no households here – and all procedures for gathering information are "standard" – no one is assigned the roast lamb, which is to say that no Susan Alsops seep out as independent, misidentified rogue perceivers. Complexly routine, the standards are fixedly identified in ways that avoid uncertainty and that set parameters of effective vision in terms of cooperative autonomy from "women" in the realm of statecraft (Sylvester, 1994a, 1998b).

When, in the "blank white spaces at the edges of print," one stumbles on Kennedy's purposive dismissal of "women" he dined with at the Alsops (at least in Reeves's rendering), one realizes the potential abyss of body pre-programming into which one stares. When one actually sees a handmaid cited as ahead of her "man" in entrapping Washington's currents, one realizes that there may be many countermemories of events and decisions submerged in citations to "men" in their limited and somewhat inflexible organizations. If so, can it be true, as Allison (1971:96) claims, that the organizational model "constitutes a marked shift in perspective" from the rational model? Does not cooperative autonomy from certain bodies link the rational and organizational decision-making models – much to the detriment of each? And do not handmaids in the organizations around the Cuban missile crisis warrant investigation on the grounds that they seep about – in many different ways – in the historical organization of power, discourse, and bodies? Without them, how can the model (can it) be decided?

Bureaucratic politics

"I'd like you to play a game of Scrabble with me," he says.

I hold myself absolutely rigid. I keep my face unmoving. So that's what's in the forbidden room! Scrabble! I want to laugh, shriek with laughter, fall off my chair. (Atwood 1985:179)

Allison's (1969:707) third model of decision making features sport-metaphored "player[s] in a central, competitive game" with high stakes. He says that "[t]he name of the game is politics: bargaining along regularized circuits among players positioned hierarchically within the government" (Allison, 1971:144). Which bodies, though, run with the ball, fumbling it, landing at the bottom of a pile-on, or pulling off a touchdown? Which ones scramble to the Scrabble board, to the board game of power words? In case the reader should not know, Allison tells us in the most straightforward of referential terms that "Men share power. Men differ concerning what must be done. The differences matter" (Allison, 1969:707).

Here is a purposively embodied construction of power. Men-bodies are invariably agents of politics; no other sex is in the game on any side. What makes for complexity in foreign policy decision making are the differences across individual body-tied men about how to solve a problem. There is no unitary community of policymakers, as in the rational model. There are not organizational ties that bind. Every man is a free agent, and in the political process that results, "one group committed to a course of action triumphs over other groups fighting for other alternatives" (Allison, 1971:145).

This model smacks of a certain Hobbesian understanding of sociality that wearies many a standpoint feminist writer. Nancy Hirschmann (1992), for one, argues that images of individuals fighting over alternatives compose a distinct myth in which human bodies are constituted as essentially separate from one another, with no built-in relational ties. They are autonomous bodies, equally wary of attack and of defection from temporary, strategic, and only voluntary alliances. Hirschmann's feminist understanding of human sociality starts with lifelong involuntary associations. She recognizes that few humans self-birth and self-rear to adulthood; few live the life of a hermit; people are always in some social situation. Men, however, are led to think they stand alone because constantly cited compulsions of proper gendering differentiate them – as a goal – from the repetitions of sex that make "mothers" "women."

In this form of "sex" disidentification, self-centered men take the field and "what moves the chess pieces is not simply the reasons that support a course of action, or the routines of organizations that enact an alternative, but the power and skill of proponents and opponents of the action in question" (Allison, 1971:145). One must stay in the game as long as possible, and the gendering process ensures that outcome by teaching the performative norms of "sex": have power and skill to shape your disidentification from the social connections into which you were born, or you will collapse into abjection yourself. "This was once the game of old women, old men, in the summers or in retirement villas . . . or of adolescents once . . . Now of course it's something . . . dangerous. Now it's indecent. Now it's something he can't do with his Wife" (Atwood, 1985:179).

Because this particular disidentification with women, with wives, is reiterated in common gendering norms and practices, at least among European-Americans, Allison feels no need to explain his words about men and power and their separate responsibilities and narrow social scope. The presumptuousness limits his work and builds a thick wall between All Men and all the others who, by implication, do not share power in ways that matter, because they have not materialized into acceptable bodies with proper gender. Hence we never read a recreation of the Cuban missile crisis from the situated standpoint of John McCone's wife, who experienced, and perhaps even influenced, the first round of the bureaucratic politics game, when her new husband bombarded the president with the famous honeymoon cables from their marriage suite in France. This is very much beside Allison's point.

Allison (1969:709) goes on to say that politics is a question of man's personality and how he "manages to stand the heat in his kitchen." He appropriates/reverses his gender metaphors again. How many "men" stand in most kitchens long enough to feel heat? Only the chefs, presumably, who tend already to be appropriators of the usual food preparation narrative that puts a certain abjected "sex" in everyday domiciles far from the "kitchen cabinets" of power. Still, there is doubleness in this appropriation: there must be power in the kitchen or researchers like Allison would not find the image sufficiently compelling to appropriate. Is it the power of creative decision making under pressure in places (uncited) where there is a "dense intersection of social relations that cannot be summarized through the terms of identity" (Butler, 1993:218)? Atwood (1985:14, emphasis added) says of handmaids whose "sex acts" are performed as cooking and cleaning Commanders' kitchens: "The *Marthas* know things, they talk among themselves, passing the unofficial news from house to house . . . they listen at doors, no doubt, and see things even with their eyes averted." Is it that "[t]he problems for the players are both narrower and broader than *the* strategic problem" (Allison, 1969:710)? There must be something powerfully unrepresentable or ambiguous about abjected labor that can be made to fit, to represent, to seep into the power "men" – invisibly.

Allison (1971:147) quotes James Forrestal: "you can no more divorce government from politics than you can separate sex from creation." More aptly, you cannot divorce politics from "sex." Reeves (1993:215) tells us at one point that "[Vice President] Johnson was accompanied by a pair of flashy secretaries no one believed were there for typing. Real typists were in the back of the plane with State Department and White House men, writing out the encouraging words that Johnson would deliver to Berliners." What if the "flashily 'sexed' secretaries" – the "real" ones who can reveal excess "sex" in the White House – defied belief in separately "sexed" places and flashed a few political messages from abjection to Johnson? That would be fairly easy to do in an unnoted way, given the ability of handmaids to ooze from abjection without announcing it, without being seen as seeping from the narrow to the broad.

Indeed, handmaids can be seen, even with "eyes averted," in the demanding, team-requiring list of bargaining tools Allison (1971:169) ascribes to bureaucratic process men of foreign policy:

> formal authority and responsibility (stemming from positions); actual control over resources necessary to carry out action; expertise and control over information that enables one to define the problem, identify options, and estimate feasibilities; control over information that enables chiefs to determine whether and in what form decisions are being implemented; the ability to affect other players' objectives in other games, including domestic political games . . .

For a player to achieve such thoroughgoing control over position, resources, and information, one must assume that he has some help.

Washington insiders seem to know about the necessity of help when a crisis looms. Reeves (1993:400) tells us that as preparations were laid for an emergency evacuation of Washington officialdom during the Cuban missile crisis, the order came down: "You are allowed to bring one secretary . . . approved personally by the President." Wives were given stickers for the windshields of their cars, "so that traffic would clear out of the way as [they] headed for a designated gathering place on the George Washington Parkway along the Potomac River. All this was to be done while air-raid sirens wailed" (p. 400). The abjected and semi-abjected were to be saved from nuclear destruction, so they could help Commanders another day.

Wails notwithstanding, there are few direct citations in Reeves (and none in Allison) to the bodies that were always present and provided for, but not fully accounted for, in the Kennedy days of missiles. Reeves (p. 426) sneaks in one other power reference:

> After it was over, Kennedy called Tiffany's, the New York jeweler, to make up small Lucite calendars showing the month of October 1962, with the thirteen days of October 16 to October 28 engraved more deeply than the other days. He wanted to give one to each of the thirty men who had sat on Ex Comm, with their initials in one corner and his, JFK, in another. Walter Hoving, the president of Tiffany's, called back and said he would pick up the cost, but didn't the President think silver might be more appropriate than plastic? Silver it was for Kennedy's men, and for two women, Jacqueline Kennedy and Evelyn Lincoln.

Obviously, we need to interrogate the narrow circle of players and personalities we usually perceive as the bodies playing bureaucratic politics. Kathy Ferguson (1984:23) argues that "[t]o be firmly located in the public realm today is, for the most part, to be embedded within bureaucratic discourse; to be firmly grounded in the nonbureaucratic is to be removed from the arenas of available public speech." How thorough, though, is the removal, the evacuation, the abjecting of the broad? We can invite greater visual and analytical acuity if we disidentify solely with the "men in the kitchen" who are trying so hard to disidentify handmaids from places of policy and are textually failing to do so.

Figures seeping

In the unliveable zones of top offices of governance, handmaids are among those servers of power that self-conscious accounts of the real fail to include; or they are the ones who appear in asides, jokes, or in ways intended to draw attention to the men. The powerful feint of man-centered power can mask the identities of people who are given the locations, skills, and the resources to make and interpret and shape key decisions. Handmaids cannot be contained. Their work makes citations to Washington decision-makers possible. They haunt power by oozing into the identificatory boundaries of "sex" that regulate the norms of position in Washington. Not without excess meaning does Atwood (1985:172) have one handmaid say of another: "She was now a loose woman." Loose "women" render models of decision making in capital places undecidable precisely because "women" are uncapturable within them.

Ironic contradictions of power, "contradictions that do not resolve into larger wholes, even dialectically . . . [make for] the tension of holding incompatible things together because both or all are necessary and true" (Haraway, 1985:65). "Handmaid" is one of those categories that can be described as "neither conceptually pure nor politically correct" (Braidotti with Butler, 1994:58); it is neither an obvious body of struggle nor a body bereft of struggle. It is a sphere of "sex act" liquidity, a cultural dilemma in and amongst representations of reality in which the abject is sited on the margin of agency: "Voices may reach us from it; but what they say to us is imbued with the obscurity of the matrix out of which they come . . ." (Atwood, 1985:394–395).

In this particular tale, the "obscurity of the matrix" is imbued with the fictions of a Kennedy White House remembered as Camelot, or as bordello, often as the golden age of a strong young man at the helm of a superpower. Counter-memory finds the fictions surrounding men and missiles in the marks left by those we might assume to be below decisional capacity. Counter-memory engages the "deferral of closure, not its resolution," a point that has been made in reference to the feminist sex–gender debate (Moore, 1995:84). Very importantly, it helps those of us interested in sighting women in politics to set a course of investigation that neither denies the importance of official women with power nor assumes they are the only ones to sight, site, and cite in Washington.

4   Reginas in international relations: occlusions, cooperations, and Zimbabwean cooperatives

This set of sightings moves geospatially and geopolitically from a Washington powerhouse to the fields and workshops of women in Zimbabwe, a country and a people that have not figured into IR's line-up of power worthies. I am fascinated with labor that (only) seems to take place in power-insignificant or -irrelevant locations of international relations, and with workers who are women. "Reginas," an earlier piece than "Handmaids' Tales," brings those interests to IR via hidden, distant, and "minor" cooperatives of Zimbabwean women, which I link to a feminist update of regime analysis.

The study grows out of twenty years of regular field research in Zimbabwe coupled with the type of regional travel that puts one into parallel orbit with the always already world-traveling Cynthia Enloe. Then again, that Zimbabwean women could teach IR a lesson or two on cooperation joins my work with Tickner's efforts to nudge IR into seeing what is has been missing of the world. I am also keenly aware of Elshtain's *Women and War* whenever I contemplate the contributions women made to Zimbabwe's ten-year war for independence, and the ways in which a conflagration that ended in 1979 still affects local understandings of "women."

I first journeyed to Zimbabwe in 1982 as a refugee from the power-centered world of IR. Plumping out my second area of Ph.D. concentration, African politics, I arrived looking for the fabled Marxism of the new Zimbabwe. There was not much evidence of it, apart from the awkward form of address government officials used among themselves – Comrade. Zimbabwe seemed to sway to the currents of Marxist rhetoric and aspiration; yet it mostly followed liberal principles of political economy using tactics of authoritarian practice transposed from the armed struggle and Rhodesian rule (Sylvester, 1991b, 2001). The inconsistencies of "Zimbabwe" grabbed my mind and my sentiments almost immediately. I kept returning.

While conducting research for "Reginas," starting as a Visiting Research Scholar in the Department of Economics at the University of Zimbabwe (1987–1988) and carrying on for years thereafter, I saw that Marxist, liberal, and authoritarian cross-pressures were also keeping gender relations unstable and fluid. Marxism had an angle on women as class-based producers; liberals were keen to grant women equal rights with men; and agents of strong-arm authoritarian methods expected women to police each other's political interests. The key issue for me was what "women" meant in this environment – to the people called women and to agencies with resources to assist "women's progress." My research therefore queries where the "women" of Mashonaland (near Harare) stand amidst the cross-pressures; what work they usually do; and the ways they have come to define themselves and their hopes. Years of fieldwork have put me in contact with well over 400 rural and urban Zimbabweans and 100 representatives of local and international agencies endeavoring to help women. The results to date appear in *Producing Women and Progress in Zimbabwe: Narratives of Identity and Work from the 1980s* (Sylvester, 2000a), though portions feature in earlier publications (Sylvester, 1994a, 1995b, 1999b).

A small slice also appears below. It shows Zimbabwean women working in two silk cooperatives and unwittingly working the edges of international political economy through contacts with European patrons and other international agencies. Mainstream IR does not see them. Its usual orientations to cooperation (minimalist neorealism, less minimalist neoliberal institutionalism, and multilateralism) cannot identify such women working new meanings of cooperation into "our" field. We might say that IR's low politics literature still manages to evade people by focusing on states, international organizations, economic decision-makers of high status, and shared norms/ideas/values that reflect those entities. To see Zimbabwean women seems to require looking through feminist lenses, and here I discuss standpoint and postmodern feminist sighting approaches – a juxtaposition that recurs throughout my journey. Along with providing ways to see cooperating women in international relations, "Reginas" bolsters IR's capacity to incorporate lessons from feminist fieldwork into regime-analytic international political economy. Contrasted to "Handmaids' Tales," then, this piece is somewhat more in the mode of bringing a feminist eye to IR than of bringing IR to feminism.

* * *

In 1987 I began a study of women, production, and progress in two provinces of Mashonaland, Zimbabwe, focusing on the meanings of "women" in relation to official notions of progress articulated across several sectors of production in that new country. During one portion of the research, I became acquainted with two silkmaking cooperatives located on the outskirts of Harare. Both were being run entirely by people called women and both engaged at that time in negotiations with the then European Economic Community over funding. There, in geospaces far removed from the central concerns of professional IR, I learned something about the ways "our" theories block certain agents and forms of cooperation from occupying the privileged inside of the discipline. This chapter is about the cooperative occlusions from cooperation that mark theories of IR and international political economy (IPE), and about some cooperative resistances to occlusion that take place beyond our usual frames of vision.

Reginas and regimes: sites of occlusion

Several years ago, Friedrich Kratochwil and John Ruggie (1986) pointed out that the theoretical emphasis on regimes, then solidifying in a corner of IR, brought into relief two sides of one coin. It enabled us to begin to appreciate the effects that regularized forms of cooperation could have on states. It also enabled us to see the ways in which regimes could become relatively autonomous from the states that created them. A parallel double casting of a different sort was emerging around the same time in feminist literatures. It was becoming clear, on the one hand, that the move to bring gender sensitivity to bear on IR was revealing previously unrecorded sites of people called women in the world (as underpaid producers in the world-system of capitalism, as commodity logos, as beneficiaries of global tourism, and so on). It was exposing the cooperative autonomy of IR theory and its regimes from the female-bodied and -named Reginas, who evoked places and tasks domestic.

This part of the chapter is based on my chapter in *The Global Economy as Political Space*, edited by Stephen Rosow, Naeem Inayatullah, and Mark Rupert. Copyright © 1994 by Lynne Rienner Publishers, Inc. Used with permission.

Feminists could see, in other words, that some realms of identity were denied relevance to places deemed international (Enloe, 1989; Sylvester, 1993b). The same could not be said of Eugenes – keepers of male-bodied images and tasks assigned to people called men. Their shadows stalked and dominated the world(s) IR studied and the world(s) IR ignored. We might say that certain gender cooperations ruled the field.

Within contemporary IR theory, there are diverse views on cooperation. Neorealism tells of states inhabiting an anarchic system and striving therein to survive – that is to say, to maintain identity via territory and self-help strategies rather than through processes of cooperation with others. Neoliberal institutionalism telescopes the ways in which an anarchic system harbors incentives for states to cooperate with each other by establishing regime "principles, norms, rules, and decision-making procedures around which actor expectations converge in a given issue-area" (Krasner, 1982:186). A focus on multilateralism now emphasizes relations among three or more states on the basis of generalized principles of conduct, an indivisibility among members of a collectivity with respect to the range of behavior in question, and a diffuse reciprocity that elevates the importance of cooperative institutions to the system (Ruggie, 1993:10–11). Peering through gender-sensitive lenses at these three approaches to cooperation, we see that the differences between them all but disappear when we consider their shared cooperations on behalf of socially constructed Eugenes and their cooperative occlusions of Reginas.[1]

Neo-realist minimalists

Kenneth Waltz's *Theory of International Politics* (1979:89) raises the question of how there can be "an order without an orderer and ... organizational effects where formal organization is lacking." Borrowing heavily from microeconomic theory, Waltz answers that order forms spontaneously from the self-interested, self-helping acts and interactions of

---

[1] These approaches do not exhaust the universe of possibilities for cooperation in mainstream IR/IPE. Ruggie (1993), for instance, suggests that we could speak of bilateralism and imperialism as generic institutional forms of cooperation in international relations. There is a longer tradition of so-called idealist writings that emphasizes the possibilities for cooperatively bringing the domestic rule of law governing liberal western states to bear on international relations. See overview in Suganami (1989). There are also functionalist and neofunctionalist writers of the international organization tradition who placed their faith in the formal processes of coordination undertaken by international governmental and nongovernmental organizations. See Kratochwil and Ruggie (1986). The approaches I discuss here simply seem most current in the field.

states bent on surviving in a system that has no central authority. Put differently, in situations where each system unit has sovereign rights of autonomy from the governing norms of every other unit, the formation of an overarching governance system is impossible. Coordination of separate and independent state actions, however, is possible. When "states retain their autonomy, each stands in a specifiable relation to the others. They form some sort of an order. We can use the term 'organization' to cover this preinstitutional condition if we think of an organization as simply a constraint" (p. 100). To Waltz (p. 109), the organization of order revolves around balances of power, international economic divisions of labor, hegemonic states of great capability "called on to do what is necessary for the world's survival,"[2] and war – "often mistakenly taken to indicate that the system itself has broken down" (pp. 195–196).

Neorealism, the broad theoretical offshoot of Waltz's reasoning, posits that "[s]tructural constraints cannot be wished away, although many fail to understand this" (p. 109). Moreover, the constraint of governance-less existence in international relations should not necessarily be wished away: "[a] self-help situation is one of high risk – of bankruptcy in the economic realm and of war in a world of free states [but] it is also one in which organizational costs are low" (p. 111). To venture beyond the deep structural imperatives of mere organization into the realm of "willingness of states to work together," says Joseph Grieco (1990:1), requires a reduction in conditions that alarm realist states; for "a state will decline to join, will leave, or will sharply limit its commitment to a cooperative arrangement if it believes that gaps in otherwise mutually positive gains favor partners" (p. 10). The emphasis on egoistic states, helpless at working together very purposively, evokes a minimalist orientation toward cooperation in international relations.

Less minimalist, neoliberal institutionalism

Neoliberal institutionalism allows that states in anarchic international relations can and must cooperate under certain conditions or face the consequences of unfettered ego (such as the crashing restrictions on trade that attend uncoordinated intercontinental air travel,

[2] Indeed, although hegemonic stability theory can seem to focus on cooperative aspects of international relations (that is, on states cooperating with a hegemon in creating regimes), in fact "[t]he most that can be said about hegemonic power is that it will seek to construct an international order in *some* form, presumably along lines that are compatible with its own international objectives and domestic structures. But in the end, that really is not saying very much" (Ruggie, 1993:25).

beggar-thy-neighbor policies, or global resource depletion). There can be cooperation under anarchy, under the security dilemma, among egoists, and after hegemony (cf., Axelrod 1981; Axelrod and Keohane 1985; Jervis 1978; Keohane 1984), because "as everyone understands by now, rational egoists making choices in the absence of effective rules or social conventions can easily fail to realize feasible joint gains, ending up with outcomes that are suboptimal (sometimes drastically suboptimal) for all parties concerned" (Young, 1988:1). Moreover, Robert Keohane distinguishes between "crude," realist-force models of hegemonic stability, which equate power with leadership, and the forms of asymmetrical cooperation that a willing hegemon promotes to achieve order. He says: "Unlike an imperial power, [the hegemon] cannot make and enforce rules without a certain degree of consent from other sovereign states" (Keohane, 1984:46).

"Cooperation," to the neoliberal institutionalist, however, is a very restricted concept that presupposes an original and perhaps more authentic condition of no cooperation. It is "the use of discord to stimulate mutual adjustment" (p. 46). "Discord" is the day-to-day consequence of inhabiting an anarchic system. "Mutual adjustments" lie in institutions that can "reduce verification costs, make relationships more iterated, and facilitate punishment for cheaters" (Grieco, 1990:33), all of which lower the likelihood that a state will be double-crossed by other states once it warily enters international contracts (Keohane, 1984:97). In turn, "conventions...enable actors to understand one another and, without explicit rules, to coordinate their behavior" (Keohane, 1989b:4).

Reciprocity is one such convention. It informally regularizes expectations among states and helps to hold anarchy in check when formal institutions cannot be rationalized. Diffuse reciprocity, in particular, enables states to reach the point where each can "contribute one's share, or behave well toward others, not because of ensuing rewards from specific actors [specific reciprocity, as in two states agreeing to reduce tariffs], but in the interests of continuing satisfactory overall results for the group of which one is a part, as a whole" (e.g., as when a state is accorded unconditional most-favoured-nation status) (p. 146). However, diffuse reciprocity cuts two ways: it can whittle away at defensiveness and thus affect key norms of state behavior, and it can expose diffuse reciprocators to exploitation if they cooperate in the absence of strong norms of obligation (as when a country free-rides on future concessions made among

its partners). A history of satisfaction with regime-coordinated reciprocity on specific issues can minimize the probability of exploitation and double-crosses by defection-minded states and help maximize
the possibilities for relational forms of autonomy in the system –
relationships in which participants gain or deepen their identity in the
process of working with others. Relational autonomy stands in contrast to the reactive form of autonomy that neorealists implicitly respect,
whereby relationship is denied in order to achieve and maintain state
identity.[3]

In neoliberal institutionalism, regimes lie in between "conventions"
and perfect conditions of "diffuse reciprocity" in deepening the institutional "governance" characteristics of the anarchic system. At the same
time, if states are self-interested actors, owing to the system being without formal governance, then the full play of regime-oriented relational
autonomy can never be. States will be inclined to cheat and defect as
long as the costs of doing so are not excessively high. Accordingly, "if cooperation is to emerge, whatever produces it must be consistent with the
principles of sovereignty and self-help" (p. 132). In this final recourse to
reactive autonomy, the would-be neoliberal difference from neorealism
ends up affirming neorealist foundations of IR.

Less minimalist multilateralism

John Ruggie (1993:12) maintains that "there is a widespread assumption
in the literature that all regimes are, ipso facto, multilateral in character [and yet] this assumption is egregiously erroneous." Regimes can
encompass only two states and they can lack the generalized principles of conduct that would make a multilateral security regime, say,
incorporate a "norm of nonaggression, uniform rules for use of sanctions to deter or punish aggression, and . . . collectively sanctioned procedures for implementing them" (p. 13). Multilateralism is a generic
form of modern institutional international relations that manifests diffuse reciprocity (such that the good of the group is valued), draws
on generalized principles of conduct, and results in a group that is
indivisible.

In the post-World War II world, multilateralism has figured prominently in the organization of the western economic order, thanks initially
to the US effort "to project the experience of the New Deal regulatory

---

[3] See Nancy Hirschmann's (1989) discussion of relational and reactive autonomy. For an
application to IR, see Sylvester (1992).

state into the international arena" (p. 30). Yet "much of the institutional inventiveness within multilateral arrangements today is coming from the institutions themselves, from platforms that arguably represent or at least speak for the collectivities at hand" (p. 34). The European Union illustrates this trend in a most visible manner; but so also do groups of multilateral players who, for example, keep the issues of global warming alive internationally (cf., Benedict et al., 1991). This phenomenon of institutionally directed agenda setting is difficult for neorealism to see, let alone accommodate. By contrast, it seems to be the neoliberal institutionalist vision come to life, only not in a causal sequence that school would recognize (i.e., with specific reciprocity between states leading to diffuse reciprocity that encourages states – the leaders of the band – to demand more regimes and to extend diffuse reciprocity).

For multilateralism, cooperation is not simply instrumental, such that states adjust their policies to account for others when it is cost-effective to do so. Cooperation "depends on a prior set of unacknowledged claims about the embeddedness of cooperative habits, shared values, and taken-for-granted rules" (Caporaso, 1993:82). These claims draw attention to the conventions that neoliberal institutionalism acknowledges, and reach beyond them. "Sovereignty is not a concept that is sensibly applied to a single state or to numerous states in isolation from one another [so much as it] is inherently a relational concept." In other words, the anarchic system of sovereign states is "a forum as well as a chessboard" (p. 78).

Because mainstream IR favors the study of state rationalities and interests, it has neglected multilateralism, with its reflectivist and relational bent (p. 78). Also, one might add, it has neglected some post-neoliberal institutionalist possibilities for exploring relational versus reactive forms of autonomy in international relations. Relational autonomy presupposes sociality and involuntary ties, such that we can imagine eviscerating our notions of separate and wary states disconnected in international realms of politics from domestic socialities. Yet when the emphasis is on "preconscious, taken-for-granted understandings" (p. 83) we also become aware of the many ways that even relational forms of cooperation may be narrow and exclusive, such that some groups are indivisible *vis-à-vis* others. That is, some groups have encrusted certain "natural" principles of conduct and these create and deepen diffuse reciprocities, but only between themselves. Reginas have been frozen out by understandings that endow the worlds of Eugenes with taken-for-granted relevance to international relations.

Gendered cooperations?

Even as the literature on cooperation becomes less minimalist, it retains an occluding tendency that weakens its scope of engagement with the worlds assigned to Reginas. Simply put, these theoretical approaches do not conceptualize sociality and power as having something to do with gender relations. Purveyors of cooperation and noncooperation in IR try to establish difference from each other, but they uniformly share disinterest in the possibility that a field's views of cooperation cooperatively draw on a limited set of human experiences. Neoliberal institutionalism lionizes regimes without examining the extent to which there is a gender regime in international relations that prevents activities we associate with Reginas from informing IR theory. That gender regime may also preclude certain bodies from entering international relations, allowing them in only as visitors who have no "embassy" to protect them in a taken-for-granted, rule-governed sphere of men.[4] Neorealists speak of the absence of cooperation in anarchy without questioning the clear absence of gender anarchy in the supposedly anarchic system. That is, Kenneth Waltz does not qualify his structure-bound IR with a sense that "man's" authority is ubiquitous in the international relations that IR theorists produce. Fascinating possibilities for probing the habits and shared values of gender cooperation in IR seem to elude even the reflectivist multilateralists. Friedrich Kratochwil (1993:445) argues that "the predominance of realism in its various forms has made it difficult to explain the not inconsiderable amount of cooperation in general," without himself even briefly noting that the field is locked into gender cooperative and occluding forms of multilateralism that no one questions.

Feminist theorizing focuses on the flaws in mainstream scholarship that appear when we consider the range, depth, and relevance of hierarchical gender relations in international relations and IR. *Standpoint* feminism, for instance, posits that theorizing would change profoundly if it were launched from the perspectives of women's lives, mediated by feminist analysis, and then built into "a morally and scientifically preferable grounding for our interpretations and explanations of nature and social life" (Harding, 1986:26). Excluded ones, this argument goes, can see through the smokescreens of "objectivity" to identify the group-preserving qualities that insiders may defend as (really) the universals

---

[4] For a further discussion of "women" as visitors to international relations, because their homes are assigned elsewhere, see Sylvester (1993b, 1994a).

of life. From that basis of insight, one can struggle to elaborate vision, correcting for distortions within it, and produce a series of successor projects to science that offer the possibility of more complete and inclusive knowledge of social dynamics.[5] *Feminist postmodernism*, by contrast to the standpoint perspective, often explores the power and authority that would enable constructs such as "cooperation" to be defined as they are in the mainstream of IR and rehearsed in monotones across ostensibly different theories. It encourages scholars to read the canonical texts and their mantra-like pronouncements with a sense of the silenced voices and double meanings that contest, estrange, and unravel the privileged commonplaces of "our" field.[6]

These two (of many) feminist approaches have their differences. Yet would either one pronounce any particular domain of sociality as anarchic? For something to be taken as true, most feminists believe it must be constituted as true within some authoritative community that pronounces "the rightful governance of human action by means other than coercion or persuasion" (Jones, 1993:161). Standpoint feminism draws attention to an authoritative community called patriarchy, which projects masculine standpoints on gender, states, regimes of international political economy, and theories of IR. Under patriarchy, anarchy hides by making commonplace the many different ways that people called men dictate the status of activities associated with "women." The postmodern turn in feminism facilitates analysis of the knowledge-power moves that delineate an authoritative boundary of inside versus the outside. It also provides evidence of countervailing knowledge-power ensembles that refuse such boundaries. Anarchy is definitely possible in a postmodern world, but only as a by-product of numerous social refusals of dominant discourse, and not because there is a lack of authority – of truth-saying power, language, and knowledge – in some domains.

Turning the tables, standpoint feminist explorations of cooperation in international relations would start by describing the ubiquitous presence of professional men and norms of masculinity in the world we study and among the studiers (Tickner, 1992). Male dominance ensures that many aspects of the theorized system are controlled, ordered, and ruled within the discourse of anarchic relations. The invisibility of

---

[5] For an elaboration of the feminist standpoint, see Hartsock (1983). For an application of it to IR, see Enloe (1989).

[6] See discussions of feminist postmodernism in Flax (1990) and Harding (1986). Elshtain (1987) uses elements of this approach.

94

"women" in international relations – or one could say the evacuation of "women" from a global human habitat – is one such manifestation of control. Gender power in IR is fixedly unipolar; it is also untheorized as such. One might say that there exists in IR circles a generalized principle of masculine standpoint that exemplifies diffuse reciprocity among in-group members of the field; and that standpoint tends to exclude realms of women from "true" international relations. Put differently, relational autonomy from feminism and women reigns among insider colleagues of IR, protected by a barrier of reactive autonomy towards outsiders.

One could argue, from a care-centered feminist perspective in particular,[7] that "[m]uch of the fabric of communal connectedness is lost in the male-rule, instrumental model" of international relations (Jones, 1993:160). More, the model occludes what could be a "search for contexts of care that do not deteriorate generate into mechanisms of blind loyalty" (p. 160). Yet one must be careful in making this argument. The construction of gender-linked standpoints relies on some communal connectedness within each gender group. The scope of connection is purportedly more gender-restricted in a masculine world than it is under feminist standpoints. But standpoint thinking adheres to a notion of truth that is itself carefully delineated from dangerous external forces.[8]

Meanwhile, practices in international relations willy-nilly defy theorized boundaries of truth and spoil models of inside/outside knowledges. For instance, the felled Berlin Wall symbolizes a situation in which a realist state does not persist with the usual forms of sovereignly separate authority and, instead, becomes connected with the standpoint of another – with painful consequences.[9] Seemingly intractable conflicts

---

[7] This take on feminist standpoint is found in Gilligan (1982) and elaborated and expanded by Tronto (1987).

[8] Kathy Ferguson (1993:12) refers to the hermeneutic project of standpoint that calls and relies upon "some version of an ontology of discovery and an epistemology of attunement."

[9] One could argue, along with neoliberal institutionalism, that a history of discord between the East and West German states boiled over for the people of East Germany once the Soviet empire began to unravel. Cooperation was the outcome. Still, the image of "women" pushing baby carriages through the Wall and living to tell their tales (instead of being shot dead on site) cannot be accommodated in neorealist and neoliberal institutionalist frameworks, because these are peopled only with decision-makers, government authorities, and an occasional statesman. In the German case, groups of people (momentarily) usurped the authority of state groups, and the latter, unable to weather the onslaught long enough to seek cooperation with the West, expired. For two glimpses of "women" in the German merger, see the exchange between Martina Fischer/Barbara Munske and Soja Fiedler in Sylvester (1993a).

between Israel and neighboring Arab states may have been perpetuated "cooperatively" through a politics that lies in between the oft-rehearsed divide (Northrup, 1989). Multilateral Europe chugs disjointedly toward unity like a family that tries to reduce internal conflict by establishing lines of authority, even though there is periodic defection by disgruntled family members.

The postmodern turn in US feminism prepares us for boundary transgressions such as these without suggesting that feminist standpoint has won out, implicitly at least, in international relations. There may be multiple standpoints that qualify as feminist, but to thinkers in the postmodern vein all such standpoints may erroneously suggest that a series of truths can be excavated if one digs deeply and hermeneutically enough (Brown 1991). What if we have multiple and mobile subjectivities that make it difficult for "women," or "men," or their standpoints to exist coherently?[10] What if genders are oppositional categories that dump residual tasks on certain groups, leaving others free to participate in crafting enterprises of western history, such as the state, the market, and international relations? Thus, what if "women" is the residual assignment signifying values, traits, and places that are not deemed public? People called women may seek fulfillment within their assignments and therefore make the invented identity seem true. But could we not say that "women" is the sum total of the stories various groups in society tell about "women," and the constraints and opportunities built around those stories? And is not the gender picture criss-crossed and hyphenated with other assignments – class, race, age, ethnicity, and nationality identities?

In posing these questions, we do not end up dashed against the rocks, reduced to elegiacs. The postmodern turn may mean that sisterhood eludes, but it also means that the male-crafted statecraft (Ashley, 1989) of international relations/IR eludes, too, dissolved into an admittedly taken-for-granted, but porous, boundary that is subject to deauthorizing activities. To say it differently, the suggestion in all these queries is that the wall of cooperations that holds a field autonomous from women comprises less than robust practices. But how to activate the subversions that lie encrusted in the gender instabilities?

World-traveling (Lugones, 1990) to "women's" cooperatives in Zimbabwe provides some clues. It suggests, *à propos* of feminist

---

[10] See Riley (1988) for the question of whether "women" exist. See Ferguson (1993) for a discussion of mobile subjectivities.

standpoint thinking, that we must keep an ear tuned to what people called women report about their lives, because some stories, whether authentic or not, have been silenced in the IR literature. We must also recognize that groups of people do not necessarily stand fixed and timeless in their identities. Our selves can shift into previously unrecognized quadrants of subjectivity, or burrow about new quadrants, as we listen to that which has been thought alien. Uma Narayan (1989:263–264) admonishes us to refuse the thesis that

> those who are differently located socially can never attain *some* understanding of our experience or *some* sympathy with our cause... Not only does this seem clearly false and perhaps even absurd, but it is probably a good idea not to have any a priori views that would imply either that all our knowledge is always capable of being communicated to every other person or that would imply that some of our knowledge is necessarily incapable of being communicated to some class of persons.

The story in the next section gives credence to this plea. It features Zimbabwean women speaking about their silkmaking cooperatives as they become entangled in identity-shifting negotiations with international donors. A strange cooperation emerges across differences. The chessboard becomes a forum in places unauthorized as sites of IR/IPE. People who have no canonical right to narrate issues of international cooperation do so anyway. Subjectivities become mobile. Funds are dispensed to the "wrong" identity. To relate the story, to dance to distant music, is to reduce some boundaries of IR to jelly.

Cooperations in Zimbabwe?

There is a mood of anxious hope radiating from the small silkmaking cooperatives, whose members have gathered in the urban township of Mabvuku. Dressed in their good clothes, the women talk nervously among themselves as they await the arrival of a delegation from the European Economic Community that will, perhaps, pronounce the words the women tell me they have been waiting for a year to hear – that Mabvuku and its sister cooperative in Glen Norah are worthy of a Z$200,000 grant to expand their operations. Meager wares, machinery, and inputs are on careful display. Nearly half the small room is taken up with cartons of graded silkworm cocoons. In one corner stands a rickety handloom readied for a demonstration and a spinning wheel loaded with silk thread. Rudimentary wall hangings, greeting cards crafted from cocoon parts, and a few nicely made articles of silk clothing stand out on the unpainted walls.

As I survey the surroundings, two European women arrive with great fanfare. These are the patrons of the cooperatives, the Greek women responsible for starting and funding the producer-cooperatives at the rate of Z$70,000 to Z$80,000 over a two-year period. They are obviously the centers of gravity here, and as one breathlessly greets me the other makes suggestions for improving the display. Nervous energy goes into last-minute details.

A more typical day at the cooperative is busy but less frenetic:

> The silkworms eat so much that we have to struggle to find enough mulberry leaves to satisfy them. Every day of feeding season, five of us take a public bus into the suburbs. We go house to house looking for mulberry trees and asking permission to take some leaves. The people there think we are mad. We stuff our bags and return, where another group spends the afternoon cleaning dust and water off the leaves – the worms are so fussy. With money from the European Community, we hope to get five hectares to plant our own trees and solve the problem of traveling so much.
>
> This cooperative is not good yet because we have the problem of finding leaves and little production. But we have learned new skills of weaving and crochet and operate like a family. The Greek women have been kind in sharing skills and social workers from the Harare City Council help. We have learned to be self-disciplined, because of a regular work schedule, and if resources become available the project will prosper and we can hire more people. Then we'll make many things, like mulberry jam and tinned mulberries. The cooperatives will keep poultry and expand the weaving.

A more typical day is also filled with high expectations:

> We'll build a factory in the future and employ men and women, although the women will manage it because the men know they have no knowledge of silk. We have many plans. It took the Ministry of Cooperatives so long to process our papers for registration that some of us were discouraged. Our possibilities for EEC funding were held up. Maybe now it will be OK.

But this is not a typical day:

"Yes, yes we understand you have been undergoing training," says one of the two male EEC representatives. "But what about the administration of these cooperatives if the two Greek women leave Zimbabwe?"

"What about establishing prices? Who does that?"

"Have you considered the costs of fencing your new land?"

"Have you had the land surveyed? Precisely how much land is required for your project?"

"Can you get the spinning equipment you need in Zimbabwe?"

"How will you market your products?"

"Can you compete in export markets?"

The Greek women answer all the questions. The local women sigh. They tell me they can neither read well nor do sophisticated mathematics.

A month later, I interview one of the EEC representatives from the Mabvuku Inquisition.

"We haven't given out any aid to Mabvuku and Glen Norah because we're waiting for the government of Zimbabwe to put together a program proposal for us on this. All our funding requires evidence that the government is willing to help the project to succeed by following through on its promises for land or sales outlets. The relevant ministries have taken well over a year on this."

"We plan to fund the two silk cooperatives separately because we want them to compete. If you're not competitive, you'll fail in six months."

"It's good to have the Greek women involved. We calculate that their advice to the cooperatives is worth about Z$1,000 a month. They're saving us money."

A year later, I return to the European Community office in Harare. The original evaluation team for the silk cooperatives has left. A representative from the new team tells me: "Ah, the silk cooperatives. You know them? Then you know that they are risky ventures. We funded them a while back, but I would never have funded them myself. Silk is a new product in Zimbabwe and we don't know if there is a market. Plus I don't like the idea that the whole thing is held together by two European women. If they decide to leave Zimbabwe, the cooperatives will fall apart. I know that."

"Then why did the EEC fund them?"

"It was all so well orchestrated as mainly a Greek-to-Greek thing. That evaluating officer you spoke to last year was Greek, you know. Plus, the team had been to those cooperatives so often. It was all like family."

When Zimbabweans threw off the yoke of Rhodesia and its absentee landlord, Britain, in 1980, the party-government of ZANU-PF promoted producer-cooperatives as one way of bringing the poor into modern "production" under national conditions of sluggish growth. However, the government waxed ambivalent about the importance of cooperatives to an economy that was based more conventionally on large-scale farming, manufacturing, and mining. This ambivalence led cooperatives into a tragically ironic, migratory existence within government authority. Cooperatives first came under the purview of the Prime Minister's Office. Then they were transferred to a ministry that dealt with lands and resettlement, as though all cooperatives were agricultural in nature, which is not the case. In 1986, an independent Ministry of Cooperatives was formed, but less than two years later it was merged with Women's Affairs and Community Development; in effect, "cooperatives" were assigned to "women." Cooperatives were then separated from Women's Affairs and turned over to a new ministry, Cooperative and Community Development. Throughout this process of creeping government defection from cooperatives, at least three hundred "women's" cooperatives were forced to struggle for survival in a setting analogous to issue anarchy, owing to the waning interest of the resource hegemon.[11]

But there has been more to producer-cooperation in Zimbabwe than government whim. Cooperatives are spaces where what is produced is neither always what a government has in mind nor what development economists count as production. One part of production entails cooperatively generated knowledge. Zimbabwean "women" who join cooperatives often tell me: "Here we help one another to think our own thoughts," or "Here we learn skills without fear," or "Here we do things by ourselves without doubting." Since knowledge is "produced by individuals in actual settings, and [is] organized by and organizing of definite social relations" (Smith, 1990:62), cooperators produce knowledge together. They cooperate, not because they are experiencing discord among themselves as they try to operate in an anarchic-seeming economy. They cooperate because they are social actors who can draw on shared values and embedded cooperative habits.

Along with knowledge, cooperatives produce a range of commodities, from school uniforms to soap, for markets that are often limited to one village or school. Their isolation from the large trade, monetary, and capital concerns that occupy theorists of IR and IPE means that the activities of cooperatives do not feature as starting points for theory in

[11] For additional discussion of cooperatives in Zimbabwe, see Sylvester (1991a, 2000a). For an overview of Zimbabwe's political economy, including gender issues, see Sylvester (1991b).

our field. Supposedly, the action lies beyond such local, within-nation activities. But look again.

"Women" who are "cooperators" in Zimbabwe have one foot in a world resonant with neorealism, where competition is valued above cooperation; one foot is in a nostalgic realm of used-to-be-household politics, where "international" and "domestic" did not cooperate; and a hand is in the till of donor agencies, where multilateral funds are funneled to local development projects. This means that these "women cooperators" are simultaneously inside and outside international political economy; inside and outside international–local regimes of aid and development; and inside and outside domestic–international arenas of managerial responsibility. It means, as a result, that their situation and responses to it warrant attention as part of our study, as part of cooperation in international relations.

So also do the responses of agencies that have resources for cooperatives. In the course of my study, I recorded a variety of cynical comments from donors about both "women" and "cooperatives," as well as remarks (mostly by "women" development agents) that indicated considerable resistance to the negative remarks. The following is only a sampler (rather than sample) of what I heard.

> Cooperatives are seen as where you go when there is nothing else to do. They're dumps for the marginal and the unemployed. If you're in a cooperative, you're a failure.
> (Man representing an international development organization)

> Men are threatened by women forming cooperatives. They might not bring in that much money, but they don't want women getting involved. Women, on the other hand, persevere.
> (Woman representing an international development organization)

> Women have always known that they were powerful, but we have been made to feel unpowerful. Now we appreciate the need to exert power. Before, marriage was a profession. Within it, women were given petty managerial responsibilities. What we want is to be on an equal basis with men, because as it stands now, even when women talk sense, their statements are rejected.   (Woman from the Ministry of Cooperatives)

> When I think of cooperatives, I think of men.
> (Man representing an international development organization)

> A cooperative has to be more than a family registering. It must be viable.   (Local woman consultant)

> "All this emphasis on women. It seems too much. I don't approve of separate activities for women. They can always just join the men."
> I ask: "Can men always just join the women?"
> Silence.
>
> (Discussion with a man from
> Mashonaland East Department of Cooperatives)

> We tend to speak of cooperatives as a strategy, but we do not see that people can be pawns in the game. (Local woman consultant)

Local "women" cooperators come into "international relations" through these oftentimes-reluctant donor agencies. The donors do not usually cooperate with cooperators in determining a project for funding. Rather, they articulate general principles, norms, and rules governing eligibility for funds and expect cooperatives to cooperate with them in a patron–client relationship that legitimates the western sense of proper business techniques. Little wonder that "people can be pawns in the game."

The then European Economic Community's Microprojects program was especially strack. Prospective recipients of funds had to demonstrate the technical, financial, and economic feasibility of their projects and provide assurances that long-run operating costs would be available locally. The projects also had to fit into one of several categories of donor priority and satisfy a lengthy list of standards, one being that proposals must be written, and written in English, even if project members were not literate or English-speaking. The rules were authoritative. Only serious business enterprises would be funded. Yet in the case under consideration here, the EEC gave generous project funding to cooperatives that insisted on a "family" identity (and we have already seen the opinion that "a cooperative has to be more than a family registering").

Local meanings of cooperation

Arguably, the members of the cooperatives visited hold two approaches to cooperation in their heads simultaneously. The first approach is instrumental: one must be proper patrons and cooperate with a donor in order to garner the funds needed to pursue projects. Members anoint the Greek sponsors to handle this form of cooperation and themselves hold back in silence during the EEC inquisition. One can think one's own thoughts while allowing others to speak the words that donors expect to hear, because the second meaning of cooperation is noninstrumental: a good cooperative operates like a good family. The co-op teaches skills to its members and nourishes their dreams. It is, in effect, a relationally autonomous site of connection and nurturance, where members are strengthened to handle discord that threatens from out beyond it. But families in Zimbabwe are no more or less idyllic than families located elsewhere.[12] Discord is common. Cooperation, as shaped by these "women," has to do with shared training in what they think of as a sheltering environment *vis-à-vis* the "out beyond." Their embeddedness in social spaces helps the cooperators to attain a state of diffuse reciprocity, *from whence members initiate the cooperative effort.*

Of course, some IR theorists will argue, righteously, that the cooperatives are not states operating under conditions of anarchy and self-help! But just as multilateralists question the sacred tree of anarchy in IR, there is a larger theoretical lesson to be pondered here. Perhaps domestic norms of cooperation, fixedly located beyond anarchy, are really inside IR, where they can dispel the mesmerizing effects of rehearsed anarchy. The inside, in other words, could have broader parameters of cooperation than many theorists of IR/IPE notice, precisely because states are embedded in ongoing and historical relationships. James Caporaso (1993:77) tells us that the basic question "is not how to cooperate and to derive rules, norms, and sociality from a rule-free, normless state of nature. Rather, the starting point is a social conception of the actors." I would add that a social starting point makes it possible for multiple subjectivities to exist in empathetic conversation with each other, such that rigid and otherly norms of eligibility can accommodate an outlaw family.

The outside and inside meet

We now confidently return to the story of Zimbabwean cooperatives as the story of marginalized insiders to IPE. The Greek sponsors come into focus as insider-outsiders. They are cast by the "women" in a parental-familial role and will, in fact, never receive tit-for-tat reciprocation for their considerable financial and training efforts. That is how it is in "families." Moreover, their trainees develop "own thoughts" on how to build an extended family – a factory they will run, "because the men know they have no knowledge of silk." (Presumably the Greek patrons will be part of the "family," but they are not explicitly mentioned.) The cooperators resist the oversupervision of a standpoint as they take in the standpoints of these empathetic others.

---

[12] When I speak of families in this context, my frame of reference is the heterosexual family. I am aware that this is a flawed, partial sense of family and yet am also aware that homosexuality among Africans in Zimbabwe has been forced underground by a relentless homophobia in the local culture and state.

Meanwhile, their patrons face oversupervision from other outside quarters. They face, first, a certain loss of racial authority by working closely with the African "other" in a country that tolerates considerable *de facto* segregation (of "cultures," the whites say). Second, as "women" they are suspect in donor circles: "I don't like the idea that the whole thing is held together by two European women." And yet, like the women cooperators, they too escape oversupervision, in their case by having one foot inside the cooperatives and the other inside the camp of EEC kith-and-kin. The first placement makes it difficult for the second foot to get a too-tight colonial grip on them and on the cooperatives through them.

The Europeans also use a Greek-to-Greek "family" relationship to justify (or simply rationalize) funding for these particular cooperatives. Such funding of a cooperative – using family norms – however, is a highly irregular way for multilateral lending agencies to bring the poor into modernity. Some shifting of identity, some mobility among multiple subjectivities, enables those inside the rules to draw on the outside realm of "family" for meaning and justification – much as the cooperators slip the boundaries between "cooperatives" and "families" in order to "make many things."

We can say that the resultant cooperations challenge a local subtext in which all cooperators are "failures," people who have not made it as sovereign individuals in the valued anarchy of the marketplace. They also face-off simultaneous oversupervision and invisibility in the theories that purport to explain cooperation, or the lack thereof, in international relations. Rather than presenting us with homegrown theory *per se*, they surprise us, not the least by indicating how Reginas in a local situation are affected by regimes affiliated with the international political economy; and how Reginas, in turn, can influence the policies of regime members.

And so?

It is an accident, one supposes, that there are Greek patrons in Zimbabwe who can develop links with Greek representatives from international relations in order to configure a family authority that overcomes adversity. Is it an accident that participants in two cooperatives have a family-style diffuse reciprocity among themselves before they seek specific reciprocity with the EEC? One cannot say. Is it accidental that the metaphor of "family" figures in the explanation for the European decision to fund the two silkmaking cooperatives? Or did a "strange" conversation take place in this Zimbabwean locale, such that "family" emerged as the point of tangency across difference? Do actors involved in international relations take their cues from socialities that exist outside the carefully demarcated realm of the international? Does international relations operate with isolated self-helpers or with socially embedded groups that connect on the basis of shared "outside" symbols? All of this is fertile research terrain.

Gender weaves in and out of the stories of cooperation in Zimbabwe and in IR. Gender is often associated only with "women," who are entreated to join those who are the ungendered humans in an enterprise of theory building that cannot include them. The invitation to drop gender as a way of knowing hides the already wielded power to exclude through gender-privileged cooperations, a power that affects the field's theory about cooperation. The multilateralists alone seem to understand that "rules, norms, and habits of cooperation [are not] exclusively . . . something external to agents (states), something that agents 'bump into' or 'run up against' as they interact with one another. Instead, they recognize that these practices are often constitutive of the identities and power of agents in the first place" (Caporaso, 1993:78).

Yet gender is an identity for both "men" and "women" in international relations that even the multilateralists powerfully occlude. They do "not-see" postmodern feminist resonances in their call to rethink the "problem of cooperation" – which is usually portrayed as a game of strategic interaction – in favor of a model of decision featuring "debate, communication, persuasion, argument, and discursive legitimation." Multilateralists overlook gender generally, even as they "do-see" that "the international system . . . is not just a collection of independent states in interaction" (p. 78).

If we are to promote the idea that "the international system is a forum as well as a chessboard," it is imperative to admit gender into the discussion. This means that not only should the Reginas of Zimbabwe speak alongside states, regimes, and multilateral agencies that are themselves the local agents of international political economy. It is also appropriate to query *masculine* gender as an identity that carries power and assumptions about cooperation. We must look outside mainstream IR for the inside, and that "outside" includes those whose lots in life are unchronicled and subversive: "We have many plans . . . It took the Ministry of Cooperatives so long to process our papers for registration that some of us were discouraged . . . Maybe now . . ."

5   The White Paper trailing

"White" developed out of more travel, this time to Australia in the mid-1990s, when I took up sequential visiting appointments at the Australian National University (in the Department of International Relations, Research School of Pacific and Asian Studies, and then in the Department of Political Science in the Faculties). At that time, there was concern in critical IR circles of the country that the government was about to issue a retrogressive defense strategy – a White Paper – for a new era. I was only vaguely aware of this planning when Graeme Cheeseman, of the Australian Defence Forces Academy (ADFA), asked me to write on gender aspects of the Paper for a volume of critical essays. I was nowhere near the right person for the job: I had little knowledge of Australia and much less sense of its defense history and policies. Furthermore, the very thought of reading an official defense document made me go pale with ennui; military policy is not "my thing." Graeme insisted, and so I stuffed the Paper into a bag as I headed for a vacation at the south coast. In pristine Moruya, New South Wales – ocean front and estuary back – I read the dread Paper. Techno-garbley, it mentioned women in only two short, obviously prescribed, sections.

The *raison d'être* behind the White Paper was fear that the United States could no longer be relied on to defend Australia's regional interests in the post-Cold War era. Australia had been as loyal to the Cold War USA as a Boy Scout to his troop. Now it defined itself as needing a military doctrine for a new time, in a region where Indonesia and China were also seeking strategic influence. The resulting White Paper tried hard to project a future working relationship with Asia, but was foiled at each turn by the sense that "those states" were so vastly different to Australia.

I knew nothing of these things in the specialist way that a strategic studies analyst "knows." As I read the White Paper, however, I experienced *déjà vu*: Australia's self-defining difference *vis-à-vis* the regional "out there" echoed aspects of Zimbabwe's and South Africa's colonial concerns about "the other." Those white settler states had been known to "resolve" racial and cultural difference using tank divisions and sjamboks, with South Africa insisting that African blacks were so different that they required separate homelands. Both fought alterities that they themselves constructed as threats to a (fictive) "White Way of Life." Now here was Australia, a white settler country convulsed over Aboriginal claims, thinking about meeting military challenges involving Asian others.

The Australian White Paper suddenly interested me as a case of white settler, postcolonial strategism. I reviewed work by Homi Bhabha, Edward Said, Arjun Appadurai, and Anne McClintock – whose writings have not yet had the wide impact they should in IR – and mixed it with postmodern feminist favorites by Judith Butler and Donna Haraway to produce "The White Paper Trailing." With standard IR cast aside in the style of Elshtain and Enloe, it arrays aspects of imperial fears and controls alongside prospects for postcolonial empathies across difference, empathy being another theme that runs through my travelogue. I now find postcolonial literatures indispensable to thinking about IR and about feminism (Sylvester, 1994a, 1995a, 1999a, 1999b, 1999c, 2000a).

The 1994 White Paper underwent refinement during the 1997 Asian Economic Crisis and after tumultuous events in Indonesia. Yet the sense of the USA holding itself aloof from the Asia-Pacific strategic picture, pushing Australia into a more activist regional role, persists; indeed, it lies behind some of Australia's more recent initiatives in East Timor. Meanwhile, ADFA has been seeking to purge its worst hypermasculinist practices, and the rest of the armed forces grapple with the endemic sexism Enloe sights around all militaries. From a feminist perspective, Australia is not alone in needing a Lavender Paper sensitive to Elshtain's concerns about chastened patriotism and Tickner's feminist convictions about alternative security. We are all trailing.

* * *

Nothing I had told him about the bleakness of the Australia psyche and the cult of death had made it seem real to him, until he'd visited the Australian War Memorial in Canberra. The central monument in a planned capital city, it represented a glorification of battle in modern warfare on a scale that encompassed every engagement ever fought

> in by Australians ... it had no counterpart in Canada, England, any society he'd ever visited. Perhaps the nearest equivalent was the City of the Dead in Egypt.
> (Conway, 1993:143)

> Australia's strategic stance is, in the broadest possible sense, defensive.
> (Australian Department of Defence, 1994:3)

The White Paper is trailing us. It is slim yet ponderous and weighty. It looms, even for those who "merely" pass through places Australian, like so many migrating birds unhomed for awhile in a flight of dissemiNations.[1] It sings out about cross-cultural difference in its many refrains of western security, repeated roundly. Defensive. It echoes the sounds (we think we hear) of waves crashing through a conch shell placed to the ear.

The White Paper is artifact. It could have presented contrary and unhomed disjunctures with the Western Way of Security, that is, with the western way of institutionalizing defense as nearly synonymous with western culture (Klein, 1988, 1994). Hereabouts, when most of the West is wintering, Australia, along with the rest of IR's South, contrarily sets the pace in summering. Hereabouts, ways of life "Asian" wrap us round Confucian values, Islam, orchids, and coups. Hereabouts, "Pacific Islanders" satisfy the grass-skirted fantasies of those who live without much sun in December; those islanders then go about their lives near the all-too-real nuclear testing, grass-incinerating grounds of the Cold and post-Cold War. Here it takes twenty-two flying hours to reach out from Sydney to London, and fourteen to reach postmodern LA. There is a matter of identity here, perhaps bleak identity, in a world constituted as the outer edge of "the" western value system. There is a proud westernness in multicultural Australia. And, not surprisingly, on the upside down of western spaces of security, there is a White Paper chirping a familiar ditty of defense.

Here, in the intervening spaces of the almost beyond-the-West, pledges of western allegiance defensively regurgitate; new monuments to defense in and against the region get designed for the twenty-first century; and future cities capable of inflicting death on Australia are tentatively (so defensively) identified close to home. Bound to a security

---

A version of this part of the chapter originally appeared in *Discourses of Danger and Dread frontiers: Australian Defence and Security thinking after the Cold War*, edited by graeme Cheeseman and Robert-Bruce, NSW Allen and Unwin, 1996.

[1] For a discussion of "unhomeliness" and "dissemiNation", see Bhabha's (1994) introduction and chapter 8.

text that renews ongoing affinities as it nods to historical and regional changes, the White Paper tries to be brave and immunomodulating of the forces that would have AUSTRALIA set itself apart from ASIA. But it trails away in logistical support capabilities, to intelligence collection and evaluation, the ready reserves, the defense science and technology organization, F-111s, C-130s, and Collins class submarines – to immunities from all manner of aliens.[2]

What to say about the hullabaloo that is the White Paper trailing? How to see its chants as ritualistic, as security fetishizations, while also making a positive contribution to bureaucratically beatified "defense policy?"

In my efforts to assess international relations theory and practice, I have stumbled on homeless places of identity and policy and place, on unlikely negotiations between contentious blocks of knowledge, on homesteads that rework the puny claims of received entitlement, on empathetic cooperations and spaces world-traveled "to be part of a revisionary time," as Homi Bhabha (1994:7) puts it. I am, all the while, a flag(s)-waving feminist living in a world that is simultaneously decentered, centered, lacking solid identities and assertive of identity to the point of death for entire cities and populations. Defensive, it is. I am skeptical about securing (what manner of) security, even in the land of "no worries, mate."

What one can say about the White Paper is that it is full of wistful and nostalgic confessions of security among friends. It indulges in vague (post)colonial paranoia about "a region" it strives tolerantly and opportunistically to befriend. Along the way, it misses chances to cooperate empathetically with those whom defense policy would put controlling fences around. It refuses contrariness, even though it is stouthearted about being different and in a different time. It is reasonable. It is modern. These things one can reveal on the road to a policy politics that takes the tricks of security seriously.

Security among friends? Confession I

Within the 167 pages of *Defending Australia 1994*, there are numerous admissions that Australia has little to fear from a once-was Hobbesian world of intrigue. The superpower struggle of the Cold War years, which

---

[2] For an IR-related discussion of immunities, immunomodulation, and international relations, see Sylvester (1994a, chapter 5). Terms are from Haraway (1991). The military phrases in this sentence come directly from the Australian defense White Paper.

occupied Australia's loyal western attention, is now so ephemeral that defense planners say, quite simply, that the threat of global war "has now faded" (Australian Department of Defence, 1994:7). There is also apparently little to fear from something called the "region," which the White Paper describes as "comparatively peaceful," because "the stable pattern of strategic relationships in Asia and the Pacific over the last twenty years has enabled economies to grow and more effective governments to evolve, while the end of the Cold War has allowed many of the tensions and conflicts of the past to be resolved or eased" (p. 7). Thus this bold, and in many ways remarkable, statement: "We believe no country at present has either a motive or an intention to attack Australia, and we have no reason to expect that any country will develop such a motive or intention" (p. 22).

Yet all is not constitutable as secure as long as change is in the air and with it shifting and disorderly relationships. And change is upon Australia no less than elsewhere in a postmodern era:

> Notwithstanding the demise of the Soviet Union and the "Eastern" bloc, there continues to be a community of nations – including Australia – bound by a common adherence to a world view that emphasises democratic values, individual liberty, respect for human rights, and free enterprise and market economies. But the notion of a Western strategic community is no longer a defining factor in ensuring global security, and is, therefore, less important for Australian strategic planning. We now see our alliance relationship with the United States primarily in the context of our shared commitment to security in the Asia-Pacific region. (p. 5)

The worldview worth securing is still unique to "the" community. There is a distinctive West. We know it by the common values that a certain "we" rehearse on behalf of everyone, unitarily, who fits. As W.J.T. Mitchell (1992:15) maintains, this West "never designates where it is, but only where it hopes to go, its 'prospects' and frontiers." It had hoped to go everywhere. Some argue that it has (Fukuyama, 1989). Australia, though, sits worriedly on the western frontier with its paper framers, who grammatically seek to reassure the antipodean reader that the boundaries of that larger community still hold, and still hold Australia.

Secondarily, and slowly, Australia is part of something it sets apart from the West and calls "the Asia-Pacific region." This is a region Australia laments: the White Paper scampers here and there in the effort to direct the neighboring outside of "the" community. It does not identify friends there quite. Rather, it identifies a "strategic environment" that at best can promote "transparency in defence policy development and force planning" (Australian Defence Department, 1994:85). Left largely unstated is the big economic advantage to Australia that goes along with being part of a "region" designated as experiencing an economic boom.

Although the United States is a friend to the last – "The United States looks to its network of bilateral alliances to maintain its continuing presence in the Western Pacific . . . [and] [w]e will facilitate, when we can, US activities and deployments in the region" (p. 99) – the North American giant has imposed conditions that throw Australia into the arms of "the region":

> the United States' engagement in the region is changing. With the collapse of the former Soviet Union, trade and economic issues will be more significant factors in its interests than in earlier decades . . . Although the United States will remain the strongest global power, the relative military strength of others in Asia will grow over time. The United States will remain a major contributor to security in the region over the next fifteen years, but it will neither seek nor accept primary responsibility for maintaining peace and stability in the region. (p. 8)

In light of a superpower's assumed retreat from some international activism, the defense analysts of Australia make many a prediction about the changes that will transpire and require accommodation. Those who think the twenty-first century may elude the confining patterns of international relations seen during the Cold War will find some comfort in references to "a more fluid and complex environment" (p. 8); but there is little comfort for the white paperers, who seem worried as they assert that "a new strategic balance will emerge in Asia to underpin peace and security" (p. 8). In between fluidity and balance of power, as in ideas sandwiched with copious fillings, the Paper waxes ominous about threats to Australia simmering in the margins of international relations: "However, ethnic and national tensions, economic rivalry, disappointed aspirations for prosperity, religious or racial conflict, or other problems could produce an unstable and potentially dangerous strategic situation in Asia and the Pacific over the next fifteen years" (p. 8).

Confession: amidst change, security is assured all around, but it is an ambiguous security. A new realist certainty will (surely) emerge eventually to guide us. Meanwhile, people messes ooze out of nation-states into international relations, bringing with them tensions, conflicts, disappointments, rivalries, problems. There is need for vigilance. There is need for defense policy, understood in conventional military terms as a plan to manage the strategic environment. There is security community in the West and conflict in the rest. Perhaps what looms ahead is the potential clash of western versus Asian and Asian-Pacific civilizations (Buzan, 1991; Huntington, 1993). The threat from those who do not know the established rules of international relations is a big nettle. International relations is supposed to be about the realm of states and balances of power revolving around states. People mucking about in the international where they should be homeless – indeed, where some of them have been historically (but apparently not successfully) unhomed – force Australia into a defensive position (Sylvester, 1993b).

And there is more to face. Challenges from within. People called "women" get a tiny section of the White Paper. Points are made about them, the main one being that they often express the intent to separate from military service before completing twenty years, something the men do not do. The tone of this section is low key, but we are made to know that "the Defence Organisation still must maintain maximum benefit in length of service from all personnel for its investment in training and education" (Australian Defence Department, 1994:65). There are new and old penances to pay. What to do about the potentially disruptive gender gap pulling at Australia's manly defense force?

In nodding to "new" uncertainties of various types, the White Paper confesses the limitations of prediction and even of old security ways. It acknowledges certain unknowns, albeit presuming that they have just emerged and were not there all along behind the violence of Cold War strategy. Simultaneously, the Paper parades its capabilities to tame the uncertainties and calls this, in effect, defense. We read: "Our planning focuses on capabilities rather than threats" (p. 22); "we should be capable, without combat assistance from other countries, of defeating any attack which could credibly be mounted against Australia" (p. 14); "Australia could be most easily attacked in the north, where our sea and air approaches are shortest, so we need to pay particular attention to defending that area" (p. 21).

Taming aims hide behind crisp and sometimes alliterative litanies of "command, control and communications"; "intelligence collection and evaluation"; "maritime patrol and response"; "air defence in maritime areas and northern approaches" (p. 30). If it were not for the many awkward, poorly executed leaps across the narrative from global to regional to local analyses and back again, one could easily be lulled into a stupor by this repetitive apologia. Confess: here, in this archaic language of capabilities lies nostalgia for a time from the orderly realist past that still can "be imagined as a real possibility for the future" (Connolly, 1991:463).[3] Hence the F-111s alongside tentative overtures to "the region." The confidence. The lack of confidence.

(Post)colonial dilemmas: Confessions II

"The United States, South Africa, Australia, Canada and New Zealand remain . . . break-away settler colonies," says Anne McClintock (1993: 295), "that have not undergone decolonisation, nor, with the exception of South Africa, are they likely to in the near future." Many in Australia seem to share with those in my US birthplace a marked ability to pretend to be postcolonial without unshackling the mindset that creates a host of others out there, beyond, who must be defended against. In the United States there are "illegal aliens," "Third World drug runners," "Mexicans without papers," "boat people," and so on. Such subject statuses make colonial temperaments nervous because their originary locations are (constituted as) somewhere beyond the culture and needs and values of "the" United States. That "these people" are with us means they have invaded and intruded or pulled at our liberal heart strings; they have refused geospatial discouragements and, voting with their feet, they have gone across, taken advantage.

For the framers of Australia's White Paper, the "beyond" is ASIA in all its monolithically geospatial permutations: Southeast Asia (particularly Indonesia, Malaysia, and Singapore), Northeast and South Asia, and the Southwest Pacific. Caution is the watchword in all the descriptions. Indonesia, for example, is said to have troubled Australia in the "turbulent 1950s and early 1960s" and now is characterized as possessing "stability, cohesion, economic growth and [a] positive approach to the region" (Australian Defence Department, 1994:87). Vietnam, another past irritant, is encouraged to participate in security dialogue processes, "as a means of encouraging that country's constructive involvement in the security affairs of the region" (p. 90).

Bhabha (1994:1) claims that "[o]ur [western] existence today is marked by a tenebrous sense of survival," because the "beyond" now becomes visibly rather than invisibly homeless; and it comes home to us unhomed. "[T]here is," he says, "a sense of disorientation, a disturbance

---

[3] For a discussion of some of the components of nuclear lulling, see Cohn (1987).

of direction, in the 'beyond': an exploratory, restless movement caught so well in the French rendition of the words *au-dela* – here and there, on all sides, *fort/da*, hither and thither, back and forth" (p. 1). This disturbance of direction pulls a White Paper away from mean orientalism. For example, there is a mighty effort therein to avoid piping the region of Australia's abode around what Edward Said (1993:138) might call "a *distribution* of geopolitical awareness into aesthetic, scholarly, economic, sociological, historical and philological texts" (emphasis in original). But the Paper does not problematize ASIA either. It alternately embraces it "as a partner in determining the strategic affairs of the region" (Australian Defence Department, 1994:85) and sets it apart from the true community of interest of which Australia is a member: "In coming years, Australia will need to do more to ensure that our strategic environment develops in ways which are consistent with our interests" (p. 16).

The Paper does not, therefore, escape a particular orientalist "*elaboration* not only of a basic geographical distinction (the world is made up of two unequal halves, Orient and Occident) but also of a whole series of 'interests' . . . it *is* rather than expresses, a certain *will* or *intention* to understand, in some cases to control, manipulate, even to incorporate, what is a manifestly different (or alternative and novel) world" (Said, 1993:138, emphasis in original). Within the Paper, there is pious advocacy of cooperative approaches to the Southwest Pacific, "within which the Pacific Island countries can help one another" (Australian Defence Department, 1994:92). There is talk of "developing the capabilities of these nations to assert and protect their sovereignty in peace" (p. 92). There is the constant assertion of intent, as in "[a] prosperous South-East Asia free from conflict and external pressures and characterised by increasing interdependence between regional countries is very much in Australia's interests" (p. 86).

The postcolonial dilemma of the Paper centers on how to interact with those outside the true community of the West, the ones who emerge now as crucial to the strategic environment of the future and yet pose "destabilizing tensions." It is a dilemma that is part of a larger, oft-expressed concern here with whether or not Australia is Asian. The press often answers that question in the negative – no, we do not share language and culture with ASIA. It also answers weakly in the positive, briefly noting shared concerns across the region that AUSTRALIA would be foolish to ignore. So it is also with the White Paper. One might imagine it setting in motion the means by which received customs of difference might be unmasked as both differences and denied similarities (there is ethnic tension, racism, and nationalism in AUSTRALIA, after all). But instead of seeking to be in the world one has assigned as ASIAN, rather than finding parts of Australia therein, the White Paper advocates processes of controlled cooperation with the not-quite-up-to-speed other (Lugones, 1990; Sylvester, 1994b).

It issues what Arjun Appadurai (1993a:331) refers to as ideoscapes, which are concatenations of "ideas, terms, and images, including 'freedom,' 'welfare,' 'rights,' 'sovereignty,' 'representation,' and the masterterm 'democracy,'" as if there were a true community of agreement on what these images mean. As if, in other words, the framers of the White Paper could manipulate the knowledge environment of the region so that "security" would come to mean the one thing that would always be in AUSTRALIA's defense interest. "The region," ASIA, the PACIFIC ISLANDS – all those nerve-racking places – would be turned into signs of successful or failed consumption of AUSTRALIAN-produced security. Each would be "helped to believe that he or she is an actor, where in fact he or she is at best a chooser" (p. 331). In this way, Australia can be part of Asia, part of The Region, and separate from it all in orientalizing, power-controlling, colonial ways.

Lest the reader think Australia is oddly monstrous in its efforts to evade the region while also imposing upon it, Appadurai (p. 334) points out that "the central feature of global culture today is the politics of the mutual effort of sameness and difference to cannibalize one another and thus to proclaim their successful hijacking of the twin Enlightenment ideas of the triumphantly universal and the resiliently particular." Whether these "twin ideas" are distinctly Enlightenment era or not may be debated. The larger point is that the framers of Australia's White Paper fit a pattern in the postmodern era in which speaking out of both sides of the mouth – of similarity and difference in mutually cannibalizing ways – is an utterly common element of global culture.

To see it in the White Paper, cast an eye at the section on the Australian alliance with the United States. Here the framers are terribly concerned to express the loyalty that earns one a place in "the" community of the West, even if this means taking on some dependence on the remaining superpower. Admitting that Australia is "sympathetic to most American values and interests" (Australian Defence Department, 1994:95), the Paper tells, for example, about intelligence sharing across the two countries: "Intelligence co-operation with the United States is fundamental to our national effort, and this will continue over the next fifteen years. Without that help, Australia's national intelligence effort would

need to be much bigger, and could not be as effective" (p. 97). It goes
on about access to high technology and maintenance of professional
military skills. In a manner approaching outright pride, it states that
the "United States looks to its network of bilateral alliances to maintain its continuing presence in the Western Pacific...We will facilitate, when we can, US activities and deployments in the region"
(p. 99).

Then, out of the other corner of the mouth, the Paper implicitly establishes Australia's difference from the United States through the emphasis on regional matters. Indeed, it claims that "[o]ur ability to defend
ourselves and contribute to regional security does much to ensure that
we are respected and helps us engage in the region by giving confidence
that we can manage uncertainty and assure our security" (p. 3). Here
self-reliance is the key, Australia's many western defense relationships
notwithstanding. Self-reliance brings respect *qua* AUSTRALIA rather
than as the Cold War leftover partner of the United States. Confidence
will manage uncertainty in "the region."

That the hijacked "universal" of western values and the "resiliently
particular" of constituted geospaces are wrapped up together does not
entirely escape the notice of White Paper framers. But there is a constant will or intention throughout the piece to understand difference
as fully consonant with *western* ways of security. Thus when we read,
"We will continue to foster, through dialogue, an accurate understanding of Australia's strategic interests and security concerns and ensure
that we in turn understand the perceptions, concerns and capabilities
of neighbouring countries" (p. 85), we wonder about the arrogant perceptions that could (inadvertently perhaps) influence this exercise in
tolerance.[4] We wonder about an Asia-Pacific that AUSTRALIA gingerly
homesteads and "worlds" in the sense of sublimating all the rich histories therein via the projection of common security needs.[5]

When we read about the "maximum benefit in length of service,"
which the Defence Force will have to extract now that women indicate
interest in short-term service, we find a set of "performance indicators to monitor achievement of greater responsibility by women in the
Defence Force" (p. 66). Given the universalizing tendency that exists
alongside particularism, we ask: responsibility for what, measured by
which criteria of sameness and difference in service? Whose standards

[4] For discussions of arrogant perceptions, see Gunning (1991–1992) and Frye (1983). Also
see Sylvester (1995a).
[5] See discussion of "worlding" in Spivak (1985).

of "cultural and institutional barriers impede women achieving senior positions in the Defence Force," and which ones will be brought to bear on the question of "why more women in the Defence Force do not seek a long-term military career" (p. 66)? In a word, whose security is enhanced by pledges "to ensure that women in the Australian Defence Force achieve their maximum potential" (p. 66)?

Similarly, "women" exist in the Australian Defence Force only to the degree that their bodies, and therefore their task assignments, are constituted as uniformly real and also as always already different than the usual standard. The bodies are womanly, which is to say historically inferior to those of men, at least for purposes of defending AUSTRALIA. Different bodies require different jobs. Such inconvenience. And then the brazen bodies take themselves out of the long-term and opt for short-run service, thus making non-sense of the pledge to ascertain how, as noted earlier, "the Defence Organisation . . . [can] gain maximum benefit in length of service from all personnel for its investment in training and education" (p. 65). These odd bods need studies, a Defence Advisory Forum on Discrimination, and achievement monitoring. Importantly, these bodies require a set of performance indicators that will, one supposes, not measure the performance of sex and gender as regulatory norms that influence identity and task assignments, perceived achievements, and career expectations (Butler, 1993). After all, "Defence aims to be widely recognised as a fair employer" (Australian Defence Department, 1994:65) and fairness initially assumes that true differences exist which subsequently can be reconciled to one true standard.

That one standard in this case is represented by a defense establishment in which "[b]oth on and off duty, [Defence Force personnel] are subject to strict disciplinary requirements, backed by the punishment provisions of the Defence Force Disciplinary Act. They must render service as ordered" (p. 57). At the same time – out of the other side of the mouth – comes the admission that "the" standard must reflect changes in the communities from which one recruits: "the Defence Force is under pressure to meet community expectations about personal freedom and equality of opportunity. This poses particular challenges for traditionally organised and disciplined Services, but these expectations must be accommodated as the Defence Force cannot be at odds with the community" (pp. 70–71).

A White Paper trails confessions of nostalgic friendship and (post)colonial dilemmas of identity, community, and "adjustment." A White Paper embraces change and maintains a defense monument to war (maybe, possibly, war will come even though we cannot find an enemy anywhere). A defensive instrument sustains defense policy. A bluster and a moment of sobriety together.

Insecuring defense

In the interstices of the White Paper's many confessions and postcolonial ambiguities lie opportunities to insecure the fences thrown up around AUSTRALIAN defense. Defense policy is always a strategy to secure the inherently insecure, the terrain of elusive assurance. It battens down the hatches against "the" storm when, in fact, storms with many centers unfold on many fronts at once in virtually all geospaces of the world (as we know it).[6] It detects overlapping pieces of war and peace in the postmodern era, but opts for the certainty of war preparations as a way of meeting the challenges. It seems that the pieces of peace around the spaces of war are problematic, not to be trusted. Alien.

Defense policy is also a way of securing the notion that Australia exists apart from its neighbors *and* within the sheltering arms of the West (for which read the United States). It is a way of securing the West, even though that West, as Mitchell (1992:15) points out, is "a half-truth, a premature generalisation, an impression." It is a way of insecuring the West too, not in any direct way, but by turning attention on the other half-truths and impressions painted in solid lines as The Region. It is a way of glorifying the standards of battle and also of disavowing war as the times may require. It is a way of being defensive about preoccupations with security, of construing the prospect of an AUSTRALIAN City of the Dead falling from the weight of ASIA AND THE PACIFIC.

The immunities set forth in the White Paper could be immunomodulated to fit a world that is never not insecure. Instead of carrying on about the latest generation of magic bullets capable of blasting the disease of complex international sociality in the late twentieth century, one could grapple with the possibility that a region whispered about with will and intent to control leads to a nostalgic form of security comprising tanks and fighter planes, ready reserves, target detection and tracking, and simulations and simulators. Signal propagation and signals acquisition, the language of alternative understandings of defense, pepper the White Paper (Australian Defence Department, 1994:127). These are meant as something concrete and not as codes for the signs that secure

---

[6] For one sense of the "world," see Der Derian (1993).

the enterprise of defense policymaking. There is nothing playful in the White Paper. Nothing facetious. Nothing ironic about preparing for an invasion that the framers think is unlikely. All those "problems" of ethnicity, religion, and so on to think about.

There are also, however, many references in the White Paper to a conversational form of politics, in which standards might be decided jointly rather than derived from "the West," the alliance with "the United States," and historical elements of the western way of security. We read: "The successful initiation of APEC and the ASEAN Regional Forum shows that the region can agree on broad goals" (p. 8); and "[w]e aim to ensure that these processes are inclusive and provide scope for the major powers of Asia and the Pacific to engage constructively with each other and with other countries of the region" (p. 85). The first ingredients emerge here of empathetic cooperation – of processes enabling (rather than cannibalizing) rich particular histories through negotiations of defense knowledge, not derivations of it from Australia's "superior" experience. But we also know that "[e]ffective military capability is essential to our defence . . . [and] the force on which we rely must be our own because our security environment and national interests are unique" (p. 3). Face the ideoscape of the (post)colonial white settler space. AUSTRALIA is presenced and immunized against all extraterritorials. There is no defencing going on, little knowledge-constitutive travel to odd "worlds" where we can, contrarily, also be ourselves.

There is value in world-traveling away from the arrogant perceptions of defensive orientalism and also away from a tourist's gaze on the other that assigns it only the interests that a western-subject-centered "I" projects (see Probyn, 1990). The tourist is the self-styled superior interacting with wildernessed natives in ways that can be, at most, sympathetic to them rather than empathetic with them. Judith Butler (1993:118) reminds us that "sympathy involves a substitution of oneself for another that may well be a colonization of the other's position *as* one's own." It is me telling you that I feel for you from a position of "I"ness. Empathy is a means by which aspects of other cultures become recognizably part of us rather than something we go on joint maneuvers to derive from ourselves for others. It turns down the volume on "our interests" that usually overdubs what others speak.

To be empathetically cooperative is to become relationally rather than reactively autonomous with those we have defined as unmistakably other, with those who are not inside "our" community, our value system. Relational autonomy establishes identity independence for oneself in and while maintaining relationships with difficult others. One does not take up permanent domicile in the other when one has empathy; one does not universalize her experience as something "I" can know absolutely, thus cannibalizing her. Rather, one appreciates the similarities that are echoes in one's independent experience. Reactive autonomy is independence gained by pitting oneself against, as in putting up boundaries and establishing separateness from, another (Marchand, 1994; Sylvester, 1992). Empathy enables respectful negotiations with contentious others because we can recognize involuntary similarities across difference as well as differences that mark independent identity (Ferguson, 1993:154). There is no arrogance of uniqueness. Precious little committed defensiveness.

It follows that empathetically cooperative defense policy does not seek amalgamations and assimilations into one Australian, western-based common security, albeit it might be possible to accentuate some similarities. Empathetic cooperation, rather, lodges in the liminal relational spaces between orientalist defensiveness and the defensiveness of those who have been turned into the oriental. It appreciates difference while simultaneously finding that many of the differences are echoes within one's own experience and identity, and are not bogeymen against whom to develop capabilities and self-reliance. Empathetically cooperative defense policy is more a will to understand than an understanding in and of itself through (some homogenizing sense of) itself alone (Sylvester, 1994a).

We can read in the White Paper that "the number of Indonesian service personnel participating in training with Australia has risen rapidly" (Australian Defence Department, 1994:88). We do not read, correspondingly, that the number of Australian personnel participating in training with Indonesia has risen at all, let alone rapidly (although we do discover that the Defence Ministers of Australia and Indonesia will now meet annually). We read of studies being formed to determine how women fare in the military. We do not read about studies that determine how the studies constitute the women and the military. These are small examples, to be sure, of the possibilities trailing the White Paper. They are also reminders that it is easier for the colonized to world-travel to Australia than it is for the Australian to world-travel the other way to knowledge. The colonized have been steeped in the lessons of adjustment to western ways of security in all matters. The colonizer is the one who will find it difficult to put aside arrogant perceptions of the bleak to work toward a less defensive posture of empathy.

Sitting on the surface of the foregoing discussion is the sense, as Tanzanian feminist Marjorie Mbilinyi (1992:35) puts it, that "our identities are not given or reducible to our origins, skin colour, or material locations. Our identities or positions are the product of struggle and they represent an achieved not an ascribed trait." The question of what we struggle against and for determines, in my view, what the achievement of identity frames. We have a White Paper. We have defense policy. In a world where struggle occurs on many fronts simultaneously and confusingly, security is not enhanced by the white defense policy struggling to protect fenced-in identity. AUSTRALIA is (A)u(S)tral(IA) – not isomorphically, but resonantly.

Defense policy can be the practice of struggle against distributive orientalism and for a shared moment of empathetically cooperative negotiation. It can be a struggle to achieve relational autonomy in a world struggling out from under all the reactiveness of a Cold War. We will still be insecure – always already so. But by listening to the whispers of the conch shell differently, we may learn how to dismantle certain memorials to the past.

6 Picturing the Cold War: an eye graft/art graft

A zigzag now in that nonlinear journey – back in time but ahead of it in thinking about places that contain gender in international relations. It is the 1950s. A rough and tumble New World America is suddenly supercharged, with ICBMs dug into Nevada landscapes and home-grown avant-garde art maneuvered to international attention. Missiles and Abstract Expressionism project the power and good taste of "the free world" and its leader. The art, no less than those missiles, also sends out lessons on the proper conduct of masculine foreign policy between states.

"Picturing the Cold War" is a newer piece, albeit with roots extending all the way back to my high school days. I audaciously joined the art club then, though I could not draw, and read art history texts (aloud) while the others sketched. One did what one could, and what I could hope to do was create words about what I saw. I looked and looked at pictures too, during regular excursions to the Yale Art Gallery in New Haven and the Wadsworth Atheneum in Hartford, making the acquaintance of illusionary Dalis, O'Keeffe pistils, yellow Van Gogh interiors, and Hopper's scenes of an eerily uncomfortable modern America. I was smitten. A little later, when New York became the day trip of choice, a Salvador Dali retrospective at the Museum of Modern Art (MOMA) planted itself inside my head. Thirty years later, when that "mad one" finally minced his way across my IR feminist pages (Sylvester, 1994a, 1999a), it was like going home.

Today, the MOMA and other art spots figure into my itineraries. For 1999–2000: the Guggenheims in New York and Bilbao, the National Museum of Women in the Arts in Washington, the Jackson Pollock Retrospective in London, Gallery Delta in Harare, the Museum of Contemporary Art in Seoul, and the Van Gogh Museum in Amsterdam. I wander art purposively, personally, professionally flat-out flabbergasted that IR has spent eighty some years not-seeing the international art that falls right into its portfolio.

In Canberra there is the National Gallery of Australia (NGA), with its rich collections of American Abstract Expressionists, Aboriginal art, and modern Australian oils. The NGA has *the* painting around which I sighted visual art connecting Cold War international relations: Pollock's *Blue Poles*. It is one of the key emblems of US efforts to influence the world in the 1950s and of Australians buying the US message in the early 1970s – looking out from verandas at the coasts to see the world seeing its good taste (Drew, 1994). *Blue Poles'* international journeys have taken it dripping out of a barn in Springs New York to Canberra, where it rested for twenty-five years, back to New York, and on to London for the Retrospective. It travels as a *naif* of international relations, a pretty (to some) picture set against skeins of manly blood, UN fiddlings in flesh tones, and the abstracted reds and blacks of trade and currency deals responsible for art going abroad. It also travels as gender emblem. Read the stories about Pollock and see Lee Krasner, his artist wife brooding in the corner of the barn, holding together the frantic, the splendid, and the falling apart artist – in her own performance piece *à la* Marie van Clausewitz and Fawn Hall. Notice how Krasner's effacement mirrors women's evisceration from American foreign policy of the Cold War era. *Blue Poles* is pretty: but look at its fractals, shattered glass, and gendered mien, its picture of the things IR contains, puts aside, cannot sight.

"Picturing the Cold War" insists on being IR while relying mostly on sources beyond IR sights, chief among them Jacques Derrida's stunning *Memoirs of the Blind*: *The Self-Portrait and Other Ruins* (1993). That extraordinary analysis of drawing the self and others through various forms of blindness evokes the drama of IR's critical traditions striving to peel scales from a field's retinas. There are others with names and work that few across IR may have read, such as Serge Guilbaut, Eva Cockcroft, Michael Leja, Annette Cox, Carol Duncan, David and Cecile Shapiro, and Whitney Chadwick. Again, though, when I look at *Blue Poles*, I can also see Enloe's whither-the-women question for international relations. Elshtain's aesthetic ways of sighting war and writing about its unanticipated contributors has me contemplating civic virtue in international art spaces. And Tickner's admonition rings – that we learn to see security and its strivings, manifestations, colors differently, better, beyond IR.

123

* * *

> ... an eye graft, the grafting of one point of view onto the other
> (Derrida, 1993:2)

There is a small but fascinating literature in art history about the ways Abstract Expressionist art became a tool in the US effort to promote the concept of the free world – and US leadership of it – during the early Cold War years (Cockcroft, 1985; Guilbaut, 1983; Kozloff, 1973). Abstract Expressionism was associated with such names as Jackson Pollock, Willem de Kooning, Clyfford Stills, Bernard Newman, and all of these, in turn, were associated with New York, the financial and cultural center of a United States climbing the heights of superpowerdom. Abstract Expressionism was the centerpiece there of the Museum of Modern Art's (MOMA) international program of exhibitions, which the Rockefellers funded in order to have it "known ... that America was not the cultural backwater that the Russians ... were trying to demonstrate that it was" (Cockcroft, 1985:39). Abstract Expressionism had CIA links too that made it possible for some of its artists, who had early leftist leanings, to be showcased in Europe as representatives of a big, vibrant, energetic, sweeping, and non-Communist US superiority. Business did not ignore Abstract Expressionism either. In 1946, the US business magazine *Fortune* ran an article on the atomic explosion at Bikini in which it claimed that abstract art "could communicate the new meaning of human experience, the incredible feeling of total disintegration" (Guilbaut, 1983:96). The article was accompanied by two abstract paintings by Ralston Crawford.

Through the late 1940s and 1950s, Abstract Expressionism was constituted, argues Serge Guilbaut (p. 85), as "a symbol for all those who had formed an idea, still rather imprecise, of the 'new America,' battling to rescue imperiled culture and the Western World." It was a battle waged and frequently won on the front of art diplomacy. Through the Cold War machinations of an unlikely cabal of government agencies, intellectuals, and influential art connoisseurs, Abstract Expressionism – a style of painting that average Americans did not like, and yet a style that has been termed "characteristically American" – became an *haute couture* representative of "Western Culture" as a whole" (p. 177).

Although there is a long and interconnected history between government agencies, private businesses, art patrons, and international exhibitions and sales,[1] there is still relatively little knowledge of the phenomenon of "art diplomacy" in international relations. IR literature has tended to focus on war and peace, conventional diplomacy, formal foreign policy decision making, balances of power, international trade and financial flows, and discourses of international relations theory (e.g. Allison, 1971; Carr, 1962; George, 1994; Gilpin, 1987; Morgenthau, 1965; Waltz, 1979). IR does venture close to the idea of cultural hegemony – understood in the Gramscian sense of a situation in which considerable popular consent is granted to leadership that contains some coercive elements – when it discusses aspects of international regimes. An international regime comprises "principles, norms, rules, and decision-making procedures around which actor expectations converge in a given issue-area" (Krasner, 1982:186). One could argue that a school or work of art becomes internationally "great" – hegemonically so – when a significant number of key actors in the transnational art world, perhaps with connections to national political circles, converge on its importance. But students of mainstream IR do not write about art regimes in the world; they prefer to focus on security regimes, such as the North Atlantic Treaty Organization, or regimes for such commodities as oil, trade, or food (e.g., Keohane, 1984).

That, in regime analysis, numerous locations, actors, and forms of global relations are out of view is not only a pity but also a distortion of what we claim to know. We claim to know a considerable amount about the Cold War from both mainstream and revisionist perspectives (e.g., Lebow and Stein, 1994). But what of knowledges outside IR's usual sources and purviews that could contribute to or challenge accepted ways of telling the Cold War stories? We already know the answer to that question. The discipline brackets itself off and builds its distinctive set of concerns and methods and sources; that, after all, is what any academic discipline is all about – the inside set off against the outside (Walker, 1993). The cost of exclusivity, though, can be – to use Jacques

---

[1] Watson (1992) is a good read on such connections, albeit rather offensive on gender issues. On page 46, he comments on Herodotus' discussion of men of humble birth in Babylon, 500 BC, being paid to take the ugly women as wives: "There is surely a case of adopting the same procedure at picture auctions: bidders would be paid to take away the misshapen rubbish, no less common among art objects than among Babylonian wives."

Derrida's (1993:3 n1) language of vision – such that a field's "potency always develops on the brink of blindness."[2] My concern with the field of IR has mostly been with the blind evacuations of an awareness of gender and of people called women from the theories and debates that constitute the discipline (despite an omnipresent performance of gender within it) (Sylvester, 1994a, 1996b). Art diplomacy on the international scene is not only a site of insight into the politics we tend to claim as "ours"; it is also a site of gendered IR: "Abstract Expressionism's aura of masculinity," says Michael Leja (1993:256), "... was a crucial component of cold war US national identity, differentiating the nation politically and culturally from a Europe portrayed as weakened and effeminate." It is a site of race politics too – of colonial international relations. Several Abstract Expressionists claimed a kinship with the art of so-called primitives, noble-*cum*-ignoble savage men and (often bare-breasted) women.[3] In an era of Free World Americanism, Abstract Expressionism's performance of gender and race would become part of the "overall style" of gestural and White virility, of an international order in which some imprimatur vision and others receive the approving gaze. Even artists with progressive dimensions c[ould] be deeply implicated in or overwhelmed by enveloping social processes (p. 331).

Fredric Jameson (1991) might say that each of these interacting components brings a cultural logic to bear on a transnational business, in which (local) signs are produced and exchanged as "art" in an (only allegedly) apolitical aesthetic arena. His view would lead our vision to a study of art diplomacy as an aspect of international political economy. Derrida (1993:17) talks about the production of art interpretations as "a

---

[2] I am taking liberties with Derrida, using him here evocatively. His discussion of blindness refers to spaces beyond contingency, to a physical condition that is often the subject of art and that lies at the heart of drawing – "the drawing is blind, if not the draftsman or draftswoman" (1993:2). He also says, however (more along the lines of the use here of blindness), that "skepticism is precisely what I've been talking to you about: the difference between believing and seeing, between believing one sees [*croire voir*] and seeing between, catching a glimpse [*entrevoir*] – or not" (p. 1). I am using his ideas to suggest the contingent nature of seeing and not-seeing, about researching and writing without seeing what one could see. I am grateful to Fiona Sampson for articulating this difference.

[3] W. Jackson Rushing (1995:21) and others claim that Abstract Expressionists rectified the decontextualized primitivism of Picasso and Matisse, where bare breasts and exotic women were taken into the western gaze. Artists such as Jackson Pollock engaged, he says, in an "intellectualized primitivism" as a "willful recontextualization of forms and myths." For a feminist look at aspects of primitivism, see Enloe (1989, chapter 3).

few of these commonplaces of our culture that often make us plunge headlong, by an excess of anticipation, into a misguided or seduced reading." Perhaps art diplomacy is a productive misguide to the usual tales of Cold War political economy. It could also be that old IR readings can be seduced by the types of warring questions that Jeanette Winterson (1995:10–11) asks in *Art Objects*: "What is this picture for? Pictures should give pleasure but this picture is making me very cross." If a misreading or partial reading of the Cold War lies in IR's camp, this does not mean that the prevailing interpretations of the coldness of propaganda, the warlike posturings, the logics of transnational Cold War business are incorrect. The question, rather, is how the logics, the overlapping spaces, the "excesses of anticipation" the cross seductions of art and international relations illuminate a Cold War in the early years of 1946–1952. Abstract Expressionism was then in its heyday and the Cold War was newly constituted, newly institutionalized, newly globalizing, newly seen, newly blinding.

Art and politics: the avant-garde

Art historians and critics interested in social aspects of art production, rather than the formal, socially detached aspects of painterly style, often talk about Abstract Expressionism as a manifestation of an avant-garde. "Avant-garde" is a French military term that conjures up the image of vanguard troops advancing into battle, carrying the responsibility of the occasion, going ahead, being the first struck down, struck blind, or the first to break through and succeed. Art theorist David Herwitz (1993:5) calls the term "capacious" and says there is room in avant-garde "for many avant-gardes." For him, the defining mark of any avant-garde is dedication "to the idea of prefiguring its artworks by philosophical theory."[4] Philosopher and art critic Arthur Danto (1981) maintains that an artwork in the avant-garde is what it is only because of the special property of theory behind it.[5] For art historian Leja (1993.22), that property includes "a set of progressive, experimental

---

[4] See his *Making Theory/Constructing Art: On the Authority of the Avant-Garde*. This perspective also informs Alwynne Mackie, *Art/Talk: Theory and Practice in Abstract Expressionism* (1989).
[5] On the nature of that theory, the biographers of Jackson Pollock attribute to the art critic Clement Greenberg the view that "[l]ike soldiers in the class struggle, artists either did or did not advance the cause; they marched either with history or against it. The art critic's job was to define the cause and, within the limits of persuasion, rally the soldiers to it" (Naifeh and White Smith, 1992:523).

commitments . . . [o]pposition to prevailing artistic standards and procedures . . . radical formal and technical innovation."

A seemingly simpler approach to avant-garde is offered by Annette
Cox (1982), who says that the avant-garde signifies art-as-politics. It is,
one could say, a modern marching outside the lines of conformity and
privilege and into what Clement Greenberg (1985:22) called the "superior consciousness of history." The avant-garde anticipates itself as
a social force more than as a maker of beauty, of pretty objects. To anticipate, says Derrida (1993:4), "guards against precipitation, it makes
advances, puts the moves on space in order to be the first to take, in order
to be forward in the movement of taking hold, making contact, or ap-
prehending." Its politics and theory, arguably – and in contradistinction
to Cox's overly simple formulation – are intertwined discursively.

Of course, "it is undoubtedly true that art is a political and social phenomenon just as other human activities and institutions are" (Mackie,
1989:3).[6] Thus, there would not be a historical period in which art existed outside politics, outside theory. Cox thinks, however, that some
moments of history are more political than others. Before the nineteenth
century, she writes, there was relatively little social anticipation of – one
might say today little political mission and assignment attached to – the
concept of "artist." Therefore, that was a relatively apolitical art era. Yet
we might say that political conventions of art at that time were such
that the authority of the past was to be recreated by an artist submerged
in respectfulness. American art, Cox (1982:18) claims, was particularly
conservative: "nineteenth century . . . painters, their patrons, and their
audience considered the fine arts to be a reflection of traditional social
and religious values and a force for civilising a barbaric nation," often
in confrontation with a number of internal "primitives." The political
loomed in those values too.

Cox claims the Romantic Movement altered (what only seems to be
an apolitical sense of) the artist as conservator of tradition. Under its
impact, the artist became endowed with genius, with heroism, even
with political insight. In the 1830s, French artists in particular began
to link their practice with radical social change and to aspire to challenge the bourgeoisie by creating disturbing art (p. 6). The goal for some
was to overthrow the privileged classes in advance of a more socialist democratic state. More modestly, artists such as Vincent Van Gogh,

---

[6] For explicit discussions of "The Politics of Art," see the special issue of *International
Political Science Review* (1991).

claims Herschel Chipp (1968:456) in *Theories of Modern Art*, were simply "disappointed with the indifference and rejection of the bourgeoisie or were troubled by the constantly widening gulf between the artist and society ... [and] desired a reintegration in which art was to serve a Utopian brotherhood of man."[7] Here were the makings of a prefigurative theory that Herwitz sees as defining an avant-garde, plus an emerging, conventionally expressed radical politics that is the *sine qua non* of avant-garde for Cox.

By the late nineteenth century, when the prospects of utopian socialism had declined, some of this avant-garde shifted ground to associate with an aesthetic form of political radicalism, that is, with "stranger and more difficult forms of art" (Cox, 1982:7). Characteristic of "strange art" was its supposed independence of reason or suspension of rationality, and its self-removal into individual expression. Abstraction especially flaunted what Greenberg (1961:133), critic and definer of modernism, called a longstanding "tendency to assume that the representational as such is superior to the non-representational as such." To understand abstraction, to be moved by it, required skills to analyze form rather than content. Those were the skills that the audiences courted by some socially progressive avant-garde movements did not possess or necessarily wish to cultivate. Thus, to produce abstraction, as Timothy Luke (1991) puts it, is to place art above audience and on a higher theoretical level. Greenberg (1985:25) explained Abstract Expressionism as a response to debased tastes of urban industrial audiences: they wished for the diversion of genuine culture but could only come up with an appreciation for "vicarious experience and faked sensations" from "popular, commercial art and literature with their chromeotypes, magazine covers, illustrations, ads, slick and pulp fiction, comics, Tin Pan Alley music, tap dancing, Hollywood movies, etc., etc." This wasteland was what the Abstract Expressionist avant-garde despised.

By the 1930s, the avant-garde that would become Abstract Expressionism commingled a subversive visual-discursive opposition to canonical and mainstream culture with a politically socialist theme. A show of support for their arts came in the form of the Depression-era Federal Art

---

[7] Utopian striving was a distinguishing philosophical component of many avant-gardes. See Herwitz (1993). That Van Gogh fits this characterization may come as something of a surprise, since we commonly think of him as mentally ill rather than as political (or also political). Chipp (1968:456) says that the "Expressionists too dreamed of a renewal of society in which art could take the place once occupied by religion ... The Constructivists felt that they were forging a weapon for a truly revolutionary art."

Project of the Works Progress Administration, which gave over 5,000 artists public aid. Many who were later associated with the New York School of Abstract Expressionism found work painting murals for public buildings. Working "outside the dealer/critic/museum system," says Whitney Chadwick (1990:297–298), male and female artists identified themselves with the labor force, with "the social realities of unemployment and life under the Depression." The US Communist Party tried to influence these artists to build social realism into Socialist Realist art; indeed, Francis Frascina (1985:100) describes Pollock at the time as "a Communist of sorts, interested in Social Realist mural art and Regionalism." Leon Trotsky (1957:170) was more to the liking of many, however, because he argued that art should be left alone to "plow the field in all directions. Personal lyrics of the very smallest scope have an absolute right to exist within the new art."

As the Great Depression eased into World War II, however, disenchantment with socialism set in. The Soviet–Nazi pact and the Soviet invasion of Finland could not be ignored. The very magazines and editors that had earlier promoted socialist ideas in art, such as *Partisan Review* and its editor Greenberg, now recoiled against socialist brutalities. As with the labor movement in the USA, the socialist art avantgarde turned away from communist inspiration and took stock. Realist regionalist art, such as that represented by Thomas Hart Benton or the Ash Can School, was one alternative. But that style seemed too nostalgic and sentimental to suit an increasingly violent, urban, industrial, and warlike era. Surrealism was another option, particularly as its main proponents were then in the USA to escape the war in Europe. Appealing in its play to irrationality, Surrealism was none the less eventually seen by America's native sons of Abstract Expressionism as academic and nineteenth century (a charge leveled in particular against Dali's mannered style), or, from a leftist framing, as potentially bourgeois (Sylvester, 1999a).

A new direction in the avant-garde emerged that was aesthetically radical but somewhat divorced from overtly radical politics. Within it, charges Leja (1993:23–24), there was "no critique of the institutional framework of art evaluation and promotion to which [the avant-garde was] subject." Symptomatic of the directional shift, and highlighting the end points of it, is a set of photographs of Jackson Pollock that Cox discusses in *Art-as-Politics*. In one, Pollock is shown helping to assemble a float for a May Day celebration in 1936 New York, a result of his work in an experimental studio run by the radical Mexican painter Davide Alfaro

Siqueiros. Siqueiros believed in creating people's art for Communist Party rallies, parades, and conventions. Cox (1982:17) writes:

> The float that Pollock worked on in the photograph portrayed the destruction of Wall Street by an angry working class. To symbolize the capitalist financiers, Pollock and the other artists constructed a large figure decorated with a swastika and holding captive in his hands the emblems of the Republican and Democratic parties. A gigantic hammer representing the power of the people periodically smashed a ticker-tape machine sending paper flying over the float.[8]

The second photo was taken fourteen years later, in 1950, by the young German photographer Hans Namuth, whom Pollock allowed into his barn studio in Long Island, New York. Pollock was now executing completely abstract webs of line produced by pouring paint off sticks onto a canvas lying on the floor. A series of Namuth photographs later printed in *Life Magazine* shows Pollock as he moved and gestured, almost dancing, around the canvas. Cox says Pollock was using the automatic drawing techniques developed by the Surrealists, who, following the ideas of Sigmund Freud, believed that spontaneous movements of the hand drew out images from the unconscious. Pollock's recent biographers suggest that the innovative technique entailed painting in the air above the canvas (Naifeh and Smith, 1992:539).

Ostensibly the photographs document a veering from revolutionary art to introspective abstractions that avoided all kitsch – Communist and non-Communist; indeed, they avoided all politics. Stephen Polcari (1993:31) argues that "[t]he political beliefs of Abstract Expressionists were ill-defined, or rather the artists tended to hold that combination of anarchist-bohemian-conservatism typical of many modern artists." Christopher Lasch (1970:44), writing more generally, talks about the thinness of Marxist ideas in the USA in the 1930s. He says that they "served as a form of cultural protest and withdrawal rather than as a method of social analysis." Cox (1982) maintains that the supposedly linear politico-artistic progression to Abstract Expressionism, which had Greenberg (1985) seeing "a path along which it would be possible to keep culture *moving* in the midst of ideological confusion and violence" (pp. 22–23, emphasis in original), was actually the Janus-face of the

---

[8] Stephen Polcari (1993:32) points out, however, that Pollock was in Siqueiros's workshop for only two months, "seemingly less for Siqueiros's politics than for the opportunity to learn the use of Duco in mural paintings . . . ." His relationship with Siqueiros terminated in a fistfight.

avant-garde revolving around itself. She maintains that "Abstract Expressionists, even in works that were totally abstract, still sought to create an art with compelling expressionist qualities and a profound commitment to intense audience response" (Cox, 1982:18). This was its continuity with itself from the Depression years. At the same time, given that a "potency always develops on the brink of blindness," like blind men, the avant-garde "must *advance*, advance or commit themselves, that is, expose themselves, run through space as if running a risk" (Derrida, 1993:3, 5, emphasis in original).[9]

The avant-garde goes "primitive"

Boldly advancing, they do not necessarily see.

Recoiling from the horrors of the Fascist period and subsequent war, some Abstract Expressionists turned more circles and directions, finding so-called primitive art resonant with the era at hand. With one stroke, they embraced myths about an always already-savage human *and* dreams of universal community. The savagery derived from their sense that harsh human nature was a transhistorical reality; but within that nature were elements of premodern nobility. W. Jackson Rushing (1995:121) maintains that "the spiritual crisis created by the failure of modernism to generate a social and political utopia, and intensified by the rise of fascism, instilled in the 'myth-makers' of the New York avant-garde a desire to transcend the particulars of history and search out universal values."

Thus Mark Rothko claimed fascination with "the archaic and the myths . . . negro sculpture . . . African fetishes, the fetishes of a bygone day which our reason would banish as superstitious"(cited in Leja, 1993:51). He and Adolph Gottlieb offered radio commentaries in 1943 about their "kinship to the art of primitive man" (p. 51). Jackson Pollock exhibited paintings of moon women and a she-wolf, which partly drew

[9] Arguably, all artists run risks – the portrait painter may get the subject "wrong," the landscape artist may be called sentimental or bucolic in temperament, the painter of petunias in pots will be subject to the charge of kitsch. All artists may fail to find a market or appreciation for their work. What sets the New York School's efforts apart from the everyday risks of being an artist was the effort to stand at some distance from the politics of the era. Greenberg (1985:23) waxes romantic when he says that this avant-garde tried in effect to create "something valid solely on its own terms in the way nature itself is valid, in the way a landscape – not its picture – is aesthetically valid; something *given*, independent of meanings, similars, or originals. Content is to be dissolved so completely into form that the work of art or literature cannot be reduced in whole or in part to anything not itself."

on Surrealist themes of the unconscious and partly reflected his own interest in Native American "primitive" forms. Barnett Newman (quoted in Rushing, 1995:130) had a particular fascination with Northwest Coast Indian painting and wrote approvingly that "[a]ll artists whether primitive or sophisticated have been involved in the handling of chaos."

The craze for "primitivism" supplied Abstract Expressionist painters with a rationale for looking to some deep past of "man" for entrée into new "strange and difficult art." In an era "so heavily weighted toward the rational, the material, science and technology that man's nonrational, spiritual side was seriously neglected" (Leja, 1993:62),[10] primitivism was evidence of the better sides of humanity (Fergusson, 1936; Robinson, 1921; Wylie, 1941). With it, one could break through what Robert Motherwell called modern man's "sense of gulf, an abyss, a void between one's lonely self and the world" (quoted in Mackie, 1989:35). And one could do so without capitulating to kitsch or to snobbery. In Newman's words (quoted in Rushing, 1995:126), there is an "answer in these works to all those who assume that modern abstract art is the esoteric exercise of a snobbish elite, for among these simple peoples, abstract art was the normal, well-understood, dominant tradition." And so, "[s]tanding on his own two feet, a blind man explores by feeling out an area that he must recognize without yet cognizing it – and what he apprehends, what he has apprehensions about, in truth, is the precipice, the fall – his having already overstepped some fatal line, his hand either bare or armed (with a fingernail, a cane, or a pencil)" (Derrida, 1993:4).

Of course, as Leja (1993:53) pointedly tells us, "[p]rimitive society has been a fundamental illusion, a pseudoscientific myth of origins fulfilling specific purposes in Western society." There is no ancillary historical point of primitivity. There is only geospatially and frequently racially denoted difference, which "primitivism" laces with orientalist references to "African," "Native American," "Pacific Islander," and "Aboriginal" art. "Women" were also "primitive," being not the "modern men" of "one's lonely self." Says Derrida (1993:5, emphasis in original): "It would seem that most of these blind men do not lose themselves in absolute wandering. These blind *men*, notice, since the illustrious blind of our culture are almost always men, the 'great blind men,' as if women perhaps saw to it never to risk their sight."

---

[10] This was not the only time so-called primitive art was appealing. Leja (1993:52) refers to it as a "recurrent and persistent feature of modern art history," but one that took on particular outlines during and following World War II.

If "the primitive" was both a retreat from and a way to know the modern politics of an age, then, surely, gender in Abstract Expressionism was *"a memory of the trait* that speculates, as in a dream, about its own possibility" (p. 3, emphasis in original). It was a primitive memory of a certain sort. Leja (1993:256) writes:

> Abstract Expressionism has been recognized, from its first accounts, as a male domain, ruled by a familiar social construction of "masculine" as tough, aggressive, sweeping, bold. The features of this art most appreciated in the critical and historical literature – scale, action, energy, space, and so on – are as T.J. Clark has noted, "operators of sexual difference," part of an "informing metaphorics of masculinity."

It need not have been like this. The turn to abstraction, to an emphasis on expression, could have performatively feminized the avant-garde in the sense of taking on board the qualities usually assigned to people called women in western society – expression, wild emotional gesture, incoherence. Similarly, turning to so-called primitive art for inspiration could have highlighted the vulnerability rather than the heroism of modernity; it could have been the view out of the hidden and seemingly insignificant corners of the world – the terror of being weaker in a barbaric age revealed. It could have ushered in appreciation of the colonized other as a maker of vision. Indeed, because Abstract Expressionism has many faces and angles, there are resonances of such themes scattered throughout it.

But by and large, the New York School was constituted as masculine and white and American. Western man was all the concern: his tragic condition was what mattered. The heroic American artist could see with special insight the pathos of the time and adapt his work to it. "It was as if the blind man were referring to himself with his arm folded back, there where a blind Narcissus, inventing a mirror without image, lets it be seen that he does not see" (Derrida, 1993:12). Enlightenment man had fallen into barbarism, into what Leja (1993: chapter 4) calls "Narcissus in chaos." Capabilities that had seemed so promising, so optimistic before the two wars (as in the literature of international relations, so idealist) had degenerated. The artist could see this. He was not blind. From Philip Wylie's *Generation of Vipers* (1941, quoted in Leja, 1993:203):

> It is time for man to make a new appraisal of himself. His failure is abject. His plans for the future are infantile. The varied forms of his civilization in this century are smashing each other ... If we do not

turn upon ourselves the terrible honesty our science has turned upon goods, we are done for. This war, this uprooting – the second – will be only a stumble on the path back to a new start in a new savagery far deeper than that of a thousand years ago.

This "man" too had been an invention, grown up and made modern after centuries of political philosophy, literature, and visual arts had given people called men the leading roles in international history (Sylvester, 1994a). "Modern man" was an individual of industry and efficiency; his "self was understood to be a rational core, unitary and central" (Leja, 1993:209); he was apt to be middle-class and Protestant; he was autonomous and had self-control – even while he dripped paint across canvases through odd gestures. That he was part primitive enabled the avant-garde to lionize elements of unconscious, elements of the unruly, the biomorphic, the unfocused, the fragmented, the not-to-be-trusted. But those same elements also marked out a route back to reassertion, heroically, of the importance of reason and self-control in stemming the tide of terror.

The power of society to compel and perform gender was turned away in reiterative and nonreflexive citations to man. Man was not a myth, not a primitive figment of the imagination, not the stories told about "men and women" in the past that could be re-evaluated in the present. Rather, modern man encrusted the performance of his "gender" and "sex" in art as the nearly natural course of events, nearly because Abstract Expressionist painting represented reality as nonrepresentable in realist forms. For example, it usually departed from the pre-World War I penchant to paint heterosexual male fantasy women, who, in the words of Carol Duncan (1973:31), "show no or few signs of human consciousness of any kind." (Duncan refers to the work of Ernst Kirchner, Edvard Munch, Kees Van Dongen, Erich Heckel, and others, for whom images of powerless, passive, arms-behind-the-head, exhibitionist women were the *sine qua non* of artistic "expression.") None the less in the poetic words of Laura Riding's (1980:24) "How Blind and Bright," we find:

> Light, visibility of light,
> Sun, visibility of sun.
> Light, sun and seeing
> Visibility of men . . .

While the emphasis on abstraction in Abstract Expressionism moved away for the most part from naked women displayed in titillating poses, this art was hardly without gender. "She" was there as the notable absence swallowed up in the "universality" of sweeps, drips, runs, cascades, and blotches. The so-called energy of Abstract Expressionism evoked the American male – rugged, large, a bit crudely spontaneous, moving in many directions at once. More telling even than that, the very need for a new subject of art "was defined exclusively as a male predicament . . . it was for men alone to resolve, transcend, or cope with" (Duncan, 1973:30). To see.

Two more photographs to consider. In one, Willem de Kooning is in front of a large canvas depicting a highly abstracted woman. Standing with legs apart and arms folded, he looks directly at the camera. His wife Elaine, also an Abstract Expressionist artist, is seated, her gaze absent-mindedly fixed on nothing in particular, her absorption turned inward. The site of the photograph is their mutual studio in 1953. The photographer is Hans Namuth. To Leja (1993:254), the photograph shows that "their hold on that space was not equally secure . . . Willem is more proprietary . . . closer to action, while Elaine stares absently, cigarette elegantly poised." Looming over both of them is one of de Kooning's (in)famous paintings of a leering, imposing, and glinty-toothed, buxom woman. "She" glares out more expressionistically than abstractly. "She" breaks the "rule" of not-seeing the women in Abstract Expressionism.

Polcari (1993:286) argues that de Kooning's women series inherited the sexual themes articulated by Joan Miró: "When I make a large female sex image, it is for me a goddess, as the birth of humanity . . . a fecundity figure, but all the same it is menacing . . . You understand well that this is humanity, it is always menacing on the right and on the left, above and below, we are menaced." We, the tragic modern artists and noble savages, are menaced by Woman – even when she is seated and cast as dream – as a male photographer defines (seeing blindly) the problem.

The second photograph shows a painting of the de Koonings done by Réné Bouché in 1955. Willem again stands in front of a canvas, but with his body turned in profile, his face thoughtful as he seems to study an adjacent painting. Elaine is seated, and once more her expression is absent-minded, self-concerned. This time, though, she looks more social than Willem. Her omnipresent cigarette frames her thoughts as earlier, but a drink idly on her lap and spirited clothes colorfully topped off with a checked scarf suggest an artsy soirée. Leja (1993:255) proffers this interpretation of the larger Abstract Expressionist scene advanced in the particularity of the painting:

> [T]he women stand as essential accessories of bohemia, their casual dress and posture helping to fill out a cultural image (or fantasy) of the male artist. They also keep that image within certain limits by confirming the heterosexuality or "masculinity" of their partners ... For the male viewer especially, she lends, in the variations illustrated here, sex appeal to the paintings and simultaneously displaces attention from the sexiness of the male artist, which might otherwise be susceptible to appreciation or questioning.

The fantasy was made flesh as few women other than wives of the principals of Abstract Expressionism sought to clamber on board this avant-garde, something that cannot be said with the same force for other artistic movements. Indeed, Lee Krasner, an Abstract Expressionist whose works are literally overpowered by her husband's – Jackson Pollock – says (in Chadwick, 1990:304), that "[w]omen were treated like cattle" at the major public meeting places for New York School painters. Krasner and Elaine de Kooning signed many of their works with initials only in a bid to minimize their gender identity. Helen Frankenthaler "dismissed gender as an issue," and yet critics constructed "a special category for her work in which color and touch are read as 'feminine' ... ceas[ed] examining it in relation to its specific historical context and linked it to an unchanging and essentialized tradition of women's work"(pp. 306–307). Man could transmogrify his transhistorical primitivism in a bid to save the modern era. He could "make a new appraisal of himself." Women were forever primitive menaces to Abstract Expressionism.[11]

Polcari (1993:287) opines that the gendered nature of some Abstract Expressionist works reflected changing attitudes toward women in the wake of World War II:

> Simply put, the war was an assault on pre-war morality. The brutality of the war altered men and women's feelings about themselves, sex, and love. [De Kooning's] *Woman I* is not just an icon of desire but of human folly, not just an ancient art-historical talisman, but an involuntary response to the recent experience of women as talismans, the wartime and GI obsession. Women and sex.

---

[11] According to Pollock's analyst, Ruth Fox, "Lee actually *caused* Jackson's [alcoholic] binges [because] she derive[d] pleasure from the pain she [was] able to inflict by precipitating the argument, the quarrel, the tension which unconsciously she [knew would] land her husband in another drinking bout" (Naifeh and Smith, 1992:687). Here is the wife, who single-handedly at times kept Pollock's career together, cast as a primitive demon.

Leja's (1993:257–258) different interpretation is that Abstract Expressionism claimed to "issue from and represent mind and experience, as these were revealed in mythic and unconscious materials and structures held to constitute the submerged foundations of human nature and being ... the specific model of the human subject it inscribed was profoundly gendered." In one interpretation the culprit is war. In the second case, there are "submerged foundations." In either case "blind men explore – and seek to foresee there where they do not see, *no longer* see, or do *not yet* see" (Derrida, 1993:5–6, emphasis in original). In either case, I would say that the gendering is primitive in form and in apologia.

The avant-garde Cold War

Leja (1993) maintains that the avant-garde is an identity cross-pressured by demands for "a" School that is marketable and by artistic interest in developing one's own unique and differentiating style within (or if need be apart from) "the" School. Eva Cockcroft (1985) claims that, in the case of the New York School, this combination of factors partly enabled Abstract Expressionism to become a pet of the Cold War. It was helped along by a variety of governmental and nongovernmental institutions and by the artists themselves; in a word, by a variety of politics chasing theories.

In the wake of World War II and America's catapult into superpowerdom and Cold War, there was parallel activity in US art circles. Media figures, such as Howard Devree and Edward Alden Jewell, advocated a position for US art in the world that would mirror the international ascendancy of the US political economy. Devree maintained in the *New York Times* that America was the most powerful country, and therefore needed to create an art that was strong and virile to replace the art of Paris. Jewell spoke of post-World War II artists avoiding foreign influences in their work and striving for a universality that would appeal to individuals everywhere (both cited in Guilbaut, 1983: 119).

These views found a counterpart in the works of intellectuals such as Walter Lippmann, who wrote in 1946 (p. 128): "Fate has willed it that America is from now on to be at the center of Western civilization rather than on the periphery ... The American idea is based on a certain image of man and his place in the universe, his reason and his will, his knowledge of good and evil, his faith in a law above all particular laws." Avant-gardist Pollock (cited in Robertson, 1961:193) was saying in 1944: "The idea of an isolated American painting, so popular in the USA during the 1930s, seems absurd to me, just as the idea of creating a purely American mathematics or physics would seem absurd . . . An American is an American and his painting would naturally be qualified by that fact, whether he wills it or not. But the basic problems of contemporary painting are independent of country." And Motherwell (cited in Miller, 1946:36) said in 1946: "art is not national . . . to be merely an American or French artist is to be nothing; to fail to overcome one's initial environment is never to reach the human."

It was in 1947 and 1948, when the Marshall and Truman Plans were being effected, that Pollock, de Kooning, and Rothko began paintings that were abstract, seemingly universal in theme, primitive (but so controlled) in approach to paint application – rather than to subject – large, expansive, and explosively virile. American, but with epochal resonance in the western world as "[t]he image of man struggling to exert control over the powerful forces within and without him" (Leja, 1993:283). More was going on, though, than mirrored thoughts and stylistic synchronizations across politics and art. In high political and art circles a conscious effort was underway to present the new USA as refined and cultured, a counterpoise to views of it abroad as graspingly materialistic and obsessed with science. An exhibit entitled "Introduction to Modern American Painting" ran in Paris in January 1947, through mostly private American largesse. It met with mixed reviews – mostly negative, in fact – from a Parisian art scene in eclipse. In March 1948, though, Greenberg declared in *Partisan Review* that American art was superior to Parisian art and of vital importance to western culture.

Stephen Spender (1948:33) went further, egging on a new art-as-politics, defining an advance: "where American policy finds dubious allies and half-hearted friends, American freedom of expression in its greatest achievements has an authenticity which can win the most vital European thought today." He went on to suggest that in the war looming against Communism, propaganda had limited use because it could not respond to real needs in the way western books and orchestras could. Spender, as Lasch (1970:72) reminds us, was a founding father of the magazine *Encounter* (1953), whose editors and contributors "showed an unshakable faith in the good intentions of the American government. It was inconceivable to them that American officials were not somehow immune to the temptations of great power." Spender and friends were freedom's avant-garde.

The race was on. The Cold War is usually spoken of in geostrategic terms: the tight bipolar balance of power, spheres of influence, massive retaliation shading into mutual assured destruction, espionage, space races, science in schools, the Berlin Wall, containment, etc., etc. We now know that the Cold War relied on other things beyond the pale of usual IR analysis. It relied on militarized gender, on constructions of "men" and "women" that could be mobilized for the propaganda "war" – and its dirty little fighting wars – against Communism (Enloe, 1993). "Men" were on the frontlines of freedom and "women" cultivated a conservative conformism at home (Elshtain, 1987). It also relied on a cultural war, which was waged first against Parisian hegemony in art and then, more expansively, more subtly in allied countries as far away as Australia, for the supremacy of US values. This cultural war – a form of diplomacy by other means – mobilized aesthetic sensibilities, subjectivities, and purses for the new art iconography of the USA – Abstract Expressionism.

The Museum of Modern Art in New York (MOMA) played a central role in the government-backed effort at cultural hegemony. MOMA was founded in 1929, mainly through the private philanthropy of the Rockefeller family. In 1939, Nelson Rockefeller became president of the museum. He left his post in 1940 to become President Roosevelt's Coordinator of the Office of Inter-American Affairs and later Assistant Secretary of State for Latin American affairs.[12] Nelson Rockefeller remained on MOMA's board during this stint of government service and returned to the presidency of the museum in 1946. During that time, MOMA became what Cockcroft describes as a minor war contractor: it fulfilled thirty-eight contracts for cultural materials for the Office of War Information and for Rockefeller's Office of Inter-American Affairs. After the war, MOMA was the major institutional supporter of Abstract Expressionism in the USA, helping to organize shows abroad and, most importantly, purchasing and showing numerous works (such as Pollock's *She-Wolf*, bought in 1944). David and Cecile Shapiro (1985:147) argue that "[e]arlier the rule had been for museums to be extremely chary

---

[12] In 1940, the government also organized a periodic "Buy American Art Week." A panel discussion held at the University of Chicago in conjunction with one of them, and broadcast by radio, featured Eleanor Roosevelt speaking on "Art and Our Warring World."

of acquiring work by living artists. Now museums not only splurged on such canvases sold to them at ever-augmenting prices; the trustees who had authorized the acquisitions became collectors of the new art." Indeed, from 1929 until 1944, the well-known art commentator Alfred H. Barr, Jr. was director of MOMA. The artistic advisor to Peggy Guggenheim, whose private gallery Art of This Century had showcased Pollock as early as 1943, "Barr was so enthusiastic about the work of the Abstract Expressionists that he often attended their informal meetings and even chaired some of their panel discussions at their meeting place, The Club, in New York City" (Cockcroft, 1985:131). In 1952 Barr, who retained his influence at MOMA, wrote an article for the *New York Times Magazine* entitled "Is Modern Art Communistic?" in which he praised Abstract Expressionism as democratic and condemned social realism in art as a mark of totalitarianism.

In 1952, the museum launched its international program, supported by the Rockefeller Brothers Fund, and out came the Abstract Expressionist works for exhibitions in London, Paris, São Paulo, and Tokyo. De Kooning could be seen at the Venice Biennale in 1948, which MOMA took over from the red-baiting State Department so that this overseas arena for US art could be maintained; Pollock paintings were there from 1950. It is ironic, the Shapiros (1985:148) comment, that "an apolitical art that arose at least in part as a reaction to didactic art, as an 'art-for-art's sake' antidote to 'art-as-a-weapon' [of the socialist years], should have become a prime political weapon." Is it so ironic? Where had the avant-garde gone if not into the pocket of the US government, the Janus face of politics and radical aesthetics – art above the audience – turned around, turned into art for the world audience of genuine culture lovers *qua* freedom lovers.

Cockcroft explains the art-as-politics-with-a-theory role of MOMA as a foil against McCarthyism. Whereas the US Congress insisted on vetting artists who officially represented the US abroad, MOMA could sponsor an exhibition without inviting congressional intervention. In 1957 a US Information Agency show of "100 American Artists of the Twentieth Century" was canceled for exhibition abroad because forty-two members of the American Federation of Arts claimed that ten artists in the show were pro-Communist. In response to the cancellation, the Rockefellers expanded their contributions to MOMA and in 1958 the show was sent abroad under the title "The New American Painting".

The CIA was similarly able to circumvent Congress on cultural matters and was inclined to do so. In a 1967 article entitled "I'm Glad the

CIA is Immoral," which ran in the *Saturday Evening Post*, the former executive secretary for MOMA (1948–1949), Thomas W. Braden, wrote about a variety of cultural tours the CIA sponsored, saying "the idea that Congress would have approved of many of our projects was about as likely as the John Birch society's approving medicare" (quoted in Cockcroft, 1985:128). Indeed, George Dondero, the Republican representative from Michigan, was next to none in his efforts to tar much of contemporary American art as a second Communist front. In a speech on August 16, 1949, he said:

> Cubism aims to destroy by designed disorder. Futurism aims to destroy by the machine myth . . . Dadaism aims to destroy by ridicule. Expressionism aims to destroy by aping the primitive and insane. Abstractionism aims to destroy by the creation of brainstorms . . . Surrealism aims to destroy by the denial of reason. (cited in Hauptman, 1973:48)

Far from being an enemy of the avant-garde, for a moment the CIA was an enlightened cold warrior, avant-garde itself, advancing to the cultural front – a guard-rail against Soviet suggestions that the USA was less than free. Cockcroft (1985:129) reasons that:

> Freed from the kinds of pressure of unsubtle red-baiting and super-jingoism applied to official governmental agencies like the United States Information Agency (USIA), CIA and MOMA cultural projects could provide the well-funded and more persuasive arguments and exhibits needed to sell the rest of the world on the benefits of life and art under capitalism.

And thus it came to be that an all-seeing cultural Cold War Cyclops was born – the one-eye, one world gaze – or at least the effort to develop it, which is never complete, never wholly hegemonic.[13] It is never as captured by what James Scott (1990:82) calls "thraldom and power," never unblind, despite the firm belief of the Shapiros (1985:147) that

> the critics and their theories, the art publications as well as the general press, the museums led by the Museum of Modern Art, the avant-garde art galleries, the clandestine functions of the CIA supported by the taxpayer, the need of artists to show and sell their work, the leveling of dissent encouraged by McCarthyism and a conformist era, the convergence of all varieties of anti-Communists and anti-Stalinists on a neutral cultural point, the cold war and the cultural weapons employed in its behalf, American postwar economic vigor and its

---

[13] Was it ironic that the prestigious $1,000 Rich-Campana prize for art went in 1947 to Abstract Expressionist William Baziotes for his painting entitled "Cyclops"?

sense of moral leadership, plus the explosion of a totally new kind of American-born painting that seemed the objective correlative of Greenberg's early announcement that "the main premises of Western art have at last migrated to the United States" – all these combined to make Abstract Expressionism the only art acceptable on a wide scale during the conforming 1950s.[14]

Art historians write of Abstract Expressionism's rapid decline in the 1960s relative to Pop Art and later postmodernist art, of a backlash against the whiteness, the masculine heroism, the sordid politics of the New York School. Supposedly its hegemony was short-lived. Yet in 1973 the not-yet-open National Gallery of Australia bought its signature painting, its centerpiece of international art, Jackson Pollock's *Blue Poles*, for a cool US$2 million – a record price for an artist who had been dead only since 1956. More than any other symbol of US art hegemony, this purchase points the power of Abstract Expressionism, of American values sent out, long after the heyday of the Cold War. It shows the lag time of art diplomatic efforts on the art front as the fruit of an earlier time is borne out of a private collector's apartment in New York and into the waiting arms of the director of Australia's premier national gallery, James Mollison. Said Pollock's biographer, Bryan Robertson, in a letter from the USA to Max Hutchison, the Australian businessman-connoisseur who helped negotiate the purchase:

> The presence of *Blue Poles* in Australia will inevitably change the course of Australian history, because it will affect the developing imagination and awareness of successive generations of Australians, at the most profound level. It will become a talisman for a great nation . . . in fact, *the arrival of Blue Poles in Australia will be similar, historically to the arrival in Russia of The Dance of Matisse in the early years of this century.* But in Australia, Pollock's statement in *Blue Poles* will take wings; whilst in Russia, the good news from Matisse was hidden for so long.
> (Robertson, 1973)

Henry Geldzahler (1973), curator of twentieth-century art for the Metropolitan Museum of Art, wrote a letter to Mollison about *Blue Poles*: "I would hate to see the painting leave the United States but, on the other hand, cultural dispersement has its value too."

---

[14] Indeed, Chadwick (1990:300) points out that "[t]he consolidation of Abstract Expressionism as the dominant practice in American modern art pushed to the margins not only women moving toward artistic maturity in other 'modern' styles during the 1940s, but also many women professionally active in what would come to be seen as 'conservative' and 'outmoded' figurative styles."

Abstract Expressionist art sent abroad carried traces of gender and race myths – the paint applications were controlled in this regard. By gazing into the waters of narcissism in the form of painting the unconscious, the primitive, the "man" of the difficult mid-twentieth century, the artist was unable, as Leja (1993:329–330) puts it, "to reveal . . . either his own overvaluation of physical beauty or the presence of the nymph Echo, who had faded into a disembodied voice as a consequence of her unrequited love for Narcissus." In analogous manner, middle-class "women" of the United States, along with "Negroes" and "Indians," faded into the frame of a conformist and white America during most of the Cold War. They were not represented much in foreign policymaking (McGlen and Sarkees, 1993; Carol Miller, 1991). Nor were they the artists whose works came to the international fore. Apparently they were too "primitive." Leja (1993:330) writes:

> That Echo was female is by no means insignificant here: artists whose identification with Abstract Expressionist subjectivity was impeded by their sex, race, or sexual preference have played a leading part in developing the critique and effecting transition. The influential work of Laurie Anderson, Barbara Kruger, Sherrie Levine, Adrian Piper, and Cindy Sherman, for example, has often explicitly criticized and undermined the white, heterosexual, male orientation of modernist subjectivity.

Similarly, the influential work of dissidents in the discipline of international relations – the critical theorists (e.g., R. Cox, 1981; Linklater, 1992), the postmodernists (e.g., Ashley and Walker, 1990a; Der Derian and Shapiro, 1989), students of culture (e.g., "Culture in International Relations," 1993), the ones who would forget IR theory (Bleiker, 1997), the ones who dare to suggest that there are many worlds that resist worlding into the US vision (Walker, 1988), the ones who speak of ecoCultures (Dyer, 1993), the literary minded (e.g., Bleiker, 2000b; Burke, 2000; Constantinou, 2000; Sylvester 2000b), the feminists (e.g., Tickner, 1992; Elshtain, 1987; Enloe, 1989) – storm barricades erected against incursions of enemy or alien knowledges into this field, into "our" stories of what is important in the Cold War. They are the avant-gardes of IR – those who have revealed the politics of the field's exclusionary agendas and have done so informed, innovatively, by theory.

The final word, though, goes to the Australian middle-class family that plunked itself in front of *Blue Poles* at the National Gallery of Australia on a cold Sunday in July 1994, and pronounced the painting – to me, who was attending my own business blindly – "repulsive, not worth the money." Indeed, *Blue Poles* has never been fully embraced by the Australian viewing public (as average Americans have not embraced Abstract Expressionism). Many Australians are seemingly blind to its value, its representations of freedom, its energy.[15] Not consenting after the fact to the political decision to purchase *Blue Poles*, not acquiescing to an aesthetic they dislike, this family and many other unconvinced Australian art viewers remind us that the hegemony of an art regime can be thin: the Gough Whitlam government, whose funds supported the purchase, was severely called to task in the media and in parliament for extravagant expenditure on an incomprehensible American painting.[16] A thin hegemony can elude efforts of experts to define "for subordinate groups what is realistic and what is not realistic" (Scott, 1990:74), in this case, ironically, what is realistic action for a government keen to imitate the culture of Narcissus and myth – the "genuine culture" of the Cold War.

Unblinding

> How bright is blind!/How bright is blind!　　　　　　(Riding, 1980:24)

What we learn from this case is that the emphasis in IR on the military and standard diplomatic and market activities of the early Cold War period – the events we rehearse with piety – smokescreen the ways that gender, race, and foreign relations of the Cold War international were being forged in and around the crucible of US avant-garde art. We learn that the CIA, which hardly has a reputation for cultural acumen, quietly fought off the efforts of other foreign policymaking agencies of the US government to prohibit certain visual artists from being represented abroad (those who had been seen with the art-as-socialist-politics wing of the Depression-era avant-garde). The CIA certainly does not deserve kudos for its efforts on behalf of art; its actions for pluralism were cynical. Writing in the *New Statesman* in 1967, Andrew Kopkind (quoted in Lasch, 1970:111) argued that "[t]he illusion of dissent was maintained: the CIA supported Socialist cold warriors, Fascist cold warriors, black and white cold warriors … But it was a sham pluralism, and it was

---

[15] Curators of international art at the gallery refer to an Australian "grocer aesthetic," in Lloyd and Desmond (1991:21).

[16] The headline of the Melbourne *Herald* for December 17, 1973 read: "Would You Pay $1.3m for This?" ($2m in US). See Barrett (2001).

utterly corrupting." Said MOMA-CIA Thomas Braden (cited p. 111), "the cold war was and is a war, fought with ideas instead of bombs." Called for, instead of praise, is a rereading of practices of particular blind men who see what other blind men, such as Dondero, would gouge out the eyes from in order to have the national and the international viewer of art not-see. Dondero: would-be Cold War hero – advancing. In Derrida's words (1993:63, emphasis in original): "For a mirror is also necessarily inscribed in the structure of self-portraits of draftsmen *drawing something else.*" Politics can mirror what avant-gardes seemingly reject. It can parody the marching of forces in advance of conformity and "progressively" experiment – cynically.

We learn, too, that a museum can be a pivotal actor in high political moments of a country's diplomacy; that international art connections can be the hidden supporting poles of bipolar politics; that the international political economy of art diplomacy is primitive, but not without sight. " 'Blue Poles' is a very pretty picture," claims Mollison (1989:3), "which is why I have never actually liked it." Is it a pretty abjected "woman" all dressed up in reds, whites, blues, and silvers? Is it *Woman I* deflated and defleshed? Is that why Mollison never liked it? Or is *Blue Poles* a sweet, nonpolitical prettiness – a horror of the avant-garde? Was it bought in an act of Australian relations international, in the controversial waning days of the Vietnam War, to induce a sense of art-for-the-people in a land geospatially distant but never far from the USA? Was it the harvest of an alliance forged before and during the Cold War? A way of jumping on the US bandwagon?

A gallery docent said that day in July 1994, to another Australian family that was in disbelief over the folly – in their view – of *Blue Poles*: "Really, do look at its size, its vitality, its freshness. It's a perfect reflection of America in the 1950s, a self-confident America. You know, the Americans are very angry at us because we got this painting from them at what is now such a good price. Think of its value in today's market. They would like it back. But we have it." "And now," says Mollison in 1989 (p. 3), "after colonial Australian [art], 'Blue Poles' is the most popular thing."

After the colonial. Popular but unloved. Irony upon irony memorializes the political eye cast internationally. "[W]ith the most intense lucidity, the seeing blind man observes himself and has others observe ..." (Derrida, 1973:57). "Eyes not looking out for eyes/Look inward and meet sight" (Riding, 1980:24).

7   Four international Dianas: Andy's tribute

On to the late 1990s and another bit of world-travel, this time to the University of Tampere, Finland and into yet a different art spot. The "sighting" section closes around a fractured woman who seems, for a while, to be an international sight recognizable anywhere and in any tone. A painterly man of world fame misses citational moments with her. But no matter, she and he are here still, as are their worldly sites that show us how unsafe it can be "out there" for traveling women and their colorful international arts. At the edges of the personal and the professional, "Four International Dianas" disabuses us of the illusions that can sustain our lives (too) in international relations.

*   *   *

Helsinki: Sunday August 31, 1997
The day starts near the markets at South Harbour. A solemn walk into town and up the hill to the Taidehalli. Heavy doors swing open to admit the crowds milling quietly outside. I enter and am immediately consoled by seeing so many familiar faces, eyes all a little glazed. The people gathering around those faces are youngish. They look around, spin around in circles even. They aren't certain what to do here. They don't know where they are to begin: the Andy Warhol Retrospective.

His things are hung around. There are shoes from the 1950s, the butter-fly stencils. Soapbox Brillos team with the ubiquitous 1960s soups. Four Maos appear from the '70s; the purple one tears at my heart. Ten Portraits of Jews of the Twentieth Century provoke. Turn a corner: Twenty

Reprinted in English from *Kosmopolis* (1998), 28, 1.

147

Marilyns; Nine Multicolored Marilyns; Four Marilyns; One Green and Pink Marilyn. Five Deaths. Suicide.

For nearly two months now, I have been in Finland adding the burdens of my English to the workload of students and academics around me. I came from Australia, which means that I don't (have to) read Finnish except for a few useful words: *ravintola* (restaurant), *Linna* (castle), *Yliopisto* (university). There aren't many English words in Tampere, anyway, save those I have brought with me. There is a TV in the university flat, and CNN works overtime to bring the news; but I am not a TV type. Days can also go by before I do a web logon. I am the only person in Helsinki, thereby – nay, perhaps in the plugged-in world – who doesn't know about an important British body terminally slammed around by a smashing German car in a dark tunnel of Paris.

I watch some Marilyns peer at several Last Suppers across the room. There are twenty of her, each done better than the one before, hard with color changes, blurring chins, now darker now lighter eyebrows. Four Marilyns then, with lips all exaggerated. Her eyes are nearly gone too. Why? So that she can elude the next image.

Blonde. Blue. Svelte, albeit getting ample, the British press had just said. Ample for a man. Ample enough for the world. Amply political of late, too, as the international princess of anti-landmines. Had been in Bosnia a previous week. Earlier in Angola. Yachted the Mediterranean in between. Perhaps saunaed in Finland – who knows? We know. Framed now, she is Dead.

See what can happen? A woman cloaked in royal anachronisms fast-paces the international. She relates "scandalously" to Egyptian Moslems and then, dedignified, lies nearly on the French road in hulking metal. Bulbs flash, but she can't "Get away from Me" now. Andy in Helsinki stalks Paris: Five Deaths, circa 1963. Three deaths 1997.

"I'd been thrilled," Warhol says, "having Kennedy as a president; he was handsome, young, smart – but it didn't bother me that much that he was dead. What bothered me was the way that the television and radio were programming everybody to feel sad" (quoted in Nilsson, 1997:33). In the 1997 dead time, the media alone couldn't dictate. The people of the world insisted on ancient rights of mourning and burial. Old royalty were made to blink and nod by masses storming the castles. Queens tried to get it right, to pop it all popularly, tolerating the Marilyn ditty recycled and reauthenticated for Diana – and sung in Westminster Abbey. People were so grateful. I heard its notes – live – while eating lunch in a Helsinki coffee bar. Andy, sitting with me and picking at the food, insisted " . . . it's beauty, and she's beautiful and if something's beautiful it's pretty colors, that's all . . . " (quoted in Mugrabin, 1997:234).

I. Beautiful pink Diana

Think soft sadness. She had been a pudgy pillow of a girl. And then, in the late twentieth century, she married a Westphalianesque prince and gave him two perfectly good boys. He wasn't nice to her, though; he loved another. Diana had taken it out on her body, had thrown up and thrown herself down stairs. She had put enemas up. She had pushed weights up and down. She had talked to shrinks. She had tried talking to the cameras. To cameras. To cameras. She was known to shed a public tear, to hold crippled children from faraway places close to her English rose heart. AIDs victims too. Mother Teresa, overshadowed at the end by the recurring Diana, had time before death to add to the image: "She helped me help the poor . . . that's beautiful."

Diana was beautiful, they say. She wore skirts a lot. Off-the-shoulder gowns. She looked up beguilingly from under blue-lidded eyes. Her smile was often lopsided, more the type of look an American girl could not help but flash out of lack of style. I have secrets, her smile admitted. Should I be here? Her eyes asked. She teased the omnivore cameras with soft queries.

Sunday Times Books, August 31, 1997: a review of Joan Smith's *Different for Girls: How Culture Creates Women*. The book apparently elaborates a holy trinity of female celebrity: Marilyn Monroe, Jackie Onassis, and Princess Diana. The common color throughout is pink, the message is vulnerability. People like their sweet icons to be in some distress. They don't like female stars when they wise up. Marilyn stayed pink, the dear; she never got wise. Madonna didn't make it to the pink list; she couldn't do sad and soft. She found a someone, an American anyone with a good body, to father her first child. Not so Diana (or Jackie). Diana birthed for love. She was a man's woman; like Marilyn, she wished for birth rather than wisdom. Diana and Marilyn and Jackie hitched themselves to men with wealth and with varying degrees of power to make things happen. They granted those men gendered affairs. And then, to soothe their own undernourished souls, the women shopped and cavorted. A toned-down Mercedes-Benz was Diana's last playground. It became a tomb she shared with the wealthy man of the moment at a dizzying millisecond of their affair.

Paint a luscious wrong image for just the right times today, Andy. Picture her mothering the boys admirably so that Man on the World Street can love a princess – or study how to be one if he so desires. Dress her up and have her look down. Not-spicy girls everywhere will know that being in the right place on the globe at the right time with the right weep might visit upon them pink princessdom. The only cost may be early death.

Like pink Marilyn, pink Diana was undereducated but smart. She failed every single O-level exam; only Einstein could do that. Diana charmed at High Table, warmed the cynics, made a go of every evening. To hell with etching her into scenes at the Bodleian. She had outside heart instead of inside mind. She had body. She had sporting hair. She touched. She swam. She was so pictured. Worried about all of it, she tenderly smiled – or bit lip.

Again and again she smiled. She smiled at everyone except, sometimes, those whose job was to snap a well-honed image – or help her in the quest to mold herself (Jephson, 2000). These she could blast, accuse, curse, discharge, run from at high speeds. She was vulnerable. She was misunderstood. She could be stalked. Britons bought it all, devoured her body every day. Americans and Australians and Finns read purloined texts and gawped at Diana pink, finding in her an old-fashioned good girl – the charity girl – of yesteryear, framed in a way that wouldn't tarnish the images they held of their own lives.

The Times, often the only source of "data" I had in Finland, and that a day or two late, told us on August 10 of the year of her death: "Diana still has the brio and the beauty to cavort with impunity wherever and with whomever she likes" (Section 4:1). Meanwhile, a try-hard ex-husband – dour, eccentric, horsy of face, blue cold – tried hard to get some respect for himself and for a longstanding mistress with blonde hair, a bust, and money. There was a problem, though: she with the name which is *pas de rose* came altogether too average-faced to fit the War-Hall retrospective. Beige framed her, no matter that she tried for a brighter pink smile. And you know Andy didn't do much beige after the 1950s, except as background.

Warhol: "after years and years of more and more 'people' in the news, you still don't know anything more about people. Maybe you know *more*, but you don't know *better*" (quoted in Hackett, 1989:509, emphasis in original). Not true, Andy. People tell us whatever these days. And, no matter, we can look at the pictures and soften. Repeat. Repeat. We can be forever sad over lost pieces of pink.

II. Silver Diana

There is a dilemma in famous living and Andy said it better than anyone. To be famous – which one wants to be for a little while at least, *n'est-ce pas*? – be a celebrity. To be a celebrity, one must be photographed repeatedly. Yet celebrities avoid photographers unless stunningly ready for them. To avoid paparazzi when one is a celebrity is to be sought ever more eagerly by their cameras. To be sought more eagerly means one can no longer compose oneself, like Twenty Marilyns could, like Mona Lisa got a chance to do. Liz too posed. Jackie couldn't always control the time and the stunning moments of flash: she'd be taken. It happens quickly. It's out of your hands. Warholian gentlemanliness – the long convention in the art world of working with a model in a studio, which Andy studiously followed in his own quirky way – evaporated in developing fluid. Pop. Zap. The candid shot.

To be famous, one is snapped boarding silvery jets, getting out of silvery Jaguars, boarding silver yachts. One is here and one is there, thanks to keepers slipping silver coins into many fingers. In the weeks before Diana's demise, she had silvered about in Britain, France (several times), Greece, off Italy. She had ample silver with her, but tried to avoid the conspicuous clink of it, in Bosnia.

The international silver stream was Diana's time in the post-prince years. And in that international it takes less than fifteen minutes for famed words to fly about heres and theres. An instant response: Hollywood actor Tom Cruise phoned in his story about being chased by the media through Pont d'Alma in Paris. He did this silver imaging between the time he heard about the crash and the time a silver princess died. He, in Los Angeles, environs somewhere American. She, showing heart in a Paris hospital. News moves like quicksilver. Speed spreads. Warhol (Hackett, 1989:511): "There was a party at the Statue of Liberty, but I'd already read publicity of me going to it so I felt it was done already."

Chased madly, the silver Diana is no longer catch of the day. The silver-seeking parasites have killed the host. Now she is white on white Mona, hanging and framed. But the media are slow to learn this lesson. On the death day itself, the BBC put no other stories or images before its world of viewers and listeners. It "broke new ground in terms of globalization . . . A fitting legacy for Diana," said the usually restrained *Financial Times.* "She belonged to the world" (Harris, September 1, 1997:7).

The world watched as Diana didn't get to sleep with her man that night, which we know she was headed to do, wanted to do, was doing willy-nilly with her new love. She didn't get to thank him for a gaudy ring sealing something. But she did have a silver last supper *à deux* at the Ritz, a spectacle most mortals do not even know how to imagine. And then, after the afterwards, she had round the clock, high diplomatic attention from silvery men. President Chirac was at the Paris hospital as Charles arrived. John Major called her an icon. Tony Blair was all blubbering emotion and even Margaret Thatcher spoke of Diana's good works, of the hope she had brought people throughout the world. Bill Clinton left a party on Martha's Vineyard when he heard the news. Spain's King Juan Carlos and his wife Sofia reported themselves extremely upset. Boris Yeltsin sent a private message. Nelson Mandela referred to the ambassador for the needy of the world. It was a global conference of mostly male condolers. Over Diana, the world's leading dignitaries turned out without rancor. This was high political dying.

It was low too. Pink flowers and handmade cards made it all kitschy and as sentimental as possible. Masses thronged makeshift memorials worldwide. It was Diana's world day, the second riveting day of her international relations. The first had come on July 29, 1981, with the wedding that attracted millions to a falsely romantic silver image.

Diana's gelatin silver smile has now been collected (collected, collected) and marked. And being marked it will be a constant presence. It will not outspeed itself quickly and Andy knows why: "When a person is the beauty of their day, and their looks are really in style, and the times change and tastes change, and ten years go by, if they keep exactly their same look and don't change anything and if they take care of themselves they'll still be a beauty" (quoted in Mugrabin, 1997:151). The silver will take care of Diana.

III. Red Di

So. This is it? One asks oneself. Immortal life for a silver woman in international relations who puts on pink? The lesson: get into a world; marry a man with a political title; be alluring but not especially sexy. Always comb your hair. Respond with sadness and physical discomfort to his infidelities. Hold your head high (but not your brazen eyes). Hug kids. Raise money. Have some flings of your own. Mother well. Buy a lot of clothes, but never in Marks and Spencer.

Diana got worlded. How worldly was she, exactly? August 10, 1997: *The Times* reporter Bob Tyrer (section 4:1) warned of "Dangerous Di." Red Diana is Di. "If the royal family had had their wits about them, the danger of an Egyptian playboy and his father being written into the lamentable Windsor soap opera would have been obvious when the Queen first gave Diana the once-over as a candidate nearly 20 years ago. For it was clear from the start that they were dealing with dangerous Di, a young woman with a taste for adventure" (p. 1). It was? I look at the forty Dianas I can see in every corner of any Finnish news agency. Some picture the nineteen-year-old humpty-dumpty who fell for a prince. Not a hint of red in chubby cheeks of 1980. Ah, but we hear – Andy, get this one – that walking down the nuptial aisle, she looked around for the not-rose in the crowd. On guard, Diana will not be the fool. She: a tell-all who tells to take care of herself. Women who take care to tell are red dangers.

Oliver James (1997:1) says the mother and father fought in front of Diana. He proffers: "Everything she had to say about Charles was true of what we know of her feelings about her father, and probably of her mother's feelings about him too." Et cetera. This is not a new story for many a person of the waning twentieth. We can all climb on to a couch and look at red spots from our pasts. Di, in hot leopard-print swimsuit on a yacht off Italy toward the end, becomes part of the roaming identity of Mohamed al-Fayed. We know his spots: Egyptian owner of a British institution, Harrods; party to a cash-for-questions scandal involving the Tories; unable to buy himself British citizenship. Once upon a time Diana took restrained Caribbean holidays with her boys. Out yachting in rising waters, instead, she becomes a dangerous new woman. And then she almost tells all to a boatload of reporters and photographers, riskily motored to with the promise of red-hot surprise.

We can't always predict the surprises, the moments when the shot comes suddenly. Overnight, Di the Hunter voids and St. Diana oxidizes on our piss-poor page. And Dodi dear? He is fated to become . . . da who? She was said to love his warmth compared with princely chills. He did something glamorous in movie production (but didn't always pay his debts); still, not bad considering that prince is perennially unemployed, a dabbler. Dodi darkly flamed. Charles pales. Di and Dodi canoodled on reddening international waters. They canoodled and canoodled. The prince still doesn't canoodle: he aches greyly at home with his off-rose.

The right princess for the wrong image? The right red heart at story's end? Andy, tell us: what did she do in the world? Ah, you know how "I forget what I said the day before, and I have to make it all up over again" (quoted in Nilsson, 1997:32).

IV. The Diana negative

Andy's four Marilyns, 1979–1986. Look at them closely. You can see mostly black spaces with some highlights of pink, red, green, blue. His Nine Multicolored Marilyns, 1979–1986, presents a similar sense. Andy repeats four more frames of Four Marilyns each. These are silver and black mostly. They are garish, but they don't necessarily mean to be so. It's just that they have no life and yet compel attention. You want to walk away from them and think about something else. You want to look elsewhere for another image. The sensation is frantic. You turn the page or walk a few steps away. Wrong direction, though: ahead is a huge negative of Marilyn. Two of them over there. Helsinki Taidehalli has become a Marilyn factory.

Famous Andy "learned that if you intended to be a famous artist, you had best efface yourself in your work and in your life, as well. Otherwise, something you might say could delimit the meaning of your work and, even if it didn't, that work would always be regarded as tinged with your name and symptomatic of your 'self' – better to be famous just for being famous and to make art on the side" (quoted in Hickey, 1997:26). The Andy face doesn't efface, though. Diana never effaced, even when she tried to mold "self" effacingly (at times). Andy made media centrally into international art. Diana made artful gestures internationally. Neither could easily be disarticulated.

A famous face is famous for . . . er, what is it famous for, Andy? For the woman, for the silver spaces speeded, for the men of international relations dropping everything to say hello and goodbye? For standing in for the famous Marilyns' just right hint of impropriety? For making us cry pinkly for a few days about other things we dare not say? For standing in for silvery Andy, whom the times miss? For nothing at all, really? For nothing at all . . . nothing . . . all?

Look, it doesn't matter. We needn't always end cynically, needn't de-limit the work so. This Diana oozed into the whole world, a place where women have not always been welcome. She did/does it by marry-ing a certain way, then through royal gender tricks and treats, fast lens changes and quick color overlays, then through the mysteries of celebrity heart.

But there is another problem: Andy can't keep up that celebrity for her these days. It's Post-Pop now. He can't do the Dianas retrospectively. Wednesday, August 31, 1983: and anyway, "I'm so mad at Scavullo. Those pictures he did of me for the Jordan Marsh catalogue, he made me look so ugly. He didn't air-brush at all, and he's an air-brush queen! But he didn't do it for me. I'd like to call him up and tell him off, but then he'd say, 'We can only work with what you give us, darling.'" (Warhol, quoted in Hackett, 1989:525).

Nerves go on edge now at the Helsinki memorial. That irritating scratchy blond is everywhere. But there are no Dianas. No Dianas! Andy faces the anxious, rebellious, demanding crowd with an effort to reassure. We will him the words: "Look," he says, "we surely can work with the material from the last supper. There's enough here for a catalogue. And it'll go international – big, big. Don't be negative. She's beautiful and if something's beautiful . . . "

Part III
Sitings

8 The emperors' theories and transformations: looking at the field through feminist lenses

The essays in Part III anchor sightings of women and gender in sites of IR and sites of feminism. The methods for doing so range across the standpoint thinking preferred by Enloe and Tickner, to postmodernism, postcolonialism, art theory, literary theory, and imaginaries of feminist world-traveling – approaches deriving mostly from intellectual developments outside the field of IR. The various siting methods help us match what we see with what we can know about international relations, and what we can be within "it."

"The Emperors' Theories" is an early effort (1991) to persuade mainstream IR to site feminist epistemologies on the inside rather than the outside of the field. The late 1980s, when I prepared this piece, were an exciting time in feminist theorizing. Sandra Harding had recently published what would become her classic statement on *The Science Question in Feminism* (1986), setting out empiricist, standpoint, and postmodernist epistemological choices. Nancy Hartsock (1985) was challenging us to choose a standpoint entry into social inquiry, based on her incorporation of feminism into Marxist political economy; meanwhile, non-Marxist, discourse analytic messages surged through Elshtain's *Women and War* (1987). These works revealed variety in feminist methods and indicated their overall relevance to fields that did not yet give feminism a passing nod.

Across the feminist methods, one could see the tendency to by-pass or fix up the positivist approaches most US graduate schools routinely taught budding political scientists. In my own case, I had five (mostly required) graduate courses in statistics and logics of inquiry in preparation for writing a quantitative dissertation that used prediction logic to array UN delegate and Secretariat perspectives on world order issues of our time. The end product was methodologically sophisticated but flat and lifeless. In effect, I had eviscerated the research participants to fit the requirements of the method. I could see faces clearly in my mind but neither those faces nor the voices that talked to me during my research were imprinted on the analysis.

People had gone missing elsewhere in American IR – and at the time I only read US IR, indeed, had not been assigned anything else in graduate school. "Our" field was then dominated by neorealist/neoliberal institutionalist debates that circled anxiously around the rising subfield of international political economy. Foreign policy analysis was a staple too, with its models of decision and events data banks. The only alternative streams of thinking in US IR came from Immanuel Wallerstein's neo-Marxist world-systems approach and the idealist World Order Models Project (WOMP). Neorealism I found unfathomable, dead. Neoliberal institutionalism seemed more promising but sacrificed people to games played under anarchy. World-systems thinking appealingly included a "periphery" in international relations and not just Great Powers; but the approach was so structure-oriented that it left little room for human agency anywhere. WOMP was abstractly futurist and *très* blokey in its organizational dynamics.

I was already traveling regularly to Zimbabwe (e.g., Sylvester, 1983, 1985), where I was well placed to see international relations from new angles. Yet it only dawned on me when I read Harding, as it separately dawned on Ann Tickner at about the same time, that the flatness of IR had to do with – and here I quote Tickner (1992:xi) – "the masculinist underpinnings of the field." How banal that discovery now sounds! Yet how difficult it was after years of IR training to see gender in a field that claimed none, to see women in texts that routinely, "naturally" featured men or inanimate states and systems. After Harding, Hartsock, and Zimbabwe, I finally knew what was missing, and, just as importantly, there were feminist methods by which to anchor IR to a more inclusive international and its *many* sites, relations, and actors.

"Emperors'" came quickly once I realized that IR was a gendered set of discourses (we called them gender-biases then) that seemed contentious but carried a common theme of distanced, masculine rationality. Keohane cited the piece in *Millennium* (1989a) during his feminist moment. Elshtain (1995) equivocated about my contention in it that *Women and War* showcased a feminist postmodernist approach; she regularly evades taxonomic placings. Some ten and more years later, I see in this early essay precursor themes to the constructivist turn of 1990s IR. I realize how far ahead of the field we were in our concerns at that moment to bring feminist values and norms to IR (bringing IR questions into feminism would occupy me, at least, soon thereafter).

*   *   *

In an international system filled with tensions, IR analysts are keenly interested in questions of continuity and discontinuity. States persist as key political entities, as does a world capitalist system of commodity production and exchange. At the same time, new actors, technological capabilities, and ecological factors impinge on the state, and a new international division of labor reshapes capacities within and between zones of a globalized economy. Although many issues surrounding international political economy are important, other equally important issues and points of tension rarely if ever cause the brows of mainstream IR theorists, particularly the structuralists among them, to furrow. Questions of men–women relations in the international system fit this category.

Conventional wisdom has it that this is a world of states, nonstate actors and market transactions. It is a world in which neither men nor women figure *per se*, the emphasis being on impersonal actors, structures, and system processes. Yet in the theories that depict this abstract system, there seems to be a structuring-out of women and their activities and an implicit structuring-in of men and their activities. There is a hidden gender to the field, and it affects how we think about empirical international relations and political economy. It inspires those of us who notice it to question the extent to which discontinuities in the global economy have cast shadows over gender continuities, transformed gender relations so that we no longer think of sex roles, or maintained and transformed this realm of system structure simultaneously.

That some of us raise these questions now has to do with what feminists have learned during the "two decades of economic, social and political challenges within a rapidly changing international political economy" (Pirages, 1990:1). Sandra Harding (1986:15) states the lessons this way:

> Feminist scholars have studied women, men, and social relations between the genders within, across, and insistently against the conceptual frameworks of the disciplines. In each area we have come to understand that what we took to be humanly inclusive problematics, concepts, theories, objective methodologies, and transcendental truths are

This part of the chapter is based on my contribution in *Transformations in the global Political Economy*, edited by Dennis Pirages and Christine Sylvester. London: Macmillan, 1990. Used with permission.

in fact far less than that. Instead, these products of thought bear the mark of their collective and individual creators, and the creators in turn have been distinctively marked as to gender, class, race, and culture.

Starting with the premise that there are gender tensions in the field of international relations and political economy, and in the larger international system, this chapter considers new conceptual horizons visible through feminist theoretical lenses. The method entails juxtaposing mainstream theories of neorealism, transnationalism, and world systems with feminist critiques of scientific research, social structure, and theory itself. The result is an exercise in the creative interplay of seemingly different levels of analysis.

Mainstream international relations and political economy
Neorealism and its precursors

Neorealism is realism updated for that era of economic interdependence that is described by transnationalists. In the realist tradition, territorial goal-seeking states are at the center of international relations. Their interests are calculated in terms of power and their behaviors can be explained rationally, that is with reference to consistently ordered preferences and cost-benefit analysis. Power is fungible, which means that it can be used to achieve results on a variety of issues without significant loss of efficacy. This is an insecure Hobbesian world, however, because the rational pursuit of state interest aggregates into a loss of security for all. Accordingly, balancing mechanisms akin to market forces operate to check the tyranny of small decisions; tangentially, they also provide frameworks for international economic relations.[1]

Transnationalists rejected realism in the 1970s as narrow, dated, and incomplete, and still see the new issues of international relations – energy, debt, pollution, population increases, shifts in comparative advantages, currency crises, third world underdevelopment – as undermining the statist model. These new arenas of political interest represent a weaving of economic activities into the very fabric of system structure, constraining state autonomy, increasing the potential for cooperation (and mutual damage) in the system, and enhancing the roles

---

[1] For a review of realist literature, see Gilpin (1986) and Mansbach and Vasquez (1981). Original realist writings include Carr (1962), Herz (1951), Morgenthau (1965), and Thompson (1960a).

of multinational corporations, common markets, commodity cartels, international trade regimes, and other nonstate actors. Transnationalists claim that states are now so well integrated into a global economic framework that it becomes sensible to speak of a transformed system.[2]

Neorealists take a position between these two extremes that tips in the direction of realism. They recognize that nonstate actors are powerful in many issue-areas, and understand that economic interactions have bound states into complex interdependence. They argue, however, that states and politics continue to shape international political economy, rather than the other way round. Nonstate actors are created by pre-existing states to help them manage interdependence; such are the origins of the IMF, OPEC, and WTO. These newer actors are noteworthy for providing arenas in which state expectations can converge. But regime creation does not signal a fundamental change in international structure: states are still key actors and the structure of the system is still anarchic, meaning oriented toward self-help. In turn, self-help in the security order still means balances of power. In the economic order there is collaboration, but it is embedded in a competitive political framework. In both realms, state behavior retains rationality, with some game theorists arguing that "no state can choose its best strategy or attain its best outcome independent of choices made by others" (Snidal, 1983:39).[3]

Neorealists think of the state-system as "very durable with only two ways to alter it, neither occurring frequently or rapidly. Within-system change is produced by a shift in the configuration of capabilities. Change of system requires the structure of anarchy transforming into a hierarchy and in the history of the modern state system, this has never occurred" (Ruggie, 1986:140).[4] The strong emphasis on continuity calls into question the transnationalist view of "the sheer momentum of processes sweeping the international polity along toward its next encounter with destiny" (p. 151). Yet neorealism locates most pressures for change at the level of system structure and makes that structure a property of its chief actors – states. This is problematic to some, because "in any social system, structural change itself ultimately has no source other than unit-level processes" (pp. 151–152).

---

[2] For a review of transnationalist literature, see Mansbach and Vasquez (1981). Original writings include Pirages (1978), S. Brown (1974), Keohane and Nye (1977), and Haas et al. (1977).
[3] See other articles in the January, 1983 issue of *World Politics* (vol. 35, no. 2), as well as Waltz (1979) and Keohane (1986).
[4] Ruggie is referring here to Waltz (1979).

Some analysts seem to circumvent the neorealist–transnationalist divide by noting situations where domestic constituencies codetermine state actions with international forces and produce limited discontinuities rather than total system transformations (Wendt, 1987). Others accord international regimes system-changing agency within or outside a framework of leadership by a hegemon (Gilpin, 1981; Haas, 1975; Keohane, 1984; Stein, 1984). There are also critiques of neorealism that take it to task for liberal-internationalist, modernist, pro-inequality, anti-struggle, and class biases (Ashley, 1986; Cox, 1986; Klein, 1987; Walker, 1987). Within a rich debate on the ways and means of a system that is both durable and changeable, there is near silence concerning the possibility that it has been the continuous preserve of men only.[5]

World-systems

The chief and oft-quoted premise of world-systems theory is that there has been only one all-encompassing international system since the sixteenth century. This global social system is fueled by a single, expanding capitalist economy and has a decentralized network of political authority through states of differing capabilities. The world-system may include other structures or logics as well, which "continually emerge and reemerge over long historical eras, encompassing and reencompassing, integrating and disintegrating, defining and redefining the roles and positions of diverse actors in a world system" (Hollist, 1981:291).[6] Key aspects of this system include core expansion, class polarization, the creation of peripheries, bureaucratization, and interstate competition.

Industrial countries comprise the core. There, capital-intensive goods and services are produced with considerable technological sophistication by skilled and semi-skilled labour. Their states also have the administrative and elite coalescence necessary to extract resources from the world and defend against challenges to their rule-setting power. Fourth world and some third world countries occupy the periphery, where the core has coerced a pattern of low-paid labor to produce primary goods, and where weak states try to hold off attacks from struggling classes as they react to shifting international market conditions over which they have no control. The semi-periphery exports primary products to core countries and core products to peripheral areas in roughly equal degrees,

[5] The outlines of a promising exception can be seen in Klein (1989) and Ashley (1989). But the promise is not fleshed out.
[6] For other discussions of world-systems, see Wallerstein (1974a, 1974b), Chase-Dunn and Robinson (1977), and other contributions to Hollist and Rosenau (1981).

under states which can be as bureaucratized as in the core, but which are less resistant to internal class pressures created by efforts to grow, adapt, and readapt. States in this zone can make decisions that move them up the hierarchy of exchange, especially when the core is in disarray owing to recession or war.

The future is not expected to be continuous with a four-hundred-year past. Many world-system analysts think we are already in the long transition to socialism, and Immanuel Wallerstein (1974b) posits that the next major structural change will come in the politics of the system as we move toward a socialist world government. The details of transition are generally secondary to the task of understanding capitalist persistence, although there is concern to probe relationships between continuities that rejuvenate the world-system and "salient discontinuities" (Hollist, 1981:291) that will propel the forces of transition. People can be agents of change in their capacities as laborers, elites, and political activists. Women enter the system, therefore, under those social categories only, and are not agents by virtue of distinctly gender-related experiences: "crudely, those who breed manpower sustain those who grow food who sustain those who grow other raw materials which sustain those involved in industrial production" (Wallerstein, 1974a:86).[7]

Critics generally sympathetic to Marxist analysis seek more information in world-systems theory about "contradictions which can lead to a system's transformation" (Cox, 1986:206) and find instead an understanding of capitalism based ultimately on the power of some individuals in some countries to order the social behavior of others in different countries. They see a neglect of "ever-changing class and nonclass processes comprising human relationships within and between nations" (Resnick et al. 1985:97). Analysts with neorealist inclinations can find the world-system reinforcingly realist: "Dutch economic hegemony in the seventeenth century was destroyed, in quintessential Realist fashion, not by the operation of the world-market system, but by the force of British and French arms" (Keohane, 1986:182). Nowhere in these critiques is there sustained discussion of gender biases and issues: the promising mention of nonclass processes simply hangs in the air and Robert Keohane's (p. 182) comment that "the insights of Realism . . . cross

[7] A contribution to this genre by Smith et al. (1988) offers numerous examples of women both as anti-systemic agents and as victims of structure. None the less, there is a tendency in this work to see the twin evils of racism and sexism as emanating from one system united and functional in its dialectics.

ideological lines" rings true as a statement of what is accepted as permanent in international relations.

Missing

Neorealism and world-systems contribute to our understanding of actors and structures that endure despite and beyond the changes and tensions associated with interdependence. Feminist theorists, though, are generally concerned with what gender invisibility in theory, and in the apparently durable actors, structures, and processes of the world, means. Where are the women in commodity agreements, food production and markets, newly industrializing countries, the fourth world, across various economic zones and in Japanese–American trade? Is their absence warranted, theoretically and empirically, or have women and their customary spheres of economic and political activity been structured out of international relations by a levels-of-analysis sleight-of-hand, which does not extend to men and their activities? What is the meaning of continuity and discontinuity in a system that does not recognize women's agency? How deep and significant can some of the changes noted by transnationalists (and later lauded by aficionados of globalization) be when they do not overturn global structures of male dominance or have enough impact to nudge mainstream theorists to take gender into account? Are not deep gender divisions deeply implicated by silence about them?

Feminist theories are diverse but generally concur that the invisibility of gender issues within mainstream social theories, and of women in "important" public domains of human existence, cannot be remedied simply by adding a pinch of woman – to the state, to capitalist processes, and to theories. Visibility requires considerable analysis of the points in the international system, and in the theories that depict it, where women's behaviors and contributions are choked off and men's are taken as the norm.

Feminist theorizing

Sandra Harding (1986) discusses three feminist theoretical epistemological approaches that reveal, examine, and correct androcentrism in mainstream theorizing: empiricism, standpoint, and postmodernism. None poses a direct and theoretically complete challenge to reigning understandings of international relations and political economy. Rather, their usefulness and relevance for us come from identifying deceptions, distortions, and systematic denials in theories which implicitly or explicitly assume that women and their activities are either beside the point or are subsumed under men's activities. Although each focuses on a different aspect of women's exclusion, there is shared conviction that the unveiling starts by plumbing the depths of social structures and conventions.

Feminist empiricism

Feminist empiricists think researchers often lack the detachment from social expectations about gender roles required to do good science. The scientific observer tries to be objective but is unknowingly influenced by prevailing views of proper roles for men and women. Jane Flax (1987:629) puts it this way:

> In a wide variety of cultures and discourses, men tend to be seen as free from or as not determined by gender relations. Thus, for example, academics do not explicitly study the psychology of men or men's history. Male academics do not worry about how being men may distort their intellectual work, while women who study gender relations are considered suspect (of triviality, if not bias).

Social science is no less free of gender influences than the "harder" sciences. In fact, social scientists tend to equate humanity with men in ways that distort theory, affect hypothesis formation, and skew the data. It has only been with the advent of feminism that scientists have the tools to see this problem. Feminist scientists, in particular, have been instrumental in finding that the objectives of science as method can be at odds with the practice, and thus with results. Carol Gilligan (1982), for example, has shown that the Kohlberg scale of moral reasoning unwittingly tests conformity to men's ethical concerns: boys, the usual subjects of the scale, think in terms of justice, unlike the girls, for whom an ethic of care may be more central.[8] If systematic biases at the problem-formulation stage go undetected, women's behaviors get lost in the residuals; worse, they can be labeled deviant and immature.

It is arguable that there are a number of analogous biases in mainstream theories of international relations and political economy. Each bias enters at the level of assumptions about structures and key actors of the system.

---

[8] Of course it is noteworthy that Gilligan's female subjects are from relatively privileged racial and class groups.

Rationality as bias

The rationality assumption, which figures so prominently in neorealism, may derive from a deep and unexamined cultural expectation that "men are supposed to be motivated by calculation of instrumental or other 'rational' considerations" (Harding, 1986:86).[9] States, economic zones, bureaucracies, trade regimes, and so on appear in theory and case-studies as personifications of Real (White) Men, that is, as receptacles of idealized western, masculine qualities. To the degree that core concepts of the field may be framed and selected for analysis because they make sense to men, this could constitute a hidden ecological fallacy of serious proportions. And that fallacy could go undetected as long as feminist women are few in number within theoretical circles and public domains that theorists of international relations study. They have been few in number too, because there is another side to the rationality of man's assumptions, a side that seems to justify the bias: women, it has been said time and again, are private beings who are motivated by conscious or unconscious emotions and feelings rather than by brain power.

With this pervasive and double-edged bias – men are rational and rationality characterizes the behavior of important social entities – states become gendered: they are autonomous and unitary actors that thrust, penetrate, and calculate their moves like high-stakes billiard players. As long as women do not occupy the high decision-making posts that aggregate into state behaviors, assumptions of rationality in politics can interact with and reinforce the socially acceptable view that politics is a men's activity. Meanwhile, examples of irrationality will be interpreted as anomalous or as really new types of rationality; for example, states become positive or negative altruists (Gowa, 1986). In that twisting way, emotional aspects of decisions are underplayed and, in a final *coup de grâce*, theory is judged on its usefulness and falsifiability, not on the degree to which the assumptions used to build it are correct (see Staniland, 1985).

The single-society bias

World-systems theorists recognize that several logics can intersect the primary economic logic of the system. Neorealists present political and economic systems as separate but interactive. Transnationalists speak of several overlapping realms of activity that produce integrative webs. In

---

[9] This section of her work reraises issues discussed in Millman and Kanter (1975).

each case, however, an obvious awareness of plurality does not extend to the gender realm. There is "the" state-system, "the" world-system, and "the" interdependent system; presumably, men and women live together within each, subscribing to shared principles, norms, and values. Feminist empiricists point out that any assumption of gender-unitary society must be validated through research. They suspect it is more common for women and men to occupy rather separate societies that only appear gender-unitary because "women more than men are forced to rationalize discomfort in order to gain economic or social/political benefits from the dominant society of men" (Harding, 1986:87).

Maria Mies (1986) explores this proposition using a feminist empiricist adaptation of world-systems theory. She traces the historical emergence of two male-identified societies in the world-system: the class society of capitalism, which world-systems theorists acknowledge, and the unacknowledged society of patriarchy. Of the two, patriarchy is older, perhaps for reasons of biology: women could produce without tools through pregnancy and lactation, while men could not and became the more tool-oriented, nature-dominating sex. Patriarchal society conditions women to be primarily household caretakers rather than keepers of the tools, symbols, and offices of the public sphere. Capitalism devalues women's traditional economic activities and remunerates women less when they become paid laborers. With this two-fisted structure in the foreground, Mies looks closely at the new international division of labor. She argues that a capitalist–patriarchal redivision of the world encourages third world women to enter income-generating export sectors, and western women, increasingly involved in non-household production, to define themselves as consumers, often of those third world products. A seeming differentiation of tasks, however, belies a commonality across both sites of women: the intensification of the sexual division of labor such that women everywhere become defined mostly, and most disceptively, as housewives. In her words:

> The housewife is the optimal labour force for capital at this juncture and not the "free proletarian", both in the underdeveloped and overdeveloped countries. Whereas the consumer-housewife in the West has to do more and more unpaid work in order to lower the costs for the realization of capital [like bringing her own bags to food stores], the producer-housewife in the colonies has to do more and more unpaid work in order to lower the production costs. Both categories of women are increasingly subjected not only to a manipulative ideology of what

a "modern", that is, "good" woman should be, but even more to direct measures of coercion, as ... visible in the Third World as far as birth control is concerned.   (Mies, 1986:126)

Women thereby form an "unintended aggregation" (Rosenau, 1981) separate from the "real" breadwinners. In revealing this separate society, Mies adds another, women-relevant logic to an already useful model of international political economy.

The functional bias

Theories of international relations and political economy also imply that a particular social entity or kind of behavior is functional for "the" state-system or for capitalism. A feminist empiricist will ask whether relationships functional for men's societies are also functional for women's societies. Harding (1986:87) raises the question of whether "beyond and across adjustments to race and class hierarchies, women are forced to accommodate their natures and activities to restrictions they have not chosen." This type of hypothesis would not leap out of neorealist discussions of functionally equivalent states or standard world-systems analyses of the changes that sustain capitalism.

The bias of impersonal actors and processes

Based on increasing awareness of bias in social science, feminist empiricists research the origins of those "impersonal" actors and processes that comprise "the" state- and world-systems. They find that both the modern state and capitalist markets were centrally involved in structuring women out of official significance. Both emerged at a time of systematic persecution of women for activities that science, religion, and budding statecraft deemed superstitious, dangerous, disorderly, and therefore to be controlled by outside authority. Midwifery, for example, was a profitable and socially useful profession until the age of science when, with assistance from a church reeling under accusations of virgin worship, it was branded as witchcraft. In parts of Europe the legal profession coalesced around the vibrant and lucrative business of witch defense or prosecution (Mies, 1986). States became war-constituted solidarities of men that transcended the realms of necessary labor where women dwelled (Elshtain, 1987; Hartsock, 1985). States enshrined the Rights of Man in the West, elsewhere through colonization, and literally empowered men to own and control all manner of property, including women

(Mies, 1986; Staudt, 1987). This is a form of protectionism that feminist empiricists would notice and investigate.

The market system worked hand-in-glove with the state in demoting women and their activities to the sphere of private property. Women are primary producers of children and the food to feed them. The market system has direct rewards only for the types of production that yield exchangeable commodities. With the rise of capitalism, women's traditional labor became part of nature, to be controlled by men. Henceforth capitalism relied on women's noncirculating production and nurturing of producer men, but defined these essential activities as external to the economic realm of significance. As Cecil Rhodes subjugated the Shona and Ndebele of Zimbabwe, European women became the subjugated Beautiful Ones in the private sphere, delicate of physique, soft and giving of temperament, and high-buttoned in starched collars.[10]

The feminist empiricist contribution

Feminist empiricist examinations of neglected evidence show that historical trends in the emerging international system were very likely misogynist as well as racist and classist. Both the state and the market became communities of men, where "power is the domination of those outside the community" (Hartsock, 1985:203), sometimes in the name of free exchange, comparative advantage, or division of labor. If the social biases these processes wrought are eliminated from scientific research, women will reappear. Their reappearance could represent a transformation of greater significance than feminist empiricists usually note. To date "women and the sphere with which they have been historically linked remain an absence that helps to make possible the much cherished 'parsimony' of the preferred model, or framework, or simulation, or analysis" (Elshtain, 1987:90–91) – or, I might add, international system.

Besides issues raised above, feminist empiricist work leads us to consider the following.

1. Whether it is accurate to focus on states and worldwide capitalist processes and not also examine the social attitudes and structures that impart a gender bias to these entities and processes.
2. Whether gender biases may result in systematically overlooking important focal points of change and continuity that have

[10] Elshtain (1987) offers this description of Victorian-age women.

to do with women's economic and political activities. Do we
posit discontinuity and transformation in ways that change the
symbols but keep the substance of patriarchy in the next world
order?

3. What interdependence means in a male-dominated political
    economy. Are neorealist states interdependent in the way
    women and men are, that is, within a structure of domination–
    subordination?

4. How we can work within science to falsify theories incorporat-
    ing so many hidden, unspeakable gender issues at the level of
    assumptions.

Feminist standpoint

Theorists of feminist standpoint offer theories and methods that reflect
lessons women learn through subjugation. They argue that centuries
of exclusion have given women perspectives on social issues that more
insightfully reveal the true structures and actors of the world than do
theories spun by representatives of the dominant group. The overarching analogy is men–women with master–slave, where the slave is
a structural extension of the master's will, yet the master thinks the
relationship is really codetermining, with slaves creating masters and
masters simultaneously creating slaves. In dyads like this, "however
well intentioned one may be, the real relations of humans with each
other and with the natural world are not visible" (Hartsock, 1985:117).[11]
To see them, one must look from the perspective of the subordinate, not
the master.

Feminist standpointers want to identify the elements of women's
voice, insight, understanding of reality, and, through political struggle as well as good feminist research, transform these elements into
"a morally and scientifically preferable grounding for our interpretations and explanations of nature and social life" (Harding, 1986:26). The
emphasis is less on women as victims of bias than on valorizing her
feminist-mediated standpoint as a point of departure in understanding
and changing her relationships to the world. There are a variety of ways
to go about this task.

---

[11] This is a point Cox (1986:207) raises as well, arguing that "[t]heory is always *for* some
purpose ... The world is seen from a standpoint definable in terms of nation or social
class, of dominance or subordination ..." His list of standpoint-constitutive influences,
however, does not include gender.

Constructing woman-culture

Some standpoint theorists seek a true story of womanhood in the spiritual realm. Mary Daly (1984), for example, recovers woman in the very concepts, words, and metaphors men have long used to demean her. Her story revolves around lusty wanderers weaving and spinning connections in the universe in ways that threaten and annoy men; hence their terms for us – nags, shrews, scolds, spinsters, and worse. She calls her method "Methodicide," and her research a project in errata to crystallize woman's experience in ways the mainstream would dismiss as a Mistake. She is bold and challenging in referring to snoolish sovereigns of sadostate who try to prevent women's escape from amnesia into ancestral Memories. Hers is a fully oppositional perspective on a world characterized first and last by structures of patriarchy. Reminding us that realism has meaning in modern philosophy as material objects existing externally to us and independently of our sense experience, she offers Realizing reason as a natural transforming elixir: "through the pursuit of Realizing reason, women realize that the restored world is an artificial product resulting from the forced compliance of 'reality' to the patriarchal male's perceptions of and designs upon 'reality'" (p. 163).[12] To enter this woman-memory, one is very likely to abandon the man's world as much as possible, rather than seek to correct its biases.

The interesting question therefore arises of whether there are entirely different ways of seeing the world of states and regimes, zones and exchanges if one "controls for" patriarchy and focuses on the political economy of matriarchy. Woman-culture also pushes a feminist empiricist point to its limits by asking: is the scientific method itself an inextricable component of man-culture?

Reconstructing gender-structuring processes

A very different approach to woman's standpoint emerges from applications of object-relations theory, the purpose of which is to understand the social structuring of gender identity through psychoanalytic method. Harding (1986:131) states the central thesis of this school:

> In cultures where most child care is performed by women, both male and female infants must individuate themselves against only women. This struggle creates different models of the self and its relation to others for those who are becoming girls and boys. Because the creation

---

[12] Daly's (1984:31) use of capitals is, in her words, "capitally irregular: it is intended to convey my meaning rather than to conform to standard usage."

of gender in the individual occurs simultaneously within the transformation of a neonate of our species into a social person, our social
identities as distinctive human beings are inseparable from our sexual
identities as female and male or our gender identities as feminine and
masculine.

Some standpoint theorists see within this systemic structural account of
socialization and social reproduction (Chodorow, 1978), materialist and
ideological components of difference.

Boy babies begin to learn affinity for abstraction and transcendence
from the moment they realize mother is biologically not-I, an object
rather than extension of self. This trauma encourages defensive responses that simultaneously deny and, in the vehemence of denial, af-
firm the material closeness in that first relationship. Patriarchal social
norms reinforce the defensive personality structuring, by determining
that proper male gendering corresponds with how extensively boys root
out, denounce, or create opposite models of, remove themselves materially from, and otherwise denigrate the concrete mother-world. Says
Hartsock (1985:241), "[t]his experience of two worlds, one valuable, if
abstract and deeply unattainable, the other useless and demeaning, if
concrete and necessary, lies at the heart of a series of dualisms – abstract/
concrete, mind/body, culture/nature, ideal/real, stasis/change. And
these dualisms are overlaid by gender; only the first of each pair is associated with the men."

In "successfully" transcending the trauma of individuation from a
woman via a retreat to the mind and away from emotional connections,
adult men maintain artificial discontinuity from the material world.
Their codes of abstract masculinity maintain a set of idealized gender
traits that keep unconscious connective longings at bay, so that these will
not inappropriately resurface and commingle subject and object into loss
of identity. Abstract masculinity shows up in Roberts's Rules of Parliamentary Procedure, which structure the emotion of meetings into over-
controlled, over-ordered relations. It may also underlie the requirement
of scientific method to achieve distance from the subject, objectivity, and
detachment from "the particularities of time and place, personal quirks,
prejudices, and interests"(Bordo, 1986:451, paraphrasing Keller, 1985).
Consider, as well, that neorealists give states a degree of realist freedom
in rationality, even as their choices become increasingly constrained by
the decisions of other states (men). Even interdependence is something
of a battle between fundamentally hostile and primordially unconnected

entities, whom, to take a phrase from Hartsock (1985:242), "one comes to know by means of opposition (even death struggle) and yet with whom one must construct a social relation in order to survive." Moreover, to assert that the global economy has been transformed, even as capitalism persists, may unconsciously model that other "transformation" of continuously connected boys into paragons of (false) autonomy as men.

Girls have different individuation experiences. Mother is biologically similar to self rather than an object, which means that the trauma of individuation comes much later when girls try to gain psychosexual maturity as autonomous adults. In infancy, the absence of a jarring discovery of mother-difference sets the stage for an empathetic identity. This is nurtured by socialization practices that equate femininity with mother-world activities of family preservation, personal involvement, and necessary labor (such as changing dirty diapers). A maturing girl thereby develops affinity for continuous connections more so than for the dichotomies and abstractions of man-world. For her, mental and manual labor go together, work is often play, the sensual can be intellectual, and change is the reworking of continuous ties.

Her different experiences may explain why many adult women seem more peace-loving than men, why they seem to avoid activities of statecraft in which "we" are in a competitive death struggle with "them" (Brock-Utne, 1985; Reardon, 1985; Ruddick, 1983). We know from the mother–child dyad that power relations are interchangeable over time rather than fixed, hierarchical, and defensively protected from decline: it is a sign of healthy child development that mother's omnipotence ebbs within less than a year of her infant's birth. As well, the preferred arena of power for women may be the local community, where there are opportunities to express caretaking morality in concrete ways (Gilligan, 1982; Hartsock, 1985).

On the downside, these gender lessons also prepare women to join a status group subordinated to men. Women can continue connecting to the point of losing ourselves and our power in mesmerizing mergers with others; we can almost seek out objects into which to pour ourselves (Rich, 1976). Ours can be a community of self-sacrificers lacking effectiveness as system challengers. This could explain the long reign of emperors and their theories – at least in the West.[13]

---

[13] Object-relations theory, and the research on which it is based, takes the western experience of gender relations as universal.

The feminist standpoint contribution

Standpoint countertheories seek expressions of womanhood in structures and processes operating at very different levels than most neorealist and world-system analysts would find relevant. None the less there are lessons there in the importance of deconstructing abstractions that may invisibly gender-mark the structures we do find relevant for study, masking the distorted relations that create them. There are also lessons in how to conceptualize transformative discontinuity as valorization in the public domain of the continuities women experience in officially less important private domains. The novel question posed is, in Hartsock's (1985:246) words, what is "the potentiality available in the actuality" of women's lived experiences or natures, and in analogous processes that connect and co-determine through mutual attraction rather than domination–subordination (also French, 1985:499)?

A set of feminized relations may be embedded in the Southern African Development Community (SADC). Designed originally to end dependence on the South African economy by building up regional infrastructures, SADC has become a mutual-attraction scheme that valorizes colonially muted voices and promises an order based on simultaneous codetermining processes of state and regional action. In contrast to the SADC logic, neorealist states collaborate as competitors seeking to extricate themselves from prisoner's dilemmas by forcing others to back down as "chickens," to take the patsy "sucker" rap, or do the "saintly" thing. Contributions to game theory bring out elements of cooperation in "tit-for-tat" strategies and considerations of "long shadows" of the future (Axelrod, 1984; Axelrod and Keohane, 1985). A feminist standpoint theorist would notice that these international relations are pseudo-personalized and that dominance masquerades as a cooperative tendency.[14]

In feminist standpoint theories, the feminist is the transformer. She enhances her agency in the world by putting her lived experiences on the same plane as, if not higher than, woman-denying authority. In this spirit, we ask:

1. Is there a woman's standpoint on international relations and political economy?

---

[14] Gowa (1986:168) notices the problem of system-dominant sources of state behavior and outcomes in Axelrod, and says it "circumscribes his book's utility for students of the field." She does not go on, however, to tie her very interesting discussion of state altruism to feminist theoretical frameworks.

2. Is there a relationship between the social construction of males as men and the topics analysts of international relations and political economy consider to be within or outside the field?

3. Are there dyads in political economy that behave as codetermined entities of the child–mother type? [15]

4. What does the search for scientific parsimony suggest about the types of actors, processes, and structures men may seek to control and/or transform?

Feminist postmodernism

Like other feminist approaches, postmodernism asks how we think, or do not think, or avoid thinking about gender (Flax, 1987).[16] Feminist postmodernists, however, advise researchers to embrace a posture of uncertainty about "the self, gender, knowledge, social relations, and culture (understood by) linear, teleological, hierarchical, holistic, or binary ways of thinking and being" (p. 622). They are the skeptics for whom "reality can have 'a' structure only from the falsely universalizing perspective of the dominant group" (pp. 633–654). They see danger in denying women behaviors that do not exemplify some true story of womanhood, as when women in the public sphere are accused of being like men. They also object to accounts of womanhood that are not sensitive to historical nuance, and that ignore the impact of class, race, and culture on identities and lived experiences. Their overarching question is: in what ways do women comprise "a" group and in what ways is the search for themes of group coherence a way of voiding diversity?

Harding (1986:189) suggests that "we should expect differences in cognitive styles and world views from peoples engaged in different kinds of social activities."[17] There are women in the armed services and "offshore women in the electronics factories in Korea" (p. 192).

---

[15] Wendt (1987) asks researchers to conceptualize states as having internal organizational structures that condition perceptions and responses, and which experience, absorb, and perhaps change in response to the intended and unintended actions of other states and agents. Both neorealists and world-systems analysis, he says, should explore "the social structural organizing principles which generate the state as a particular kind of social actor" (p. 366). He uses both the master–slave and the child–parent dyads to illustrate codetermining entities, without citing feminist literatures that explicitly discuss these relationships. If mainstream researchers take Wendt's advice but do not consult feminist literature, they may fail to expose dominating sides of some only apparently codetermining entities.

[16] There is now a lively debate about whether gender is what feminism is about. See discussion in Chapter 3, "Handmaids' Tales" and also Butler (2001).

[17] Some standpointers share this position and speak of multiple standpoints. See Hartsock (1985). Also see discussion in Sylvester (1987).

There are subsistence food producing women in Africa and luxury consumer women in the United States. Margaret Thatcher was at the head of a state, female economists are in the employ of the IMF, and some Caribbean women are in the sex industry. There are western middle-class-mother-feminist-peace-activists and peasant-combatant literacy teachers in Southern Africa. Are we more alike than different? Do we compose a standpoint?

Harding thinks not. In her view, "if there can be 'a' feminist standpoint, it can only be whatever emerges from the political struggles of 'oppositional consciousnesses' – oppositional precisely to the longing for 'one true story'" (p. 193) and "the culturally dominant forces for unitarianism" (p. 247) that lead us to believe that there is such a thing. It is theoretically preferable to accept the notion of permanent partiality and to explore intersecting, contradictory, and simultaneous realities within a pro-women framework. Other critical streams, including world order and peace studies, have pecked away at mainstream international relations for years and offered a range of alternatives. Feminist postmodernism, however, stands alone in seeking to deconstruct more than it prescribes and in focusing on women as the subject of deconstruction.

Smashing the stereotypes

Jean Bethke Elshtain (1987) demonstrates one postmodernist approach in a study of *Women and War*. She embeds an assessment of the realist tradition of international relations in a broader treatment of "war as an object of discourse central to historic understandings of politics in the West" (p. x). Her method entails exploring the political claims and social identities deeded to us through war stories. She realizes that this is unorthodox, as is her nontheoretical approach, but claims it is important "to remain open to one's subject matter, to see where it is going and follow – not to impose a prefabricated formula over diverse and paradoxical material" (p. xi). On these grounds, she takes "[p]rofessionalized IR discourse" to task as "one of the most dubious of many dubious sciences that present truth claims that mask the power plays embedded in the discourse and in the practices it legitimates" (p. 91).

She also takes to task the commonplace and standpoint-constitutive assumption that Real Women have no yearnings for war. She speaks of her own youthful identity with soldiers' tales and recalls a nurse veteran of Vietnam saying: "I think about Vietnam often and I find myself wishing I was back there" (p. 10). To Elshtain, "wars destroy and bring into being men *and* women as particular *identities* by canalizing energy and giving permission to narrate" (p. 166, emphasis in original). That IR hands war over to men – making it their creation and responsibility – means women involved in war fade too far into the background.

Elshtain's concerns may seem a far cry from the topics suggested by neorealist, transnationalist, and world-systems writings, but they are not. She is suggesting a way of including the heretofore excluded by questioning the limited categories of acceptable identities in stories where soldiers are on the battlefront and women are on the homefront (and where there are statesmen and first ladies). She says there are many "historical amputations that excise many alternatives, male and female" (p. 171). Her humanistic even-handedness in seeing men and women in war may be problematic (Sylvester, 1989), but Elshtain helps us think creatively and more accurately about the amputations that must have taken place for women's activities to be so structured out of mainstream international relations and for men's activities to be so stage-center. As Elshtain (1987:171) says, "if this is where we are *at*, where have we *been?*"

The feminist postmodernist contribution

Feminist postmodernism asks us to think of the multiple realities hidden by any True Story of Reality, and about the ways that story can promote oppressive conformity and discourage criticism and action for change. It inspires us to ask:

1. What stories have we accepted about men that deny women agency in war, capitalism, state decisions, and so on?
2. In what ways are women battling patriarchal international relations and political economy today? How many women-logics are there in how many different systems?
3. What are all the salient divisions of labor within and between the entities we study? Relatedly, how are "understandings of gender relations, self and theory partially constituted in and through the experiences of living in a culture in which asymmetric race relations are a central organising principle of society" (Flax, 1987:640)?

Transformations?

Feminist and mainstream theorists may seem to talk past one another, because their frameworks, levels of analysis, and foci are very different. There are points of nexus, however, that could bring accuracy through inclusiveness to theories of international relations and political economy.

The empiricists tell us that bias enters theory building when gender is uncritically projected on to the world and becomes a basis for identifying "significant reality." In "our" field, masculine preserves are well depicted in "our" theories. The theorists, however, do not acknowledge the gendering of international relations, and this subterfuge makes it difficult to talk about transformation: how many ways are there to rearrange systems and, notwithstanding laments about their harmful aspects, maintain masculine privilege? There are limits to the very parameters of change. States persist – Men lead.

Standpoint theorists tell us it is not just that theorists fail to ask how gender experiences and expectations may impinge on the claims of scientific accuracy, universality, coherence, and completeness. They fail to ask how the world looks from the vantage point of any outside group. Henry Kissinger once said: "For me, women are only amusing, a hobby. No one spends too much time on a hobby" (quoted in Jaggar and Rothenberg, 1984:81). Few men in IR may answer, Amen; yet "our" frameworks of analysis propagate the dualisms that make a particularly offensive work/hobby distinction possible. Women's activities occupy space at the lower end of the public/private dichotomy. As a group, women are either the Beautiful Irrelevant Ones or the Overbreeding Ones; I suppose women academics are the Exceptional Ones. If dualisms reconstruct the world from a master's standpoint, then we should not be surprised to discover resistance to any notion that structural transformation is, at root, a bringing-in process for all those who are "not-I." The world of "her" may be quite different from "his": she may experience power both as male dominance and as the mutual attraction of the mother–child dyad; states may be more symbols than reality, such that community is the empirical point of reference and action; markets may figure as places to gather as well as to sell and buy; games may be what children play with great abandon of rationality and considerable pleasure.

Feminist postmodernists tell us that the world of "her" is not unitary or ideal. We should not seek "a" framework for understanding "her" or anything else right now, or a consequence may be that we merely elevate one of the patriarchy-battered perspectives to a position of privileged insight. At this moment of flux, to transform is to deconstruct and fragment all potentially tyrannical coherences into partialities. Although feminist theorists will disagree on the questions we should introduce to the study of international relations and political economy, and on the methods to improve the field, few will disagree with the proposition that there are many relations masked within official international relations. This is a clue to the transformation puzzle that no other tradition of analysis offers. How a gender dethroning can occur, how it would interact with other changes, are issues mainstream theorists might explore in dawning recognition that their theories are more similar than different in the issues they evade.

9 Feminists and realists view autonomy and obligation in international relations

I wrote the next essay for the major conference on Gender and International Relations that Ann Tickner conceived, won a Ford Foundation grant to fund, and hosted in 1990 with Peggy McIntosh at the Center for Research on Women of Wellesley College. Several layers of invited academics presented papers at this affair. Some were in what seemed then to be the fledgling feminist IR crowd (Tickner, Elshtain, Enloe, myself, Rebecca Grant, Spike Peterson, Robert Keohane, and Richard Ashley); each had participated in at least one of the two earlier conferences at the London School of Economics and Political Science (1988) and the University of Southern California (1989). In a second group were Ann Sisson Runyan, Mary Ann Tetreault, Craig Murphy, Carol Cohn, and R.B.J. Walker, who may not have been at earlier conferences but some or all of whose writings would later be identified with feminist IR. Then there were notables from IR, who contributed just that one time to the new endeavor: Hayward Alker, Mary Katzenstein, and Celeste Wallander. Several invited participants from outside IR also presented: Theda Skocpol, Beverley Grier, Mona Harrington, Joan Tronto, Ariti Rao, and Lois Wasserspring. That there were no representatives of British, European, or Australian IR at the conference – let alone from much of the world – did not strike most of us, I surmise, as strange.

Along with the intellectual stimulation of the conference, which was non-stop and occasionally harrowing, I remember the cocktail party Nannerl Keohane put on for us as then president of Wellesley College. The September evening was unusually stormy – the tail end of a hurricane. Having declined to take the provided transportation to the Keohane residence, Ashley and Walker turned up soaked to the skin. The two also declined Robert Keohane's offer of dry clothing and proceeded, if I recall, to sit down on a damask sofa, hair plastered to their skulls, pants clinging, and shoes squishing.

For complicated reasons, Tickner did not end up editing the book that came out of her momentous conference (Peterson, 1992). She did, however, set the tone for the gathering by asking participants to discuss the proposition, and its implications, of a world of states and international politics reflective of men's experience. I was then engrossed in a new feminist analysis of liberal theory written by Nancy Hirschmann (1992), which addressed the ways freedom and obligation would have to be rethought within liberal theory if we brought feminist psychoanalytic insights about gender formation to bear. Hirschmann's writings, together with Carole Pateman's (1988) work on the sexual contract within the social contract underlying liberal governance, set me thinking about the IR credo of (masculine) autonomous states in anarchy, cooperating or not depending on the theory. I had also newly digested Enloe's *Bananas, Beaches, and Bases* (1989) and was influenced by the many examples she provided of men practicing international relations while leaning heavily on the uncited work of women minions.

In something of a flash, the various pieces comprising this paper came together and the final draft was completed while I was a senior visiting scholar at the Center for International Studies, University of Southern California. Somewhat revised here, the main points remain. I suggest that masculine gender identity may be implicated in issues of autonomy raised in realist IR. It may arise from what psychoanalytic feminism identifies as different gendering processes across the sexes. By anchoring concepts such as "autonomy" to gendered experiences and resultant standpoints, it becomes theoretically compelling to resite realist IR around neglected relational activities. In this piece I journey simultaneously as a feminist-influenced voice in IR and as a student of IR brought to feminist questions of sociality and standpoint.

* * *

... and the gravest problems arise from theories of the world founded upon a conception of man that is concealed and for this reason never examined. (Thompson, 1960a:1)

This chapter explores concealments of autonomous and minimally obligated man – and gender more generally – in realist international relations theory and practice. It also reveals activities by women in international relations that subvert realist autonomies and rewrite obligations in more feminist ways.

The seemingly generic term "realist" has been posed as a way of "examining reality as it really is – without subscribing to Realist assumptions" (Keohane, 1989b:68, n17). In practice, however, realism can smokescreen Realist strivings for autonomy from "men's" and "women's" "real" experiences of relationships and unchosen obligations, thereby reinforcing, in unexpected ways, the view proffered by Hedley Bull and Carsten Holbraad (in Wight, Bull and Holbraad, 1978: 20), that "international relations is not one of those subjects in which it can be assumed that new studies represent an advance on old ones."

The Realist-realist gender concealments may have to do with shared groundings in liberalism (Stein, 1990).[1] The feminist writings of Nancy Hirschmann, Carole Pateman, and Cynthia Enloe help us see how that connection works and how certain forms of liberal thought can erase women from spheres of significance. Hirschmann (1989) traces the unacknowledged gendering of freedom, recognition, and obligation in western liberal theory to defensiveness experienced by males in the process of becoming properly gendered as men; one sees within her treatise the origins of defensively positionalist realist states.[2] Pateman (1988) writes about a conquest-based sexual contract predating the hypothetical liberal social contract that brought Leviathans into existence; both contracts are alive today within the gendered operations of many neorealist and neoliberal institutionalist regimes. Enloe (1989) offers glimpses of women engaged in liberal exchanges and reciprocities that should figure into realist theories of international relations, but do not; she argues in effect that viewing these activities from women's standpoints reveals the false gender blindness of the realist imperium and makes it more difficult for the rule of emperors to continue.

There are other clues to disguised gender in Realist-realist overlaps and skepticisms that complicate and enrich, order and disorder everyone's theories and arguments; and there are concrete actions that women engage in within international relations that reveal the limitations

---

Revised from: *Gendered States: Feminist (Re) Visions of International Relations Theory*, edited by V. Spike Peterson. Copyright © 1992 by Lynne Rienner Press, Inc. Used with permission.

[1] This is not an uncontroversial claim. James Dougherty and Robert Pfaltzgraff (1990:7) describe realism as "basically conservative, empirical, prudent, suspicious of idealistic principles, and respectful of the lessons of history." Postmodernist critics tend to emphasize that there is no one direction of thought in any theory; rather the directions are created through community readings. See R.B.J. Walker (1987).

[2] Joseph Grieco (1990:10) defines defensive positionalist as a state that wants "to know what the impact will be of virtually any relationship on [its] relative defensive capabilities."

of our usual understandings of the field. After exploring the meanings of autonomy and obligation presented by Hirschmann, Pateman, Enloe, and others, compared with meanings encrusted in IR theory, this paper turns "strangely" onto highly contextualized terrains where women operate in, around, and against realist forms of autonomy and obligation in everyday international relations. The discussion provides gender "takes" on James Keeley's (1990:93) point that "disorder and resistance can persist in the face of realist ordering or be created by it," and suggests ways that seemingly insignificant disorderings begin to recast a field.

Feminist issues of autonomy and obligation

Nancy Hirschmann addresses the tendency of consent theorists to make "obligation" an inferior second term to "freedom," and probes the related and gendered meanings of "autonomy" that give rise to this practice. She implicitly agrees with arguments casting social contract liberalism as a politics of negativity. In Benjamin Barber's (1989:59) terms, this politics has "enthroned not simply the individual but the individual defined by his perimeters, his parapets, and his entrenched solitude." To Hirschmann the negativity has to do with equations in liberal theory of "individuals" with men – a connection Barber's statement reveals. She argues that masculine identity is embedded in notions of inherently and naturally free individuals, and, correlatively, in the idea that "the only legitimate limitations are those imposed by the self" (Hirschmann, 1989:1227).

Feminist standpoint offers women's common experiences of subordination in public life both as unfortunate and as opportunities to view reality in different and more accurate ways.[3] Hirschmann's concern is to move backwards to the sources of masculine dominance in early gendering experiences and forward to the social distortions adult masculine enterprises often uphold as truth. Her feminist psychoanalytic account begins with a young infant unconsciously believing that its mother's body is coterminous with his own, only to discover through maturational processes that he cannot be "subsumed in the one who supplies [its] needs, who is most generally across cultures, female" (p. 1230). For boys, that discovery begins a struggle to suppress original psychic

---

[3] See discussion of feminist standpoint in Harding (1986). For an application to international relations, see Sylvester (1990).

femaleness. The path of struggle is not foreordained in "nature," but rather conforms to cultural notions that gender is an exclusive category of identity that must be learned. Becoming male entails an exaggerated emphasis on separation: "a boy defines himself against the mother, as 'not-mother' " (p. 1230). She becomes an object of difference, an "other," as he develops "a conception of agency that abstracts individual will (the ability to make choices and act on them) out of the context of the social relationships within which it develops and within which it is exercised, because it sees those relationships as threatening by definition" (p. 1231).[4]

The properly gendered man then denies the roots of a defensive gender identity and embraces as normal a form of social autonomy that is, "a separateness and independence that is a reaction against others" (pp. 1230–1231). In public society, the reactively autonomous mental stance creates "discrete and controlled points of contact, only through rule-governed and role-defined structures" (p. 1238). It reconnects separate and wary individuals through formal "rights" and creates obligations as chosen restraints on what Nancy Rosenblum (1987:29) describes as "a masterless person, free of deference and ascriptive attachments and privileges, though not without norms and attachments altogether."[5] Nonvoluntary consent becomes oxymoronic when, in fact, the basis for a model of voluntary consent is a set of gender rules that men learn involuntarily.

Liberal political theory, in other words, extends a particular gendering experience into the norms of western society. The cast of masculine reactive autonomy appears in stories of abstract social contracts entered into, seemingly, says Christine Di Stefano (1983:639), by "orphans who have reared themselves, whose desires are situated within and reflect nothing but independently generated movement." Realist international relations theory follows in this mold, even as it focuses on those anarchic spaces that elude social contract. It depicts states as primitive "individuals" (Wendt and Duvall, 1989:55) separated from history and others by

[4] Terry Eagleton (1990:91) uses a similar argument to describe Immanuel Kant's aesthetic representation of the sublime, noting that "to attain full moral stature we must be wrenched from the maternal pleasures of Nature and experience in the majesty of the sublime the sense of an infinite totality to which our feeble imaginations will never be equal ... In the sublime, morality and feeling for once come together but in negative style: What we feel is how immeasurably Reason transcends the senses, and thus how radically 'unaesthetic' our true freedom, dignity, and autonomy are."

[5] Michel Foucault (1973) would find the projection of men's lived experiences on the world symptomatic less of lessons from childhood than of general modernist tendencies to construct regimes of knowledge-power establishing authority for certain practices. See Ashley's (1989) discussion of Foucault's ideas as relevant to international relations.

loner rights of sovereignty – backed up, for good measure, by military hardware, and involved in international conventions and institutions only on a voluntary basis.

The world looks different to girls, because they are mothered by phys-ically similar beings and face no social messages to be unlike mother in order to attain proper status as women. A girl thereby develops a sense of empathetic connection to the world: "self and other will constitute a continuum for her" (Hirschmann, 1989:1230). This does not mean she is free of struggles to differentiate from mother; those tend to occur in adolescence, when issues of psychosexual individuality come to the fore. It does mean that experiences associated with being mothered by a physical similar, in combination with social reinforcements of mother–daughter sameness, contribute to a sense of relational autonomy. Girls and then women find their identity within the context of relationships rather than in opposition to them.

If this is so, then many of the relationally grounded obligations women assume also fail to fit the liberal model of chosen restraints one can disavow if it is in one's interest to do so. Feminine differentiation is "a particular way of being connected to others" (Chodorow, 1978:107), and often that connection takes the form of childcare or of responsibil-ity for children abandoned or disavowed by their fathers. In a piece for the *Village Voice*, Enloe (1990:29) argues that such responsibilities are the basis of media comminglings of "womenandchildren" into connected word symbols, victims, and dependants that states are supposed to pro-tect in an international crisis. The melding of bodies of women into bodies of children suggests that women have unchosen obligations; but it also denigrates the content of those obligations by presenting women as hobbled people who must, themselves, be a bit childlike *vis-à-vis* the tough realities of international relations.

How do adult men come to dominate women and to denigrate their own obligations after "escaping" psychic femaleness? Feminist psycho-analytic thinking implies that patriarchal right derives from women's position as mothers: as long as primary caretaking falls to women, iden-tity differentiation occurs first against her and then against others. Pate-man (1988:34), however, argues that "the meaning and value accorded to motherhood in civil society is ... a consequence of the patriarchal construction of sexual difference as political difference." This construc-tion has origins in a symbolic sexual contract that subordinated women before the social contract came into effect. The social contract divided sociality into public and private realms – state and civil society – and the pre-existing sexual contract contributed the idea that "the private sphere is part of civil society but is separated from the 'civil' sphere" (p. 11).

Pateman (pp. 47–48) reconstructs the sexual contract to show the basis of women's later subordination in society:

> Hobbes states in *Leviathan* that in the war of all against all "there is no man who can hope by his own strength, or wit, to defend himself from destruction, without the help of confederates." But how can such a protective confederation be formed in the natural condition when there is an acute problem of keeping agreements [owing to the isolation and mutual wariness of all]? The answer is that confederations are formed by conquest, and, once formed, are called "families." ... In *Leviathan* ... a family "consists of a man, and his children: or of a man and his servants; or of a man and his children, and servants together; wherein the father or master is the sovereign". ... If one male individual manages to conquer another in the state of nature the conqueror will have obtained a servant ... [If] a male individual manages to conquer a female individual [t]o protect her life she will enter into a contract of subjection – and so she too becomes the servant of a master ...

Thus, in a condition free of systemic domination-subordination relations, the conquest of women does indeed occur with motherhood. But in this case, mother is equal to men, though she must defend her infant and herself in the state of nature. Defending two people, one of whom is helpless, disadvantages women *vis-à-vis* unfettered or confederation-strengthened men, and we are conquered. Conquered peoples become politically subordinate; gendering processes root out that subordinate psychic femininity in boys.[6]

This Hobbesian story explains why men are dominant forces inside families that are ostensibly outside the important realms of civil society. It has it that men exclude women from participation in the original

---

[6] Women are the ones fettered by infants in the war of all against all because Hobbes (1966:116, quoted in Pateman, 1988:44) initially grants them (family-less) mother rights: "every woman that bears children, becomes both a *mother* and a *lord* [over the child]." In return for her nurturing, the child "agrees" that "being grown to full age he become not her enemy" (p. 44). Thus the mother–child relationship is a contract that eventually wins for the mother an ally in the war of all against all. Presumably, having an ally reduces the likelihood that she will be conquered; yet, given the logic of the argument, she never makes it to that point without falling under a master, because the child is a free rider for many years. Men conquered by other men also become servants in Hobbes' scheme of things. That they are later released and women are not implicates the marriage contract as the vehicle of servitude for civic women.

social contract and thereafter from public spaces deemed by men as "significant." It reinforces Hirschmann's (1989:1240) sense that "voluntarist theories of obligation can be read, at least in part as theories of power, with power conceived as domination."

A different approach to knowledge and power starts from women's more relationally oriented world. For girls, the process of attaining identity involves less defensiveness; the Rubicons dividing self from others, and creating sovereigns and servants, threaten less. This may be the reason Hobbes' "family" women later "consent" to enter marriage contracts in civil society: the conqueror is not an alien so much as he is a potential community member. Properly gendered boys, meanwhile, have difficulty seeing that the autonomous self is already connected rather than also connected (Di Stefano, 1990:36). They have difficulty conceptualizing choiceless sociality. None the less, relational autonomy incorporates the experiences of both sexes – whether "he" sees the links or not – and forms a reasonable starting point for a liberal theory in which obligation accounts for "the very human experience of choicelessness, and for the fact – so adamantly denied by consent and social contract theory – that choices exist in contexts" of relationship (Hirschmann, 1989:1241).

Enloe's *Bananas, Beaches, and Bases* is different in scope and approach to the political theories elaborated by Hirschmann and Pateman; and yet it parallels their ideas nicely. Enloe offers an extended look at women's contributions to international relations and argues that realist practice depends on, but is presented as autonomous from, activities of and obligations to women. "Our" field is normally silent about the theoretical implications of women's embeddedness in international relations – as representatives of imperialism, as workers in global factories, as marketing logos affixed to export products, and so forth. To Enloe (1989:4, emphasis in original):

> Women's roles in creating and sustaining international politics have been treated as if they were "natural" and thus not worthy of investigation. Consequently, how the conduct of international politics has *depended* on men's control of women has been left unexamined. This has meant that those wielding influence over foreign policy have escaped responsibility for how women have been affected by international relations.

In keeping gender off the agenda and isolated from the realm of significance, realism reveals "how *much* power it takes to maintain the international political system in its present form" (p. 3), and how much this power "hides the workings of both femininity and masculinity" (p. 11). For example, in order to preserve state sovereignty, governments rely on masculinized and feminized sacrifice to sustain a readiness for war. Masculinized sacrifice wins honor through battle, while feminized sacrifice at home is considered second order (except by Jean-Jacques Rousseau) – references to patriotic mothers and the odd tribute to women combatants notwithstanding (Elshtain, 1987).

Although Enloe does not say it directly, the bedrock issue for her, as for Hirschmann, seems to be obligation and the falsely unitary concept of reactive autonomy that denies or buries international relationships in the language of liberal exchange-oriented contracts. The alternatives may lie on the unexplored cusp of reactive and relational autonomy, where for Enloe the international is personal and for Hirschmann (1989:1242) "the point is to call attention to the fact that men already *are* consensually obligated in many ways and that these obligations are appropriate to human relations but our public ideology will not allow us to recognize this fact."

Autonomy and obligation in international relations theory

The texts of classical Realism establish reactive autonomy as a norm of international relations; and since Realism has been hegemonic, some claim, for three hundred years (Gilpin, 1981:7; Holsti, 1985:vii), its stance on this matter fills many spaces. In the work of Hans J. Morgenthau (1965:11–12), for example, autonomy figures directly into the sixth principle of political realism:

> Intellectually the political realist maintains the autonomy of the political sphere, as the economist, the lawyer, the moralist maintains theirs ... the political realist is not unaware of the existence and relevance of standards of thought other than political ones [but] [a]s a political realist, he cannot but subordinate those other standards to those of politics.

Initially the domain of the "individual" political realist, his reactive autonomy is transposed on to the state. That state is "free to manage its internal and external affairs according to its discretion, in so far as it is not limited by treaty or what we have earlier called common or necessary international law" (p. 315). Obligations are approved warily: "No nation has the right, in the absence of treaty obligations to the contrary, to tell any other nation what laws it should enact and enforce, let alone enact and enforce them on the latter's territory" (p. 315). While both of these postures prevent social fusion, a condition of subverted relationship, they also enable one heroic egoist to destabilize those few obligations to others that arise in realist international relations: "without my consent your decision does not bind me . . . [and] without my consent there is no decision" (p. 315). Each state is thus a heroic exhibitionist using its sovereign privatization as a public act to stand aloof from or to thwart other would-be conquering heroes (see Rosenblum, 1987: chapter 5). That sovereignty is a romantic fiction or breached principle – often violated, in fact, by *realpolitik* decision-makers – seems to have little impact on the abstract theoretical point.

Realists often look askance at interdependence because it connotes to them "some degree of vulnerability by one party to another" (Viotti and Kauppi, 1987:56). What is to be avoided is a situation that gives a state power over another, for then conflict is likely to result rather than cooperation. Hence, in relationships among states, "just as in households or community conflicts, one way to establish peace is to eliminate or minimize contact among opponents or potential adversaries. Separation from other units, if that were possible, would mean less contact and thus less conflict" (p. 57, paraphrasing Spiegel and Waltz, 1971:454–474). Indeed, it is in the household, say feminist revealers, that the realist has honed his separation skills so that the impossible becomes the norm.

Richard Ashley (1981:214) argues that Morgenthau does leave room for statesmen and theorists to reinterpret the community tradition of realism in ways that reflect "the internal history of the community and its internalized context." Conceptions of man are part of that internalized context, but they are "concealed and for this reason never examined" because realism is autonomous from most community identities and interpretations. Again to quote Morgenthau (1965:103), "the great mass of the population is to a much greater extent the object of power than it is its wielder."[7] This view resonates with Antonio Gramsci's

[7] This means that realism features "a kind of dialogue that is echoed in many a male-dominant marriage . . . [wherein] the dependent female . . . is asked to maintain and adjust the intersubjective understandings, values, and ethics of the whole family in accord with the demands and opportunities emerging from the 'man's world'" (Ashley, 1984:225). Yet this gender imbalance in power casts doubt on Ashley's claim that the hermeneutic dialogue has been bounded by the addition of technical realism's stylized form and concerns; rather, parts of a potential dialogue are bounded by realism's internal gender concealments.

(1971:246) sense that a state achieving that delicate combination of consent and coercion associated with liberal hegemony becomes the outer ditch of civil society, its bureaucracy "the crystallization of the leading personnel – which exercises coercive power, and at a certain point becomes a caste."[8]

In the hidden Realist story of international relations, man is metaphorically fused to his state to form an entity celebratory of freedom in the world while obligated by social contract to protect nationals from international anarchy. The he-state draws some identity from multiple relational ties with the society under contract, but it also, and not insignificantly, identifies with other he-states operating in spaces beyond contracts. Relational autonomy embedded in the domestic sphere can thus square off against the "freedom" gained from anarchic international relations, and, in cases such as Italy during World War II, the USA in Vietnam, or the break up of the Soviet Union, relational autonomies at home can lose.

Schools of thought representing differences within Realism also maintain disconnections from noncaste populations and freedom from gender-aware interpretations. Hegemonic stability story suggests that international order is best ensured when one of the most heavily resourced states – truly the heroic individualist – assumes leadership and provides collective goods for otherwise conflictual sovereign states. It evokes the hegemonic mother of a boy's earliest memories and fears as the good state acting obligingly to rid a world to which it is connected of harmful vulnerabilities. Yet the hegemon conducts its relations at discrete and controlled points of contact through rule-governed and role-defined structures – regimes – within a competitive political framework where would-be defectors defer to the high costs of cheating (Kindleberger, 1973; also Gilpin, 1981). Moreover, "many of the gains from hegemony have been less in the line of collective goods than private ones, accruing primarily to the hegemon and thus helping maintain its hegemony" (Russett, 1985:208). Regime contracts thus tip the benefits toward already strong parties in a neurotic and inappropriate parody of mothering.

Tellingly confused autonomies and obligations also line *Man, the State, and War*, Kenneth Waltz's (1959) nearly neorealist celebration of an

[8] Robert Keohane (1984:32) points out that "[m]any Marxian interpretations of hegemony turn out to bear an uncanny resemblance to Realist ideas, using different language to make similar points."

anarchic state system.[9] There, state policies demonstrate interdependence along lines described in Rousseau's metaphor of the stag hunt. There is no automatic mechanism to adjust clashing interests, and so balances form in which the freedom of choice of any one state is limited by the actions of all others. Waltz simultaneously maintains that "pursuing a balance-of-power is still a matter of choice," and that "the alternatives are those of probable suicide on the one hand and the active playing of the power-politics game on the other" (p. 205). He also says, in a statement resonant with feminist psychoanalytic understandings of men's choiceless relations, that:

> the balance of power is not so much imposed by statesmen on events as it is imposed by events on statesmen. It is not to be eliminated by declamation but, if it is to be eliminated at all, by altering the circumstances that produce it. The circumstances are simply the existence of a number of independent states that wish to remain independent. Freedom is implied in the word "independence" but so is the necessity of self-reliance. (p. 209)

Waltz throws authorship of the balance "problem" on to abstract "events" man is simply forced to confront (as when a boy baby must confront the otherness of the mother's body). To alter the circumstances of balance of power requires that its analysts recognize false independence and autonomy. One cannot continue to assume that states exist prior to relationships they have been in, or that they manage to achieve autonomy from interdependencies that blur domestic and international boundaries (for example, from domestic banks that operate internationally or from women who work in support roles for international organizations). These old yarns leave states backed up defensively against domestic spaces, where women's experiences cast shadows across the lines, and forever facing "the residual zone of historical determinacy still to be brought under control in the name of reasoning man" (Ashley, 1989:286). As long as there are IR community concealments of the man in the state and his domestication of women, there is little likelihood that realists can correct state fantasies of independence. Everything gets stuck.

---

[9] Viotti and Kauppi (1987:599) define neorealism as "a label applied to those realists who are interested in explaining state behavior under conditions of anarchy and who emphasize the importance of the structure of the international system and how this influences and constrains state behavior. The term may also have negative connotations in the eyes of some critics who claim that the neorealists have neglected the importance of values and norms as stressed by earlier realists such as Hans Morgenthau."

In Waltz's (1979) *Theory of International Politics*, the anarchic dynamics of the system triumph and have an unchosen leveling effect on states, rendering those (id)entities functionally similar and somewhat predictable. Foundational sameness, we learn from feminist psychoanalytic writings, can enhance empathy. Indeed, to some (Keohane, 1989b:41), Waltz's neorealist states "determine their interests and strategies on the basis of calculations about their own positions in the system," and can find mutual predictable interest in formal associations or regimes. Neorealist associations, however, are arenas of defensive vigilance that tilt states in the direction of reactive autonomy. Waltz (1979:105) writes: "In a self-help system each of the units spends a portion of its effort, not in forwarding its own good, but in providing the means of protecting itself against others." The result is that "interdependence is always a marginal affair" (Waltz, 1970:206). Waltz's structure tames relational autonomy.

Robert Keohane accurately argues, I submit, that neorealism fails to take into account institutional characteristics of the system and therefore provides no way for the system of relations to change except when the capabilities of states change. To understand world politics, we must explore the ways institutions emerge and "affect incentives facing states" (Keohane, 1989b:11). In his account, regime formation is a process of cooperation "that involves the use of discord to stimulate mutual adjustment" (Keohane, 1984:46).[10] Through planning and negotiation, using a variety of resources, and calling upon pre-existing conventions, without which communication would be difficult, "decisions involving international regimes [become] in some meaningful sense voluntary" (Keohane, 1989b:104). Once regimes form, often "in the utilitarian social contract tradition" (p. 101), they can connect self-helpers by offering high quality information to policymakers and by developing norms of honesty and straightforwardness that participants can internalize to counter realist values.

State obligations initially chosen on the basis of specific reciprocities can metamorphose into "regime-supporting behavior[s deemed] ... beneficial to us even though we have no convincing evidence to that effect" (p. 114). The attainment of this diffuse reciprocity enables states

---

[10] At the time I first wrote, I hoped that this would not be Keohane's final statement on the issue, since in "International Relations Theory: Contributions of a Feminist Standpoint" (Keohane, 1989a) he raised questions about reciprocity that hint at cooperation through empathy. Yet, instead of elaborating these inchoate feminist ideas, Keohane later turned sulky about feminist IR (1998).

to "contribute one's share, or behave well toward others ... in the interests of continuing satisfactory overall results for the group of which one is a part, as a whole" (p. 146). Although Keohane notes that "diffuse reciprocity in the absence of strong norms of obligation exposes its practitioners to the threat of exploitation" (p. 149), his neoliberal institutionalist framework offers promising relational innovations.

But there is a dilemma built into it as well. Among *a priori* sovereign identities, each entity may be leery of decisions that could alter the structure of the system and undermine reactive autonomy (the British concern about a united Europe). Functionalists of old had an answer to such identity crises: put the matter in the hands of Lilliputian technocrats, who will enmesh Gulliver in unobtrusive relational ties. Under neoliberal institutionalism, sneaked interdependencies come alive but are quickly restrained: only after states reach a threshold of satisfaction with chosen obligations to one another (specific reciprocities) can they be tempted into diffuse reciprocity. Thus the neoliberal difference from realism is hidebound to realist vigilances. Unchosen obligation is tamed.

Other schools of thought in international relations base their prospects on similar unleashings and tamings. World order analysts, for instance, admonish us to break with state-centric understandings of power and interest; but some among them would replace that "reality" with an international society of "man" (Holsti, 1985:47).[11] Then there are deconstructors who reveal many concealed power moves in international relations but have yet to undertake systematic deconstructions of gender in realist literatures;[12] man thereby retains "his privileged place as the sole author and principal character in their stories" (Flax, 1990:226).

[11] This is Holsti's encapsulation of work in the World Order Models Project genre. WOMP literature evokes voices of the oppressed, including women, but has tended to espouse a humanist future, a term feminists find historically justifying of men-centered cultures. See Sylvester (1987). However, Walker (1988:xii) argues that "groups like WOMP, journals like *Alternatives*, as well as the work of peace researchers and alternative development groups, have provided some of the few spaces in which fundamental questions about the interconnected and global character of contemporary human life could be raised in a critical manner at all." That global civilization relies in part on women's struggles is a theme more evident in his *One World, Many Worlds* than in most previous world order writings.

[12] One notices an earnest, but none the less passing, nod at feminist concern in the special issue of *International Studies Quarterly*, edited by Ashley and Walker (1990a) on "Speaking the Language of Exile: Dissident Thought in International Studies." There, women are mentioned as suffering exile from professionalized international relations, but our dilemmas are not considered important enough to warrant article-length treatment by a feminist.

Although post-international relations theories are also promising, they likewise are not awake to the issue of gender in international relations. In one case the tropes of autonomy trot out to indicate how foreign activities undertaken by social groups in industrialized societies now pose "autonomy and interdependence [as] constituent aspects of the position held by social groups or their directing elites respectively in relation to the national-political actors" (Link, 1989:104). One looks in vain for women and men in these autonomous social groups and for notions of obligation that are less tied to calculated outcomes. One wonders whether this is another case of masculinity concealed in international (post-international, transnational) relations.[13]

In perusing vast realist literatures, even in this cursory way, feminist standpointers notice the recurrences of reactive autonomy and minimal obligations in ostensibly gender-free international relations. This is the quality that binds realism, neorealism, and neoliberal institutionalism to one another. What strategies can disorder and destabilize the entrenched concealments?

Women in the interstices of realist autonomy and obligation

At the intersections of theory and day-to-day realities of realist practice we can locate sites of women's struggles with, through, and against the reactively stuck state and the community of realism that theory both constructs and reflects. The sites and the struggles are empirically visible – Enloe has sighted them. And yet they are hidden from view when one engages in theoretical flights of freedom from obligations to the supporting actors of the drama. To reveal women's concrete struggles is to challenge the realist story of reactive autonomy and its corollary that gender is insignificant to international relations. It is to take up Sarah Brown's (1988:461) suggestion that "the proper object and purpose of the study of international relations is the identification and explanation of social stratification and of inequality as structured at the level of global relations." It is to join realism's experience-based castings of a field – its

---

[13] There is considerable room in James Rosenau's (1990:xiv) framework of postinternational relations to insert feminist standpoints on relational autonomy, because he seeks to move "beyond the interaction of states and...into the wellsprings of national and local politics as well as into the ways in which individual orientations and actions are translated into collective outcomes."

partialities orchestrated into the grand production – to other sites of experience and production.

The first site features activities complicit with realism that actually subvert the reign of reactive autonomy and disorder realist expectations. Fawn Hall is at this site, where she helps a realist engineer of foreign policy pursue his voluntary association with the Contras, and protects him from government agencies acting to reconnect him to the sphere of legal obligation. Her shreddings feed his fantasy of mastering history, something that eluded him during the Vietnam War, when "we were winning but the press was portraying our victories as defeats" (quoted in Morgan, 1989:174). Her testimonies before Congress uphold a heroic script of old realism enlivened by a patriotic man, and in her private choice of a Contra lover, she commingles the personal with the international in ways that are not supposed to figure into the world of realism. Hall's actions are ostensibly on the side of realist triumphs. But her relational autonomies within realism alienate her twice from the field she serves: first, from the realist state that seeks to tame her boss; and second, from the liberal realm of privacy that is supposedly the location of romantic secrets. At the same time she is twice obligated to realism – through her identification with North's division of sociality into us/them and insiders/outsiders, and through the Contra lover as heroic state in formation (adapted from Waltzer, 1970:221 and Morgan, 1989: chapter 2). Her actions do not change history, but they do reveal that the realist community is susceptible to internal subversions at the hands of loyal women. This is a crucial revealing if one is to recast realism as a partial view of the world.

At this site we can also identify diplomats' wives, who daily serve realist politics and have done so until recently in the absence of recognition. These unpaid servants of national interest create conditions of cosy relational autonomy. For men who incline towards reactivity in the diplomatic arena, their wives make the conduct of affairs of state sociable, and do so not because they are recruited by the state, but because the marriage contract carries the private obligations of servants into the public arena of conquerors. As a result of lobbying by the Association of American Foreign Service Wives, the US State Department in 1972 declared the foreign service wife a private person. This "new" status conflated her previous duties with a kind of ceremonial independence from them. Choiceless obligations in her wifely tasks did not end, because the sexual contract was still in force; but the end of liberal rights was served. This outcome underscores feminist cautions about the coop(t)erative potential of liberalism even as it reveals its realist-thumping potential (see Brown, 1988:461–464; Eisenstein, 1981).

The next site of women in international relations comes into view when we examine workplaces of the state in international relations. "Nearly ninety per cent of the secretaries and clerical personnel at the World Bank are women, but women occupy less than 3 per cent of its 'senior level' positions" (Enloc, 1989:120). In 1984 the female staff at the United Nations "made up more than half of the Secretary General's staff, but held only 22.3 per cent of the professional international civil-service posts, as compared with 83 per cent of its clerical and secretarial jobs" (p. 121). How can women be so nonrecognizable within organizations that exist to tame uncooperative aspects of the realist world?

We might begin by following Pateman's (1988) lead in suggesting that the sexual contract underlying liberal theory simply makes its way into international contracts negotiated by realist states, as do other dominance-subordination relations; for example, the formerly contracted terms of colonialism are the basis of today's North–South statuses. It is also possible, from a feminist psychoanalytic view, that relationally trained women accept lower professional positions in the hope that their contributions will advance the interests of the group (the organization) as a whole and will be reciprocated in due time. A diffusely cooperative sense of obligation does not work, however, in contexts where a field of study and its community of practitioners recognize no particular obligations to women and to their characteristic ways of relating. The regimists are "free" to operate inside international organizations under the self-interested norms of their realist masters. Diffuse reciprocators, who behave in more generously obligated ways, become exploited.

Keohane (1989b:150) argues that "repayment of political and economic debts in a strictly bilateral context may increase confidence, enabling actors to take a broader view of their common interests." Payment of debts to women regime workers would, by this logic, nurture a (gender-bilateral) practice of common obligation. Notwithstanding a Coordinator for the Improvement of the Status of Women in the Secretariat of the United Nations, and attention to women during the United Nations Decade for Women, the debts remain largely unpaid. When gender is considered, neoliberal institutionalist theory is only partially helpful in understanding regimes. To bring women in, however, could transform rather than modify that theory.[14]

At a third site in international relations, women give up on liberal struggles against the liberal-realist oppressor and embrace post-hegemonic processes aimed at promoting transformed rather than reciprocated obligations. Their actions feature what Hirschmann (1992: chapter 6, 2-3, typescript) refers to as "working out the content of obligations within the context of connection ... [rather than attempting] to predefine feminist obligation ... in the standard fashion of analytic philosophy." The connections are with women, and that move acknowledges the importance of bringing absent presences into theory and practice, not simply in the sense of "allowing voices to express themselves [as women advocacy groups in international regimes do] but helping them realize their expression, and attempting to see and understand the world from these other perspectives" (chapter 6, 6).

Enloe briefly mentions one such case in relationships between women soldiers and military wives across boundaries of realist military practice. The basis of this defiance of convention is, ironically, the realist state's unconventional invitation to women soldiers to be more than the absent or protected ones of yore, while designating them as less than military men in the tasks they can perform. Military women emerge in between to assume highly technological support tasks in a military suffering the effects of too few good men. As they respond to these liberal "opportunities," some women find more in common with wives than with insider career peers. There is a certain choicelessness woven into their context, and in that choicelessness is an opportunity to rescript the type of military–civilian autonomy that has long prevented military people from crossing lines of status.

Women's peace encampments of the 1980s also occupied this site, taking a hand in revealing realist security as permeable and oppressive. Their efforts took shape in response to contracts forged between the USA and its European allies to bring new nuclear weapons to already

---

[14] In order for the theory truly to distinguish itself from realism, it would have to break from a convention of cooperative autonomy in realist international relations to which it also subscribes. This convention rehearses "anarchy" as a necessary prerequisite for rational action in international relations. If the crutch of cooperative autonomy were kicked away, diffuse reciprocity would be revealed as the acceptance of similarities between elite men as the basis of the "group," for the good of which regimes form. Recast the "group" and the implications for regimes and their chroniclers could be profound. See Sylvester (1994a).

missile-clogged countries. Some women, who supposedly have no agency in international relations, protested these contracts in ways that demonstrated the weaknesses of nuclear defenses: they public(ized) the private movements of US "secret" convoys carrying cruise missiles to points of deployment throughout the UK; they mixed the metaphors of war and peace by painting peace signs on convoy trucks and putting implements of domesticity (potatoes) up truck exhaust pipes; and they climbed into convoy vehicles and rode along with autonomous military men (Kirk, 1989a:11).

In the process of formulating such strategies, encampers developed nonhierarchical, nonlinear, and nonreciprocal methods of decision making to anticipate "a simple, peaceful, postnuclear society" (p. 11). Their methods were not bereft of discord nor were their strategies totally new; but neither were these activists beholden to received conventions:

> At the peace camp each woman does what she thinks is necessary, so there are no rosters or lists of who has to do what ... This is very unfamiliar to some people, who exclaim in frustration, "why don't they *organize* something?" To their credit, women at the camp have not given in to this demand but have created a space that allows many women to ask instead, "What do *I* want to do?" Some feel alienated and do not return, but others become much more autonomous and effective than they would if they merely followed other people's directives. (Kirk, 1989b: 264)

In a more realist context, a situation of every woman doing what she thinks is necessary would suggest that each was a victim of anarchic structure and had to rely on self-help strategies until conventions and then contractual agreements could bring stable relations. Indeed, some camp women recount how in the absence of rule-governed behaviors at the Seneca Women's Peace Camp, a free-rider problem emerged; "suckers" ended up doing more work, thereby experiencing burnout and resentment (Schwartz-Shea and Burrington, 1990), even though the logic of the exercise was to recast politics instead of rehearsing old rules of organization. Free-riding, though, also produced some innovative decision-making procedures:

> The meeting started out with hard-line opposing views and consensus seemed unlikely. But acting on the suggestion of a participant to break into smaller circles of like opinion, including a middle-ground group, and create a circle within a circle, each group taking its turn, the discussion proceeded. Without fear of judgement now, because speaking

with those with whom we felt most at ease – while the others listened in. And so speaking more deeply than before. When we formed one large circle again, the talk was no longer strained ... And consensus, to the astonishment of all, I think, was reached easily.

(Linton, 1989:243)

A meeting such as that, recorded in such "strange" incoherent language, differs both from the realist bargaining environment, with its "free-riders" and "suckers," and from what Hirschmann (1992: chapter 6, 7, typescript) describes as "liberal dialogue." She says: "Liberal dialogue of political theory is an interaction of two totally separate individuals who have particular points of view and try to win by convincing the other person: it again replicates the struggle for recognition, to have your views recognized without recognizing the other." The Seneca meeting model features, instead, a conversation that proceeds from the assumption that "people will really listen to what others say, will attempt to incorporate those views into themselves, and indeed become somewhat transformed by that incorporation" (chapter 6, 8). Such techniques provide spaces for political action in between reactive and relational autonomies, in between chosen and unchosen obligations. They do not banish all problems of sociality, such as "free-riding," because women who come to adulthood following relational scripts may rebel against them as restrictive; or, suffering the ill-effects of systematic denigrations of relationship, women may take care not to caretake. The peace camps were real arenas of sociality rather than restricted places of coercive contracts (entailing the punishment of defectors) or of impossible goody-goodyism.

When women peace campers stepped into agency in international relations – often taking their children with them – the outer ditch was threatened with having neither defenders nor defense against such insubordinating tactics. Women should form more "strange" conversations at the fence of realist defense, including conversations with diplomats' wives, women serving in national militaries, and women caught in regimes. A messy and surely unrul(y) alliance such as this would demonstrate generalized commitment to a different "group" than realist theory recognizes. Women's politically significant relationships would help develop obligation across different standpoints based on listening to what "others" to realism say about international relations. Theory written from various points within this alliance would undoubtedly rattle realism's cage.

Another recasting

The exercise of revealing concealed sites of women's struggles in, with, and against liberal-realist international relations shows not only that men and women are already connected to the field. It also shows that realism is simultaneously ordered and disordered by women's activities in relation to the activities of masculine theorists, states, and organizations. Reinscribers of realist international relations must note simultaneous power directions and read them back to their homeplaces and ahead to their outlets (Enloe, 1989:196). Consider what happens to one neorealist analysis when its gender concealments are methodologically read in that way.

Zeev Maoz (1989) argues that when a strong state enhances its power by acquiring extra resources, it may end up losing control over outcomes. This happened to Turkey during the Balkan wars of 1912–1913 and to Israel after its invasion of Lebanon in 1982. Added resources enabled such states to do things they could not have done previously, and this altered their preference structure and the stakes for other self-helping states. The resource inferiors then ganged up against the newly superior states in order to limit further power-aggrandizing activities.

Women are nonrecognized resources for realist states, ranking with oil, geography, industrial capacity, and military preparedness as potential contributors to national power. When an already strong state seeks more power by appropriating more women to its cause – as the United States might be perceived to have done by sending mothers to the Persian War front – what might be the international consequences? What are the results when the United States continuously taps into the voluntarism of women living around its overseas military bases in order to comfort its troops? What types of women-aggrandizing actions reorder strong state preferences, and when, if ever, do such power moves become worthy of disordering confrontations by "inferior" states? Are we talking across levels of analysis inappropriately, or do such levels serve to mask the complicated relationships that deny national power variables their autonomy?

Some precedents exist in international relations for gang-ups against people–aggrandizing state behaviors. When the Soviet state tried appropriating Jewish citizens to itself by preventing their ease of emigration in the 1970s, strong and less strong states (Israel) ganged up against it. Their response may be explained by many factors, including the high levels of education found among many seeking to leave the Soviet Union.[15] What about contexts in which the ganging-up states have little hope of, or little to gain by, appropriating the victims for themselves? Do they still "see" the resource appropriation and calculate it as potentially productive of new and dangerous priorities? Do they still gang up?

When the South African state repeatedly appropriated rural black women as a social security service for migrant laborers, this aggrandizement was not interpreted by anti-apartheid states as a state effort to free up funds for other power moves. When black men were detained without trial, or after trials of dubious validity, however, a moderate ganging-up cry could be heard in the capitals of Europe and North America. The freeing of Nelson Mandela was the *cause célèbre*, not campaigns to free women from servitude to the white power state, even though few ganging-up states would seek to appropriate Mandela for their own power.

On the one hand, none of this is unexpected. It took a female member of the European Parliament to see that the multilaterally negotiated Multi-Fiber Agreement (MFA) would "allow multinational companies to exploit women" (Ashworth, 1988:499). Why would unilateral power moves against women come to anyone's notice? Indeed, "systematic violence against women is treated as 'customary' or as a 'private matter,' and thus immune to international condemnation" (Peterson, 1990:305). Women are seemingly not resources of the state because women-autonomous realists do not name them as such. On the other hand, revealing women as resources shows that Maoz's thesis is partial and perhaps inaccurate unless he can explain why this resource does not fit predictions based on other types of resources. Future research needs to specify the types of resource appropriations that can lead a strong state to lose control over outcomes.

But let us not stop with this point. Rather let us play out Maoz's IR logic on feminist rather than realist terms. Let us call the "inferior" actors feminist organizations and theorists and the "strong" actors realist theorists and states. Maoz (1989:246) claims that strong actors can lose control over outcomes by failing "to attribute to opponents the ability to adjust their strategies to an environment in which they become increasingly inferior." From the foregoing analysis, it is clear that

---

[15] I am grateful to Eileen Crumm for this point.

realist efforts to appropriate wives for the foreign service resulted in a movement by equality-minded women to gang up on several offending strong states, primarily the United States and Great Britain. Similarly, instead of acting as proper "base women"– offering succor to US troops in the United Kingdom – Greenham Common women dashed the convention of realist womanhood. That Enloe then revealed both cases and others for all to read shows that women-appropriating actions by states may be disordered by ganging-up activities at the cusp of that infamous domestic/international dichotomy. Perhaps the Maoz argument can be redeemed by sighting and siting more players and resources within international relations.

Feminists and women strugglers might not win theory in the decisive ways realists find significant; after all, Greenham Common women did not prevail on their own against theater nuclear weapons in the UK. If one stands at the nexus of the win/lose dichotomy, however, one can lose the effort to command international relations and win new self-confidence and political skills for future international challenges. To think in terms of absolute success or failure, of theory take-overs versus realist retrenchments, is to be governed by the reactively autonomous habit of establishing identity against and in opposition to others. It is also to reinforce realist international relations as a totality to be supplanted completely, rather than as a partial reality to be filled out by the standpoints of women.

A chorus of concluding objections

The "theories we use to understand and explain the world of international politics [are] not divorced from who does the theorizing" (Holsti, 1985:viii) and the practice. Until now, an assortment of realisms have dominated the theoretical and practical aspects of international relations, projecting a certain sense of autonomy on to larger playing fields while denying that gender suits up at all. Feminist standpoint epistemology, reflecting feminist psychoanalytic theorizing, usefully reveals hidden conceptions of man in realism, alerts us to a community in reactive autonomy from women, and helps locate theory-subverting activities inside IR.

A standpoint feminist, however, can anticipate a bevy of complaints about this exercise. First, there could be the cry of confounded levels of analysis in moving from individuals to states, from infant gendering to social theory, from Chiquita Banana, perhaps, to WTO. Gendering lessons in infancy and youth must be separated from phenomena associated with the abstract level of the international system. This particular concern, though, illustrates reactive autonomy in the practices of science. Concern to separate phenomena into discrete and independent categories of analysis leads to artificial islands of sociality that can only be reattached through statistical bridging mechanisms. Research that questions the accuracy of separability assumptions may reveal that the warning cry of ecological fallacy – Confound Not the Levels of Analysis – masks interconnected power relations. Hirschmann, Pateman, and Enloe implicitly unravel the conventional prohibition against juxtaposing levels of analysis to reveal a power text and to carve out some space for more accurate social theory.

Second, IR could argue that the feminist standpoint approach jumps the gender-blind tracks of mainstream theory and takes off in a biased, pro-women, opposite direction. The issue, though, is bigger than women vs men since gender meanings and relations are subject to historical change and therefore are indeterminate (Riley, 1988). IR might be difficult to sort out by *any* single inherited subject status, be it state, organization, gender, class, or race. Moreover, since psychoanalytic thinking is a western metanarrative that sweeps everyone into one mold of human being without concern for cultural difference, its guiding logics may offer ethnocentric foundations for feminist standpoint thinking. Feminist postmodernist arguments with standpoint thinking lead us to the view that we do not want to author a new script to replace the old realist one. What we all need is some sensitivity to relational autonomies as a way of halting ritualized reactive strivings.

All these arguments warn against old and new ethnocentricities presented as the truth. In proceeding with feminist IR, it behoves us to investigate a wide range of locally understood autonomies and obligations and to use them to recast "our" world, "refus[ing] to see *all* right and good on one side only" (Elshtain, 1987:257). A more modest project calls for skepticism toward bandwagoning standpoints that would smite that realist (or, from a Realist perspective, the misguided postmodernist) with the certainty of an emperor. It foregrounds autonomies and obligations by focusing on sited struggles rather than stereotypes about what is relational and what is reactive.

We need not shatter the realist window in the course of this exercise, because constructs such as "reciprocity" instruct us about conditions that may inspire some groups to exit relationships, reject caring rescriptings, and/or manipulate agreements. We do need to explain to those who want us to replace realism with something else, however, that we are not talking about talking about feminist international relations. We are adding a new set of methods and partial views to the picture. The revelations, though "strange," are realist-disordering and space-opening – for women, theory, and alternative practice.

10 Some dangers in merging feminist and peace projects

Here is a plunge into and around war via siting issues of feminism, women's identities, and peace. I ask: are women peace-loving? Can we build peace projects on the backs of women more so than men? Feminists have taken sides on this issue for at least sixteen years. Standpoint feminism, which anchors social theory to women's gendering experiences and daily activities, often suggests that aspects of women's lives render them less aggressive than men and less likely to support wars. Feminist postmodernism, chary of sharp characterizations of "women," insists that gender traits are not authentic so much as discursively repetitive about which bodies belong where doing what. "Some Dangers" compares the two feminist ways of considering the women question around feminist peace concerns, and comes away appreciative of postmodern skepticisms *vis-à-vis* maternal standpoint thinking.

Nancy Hirschmann's (1992) psychoanalytic version of standpoint thinking, in which adult gender inclinations tend to reflect preconscious attachments and differentiations of body identity reinforced by social instruction, still stands as one of the best. There is danger, however, in predicting adult behavior from pre-adult influences or in suggesting that men and women everywhere have imbibed the same early gendering lessons. It is thus unwise for feminists to assign peace to women on the basis of gender-reinforcing links to a similar-sex mother (to say nothing of instances in which mother is a man). Jean Elshtain, herself a maternal feminist (among other things), shows us war and peace sewn together around war and its narrative assignments. In fact, many of the women she sights have been caught up in enthusiasms of armed civic virtue. Enloe regularly catches women wearing khaki. The history of the western women's movement offers instances of feminist "wars" between 1970s radicals, liberals, Marxists, and socialists. There are wars in our own families. Why, then, would we anchor women in peace?

To pursue this question further, I read peace feminist Betty Reardon's *Sexism and the War System* (1985) and compared its points and methods with those of Sandra Harding's more postmodernist side-taking in *The Science Question in Feminism* (1986). Reardon has it that women and men share positive and negative characteristics, including a positive concern for peace. She wants to base a feminist peace project on the positive peace potential harbored in men and, from her feminist standpoint perspective, activated mostly by feminist women. Harding sees dangers in striving for a coherent project – for peace or for anything else – based on presumed truths about human attachments, ways of knowing, and shared values. There is a particular message for IR in this older debate. Marysia Zalewski (1995) asks: "Well, What is the Feminist Perspective on Bosnia?" Some scholars in IR think feminism is a monolith and therefore has "a" position on everything, including peace. Comparative feminist discussions dispel that myth.

I have tampered with the essay that follows to remove passé illustrations, but the main point remains: it is important to avoid amalgamating seemingly like-minded subjects, movements, and theories if in doing so we risk erasing, benignly tolerating, or ignoring different modalities of being and knowing (also Sylvester, 1993c, 1993d). IR could work harder to site feminist contributions on the peace issue within its agendas – by disputing varied feminist claims, citing their wisdoms, or making gender in war and (democratic) peace research explicit.

* * *

> Feminists and peace researchers are currently faced with what I argue is a crucial choice in the development of human knowledge and human society. Whether they choose (as I argue they should) to merge their perspectives, modes of inquiry, and strategies for action or to continue on their distinctly separate but significantly parallel paths can make a profound difference in both epistemology, and politics – particularly the politics of transformation. (Reardon, 1985:1)

> At this point, I need to remind the reader that from the theoretical perspective of this study, tensions, contradictions, and ambivalences within and between theories are not always bad. Coherent theories in an obviously incoherent world are either silly and uninteresting or oppressive and problematic, depending upon the degree of hegemony

they manage to achieve. Coherent theories in an *apparently* coherent world are even more dangerous, for the world is always more complex than such unfortunately hegemonous theories can grasp.

(Harding, 1986:164)

Betty Reardon's interest in merging feminism and peace research into a more coherent successor to the science, structures, and practices of war underlies her stimulating treatise on *Sexism and the War System.* Sandra Harding's concern to resist obvious temptations to resolve theoretical ambivalences in feminism through a search for coherence echoes throughout her important contribution on *The Science Question in Feminism.* Both books might be considered required reading for all who strive to give coherence and practicality to their concern for global peace, and who often tacitly believe that women are more peaceable than men. These are also useful texts for pundits of IR to ponder, for they suggest something about the engines that keep various war enterprises and peace protests going.

Harding writes in the postmodern vein. She offers a posture of skepticism about any approach to epistemology that offers one true study of women, one essentialized feminine standpoint, or, more generally – to use Jane Flax's words (cited in Harding, 1986:27–28) – "a universal (or universalizing claim) about the existence, nature and powers of reason, progress, science, language and the 'subject/self.'" Hewing to "correct" behaviors often induces resistance to the power of assignment and emplacement; or there is the disappointment of being unable to be "true," owing to competing claims on one's energies and identities.

Reardon's perspective is more eclectic. She argues that there is something called feminine authenticity, and that concern for peace is part of being an authentic woman. This position suggests that a self-evident feminine nature exists and can be valorized as a positive force for change. She believes that "good" science is a good methodological vehicle for uncovering the truths of nature: the self-evident can be proved. There is also a streak of conservative postfeminism in her argument that a more peaceful world will promote human wholeness and eclipse the need for a separate, possibly divisive, women's movement. Amidst arguments that pull in several directions, Reardon looks for positive coherence from a reconciliation of feminism and peace studies that can transform two coherently negative, interconnected projects – sexism and the war system.

Revised from: *Alternatives: Social Transformation and Humane Governance*, 12, 4, 1987. Copyright © 1987 by Alternatives. Used with permission of The World Order Model Project and Lynne Rienner Press, Inc.

I argue here that there are too many healthy ambiguities surrounding women and what they are, and within feminist theories about them, for there to be any healthy reconciliation of feminist and peace projects. There are theoretical differences concerning the nature of women's experiences and differences of view among "real women" about violence. With women's identities increasingly crowded and fractured, arguments on behalf of a merged feminist/peace project may seem coherent but too simple, compelling but revelatory of only some varieties of feminism, well-intentioned but potentially tyrannical.

A case for merging feminist and peace projects

Reardon argues that women often are standard-bearers of peace, their antimilitarism setting the tone and influencing the strategies of groups such as the Greens, Women's Pentagon Action, Greenham Common, The Women for Peace Movement, and The Peace People. These activist women "represent the systematic, inevitable emergence (often sparked by desperation) of feminine private values into the masculine public sphere" (Reardon, 1985:61). Their efforts, however, yield only partial recognition. Male-dominated peace research and world order studies omit women from their purview, marginalize them by focusing more on the horrors of nuclear warfare than on those of rape, or simply fail to attract peace women to masculinist-oriented research enterprises – such as the World Order Models Project – in the same numbers as men. Reardon argues that by broadening peace research to be responsive to women, theories and projects of peace will be enriched. The very process of merging the two projects will bring changes in interpersonal relations that, if replicated on a global level, could move the species toward an attainable and just peace free of direct and structural forms of violence.

Reardon's proposed merger would join the "acceptable" components only in the range of gendered human values. Acceptable values are "positive." Held by men and women in common, though in different forms, these promote noncoercive power relations among sexes, nations, and social groups. Paraphrasing Irma Garcia Chafardet, Reardon (1985:3) writes that positive values are not just better guidelines for living than negative values. They are more authentically human:

> The positive values derive from the authentic attributes and are those that are conducive to the full realization of the human potential in both individuals and society. The negative values derive from the distorted attributes and are those that stifle and crush portions of human and

social development. They are the values that underlie stereotypes and rationalize discrimination and oppression.

Positive masculine values derive from early gender lessons that teach boys to be properly objective, abstract, and structural in their concern for peace, economic wellbeing, social justice, and ecological balance. Positive feminist values reveal women's lessons in interpersonal relations, connection, and, by implication, affective (emotional and intuitive) rationality. Included are concern for diversity, cooperation, caring, equality, fairness, and love. Under the authenticity argument, all these values are expressions of experiences that lie buried or ignored under layers of social distortion.

Feminine positive values are most in need of recovery and revalorization, not only because they have been the most systematically denigrated, but because they hold the key to successful peace projects. Only these gendered values can effectively reveal the violence of sexism as well as the war-prone structures and practices that merchants of inauthentic experience – the men and women who march to the drumbeats of such negative values as dominance, competition, hierarchy, and control – champion. The infusion of positive feminine values can fill empty spaces in positive masculine analyses, where male peace researchers have had a hard time siting women.

Positive gender attributes guide the currently separate projects of the women's movement and the peace movement. The international women's movement strives to bring "women's participation and perspectives into the spheres of politics, intellectual activities, the economy, and society in general" (Reardon, 1985:24). The international peace movement strives to transform large, impersonal structures of the war system to maximize abstract human values. Feminism can bridge the two because, while promoting understanding of women's subjugation and working to end it, feminists also "insist that women need not adopt or manifest masculine values and behaviors to assert equality, nor do they devalue feminine characteristics, values, and capacities" (p. 20).

The actual political logistics of the merger are vague. Presumably, there is a noisy and conflictual, but ultimately coherent and nonviolent, dialogue undertaken by representatives of the two projects. Discussions culminate in a new discourse and successor project that resembles but outstrips existing peace and feminist enterprises. It is useful to think of Reardon's successor feminist/peace project as capable of attaining hegemony and becoming "a minimally coercive synthesis of intellectual and moral leadership which, through ideology, becomes the organic cement unifying an historical bloc" (Laclau and Mouffe, 1985:67). On the road to hegemony, there is considerable personal change, sharing of an ensemble of ideas and values, and projections of noncoercive change on to the larger political agendas of international relations. The process also requires struggle to bring down offensive structures and achieve "the conditions of justice and equity necessary for the absence of war" (Reardon, 1985:63). It does not, however, require the exercise of collective or individual violence and warriorism. Even to use the words of war is to reinforce thought processes that contribute to the war system. Thus, nowhere in *Sexism and the War System* does Reardon suggest that violence, armed battle, or warlike abstractions are authentic.

Reardon's contradictions go to the heart of differences within feminism on how to conceptualize, study, and overturn the foundations of androcentric thinking and behavior. Those inclined to label values as positive and negative follow in the Enlightenment legacy of establishing categories and assigning lesser and greater characteristics to them. Here, negative values signify false consciousness *vis-à-vis* higher-placed positive attributes that are truly human. It is difficult to reconcile species unity with gender difference in this mode of thought, unless one category is subordinated to the other. Unity around peace values could cancel out lived experiences that produce varied vocabularies and standpoints on what is authentic and eventually peaceful. Reardon tries to get around this by calling positive values authentic and seeing concern for peace as part of the often hidden, but none the less "true" and permanent, story of masculine and feminine aspiration.

But there is tension at the fulcrum. To uncover that story and overcome dualisms, which have elevated men to positions over women and fostered war science over peace, Reardon momentarily privileges feminists. She thinks feminism promotes more interpersonal politics than even peace-loving men can usually manage and, therefore, will provide the means to turn abstract ideals into real programs. But feminism worries her too because it divides along various lines of reasoning about women and seems incapable of humanist resolution. Reardon's dilemma is not hers alone. Feminists have paused many times around the question of whether reason is friend or foe of women. Di Stefano (1986:1) explains:

> As the beneficiaries, feminists have proceeded as the rebellious and yet still dutiful daughters to develop criticism aimed at the

less-than-rational justifications for sexism in modern Western culture. As the victims, we have protested against the assumption that every woman should want to become an ascetic version of the Everyman, and for a new vocabulary of reason, identity, and politics. Most of us, I suspect, identify simultaneously with the victim and the beneficiary, and have adopted the strategies and outlook of both, singly and in combination, to combat sexism and advance the interests of women.

Reardon hopes humanist reason will prevail over feminist rebellions against good, authentic outcomes. She says:

> Feminism, as it is used here, is one component of a wider humanism conceived as opposition to oppression. It is a belief system that opposes all forms and manifestations of sexism, seeks to abolish them, and assumes that such abolition requires the full and equitable integration of women into all spheres of human activity. Collaterally, it includes the belief that such integration is also necessary to abolish the war system. (Reardon, 1985:25-6)

Reardon's struggle to reconcile feminism and peace projects thus reveals a master move: the merger rests on a stereotypical self-sacrificing act by feminists. They are leaders of a new discourse and project; indeed their efforts seem to be indispensable to it. In the end, though, a leading/caretaking feminism spills its wisdom into a hegemony of humanism and happily expires. Put differently, feminists eagerly lead the death march of their own movement. There are no women warriors running amok to argue against collective self-immolation in the name of "a" species good. That is, there are eventually no nonpeaceful, feminist identities to inspire war on aspects of the humanist establishment that may deny women power – as energy, capacity, competence, and effectiveness of individuals and communities (Hartsock, 1985). There are no rebellious feminists creating dangerous, disorderly, and somewhat irrational orders within the order (Hartsock, 1982). Rather, contemporary feminists, not themselves Everymen, find the formula to construct Him.

Another way to look at the merger

Harding's *The Science Question in Feminism* does not address Reardon's arguments directly. It presents a sustained discussion of reasons why reconciliatory projects, such as Reardon advocates, could be ill advised.

Harding (1986) supports feminist empiricist efforts to bring women into scientific inquiry because she is critical of science as currently an androcentric activity. Science claims to be objective and nongendered in its procedures and techniques and yet builds in aspects of white, professional men's emphasis on rationality and inclination to compartmentalize knowledge. Readers need only think of the assumptions underlying dependent and independent variables to see her point: one variable (voting) is explained by (correlated to) the other (sex) as if the two were entirely separate and isolated phenomena rather than historically codetermined or at least interactive. The idea that women can develop their ways of knowing into "a" feminist standpoint – "a morally and scientifically preferable grounding for our interpretations and explanations of nature and social life" (p. 26) – is not one she embraces either in *The Science Question*. She argues that there is not necessarily one true story of womanhood to struggle for but rather fractured identities that give rise to exhilaratingly plural standpoints on the world.

Harding's position differs considerably from Reardon's. The originality of her feminist postmodernist view applied to issues of women and peace can be appreciated if we contrast it with single-standpoint arguments.

Feminist standpoint perspectives

"Somehow living/longing through, above, before, and beyond it, thousands of women struggle to re-member ourselves and our history, to sustain and intensify a biophilic consciousness": Mary Daly (1984:ix) quests to re-member what she terms the Lusty Wanderers of the Realms of Pure Lust and to separate them from the demonic attackers of Aggression and Obsession. Historical linguistics is her vehicle for recovering what she posits as essential in the experience of women. She reclaims words such as spinster, shrew, hag, and bitch from derogatory masculinist usage and reconstructs women through them as lusty weavers and spinners who shrewdly connect the universe. Daly's nature-based approach is not the only way of conceptualizing standpoint. Some literary critics habitually referred to as French have a view of *la différence féminine* expressed in metaphors or poetic modes of speech ("the poetic task is a maternal pursuit" [Irigaray, 1984:27]) and/or in the body of women ("the essence of femininity lies in the womb" [Cixous, 1980:122]). They look for the foundations of shared standpoint in the common bodily forms and activities that comprise sexual difference. Object-relations theorists, such as Nancy Chodorow (1978) and Dorothy Dinnerstein (1976), postulate that women have a sense of connectedness – a fundamental discomfiture with dualisms – owing to experiences of individuation that begin in infancy.

214

Standpoint approaches take on explicit maternal tones in the works of feminists who oppose militarism. Dinnerstein (1976) suggests that because masculine gender identity forms in opposition to the mother, men tend to create elaborate rules of social interaction that substitute for genuine interest in and connection with people. Out of this separation comes the possibility of, if not the actual taste for, impersonal projects of war. By contrast, Sara Ruddick (1983:479) suggests that women are less prone to warlike abstractions and soldierly behaviors because they learn special lessons in their mother's houses:

> Women are daughters who learn from their mothers the activity of preservative love and the maternal thinking that arises from it. These "lessons" from her mother's house, can shape a daughter's intellectual and emotional life even if she rejects the activity, its thinking, or, for that matter, the mother herself. Preservative love is opposed in its fundamental values to military strategy. Maternal theories of conflict are more pacifist than militaristic. A daughter, one might say, has been trained to be unsoldierly.

Maternal imagery recurs in the writings and activities of feminist peace-seekers. Birgit Brock-Utne (1985:73–82) ponders the challenges mothers face when they try to intervene in the gendering process to counteract masculine, violent, and competitive behaviors in their sons. Shibokusa women in Japan disrupt military exercises under the rationale that "we are strong because we are close to the earth and we know what matters" (Caldecott, cited in Brock-utne 1985:57). As for biologically childless mothers imparting lessons in preservative love, the late Mother Teresa stands as an ultimate teacher.

A few standpoint feminists argue that women whose behaviors contradict maternal and/or deep psychological concerns for connectedness suffer from false consciousness. Just as Reardon relegates anti-peace activities by women to the sphere of negative values, confirmed peacekeeper Brock-Utne (p. 33) finds that "women who 'succeed' in the patriarchal societies of today are usually not very different from men: they would not be allowed top positions if they were." That the climb is fraught at every ring, or that it is accompanied by ambiguities and ambivalences within a mother's head (Friday, 1977) or behaviors can be problematic for standpoint theorists to explain. Moreover, differences of race, class, age, national experience, occupation, and religion can unify into "a" standpoint only by assuming that individuation experiences, mothering, and being daughters in mother's houses are more common determinants of women's "real" orientations than are aspects of social positionality. In her moments as a standpoint theorist, Reardon falls into the empiricist-cum-standpoint trap of nearly invalidating the experiences of women who exhibit different values than the ones she asserts as authentic. She places these on the wrong side of a constructed positive–negative dualism.

Harding (1986:189) suggests that "we should expect differences in cognitive styles and worldviews from peoples engaged in different kinds of social activities." Without this recognition, politically charged macro-theories feed repressive intolerance for deviations from a norm. Thus, if the "true" story does not fit the woman, something is wrong with her. If she disagrees with a politics of feminist harmony (or more recently in the 1990s, with a feminist politics of difference [Sylvester, 1995a]), she can be labeled anti-feminist or inappropriate in her analyses; or she can be "given space," which is to say she can be encouraged *and* ignored. These women are not necessarily part of the problem of war and sexism. Harding (1986:193) argues that "if there can be 'a' feminist standpoint, it can only be whatever emerges from the political struggles of 'oppositional consciousness' – oppositional precisely to the longing for 'one true story' and 'the culturally dominant forces of unitarianism'" (p. 247) that lead us to believe there is such a thing.

A plethora of standpoints

In lieu of authentic standpoint, we might conceptualize a plethora of feminist standpoints, each reflecting aspects of the differing lived experiences and multiple fractured identities women have in the contemporary era, and the many political struggles to which these identities give rise. There are western-middle-class-mother-feminist-peace activists and Zimbabwean-peasant-mothers-postcolonialist-trade unionists-ex-guerrillas. International conferences demonstrate that when western feminists ignore important differences between women in the name of solidarity, they face strong resistance from Third World women. Recognition of differences, therefore, leads to a notion of solidarity that means "fidelity to certain parameters of dissonance within and between the assumptions of these discourses" (Harding, 1986:246). It rests on a certain foundational incoherence that could be prematurely resolved or remedied through any merger of "a" feminist project with "a" peace project.

This is a position with which Reardon and those who link women with peace could be uncomfortable. Reardon (1995:68-69) says that

> many Euro-American feminists are perceived by Marxist and Third World feminists as being themselves part of the problem, because they fail to challenge the global political and economic structures that oppress the Third World. Their refusal to accept capitalism as the major oppressing force and to analyze women's oppression as a class problem is a point of contention with Marxist feminists. Unless some resolution can be reached, such perceived conflicts of interest can be a serious obstacle to the achievement of the preferred worlds of all concerned.

For her, incoherence is "a commonly experienced stage in the 'conscientization' of most oppressed groups and a necessary, though not sufficient, component of the analysis of any case of oppression" (p. 69). But it should not persist: "I believe that the prolongation of that stage is a potentially destructive fixation, one that could impede significant social change" (p. 24). In streams of postmodernism, by contrast, representatives of multiple standpoints sustain their contradictions (Ferguson, 1993) or seek to decide rather than derive ways of knowing through democratic processes (Brown, 1991).

There is obviously considerable difference of opinion among feminists as to the proper way to understand women's experiences. The maternal single-standpoint thinkers offer a strong and welcome perspective on women and peace that has hitherto been excluded from masculine peace studies. Other theorists point to additional aspects of women's experiences that have not been considered in scientific research. In postmodernist approaches, difference of opinion is a reason for an aware cacophony that dissembles any notion of authentic feminism. Absent a single standpoint, the shame-on-you-Margaret-Thatcher style of feminism looks lame. Women disagreeing with but respecting other women, without knee-jerk appeals to consensus or angry charges of ill will, is aware cacophony.

Considering women warrior standpoints

At the fulcrum of feminism and peace, the challenge is to consider many plausible relationships between women, struggle, and peace. As a start, it might be useful to name and come to terms with women who are not uniformly positive on nonviolence. Numerous Third World women have contributed to national liberation movements around the world. In the Zimbabwean armed struggle alone, women comprised "about one

217

third of the Zimbabwe African National Liberation Army (ZANLA)" (Mugabe, cited in Lapchick and Urdang, 1982:101) and about 2150 in the army of the Zimbabwe African People's Union (ZAPU) (Ngwenya, cited p. 106). Many women elsewhere are part of urban police forces and national militaries. Others join violent protests (recently against the IMF/World Bank), or engage in Greenham Common-like sabotage on behalf of women. Women work within violent paradigms. How can we make feminist sense of this?

Women in the armed and police services of male-dominated states, and women otherwise engaged who manifest qualities of unusual courage, perseverance, and feistiness make careers of defending public realms that have "always been defined in opposition to dangerous, disorderly, and irrational forces . . . consistently conceptualized as female" (Hartstock, 1982:283). They may break the feminine mold without fighting gender relations in their societies. Others – I call them women warriors – hold to a state of mind and struggle that emphasizes energy, capacity, competence, and effectiveness in the service of women. This may entail fighting in seemingly unarmed ways against the myriad forces threatening women, or it may mean bearing arms in a national liberation struggle. The key is that they, along with "peoples engaged in struggles against imperialism and masculine dominance, are conceptualizing their labor and experience counter to their rulers' conceptions" (Harding, 1986:188). And they are doing so for women.

From whence do such countering women warrior identities spring? There are many plausible sources, all of which need exploration. Consider two paths: living as a daughter in a woman warrior-inclined mother's house; and living in political conditions that make women's lives expendable.

Women warrior contingencies of personal biography

In my family, and doubtless in many others, a Mother provided her daughter with inchoate lessons in woman warriorism. Mother was an unknowing warrior with a mixed set of loyalties. She was a gender conservative, who suggested that her daughter "let men win at tennis – men have fragile egos, you know." Yet she also took care of the household and trained me to rely on myself and not on men for my identity. Regularly, she gave me the mortgage payment to carry to the downtown bank, her words ringing in my ears: "now don't lose this check or the bank will take away the house." There I was, out in the domain of finance capital, where little girls did not then frolic. On my returning home, mother would either be battling my father or out battling for a local cause – for sidewalks to the local primary school or against opening stores on Sundays. Her house offered countless contradictory lessons about women taking charge and fighting the public and private wills of men.

Meanwhile, my father's house prepared me for private-sphere wars of attrition. A perpetually worn-down man, the victim of child abuse and of the warrior he had married, father conceded defeat stunningly by abandoning us when I was twelve. When he left, my mother and I were torn between feeling embarrassed at the nonconformity thrust on us and defiantly warring against sudden poverty. I now know that working-class and Third World women and children are left all the time by men who "forget" to support their offspring. Moreover, in an era of middle-class latchkey households, many working-mother-single-parents teach their children to handle potentially threatening strangers at the door, lurking household calamities, *and* the mortgage check. In these cases, daughters are in their mother's houses, to be sure. But they are not encouraged there to develop modes of thought antithetical to warlike battles against poverty or property repossession or, sometimes, fathers.

No doubt these struggles are hard on children because they rage in isolated, overly privatized family units of the West, and because too much early responsibility can overwhelm a child's developmental capacities. It is not a romantic experience, and my point is not to praise nervous, inconsistent mothering or to minimize the unhealthy consequences of abandonment by fathers or by states that do not insist on father support. Rather, it is to suggest that such events are part of lived experience for many women. Possibly they train daughters for a type of awareness that has, as one important component, a sense of how to fight to survive on one's own terms. Such lessons would be aspects of that preservative love Ruddick (1983) identifies. Yet in the spirit of aware cacophony, it is not necessary to reduce all lessons learned in all mother's houses to a single theme of this sort, especially since some mothers can dismantle – for good or ill – as much as they preserve. Nancy Friday (1977) reminds us that the idealization of motherhood is a recent invention, one that conservative postfeminists would like to enshrine as the politically proper interpretation of womanhood.

Several questions about the intersection of warrior feminism and peace follow from contingencies of personal biography. Could peace-oriented feminists be daughters who were kept away from the unruly public sphere within their mothers' houses? Alternatively, are the peaceful ones the rebels against harsh contingencies of personal biography that entailed considerable conflict? Would the private sphere daughter be more or less likely to join collective peace struggles than the one comfortable with conflict between public and private spheres or conflict within the former? Is it useful to think of one type of daughter as displaying positive feminine values or holding a moral high ground? Finally, is it possible that women warriors are neurotic, inauthentic, abnormal victims of false consciousness; or have they simply been unnamed within existing feminist and peace paradigms because their behaviors do not seem to support the cause? We obviously need to know more about women dwelling at and far from the fulcrum if we are to think about merging peace and feminism.

Women warriors and national contingencies

What of armed women of civic virtue, some professing to be feminists, who kill others in national liberation struggles? Clearly these women smash the icons of peace feminists. Do they have women warrior identities or are such people simply warriors at the service of patriarchy? This is not an easy set of questions to answer, as Elshtain knows from her study of *Women and War* (1987). Yet there might be a trussed-up dichotomy here. I argue that whether the war system is reinforced by their actions, thwarted, or altered, killing is such a pervasive part of lived reality for many women of the world that we must bend over backward to avoid treating their situations as "other," where no useful labor takes place and no contribution is made to our thinking on peace and feminism.

Stephanie Urdang (1979) interviewed women combatants in several African liberation movements and reports that they fought both as women, for their right to be equal to men, and as colonized and oppressed groups seeking to end foreign tyranny. Interviews I conducted with men from Zimbabwe's war indicate that women's labor of combat was highly valued, and Teurai Ropa Nhonga, an ex-combatant in the Zimbabwean government, speaks respectfully of women's deep commitment and total involvement "in every sphere of the armed revolutionary struggle" (cited in Lapchick and Urdang, 1982:107). In her words:

> In the frontline they transport war materials to the battlefield and . . .
> fight their way through enemy territory . . . They do politicization work
> among the masses . . . They teach the masses how to hide wounded

> Comrades, hide war materials and carry out intelligence reports be-
> hind enemy lines ... At the rear our women Comrades' tasks are even
> more extensive. They are involved in the work of every department as
> commanders, military instructors, commissars, medical corps, teach-
> ers, drivers, mechanics, cooks, in logistical supplies, information and
> publicity, as administrative cadres. There is no department where their
> beneficial presence is not felt.

Still, why engage in this type of labor to gain one's own and/or collective rights? The power it rests on is dominance, and it often suc-
ceeds only in replacing one set of patriarchal rulers with another. We
noted earlier that Harding sees struggles against colonialism as turning
rulers' expectations on their heads. She says, "it is precisely the disappearance of other-conceptualized labor and experience that permits the
emergence of Africanism and feminism" (Harding, 1986:188). Guerrilla
warfare, the usual form of combat in national liberation, can be less
other-conceptualized than the labor of combat under the flag of an established state. Guerrillas are everyday people of all ages, who work
together to challenge established states. Conventional soldiers are pro-
fessionals, separated from civilians, who are used to dominate or hold off
the domination of other states and would-be states. Guerrillas usually
envision liberation as a process of freeing and then transforming their
societies to suit local rather than international purposes. Conventional
soldiers have visions in the service of the dominant order and try to
conduct orderly war. Guerrilla war makes use of seemingly disorderly,
irrational, and dangerous techniques.

When women join liberation efforts, they participate in a social process that purports to change colonial power relations through energy,
proven capacity, competence, and war. Guerrilla warfare provides opportunities for them to change their usual labor, to define and exert their
own power, and to influence agendas usually controlled by colonial
governments and men at home. Women might even be likely candidates
for guerrilla warfare in situations where colonial governments render
women's lives, and those of their children, more expendable than the
lives of men. In Rhodesia (Zimbabwe), colonial policy increasingly
impinged on women's lives after World War II by promoting an
urban male proletariat. Heretofore, women reproduced men's labor by
providing primitive social security in rural areas while men worked
in the cities. After the war, women could join their husbands in urban
townships, but to do so they usually separated themselves from subsistence agriculture and found new work in less remunerative informal

sectors. In South Africa, apartheid legislation set up tribal homelands and stocked them with women, children, aged, and other superfluous appendages to the important (but abused) urban worker men.

We might think that women in such situations easily develop women warrior identities and turn those into political victories. Yet such women undoubtedly link their warrior identity to many aspirations and outcomes. Some may take up arms in order to escape oppressive personal situations, or to have an adventure. Some may fight for a humanist future in which women become written into the scripts of Everyman. Some may fight violently against patriarchal order and its sexual division of labor; or to prevent a range of patriarchs from monopolizing economic and political power as their historical right in the new society (women warriors as armed lobby group).

Whatever the reasons why they kill, armed women warriors do not usually get their wishes or their due after the smoke clears. In Southern Africa, such women were barely more conspicuous in public roles; for example, ten years into Mozambique's independence, women comprised only about 12 percent of the National People's Assembly. Public invisibility does not mean that women cannot exert visible power. Yet the realm of national governance controls resources, sets policies, and prescribes proper citizen behavior. If the state is the realm of men, as I argue in chapter 9, then women are always already precluded, even it they join men in the chief proving ground of the state – war. When women do war, it is interesting to note that they do not set postwar power-sharing as a condition for their participation in combat. Men are thus free to distribute rewards to fellow comrades and to insist on returning home to "proper" women of the *status quo ante*. Indeed, when I asked men recently returned from the independence struggle in Zimbabwe what they thought of women combatants as future wives, they seemed to find the relationship I was suggesting farfetched. One said, "They have ideas now."

Zimbabwean women ex-combatants told me regretfully that few men wanted to marry them. Women warriors may have wanted to battle patriarchal aspects of the local family (Kriger, 1992), but this exclusion from marriage – a high valued state in Zimbabwe – was imposed by men and then rubbed in later by the voice of the heroic leader saying: "married women especially must concern themselves with setting a positive example to the younger single women and show them in practice that marriage is an incentive for the pursuit of revolutionary tasks" (Machel, 1974:33). Thus, when women changed their usual labor and joined war they did not necessarily change the expectations of masculine society. Yet some women ex-combatants say they learned something from this experience. One Zimbabwean recently told me: "I have a freer hand than most women; I can do different things in life – not have so many babies – and not feel ashamed." There is useful incoherence here.

Concludings

Ambiguous incoherence does not lend itself to easy conclusions and glib parting words. This is a point worth considering as any paradigm for peace unfolds – if it unfolds. Paradigms put order into untidy universes (Sylvester, 2000c). At a time when woman is women and gender is posited as having no referents, how can, and why should, the feminist/peace fulcrum be tidied up and rendered paradigmatic?

Women warrior identities illustrate the problem with premature coherence. A woman warrior does not fully articulate to international peace efforts and to some feminist projects. But "she" exists, and in several forms. It might be as unjust to squeeze "her" or to turn her into a new model of Everywomen as warrior. One danger is further marginalization of a potentially common experience, relegating women warriors to the status of odd "others." There may also be some temptation to see women warrior identities in Everywoman, thereby renewing the search for feminine authenticity.

To appreciate the variety of women's relationships to peace it is important to end the quest for One True Story and to valorize feminism *vis-à-vis* humanist ideologies that would subsume "her" in other histories. Women warriors are proof that there is no one story of women as peace-lovers; and the fate of some armed women warriors teaches us that reasoned self-sacrifice, in the absence of a practiced alternative power, does not necessarily bring about a humanism that includes women. In endorsing women's many voices, we recognize incoherence in a postmodern world and seek solidarities across difference that are just and respectful even if they are not peaceful.

11   Gendered development imaginaries: shall we dance, Pygmalion?

In 1996 I sold house and car, packed belongings, and moved to Australia. At the National Centre for Development Studies, Australian National University (ANU), I continued my research, worked with postgraduate students from around the world, and took on development consultancies. That the move resited me topically, to some degree, as well as geospatially sent some whispers over the seas that "she has dropped out of IR." I had a giggle at the thought. For a new landscape of international relations appeared before me, full of Asia and the Pacific, full of southern hemispheric contrariness to northern norms, and blessedly free of American self-importance.

Doing development is a spin-off of many years of research in Southern Africa. After relocating to Australia, though, I found my work taking me as much to Korea, Thailand, and Indonesia as to Zimbabwe. I watched globalization affecting places I barely knew before – Bhutan, Fiji, the Maldives, Papua New Guinea. Wandering in the spirit of a Cynthia Enloe, albeit with development dilemmas in briefcase and development critiques in my mind, I have come to wonder incessantly about the women that mainstream IR scholars still have trouble locating – at all, let alone in an international development portfolio. Gone missing in some of IR, women of these regions regularly appear in the work of ANU colleagues (e.g., Jolly and Ram, 1998; Law, 2000; Pettman, 1996a) – though Africa is disturbingly out of sight across Australian academia.

This essay, one of the most recent in the book, touches my tensions with development studies and its international relations of gender. It travels around, back to places and words of Victorian and Edwardian times, and ahead from the imperium to practices of help comprising contemporary development. It draws on Bernard Shaw's *Pygmalion* (1957) and Anna Leonowens's *English Governess at the Siamese Court* (1954), as well as Jan Nederveen Pieterse's (1998) insights on development paradigms and Marianne Gronemeyer's (1992) tragic wit on the nature of development help. Britain, Thailand, the USA, and Zimbabwe take up places amidst global norms of assistance that hit with the discursive and monied force of invasion. A response to the bombardments comes from an unlikely spot for IR and cognate development studies – feminist analysis of imaginative literatures, where fiction and fact can mix nuggets of feminist wisdom in and amongst the farce. In bringing IR/development to fiction again for inspiration, I try to move them both – "come now, pack your bags" – to more postcolonial mind- and place-sites.

* * *

> . . . the change wrought by Professor Higgins in the flower-girl is neither impossible nor uncommon . . . But the thing has to be done scientifically, or the last state of the aspirant may be worse than the first . . . They must learn their alphabet over again, and different, and from a phonetic expert. Imitation will only make them ridiculous.   (Shaw, 1957:5)

> Madam: We are in good pleasure, and satisfaction in heart, that you are in willingness to undertake the education of our beloved royal children. And we hope that in doing your education on us and on our children (whom English call inhabitants of benighted land) you will do your best endeavor for knowledge of English language, science, and literature . . .
> (Maha Mongkut, King of Siam, cited in Leonowens, 1954:vii)

The Edwardian creation, Henry Higgins, develops a flower girl into a proper English speaker, ostensibly so she can work in a shop instead of on the street. In fact, he wagers with a friend about finally passing her off as a West End gentlewoman; the development concern is with his own prowess rather than her future. Halfway round the world the British wager they can effect similar change among "benighted" colonial subjects through "indirect rule," a form of administration that insists difference be respected more than its rule-governed training suggests it is.

Shaw's Eliza Doolittle becomes a success among the idle upper classes yet fails to earn from her teacher, Henry Higgins, the respect others begin to accord her. Elites from the colonies, trained abroad in the ways of administration, win the admiration of their countrymen and -women as they engineer modern postcolonies; meanwhile, departing colonists say that conversions of peasants to parliamentarians are not complete, just as Higgins believes he knows the "ridiculous" behind Eliza's changed language and manners.

In 1862 Englishwoman Anna Leonowens receives the request of King Mongkut, of what is now Thailand, to teach his children and harem wives the language, science, and literature of the English West. Having already spent time in India and Singapore, Leonowens takes off for Siam to become one of few western women privy to what she calls the palace inside. The sights alternately seduce her and suggest to her mind a whimsical cruelty. In a country that neither Britain nor France manages to bring under imperial command, Leonowens sets about with considerable industry to reel in the escapees to correct human (European) values.

The Leonowens text is a poetically written account of imperial aspirations of a cultural and moral type, wrapped in crinoline skirts and tied to motherhood. Shaw's imaginative play about a man developing an improved woman is set in London after the turn of the century and concerns social issues that occupied the imperial mind. The essay before us concerns contemporary development imaginaries and three development agencies that operate programs for women in Zimbabwe. Why take a meandering journey through literature in order to get to the central issues? That is, what links imaginative imperial writings and contemporary imaginaries of development?

Writing in the introduction to *The Fiction of Imperialism*, Phillip Darby (1998:1) asks a similar question: "what do we learn by reading fiction that is missing from the conventional political and historical sources?" He elaborates answers throughout the book but says early on that imaginative literature "is implicated in the processes of imperial expansion and ... is used to advance decolonization in a variety of forms" (p. 2). The missions Higgins and Leonowens embrace portray an imaginary of overseas "help" that marked the late imperial era; *and* they depict forms of decolonizing help seen today in the work of some development organizations operating in postcolonial settings. The link is this: imperial stories, read in tandem with certain contemporary development practices, reveal the inability of many international helpers to read themselves into the communities they help. The imperial imaginary, and its fraught outcomes, thus continues into the twenty-first century. Here, I elaborate elements of the imperial–contemporary "helping" imaginary and consider the marks it has left on the work of three agencies in postcolonial Zimbabwe: Silveira House, Partnership for Productivity, and the Zimbabwe Women's Bureau.

Imagining development help

Imperial literatures help us see that international development help can be of a certain recurring sort. It can tempt, tantalize, chastise subjects and create a desiring but always disappointing other who reaches for help and is doomed to not-receive it quite from the helper. Deborah Kerr leads the dancing King of Siam in the 1950s cinematic version of the Leonowens story. Higgins sets out to lead Eliza into a social whirligig of his own imaginative creation. Today, development practices rely on helpers instructing those with "deficits" of various sorts to sustain themselves in the western way of life. All the lessons are stiff and more than a little influenced by gender, class, and race.

Help

The issue is how to help appropriately. From the late nineteenth century people have sought out expertise and have greeted the expert as one who can, as Jane Parpart (1995:223, emphasis added) puts it, "define *and transmit* the scientific knowledge/truth needed by the modern world." The usual pipeline, we know, has been from North to South, from core to periphery, from "civilization" to "primitivism." Malaysia now invests in Zimbabwe, but postcolonies still turn to the expert West "ready to participate in the adventure of progressive modern development" (p. 224). Leonowens's international expertise is purchased locally for a royal entourage. Eliza Doolittle gets a class-superior expert in London manners of the time. The author of each tale is an advocate of the type of help that features in his or her story: Shaw writes (1957:1) "[t]he reformer we need most today is an energetic phonetic enthusiast: that is why I have made such a one the hero of a popular play." Travel writer Freya Stark (introduction to Leonowens, 1953:xiii) opens Leonowens's *Siamese Harem Life* lauding "the intimate, poignantly matter-of-fact accounts" we are about to read. Leonowens is an expert.

Literature has its ironics. In the Shaw and Leonowens tales, the helper is meant to be superior to the ones helped; but as events unfold, helper and helped become intertwined in a tense development script. Neither the flower girl nor the king transforms under expert training into "a" proper subject of development – one who takes in the lessons and uses them as intended by the teachers. Both take up the help they request and take in those lessons on their own terms, annoyed at the instructors by the end – albeit also willing to stay in contact with them.

227

The instructors in these tales exit without convincing the reader that their development missions have been well conceived let alone accomplished. It is especially the case that the instructors' lives seem little changed by the encounters. Higgins and Leonowens wax lyrically judgmental about those they help, but speak of themselves in and amongst those others with cultural distance, separation, righteous anger, fear, or perplexity. The experts make things happen and yet are not in the picture quite; at least they think they are not. Higgins exits a pitiful prig who cannot relate to any woman other than his mother. He is an anti-hero, a curd – his creature surpasses him in civilization. As for Leonowens, Caren Kaplan (1995:45) tells us that "recent scholarship casts suspicion on the factual nature of Leonowens's narrative of her life in the Nang Harem and recalls earlier protests against the publication of the memoirs." Heonowens, the expert is outside her own story of development.

The late Julius Nyerere (cited in Esteva, 1992:7) "proposed that development be thought of as the political mobilization of a people for attaining their own objectives." He did not specify the mobilizing agents, and how their own lives would develop as a result of their efforts on behalf of others; one presumes he had the state in mind for the mobilizing role. Yet Nyerere hinted at an approach to development that could be alternative to approaches that emphasized the large-scale, externally guided, economic improvements of the day. A range of alternative development approaches did gain ground in the early 1970s.[1] Feminists, environmentalists, postmodernists, and others – including the World Bank under Robert McNamara – who introduced there the Basic Needs approach – succeeded in siting some development activities around enhanced human capacity as a goal or value. Their metaphors of development pictured average rural people – the poetically named "grassroots" – becoming agents of development in partnership with those offering help (Sylvester, 2000b). Put differently, rather than creating conditions for macroeconomic change, alternative development came to prize local planning and implementation, while not entirely ignoring larger institutional and global challenges (Sheth, 1987).

Jan Nederveen Pieterse (1998:345) maintains that "in the 1990s, unlike the 1970s, the big hiatus no longer runs between mainstream and

---

[1] Their advance came amidst furious debates between modernization theorists and critics of the dependency school, which led the development field into a well-publicized impasse. For overviews of development theories and eras, see Arndt (1987), Leys (1996), and Rapley (1996).

alternative development, but between human development and structural adjustment, or, in other words, between two forms of mainstream development ..." What this means is that the mainstream has recognized the bottom-up logic of alternative development as at least a legitimate metaphor for help and has assigned such activity mostly to nongovernmental organizations and some UN agencies. Meanwhile, the structural adjustment wing, centered around the International Monetary Fund and the contemporary World Bank, carries on the tradition of macroeconomic development, adding on programs for "best practice" governance and monetary policy.

Although Eliza Doolittle and Maha Mongkut are of the imperialist rather than the development period, the actions of both resonate with the alternative development imaginary of today. Both sought outside expertise to attain goals they themselves set to enhance their own (and their charges') capacity and agency. Doolittle (Shaw, 1957:23) says: "I want to be a lady in a flower shop stead of sellin at the corner of Tottenham Court Road. But they wont take me unless I can talk more genteel. He [Higgins] said he could teach me." She is insecure, blustery. Mongkut (Leonowens, 1954:vii), as we recall, is "in good pleasure and satisfaction in heart, that you [Leonowens] are in willingness to undertake the education of our beloved royal children." At the first audience with Leonowens, he clarifies the nature of the help he needs with the air of one who is merely hiring domestic help (p. 48):

> "I have sixty-seven children," said his Majesty ... "You shall educate them, and as many of my wives, likewise, as may wish to learn English. And I have much correspondence in which you must assist me. And, moreover, I have much difficulty for reading and translating French letters ... And furthermore, I have by every mail foreign letters whose writing is not easily read by me. You shall copy on round hand, for my readily perusal thereof."

These texts of help-seeking show variegated expectations, shaded rather than straightforward requests. Yet the issue of help-giving and -taking lies at the heart of the stories.

Marianne Gronemeyer (1992:54) writes, with respect to development work, that "the cry for help of a person in need, is rarely any longer the occasion for help. Help is much more often the indispensable, compulsory consequence of a need for help that has been diagnosed from without." In arguing this point, she does not draw a distinction between the structural adjustment wing of the field and alternative elements of development that focus on grassroots participation. She encompasses both by arguing that "[d]evelopment help inherited the missionary idea, with its accursed crusade to win converts and mania for redemption . . . the modern missionary idea still declares that a shortfall of civilization must be remedied, an incorrect historical development corrected, an excessively slow pace accelerated" (p. 66).

Higgins and Leonowens are full of missionary zeal to create others in the image of themselves. At the start of *Pygmalion* Higgins shows off his ability to place every accent he hears in a crowd, including Eliza Doolittle's, while taking notes and commenting on figures of speech new to him. In explaining himself to onlookers it is he, rather than the speakers with "odd" accents, who names a problem. He then thrusts himself forward as the one who can help overcome their deficiency. Eliza Doolittle is instantaneously uncomfortable with her being, eager to improve herself through the tantalizing promises of the professional note-taker. Mongkut is somewhat different in his petition for help. Already in command of considerable English, and capable enough to hold off formal European colonialism, he takes instruction mostly for his children and wives – only some for himself.

Gronemeyer (p. 58) writes that in the nineteenth century, help "became completely the subject matter of educational strategies. It was good for the poor, for industry, and for the tidy aesthetic of bourgeois societies. More recently, Arif Dirlik (1994:329) has talked about the wisdom of "reveal[ing] societies globally in their complex heterogeneity and contingency." Leonowens and Higgins, aware of heterogeneity, wish to instruct it away. Leonowens (1954:63) is especially clear on this point: "I think the day is not far off when the enlightening influences applied to them, and accepted through their willingness, not only to receive instruction from Europeans, but even to adopt in a measure their customs and their habits of thought, will raise them to the rank of a superior nation." Higgins is attracted to the prospect of helping Doolittle because "She's so deliciously low – so horribly dirty –" (Shaw, 1957:26).

The meeting of a crusading imperial creationist and a person self-motivated to seek instructional help does not always end up felicitous, whether in London or in Siam. There are clashing perspectives on the problematic and on ways to deal with it. There are unexpected processes, intermeshings, and outcomes. There is also the matter of pay. Gronemeyer (1992:53) reminds us that in old stories of good Samaritans who bind wounds or distribute food, help is offered as "pity in the face of the need of another."[2] Today, philanthropists receive hefty tax benefits for helping. With the increasing possibility of being shot or taken hostage, some humanitarian aid workers pay security forces for protection as they go about helping those in need. Structural adjustment programs calculate ideological and policy-aligning payments while professional note-takers, akin to Professor Higgins, record the ways helped governments abide by stipulated conditions. Bilateral development aid explicitly links upto trade and/or political forms of payment. The helper does not expect that participating in the development endeavor will change him or her in proportion to the change s/he is meant to leave behind for others (although institutions giving help may change).[3] Helper is paid for the work as a professionalized money-earning money-giving matter. Doolittle pays Higgins a shilling for his services. Leonowens gets a salary and living quarters (but shifts houses twice before accepting space in the environs of the local royal harem[4]).

I want to argue that when the help stays aloof from those helped, as is usual in contemporary development work, the problematic thereby created is imperialist instruction instead of heterogeneous learning. To appreciate this point, it is useful to turn to a contemporary example, in this case the first of three nongovernmental organizations I studied *circa* 1990 (and revisited in 1999) in Zimbabwe (see Sylvester, 2000a, 2001).

Silveira House helps

Silveira House is a Zimbabwean nongovernmental organization affiliated with the Roman Catholic Church. It began its activities during Zimbabwe's colonial period, first as a rural credit organization and, after independence in 1980, as a multifaceted development agency. At the time I was most in contact with it, in 1988–1990, its programming in rural areas of Mashonaland included youth projects, agricultural training, cooperatives, and courses in industrial relations, dress-making, arts and crafts, civics, and executive leadership. Silveira House aimed to help the poorest rural people, including the poorest women, especially those who were being encouraged by the government to form cooperatives.

Staff reported that Silveira had developed a strong cooperative focus after independence, because, as one said, "the philosophy and ideology

[2] For a discussion of pity and humanitarianism, see Boltanski (1999).
[3] One thinks of the monumental ways the original Bretton Woods institutions were changed by the advent of postcolonial economies. At minimum, they changed from lenders to Europe to chief institutions of multilateral aid to the Third World.
[4] For a discussion of misconceptions about harem life, see Grewal (1996).

of cooperatives was the result of a hasty decision by government. It is necessary to step back and orient people on the rationale for cooperatives, a step the government did not take." The government rationales for starting cooperatives were many, from leading a transition to socialist modes of production, to income-generation in rural areas, to encouraging liberal entrepreneurism (Sylvester, 1991b). Silveira House helpers added their own views: "We want cooperatives to benefit individuals because we don't believe in the stated cooperative principles that emphasize collectivism. It's terrible if people don't get to own anything." Shades of Leonowens standing next to Henry Higgins, one told me: "We are trying to develop morals."

Silveira House personnel were mostly men and those they helped through their cooperatives division were overwhelmingly women, owing to the continuing colonial practice of male labor migration to cities. One might imagine the bush of Zimbabwe as a series of unsplendid harems of women and children living mostly apart from men but at their service. The helping men from Silveira had to step into that "harem" in order to help it, something only important men of Mongkut's royal family could do in Siam. Although Southern Africans do not think in terms of harems, that imaginary from a far-off place directs our attention to special men who enter an area of difference that is presumed to be waiting for assistance (rather than seen as produced as waiting by those who help).

As I accompanied Silveira personnel to cooperatives, I saw few signs that the helpers imagined themselves within the communities of women they helped. Mere visitors on "a moral or scientific expedition, justifying Western imperialism and its invasive tactics" (Kaplan, 1995:37), we politely inquired about local wellbeing and problems. Distance also figured into the content of courses Silveira House held on the principles and practices of cooperative management. The classes I observed were full of men as teachers and learners, despite a proliferation of women's cooperatives and the admission by Silveira staff that "most members of cooperatives are women." The few women attending the courses were quiet and sat apart from the men, often ignored by the teacher and by fellow cooperators during discussions. Issues of gender equity in cooperatives did not come up in class, which means that difficulties confronting women, such as balancing household obligations and cooperative tasks, appeared only as ghosts in the discussions. Men talked to men about the needs of men, as though "women" did not exist. The would-be helpers could not intervene because, like Leonowens

(1954:82), they were "sitting at one end of the table in my schoolroom . . . I felt as though we were twenty thousand miles away from the world that lay but a twenty minutes' walk from the door."

Only one moment occurred during my research when Silveira personnel tentatively embraced change and mutual help with helped communities. A ranking member of the organization confided that "we have the idea of creating a rural bank for the people. To do this, Silveira may have to restructure ourselves." He did not elaborate the point. I thought of a restructuring that could reduce hierarchy in helping relationships but suspected that he had in mind tightened hierarchy modeled on commercial banking. By the mid-1990s Silveira House had shifted its priorities from cooperatives to microenterprises and microcredit programs. They had indeed restructured themselves. The question of how Silveira's "harem" relationship with women in cooperatives might be changed, however, how mutuality and contingency might be established with communities helped, remained unarticulated.

Siting more women in help

The male creator that forms the basis of the Pygmalion story by Ovid and Shaw reverses the performance of creation among humans: usually man comes out of woman and both sexes rely on each other's "natural" performance in creation to mark the ways of gender in the world at large. The rearrangement of a story that usually accords women considerable power is what Beverley Thiele (1986) calls an act of appropriation/reversal of gender. Leonowens reappropriates the creation myth by striving to give birth to an enlightened king. Higgins steals it back for wizardly men creating women. In the backgrounds of both imperial stories, some women can sight the reversals. Mrs. Higgins, in particular, sees the masculine posturing that underlies her son's performance and tries to instruct him, and his softer accomplice, Pickering, in the fine art of human development.

> MRS. HIGGINS. Eliza came to me this morning. She told me of the brutal way you two treated her.
> HIGGINS. [*bounding up*] What?
> PICKERING. [*rising also*] My dear Mrs Higgins, she's been telling you stories. We didn't treat her brutally. We hardly said a word to her . . .
> (Shaw, 1957:89)

Writes Timothy Vesonder (1977:42) about Shaw's characters: "Just as the classical hero received help from gods, friends and benevolent spirits, the Shavian hero receives necessary assistance," here from his mother. She reveals the secret that masculine creators have limited ability to read their own ripping metaphors and are something of the buffoon.

At the Siamese court, Leonowens inadvertently depicts local, reappropriating assistants showing up her limitations. Tuptim is the favorite concubine of Majesty until she runs off to pursue her Buddhist inclinations in the proximity of a priest to whom she was once affianced. Her retreat to a place where a former love is now a humble priest, and her modesty once there, insults the king's privilege. Leonowens tries to intercede on Tuptim's behalf but Mongkut responds as to the laughed-at Eliza in London: "'You are mad,' said the monarch; and fixing a cold stare upon me, he burst out laughing in my face" (Leonowens, 1953:28). Leonowens prevails for the moment by returning the look of arrogant Majesty with her own "inexpressible horror of the man" (p. 28). Tuptim, the ironic-tragic assistant in Anna's civilizing mission, most clearly prevails, though, and does so fully within the rubric of her society's norms and meanings. Facing death by fire, Tuptim and her priest silence frenzied crowds with a calm certainty. Their mutually contingent demise is memorialized afterwards by the repentant Majesty, who orders a public monument to them.[5]

Leonowens (1954:viii) can recognize some limitations of imperial creationism: "I have to confess with sorrow and shame, how far we, with all our boasted enlightenment, fall short, in true nobility and piety, of some of our 'benighted' sisters of the East." Despite the assistants who endeavor to add a humanitarian edge to his creative mission, Higgins bows out with defensive masculinity. Shaw (1957:118) tries to explain that in Ovid's *Metamorphoses*, "Galatea never does quite like Pygmalion: his relation to her is too godlike to be altogether agreeable." But Higgins is the one who does not quite like Eliza, owing to his inability to satisfy her desire to achieve a more contingent relational autonomy, whereby she can explore her new hyphenated identities without subordinating herself to him. He wants her to remain in his household on the terms of a servant to a reactively autonomous Majesty. She prevails, which means that she leaves but the two maintain the contact of equals: "He storms and bullies and derides; but she stands up to him" (p. 118). It is a tense metaphor of partnership, and Higgins does not seem to realize his part in it. A parallel problem of contingency unrecognized and of

---

[5] Griswold (1961) argues against the depiction of burning as a common punishment in Siam and also queries why a drama of epic proportions, such as the Tuptim story, would not be mentioned in oral or written sources.

creationism dressed as anti-conquest, grows up around the second case of alternative development practice in Zimbabwe.

Partnership for Productivity: Pygmalionesque gender help

Partnership for Productivity (PFP), a US-based NGO founded in 1984, followed the alternative philosophy of "giving people who want self-reliance the right tools so they can be productive." That goal has the modernist ring of human development through economic production for profit, as opposed to making something for use. At the same time, an emphasis on helping "people who want self-reliance" suggests that the organization does not engage in acts of crusading conversion. PFP seems to produce producers out of people who think about doing grander things, but who sense, like Eliza, that a little help is needed. Said a high-ranking woman working for the PFP in Harare: "it's a matter of diverting their images of themselves to production. When this happens there is much energy." She offered this example:

> Women in the Chipinge area came forward with a uniform-making project for which they wanted funding. PFP sent instructors because these women were not experienced in needlework. They can now make the uniforms required for government schools and also sew husband's clothes when they tear. Prior to this, husbands were sending clothes to tailors when work was needed on them. They think of themselves now as tailors, as producers.

These women "came forward," first of all, for "funding." PFP's revolving funds provided up to Z$200,000 to enterprises of fifty people to buy tools and thereby develop a credit history. The organization did not go out recruiting possible recipients any more than Higgins sought out Eliza as a client. The staff believed that when people know a service exists, they will come forward if they are motivated to enhance their modern capacities as producers. Then, instruction becomes important. The women from Chipinge get funding and they get instruction in needlework.

An unexpected outcome of this help, which seems to please the woman telling the story, is that the women can now "sew husband's clothes when they tear." My mind travels to Ann Tickner's story (in the introduction to this book) of being told that getting a Ph.D. is a good idea because she can then help her husband with his work. It is a comment that also evokes Eliza Doolittle's dilemma of how to use instruction in proper English for her own material benefit rather than to benefit Higgins's ego. That the helper from PFP says nothing about whether the added sewing finds compensation in men taking up tasks that help the

women is like Higgins teaching Eliza new skills and then asking her to
be his servant. Is skills instruction for women a matter of enhancing
their capacity to service men's needs? (Where is Mrs. Higgins when we
need her?)

A related issue is how PFP personnel see themselves in relation to
those they help. One woman representative said that PFP "identifies a
need in an area . . . and once a client appears, our people are constantly in
the field, monitoring; but, PFP is there for a certain time and then it with-
draws. We don't believe in fixing problems for our clients, but rather on
advising them on strategies to pursue. This is the best way to keep them
independent." Henry Higgins also identified a "need in an area" and
waited for someone to come forward for his help. He then monitored
the one who came forward until she serviced his wager, thereafter re-
treating to his own world of concerns. He left her, as Mrs. Higgins and
Doolittle herself came to realize, with neither the language appropriate
to the station she had sought – a flower shop – nor the wherewithal to
support herself in a new way. Eliza wanted him to work with her difference and he wanted her to bring him his slippers. We could turn all
this around by imagining an agent of instruction as ontologically rather
than epistemologically within the helped community, which is a matter
not of monitoring but of engagement.

PFP is not ready for this. The representative tells me that "if a machine breaks down, the women may be at a loss; they take fright from
little obstacles and lose energy." The instructed producer is expected
to respond energetically to new opportunities and not suffer any instances of perplex or loss of motivation to push on: "A typical failure
comes from ambivalence, when women decide they don't really want
to follow through and don't put in much effort." The helper owns up to
no ongoing responsibility in either of these situations. She equates ambivalence with disinterest, lack of hard work, and the real villain – low
motivation. The direction is upwards as agencies provide the tools that
will quickly graduate their students into new lives of independence and
capacity. Yet why would a helped woman be at a loss when the machine
breaks unless the relationship between instructor and instructee is one
of unfulfilled contingency?

In other comments this woman representative of PFP appears more
sympathetically sited, although disinclined to locate herself in the story
she relates. She says impersonally: "Often there's a loss of confidence
because the women are pioneers in the rural areas and are isolated.
There's no one to talk over their problems. This causes them to lose

faith." To lose faith or to find themselves in some interesting middle between past and present identities?

> PICKERING. . . . You wont relapse, will you?
> LIZA. No: Not now. Never again. I have learnt my lesson. I dont believe I could utter one of the old sounds if I tried. [*Doolittle* [her father] *touches her on her left shoulder. She drops her work, losing her self-possession utterly, at the spectacle of her father's splendour*] A-a-a-a-a-ah-ow-ooh!
> (Shaw, 1970:128–129)

Leonowens (1954:69) tells of a harem woman studying English, who "demanded to be steered at once into the mid-ocean of the book; but when I left her without pilot in an archipelago of hard words, she soon showed signals of distress." The helpers do not see themselves as hybrid with, and changing alongside, these pioneers of postcolonial hybridity. They carry on with some sympathy, but empathetic cooperation (Sylvester, 1994b) requires mutual engagement, and that is not part of the usual development project cycle.

Is Partnership for Productivity a partner in the sense of swaying together with the music of the helped, or a partner to imaginaries of imperial creationism? The organization carefully knows that it must not lead those with whom it dances: "If you say your priority is bakeries, people will suddenly change their project to bakeries." It is aware that clients may try to figure out what the donor wants to hear rather than step forward with their own needs. "If you say, do you think this is the best way, they'll say yes, yes. There's a word politics in working with people: if you use the right words, there's no problem." Gendered development imaginaries identify a need, find a word to articulate it, and step back to wait and watch the helper assuring herself that she is handling it well (Sylvester, 2000b).

PFP personnel did not express scorn for those helped, or for the types of enterprises (usually cooperatives) their clients wished to establish. In this they set themselves apart from many others in Zimbabwe.[6] Their development values were alternative and their "following" techniques were somewhat attuned to partnership. Overall, though, the alternatives were not different enough, and differently pursued enough, to produce an awareness of contingent partner relations of development. That is, although contingencies ran throughout the agency–community relationship, mutuality was not established in a way that enabled helpers to read and represent themselves in the interpenetrating stories of fortune.

[6] For less flattering NGO comments about clients see Sylvester (1991a).

Imagining Development: the Zimbabwe Women's Bureau

The discussion so far suggests that the mantle of one-sided imperial creationism, which masks the contingent aspects in *Pygmalion* and *The English Governess in the Siamese Court*, persists in the words and actions of some alternative development organizations. According to Pieterse (1998:345, emphasis in the original), alternative development "broadly shar[es] the same *goals* as mainstream development but us[es] different *means*, participatory and people-centred." Silveira House and Partnership for Productivity worked to define a deficit and to help others supersede it, using means that, on the surface at least, were participatory. One organization danced differently within the community it sought to help, though, and still stands today as a model of a partnership that is ontologically engaged. That organization is the Zimbabwe Women's Bureau.

It took just five minutes for the then head of the Zimbabwe Women's Bureau (ZWB), a local NGO, to tell me: "We aim to help women see themselves as themselves." She amplified that provocative thought with an anti-expert one-liner: "No one can do anything for you." She then ran contingent development up the flagpole as an organizational goal: "We want to provide a platform to learn from and mix with other women." Here were the sounds of development as partnership, where the leading party embraces the prospect of mutuality. It was unusual to hear such refrains in the Zimbabwean NGO community.

ZWB began in 1978 when academic, business, and activist black women, in the tradition of instructing others, "wanted to raise the level of awareness of women in the country, especially rural women." The means brought to this common end put an indelible imprint on the organization: "At the time there was censorship in Rhodesia and letters were read; so we thought of using the churches as meeting places to talk. If asked, we'd say we were a prayer group and the Rhodesian Front wouldn't suspect anything. We saw that women go to church and pray but knew that this wouldn't help them. They had to talk about their problems." From the subterfuge of prayer groups, the organization developed an infrastructure of women who went out to rural areas after independence to survey local women's perspectives. The survey yielded both the well-regarded book called *We Carry a Heavy Load* (Zimbabwe Women's Bureau, 1981)[7] and, from what representatives told me, also a

---

[7] That survey was updated eleven years later. See Zimbabwe Women's Bureau (1992).

world of insight into the concerns of average Zimbabwean women: "We finally saw the issues," they said, "such as women not having their own property or a chance to get credit without a husband's guarantee."

The organization sponsored district, regional, and national workshops to discuss the survey. "Everywhere we went women were outspoken: they wanted more in their lives – more respect from men, more power, more freedom from gender expectations about women, and more money." ZWB worked with women to establish the viable income-generating projects jointly sought, and later formed a training program to transform the loose projects into registered cooperatives. This organization pursued the alternative development goal of grassroots participation *and* went beyond it into forms of help that embraced mutual learning as means and outcome. It swayed together with the clients, and the payback was, in the words of one: "Rural women say they now know what to look for. They are saying: 'I'm clever too.'"

One would be hard-pressed to imagine Leonowens canvassing her charges before planning the school curriculum in Siam. In her instructional garb she resembled the later Higgins: "my scholars were ranged in chairs around the long table, with Webster's far-famed spelling books before them, repeating audibly after me the letters of the alphabet" (Leonowens, 1954:69). It would be difficult to imagine Higgins learning and mixing with those around him rather than always taking notes about them. He mocks the still "ridiculous" Eliza when she proposes to support herself in the future by teaching others:

> HIGGINS. Whatll you teach, in heaven's name?
> LIZA. What you taught me. I'll teach phonetics.
> HIGGINS. Ha! ha! ha!
>
> (Shaw, 1957:103)

ZWB concerned itself with learning methods by which to hear local goals of development and advance those goals. None the less, the educated leaders of ZWB held strong and sometimes radical views of their own about gender relations in Zimbabwe. One representative told me that "women should not work for men, both should work." They said, "it's hopeless to speak of women's rights to women only, because women have been exploited by men and through their laws." They said, "we don't employ men at the field level of our work because it can cause social problems – when teaching women you don't want men there to stifle them. At other times, men should be there." Some had dreamed about cooperatives for women before the government devised its program.

Undoubtedly the individual views made their way into broader ZWB work, just as Leonowens and Higgins were influenced by the way they imagined their situations. At the same time, the standpoints ZWB staff expressed did not lead them to specific answers *for* rural women's problems. ZWB people reminded me that "no one can come up with solutions for us as women." Thus their education programs did not instruct so much as ask women to "come up with your own questions and find your own solutions or invite a resource person to help you. Don't let people speak for you. After all, someone else's problem doesn't stop them from eating."

These were assistants in the mode of Mrs. Higgins helping expert Henry to see and analyze himself. They were the Tuptims to Leonowens's self-righteousness. Rather than speaking on behalf of someone in distress or need, there was and is an ethos at ZWB that it is reasonable to know the social problems in a community and have views about them; but one cannot presume to know what those seeking help need and want and should have. Silveira House did not display such mutuality in its work, and Partnership for Productivity partnered from some social distance; both exhibited a certain presumptuousness about those to be helped. Being more of a facilitating organization, the Zimbabwe Women's Bureau avoided one problem Pieterse (1998:347) has identified with alternative development: "postconventional ideas and approaches are straitjacketed in conventional political imaginaries."

Literature implicating development and gender

Two helping tales from the imperial past implicate development themes of today. In one, a feisty English governess works to make a civilizing dent on "barbarian" majesty with actions that, in Kaplan's (1995:48) words, "speak to the desire for a good mother or a powerful woman who can stand up to patriarchal authority." In the second story, Shaw features a male expert creating a woman who speaks with the right accent and says things middle-class Edwardians value. Three other stories about help in the postcolonial present interweave these. Two of the latter mimic one-sided imaginaries of help found in imperial literature, rather than seeking out local helping strategies and mixing in with these. One agency stands out by crafting a text out of local stories, into which the helpers themselves enfold.

Into this postcolonial era spills some of the crude creation missions one finds in *Pygmalion* and *The English Governess at the Siamese Court,* despite talk of development cooperation, partnership, participation. Even champions of alternative development can mime a metropolitan innocence that masks hegemonic attitude about bestowing development on those requesting help. The helped are rarely fully bestowed. The helper maintains directive agency as part of the imperial instructional logic, and thus creates a desiring but always disappointing (made ridiculous) other. Being in a directive role difficult to relinquish, the helper is not readily able to imagine the development *gestalt* of the helped and enter it. These themes spring to our eyes when we read fiction and they remain hidden and deniable in the development "facts."

The Zimbabwe Women's Bureau stretches the imperial imaginary of development help by recognizing and welcoming contingent development. That particular agency may not be statistically representative; the spokeswomen I interviewed may be anomalous; undoubtedly the organization is flawed in ways I could not observe. Its helping scripts, however, when read alongside imperial stories, can stimulate our imaginations to see and correct our imperious assumptions:

> MRS. HIGGINS. You certainly are a pretty pair of babies, playing with your live doll.
> HIGGINS. Playing! The hardest job I ever tackled: make no mistake about that, mother. But you have no idea how frightfully interesting it is to take a human being and change her into a quite different human being . . .
>
> (Shaw, 1957:63–64)

12 Empathetic cooperation: a feminist method for IR

As we end the section on sites that enable feminism within IR and IR within feminism, several themes and tributes from earlier essays gather in a final "empathetic" place. Elshtain's and Enloe's styles, the sources they use, and types of connections and arguments they make all assert themselves around me. Both scholars are good at ducking in and out of private and public spheres to find the transversal points, people, patterns of authority, and political outcomes that comprise international relations – and there is that constructivist theme again. As my journey continues, however, it also becomes clear to me that we must both enlarge and be scrupulously rigorous within our methodological repertory. Elshtain, Enloe, and Tickner were silent about the precise feminist approaches that informed their early research, although readers can see that Enloe and Tickner displayed feminist standpoint thinking while *Women and War* raised feminist postmodernist identity concerns. In the essays composing this section, I reach for specificity in between standpoint and postmodernist ways of siting feminist knowledge, wary of impaling women on the spears that thrust at both sites.

Standpoint feminism remains the approach that puts women front and center for a change – and I gulp in the sweet air around that – instead of dropping "her" in some back lot of social theory. Yet I am not convinced that once her raw experience is mediated by feminism *per se*, it becomes what some standpointers claim of it – the preferred way of investigating the world (see Harding, 1991). I worry that well-intentioned feminist input actually leavens experience somewhat by pulling from it some points and leaving the rest to another social tradition to retrieve. Also, does not the type of feminist standpoint we bring affect the outcome? If I have a standpoint on oppression because I am poor, how does it (does it?) come out differently if mediated by sexual difference, Marxist, liberal, or postmodernist feminism? Is a feminist mediation (and which one?) of a white middle-class woman's standpoint more error-free than a postcolonial mediation? Am I wrongly posing what is by now a strong multiculturally based feminist enterprise, in which we know that "no single map or collection of them can perfectly reflect 'reality'" (Harding, 1998:190)? The location issue in feminism, as Harding puts it, is unstable, shifting, and widely dispersed – and that is one of its strengths and a weakness as it meets up with a professional IR that is also moving. A little more feminist IR/IR feminist theorizing would help overcome the sense that standpoint thinking sets up simultaneously as Archimedean and as relativist.

If standpoint is problematic, some postmodernist claims also make me wonder. I watch millennial protests against the World Bank, the World Trade Organization, and the IMF and notice that the mostly young protesters who are interviewed do not equivocate or present the ironic distance and ambivalences that we associate with postmodern identities. They are out there in the streets the way feminists were in the 1960s – before we knew that problems of voice arose when one screamed too loudly. This time the targets are politics-appropriating corporate strategies, which protesters have themselves experienced (Klein, 1999), globalization, and structural adjustment policies that affect strangers in distant places. The protesters may have complex pictures in their minds of how development capitalism works, but one does not see as much evidence of a postmodern awareness that people everywhere have multiple identities and wishes that cannot be "captured" *en toto* by "a" modern, western empathy (or capitalism). In hippy garb of yesterday, they perform a modern spectacle of protest in a transnational advocacy mode. Some impress me; and yet I worry about all the standpoints that could not get to the protests and also be heard (Scholte, 2000).

Other nettles. Zaki Laidi (1998:1) argues that we are in an era that has no particular meaning: "Our feeling of an exceptionally strong change in world order after the fall of the Berlin Wall is coupled with our equally enormous inability to interpret it, to give it meaning. Though all the upheavals we experience daily can have several meanings, nothing indicates they have a meaning, if by meaning we imply the triple notion of foundation, unity, and final goal." Yet late twentieth-century international politics still display some foundational unities around gender themes (which Laidi might have seen had he taken gender into account). At the eve of the western millennium, an Air India plane sat on a runway in southern Afghanistan awaiting some move that would end a hijacking. As of old, many womenandchildren but few men had been allowed off the plane. Bosnia in the 1990s re-presented the old spectacle of rape as a military strategy. More recently, women huddled in cold cellars in Chechnya while men tried to fend off Russians in an exercise as old as the hills – valiant and futile – rather than through new politics (at least from what I could see). Whither the falling apart of gender metanarratives, of war metanarratives in this postmodern era? The forms and goals may change, but the gender foundations and unities can remain unmoved – and full of meaning. Put differently, in some corners of international relations, "women" remains right where it has always been sited – in alternating neglect and atrocities.

Tensions between standpoint and postmodern feminism, enlivened by postcolonial feminist challenges of recent years, lead us to query where in feminism the various IR questions should attach in the future. For me, they already site at a moving fulcrum that feminists must be able both to follow and to shape through their mastery of appropriate theories and methods. In "Empathetic Cooperation," I argue that empathy – as a feminist-resonating epistemological method with some ontological overtones – is required to carry off the transversal research strategies that compose that fulcrum. Empathetic cooperation has emerged several times across this feminist journey and is systematized here. My outline of it reflects a history of participation in the feminist politics of the late 1960s and 1970s and a chastening when those power feminisms fragmented in the 1980s and 1990s to step more carefully around each other and the world. While greatly admiring the more recent feminist embrace of difference, and recognizing it as a required corrective to what Elshtain (1993) refers to as the narratives of closure of earlier days, I have also sought a method by which to massage differences into something that can be publicly powerful and not merely celebratory of separate spaces for voice (Sylvester, 1995a).

Below, I formally present "empathetic cooperation" as a feminist method for managing, working with, respecting, and surpassing rigid standpoints, positions, and issues without snuffing out difference. I lean on Elshtain and Enloe for many of the ideas, but also present Judith Butler, Kathy Ferguson, Trinh Minh-ha, everyday women at Greenham Common Peace Camp, and, at the other end of the world, Zimbabwean women in their local production sites. The chapter is a summary effort to read various feminisms into IR and vice versa around responsible feminist negotiators, who are mindful that their sense of difference "out there" is affected by movements in their own subjectivities and shifts and mobilities in the uncapturable "other."

* * *

An increasing number of feminist analysts have drawn attention to the "women"-eclipsing cast of mainstream theories of international relations (IR) (Elshtain, 1987; Enloe, 1989, 1993; Grant and Newland, 1991; Peterson, 1992; Tickner, 1992). I have argued that the gendering of IR as a masculine realm of knowledge reflects a longstanding, albeit tacit, regime in the field that rehearses rules, norms, and expectations of western professional "men" and ignores people and traits associated with "women" (Sylvester, 1993b, 1994a).[1] In IR literatures there are statesmen, soldiers, despots, terrorists, decision-makers, and impersonal structures bereft of human agency. "Women" may be written about in this realm of "men" if their behaviors have been sufficiently regime-supportive to gain them entry into the designated politics of the international.[2] "Women" who deviate from the norms of IR wander the field unnoticed and untheorized – as the Chiquita Bananas of international political economy, the Pocahontases of diplomatic practice, the companions for warriors on military bases, the Beautiful Souls who weep at the walls of war and then retreat to their proper place elsewhere, or the abstract "mother countries" that comprise the international system (Elshtain, 1987; Enloe, 1989). Refused places and tasks that theorists deem central to the constitution of international relations, most "women," in fact, are homeless in the canons of IR knowledge.

There is some irony to this. IR is a scholarly field that evidences considerable disagreement over its own fundamentals (Ferguson and Mansbach, 1988). It is a field that has been constituted and reconstituted through a series of ongoing debates, the third of which is now shading into a fourth (Price and Reus-Smit, 1998). Despite all the discussion, it is

Revised from *Millennium: Journal of International Studies* (1994) 23, 2. Millennium Publishing group. Used with permission.
[1] Commonplace gender designations do not necessarily signify true, essential, meaningful, authentic, and singular identities. "Women," for example, is associated with the private sphere of caretaking, while "men" is entitled to inhabit and manage public spaces. Individuals may break the usual "rules" without undermining the general tendency of affixing associations to the two genders. However, some men and women find meaning, identity, and fulfillment in their gender statuses and some feminist theorists insist that real women must be seen and taken seriously. When men and women appear in the text without inverted commas, it is to signify an absence of doubt in that context concerning the fundamental meaning of gender.
[2] For a discussion of masculinity as an appropriating force in international relations, see Morgan (1989).

evident that the bodies, assigned places, and evocations of "women" are unproblematically marginalized, if not put out of place entirely, in practices and in most literatures that purport to describe, understand, and debate international relations. A conversation, to say nothing of a debate, on gender and IR has simply not occupied any center stage of the field.[3]

Feminist theorizing offers numerous reasons to strive for greater inclusivity in theory; among them are the possibility of less biased, less partial understandings of the world, the possibility of greater justice in theory and practice, and the possibility that we discover, through the binoculars of gender research, that our very categories of identity and attachment are habits rather than realities. Feminist theorizing also suggests ways of activating these possibilities rather than keeping them at a theoretical level. Perhaps women's daily activities, assignments, and maybe even ways of knowing and being – which are mostly outside the scrutiny of conventional social theory – could fill gaps in knowledge created through the never impartial gaze of science. Perhaps notions of objectivity could be renegotiated as characteristics of the social context of the researcher, rather than remain the artifact left when we separate ontology from epistemology, the knower from the known, the dailiness of the private sector, where people called women are said to dwell, from the rational exemplar of proper science "out there." Then again, perhaps we should ask the question Simone de Beauvoir (1952:xv) posed fifty years ago: "Are there women, really?" For if one settles into the identity of woman (or invents oneself as woman) to learn about the world anew, yet "woman" is a socially invented category to begin with, what is one doing if not celebrating gender performance as deep authenticity?[4] It would, perhaps, be preferable to query the social constitution of gender in all fields of knowledge, and move away from inherited identity strait-jackets, rather than grant authority to invented social statuses.

Bearing these vexing feminist issues in mind, I ask whether it is possible to rescript IR to be more gender-inclusive without wedding us perilously to a "women's" international relations.[5] If we imagine that

[3] It is instructive that Tickner (1997) makes the same observation in a later piece.
[4] "To the extent that a term is performative, it does not merely refer, but acts in some way to constitute that which it enunciates" (Butler, 1993:217).
[5] Calling for greater inclusivity does not imply that full inclusion is possible. Says Butler (1993:221): "That there can be no final or complete inclusivity is thus a function of the complexity and historicity of a social field that can never be summarized by any given description, and that, for democratic reasons, ought never to be."

women do not exist, what would "an" IR based on "her" standpoint be? If we say that women do exist, might we not risk writing some stony standards against which to measure and punish false texts and heretics?[6] If we say that "women" merely exist as receptacles of qualities that are not valorized in the public sphere, then what is to prevent the re-emergence of an equally invented masculine IR to contest for "IR?" I want theorists of IR to take seriously the situated and shifting frames of knowledge that race across the eyes of disenfranchised groups. But I do not want to say that those groups have a monopoly of insight or that, in fact, there are no groups of (real) "women" to sight. I prefer to snuggle into tensions at the fulcrums of feminist representations of "women" and explore therein a borderland method to rescript knowledge, eschewing the jump to one or the other side of a needlessly dichotomized debate about women versus "women."

The method I particularly want to explore is one I term empathetic cooperation. It is a process of positional slippage that occurs when one listens seriously to the concerns, fears, and agendas of those one is unaccustomed to heeding when building social theory, taking on board rather than dismissing, finding in the concerns of others borderlands of one's own concerns and fears (Sylvester, 1994a). Conversational processes of empathetic cooperation heighten the tensions that one (or a whole field) would like to ignore, making it more difficult to think of a fixed starting place for theory. Empathetic cooperation can also be a research gaze that enables us to read the texts of practice more inclusively because we can identify "strange" slippages, conversations, locations, and perspectives that already defy the official menu of international relations, although they often go unnoticed. Both applications of the term come into play in the following pages.

Unempathetic denials of women in IR

Chris Brown (1992a) argues that normative IR should not just be about the moral dimensions of theory, but about questioning meaning and

---

[6] Butler (1993:18-19) frames this dilemma as follows: "On the one hand, any analysis which foregrounds one vector of power over another will doubtless become vulnerable to criticisms that it not only ignores or devalues the others, but that its own constructions depend on the exclusion of the others in order to proceed. On the other hand, any analysis which pretends to be able to encompass every vector of power runs the risk of a certain epistemological imperialism which consists in the presupposition that any given writer might fully stand for and explain the complexities of contemporary power."

interpretation generated by the discipline as a whole. All forms of feminist theorizing are normative, in the sense that they help us to question certain meanings and interpretations in IR theory, because many are concerned, says Jane Flax (1987:622) with "gender relations . . . how we think or do not think . . . about them" (or avoid thinking about gender). However, one does not have to be a feminist theorist to issue normative gender pronouncements. Indeed, the contemporary mainstream field of IR is encrusted with gendered understandings of who belongs properly where in the political relations that comprise the international.

It is relatively easy to see that Machiavelli had an angle on gender when he entitled a chapter in *Discourses* "How States are Ruined on Account of Women." He argued that women tempt men to mix private affairs and public matters in ways that presumably reduce a prince's rationality – and prince (along with advisors) is indisputably assigned the job of knowing politics. Years later, Louis XIV made that linkage crystal clear, audaciously declaring that *l'état c'est moi*, that the state is a certain man, that knowledge of the state is limited to knowing about powerful men. In between those respective eras of theorizing, and following them, lie a host of stories about masculinized knowledge in the politics of statecraft, which theorists of IR have borrowed or simply presumed to hold true in the invented spaces of the international. Thomas Hobbes, for instance, presents biological women as strong and cunning in the state of imagined nature, truly the equals of biological men. But he does not let this condition of equality stand. To women he gives an assignment that handicaps their efforts to fight as the equals of men in those periodic wars of all against all. That assignment is mother-rights to children. Defending themselves and children against men who do not have involuntary obligations to weaker parties – men who step forth as individuals – women are conquered. Conquered peoples cannot know the social contract in the same way the conquerors can, because they are not freestanding individuals. Along with some men who have the misfortune, rather than the destiny, of being handicapped in war, "women" are conquered and brought into the social contract in an ambiguous relationship to citizenship and rights (Pateman, 1988). Conquered men are eventually released from servitude through various amendments to their contracts: in the United States we remember the fourteenth and fifteenth amendments to the constitution in this light; elsewhere, various independence arrangements released conquered colonies of men from direct imperial servitude. Yet today, well after the second sex has achieved technical citizenship in most sites in the world, people called women who succeed in public office – those who refuse to accept the idea that states are ruined on account of women – are exceptions to the knowledge of men ruling, which means they still have an anomalous place in politics and not a usual place (Caroll, 1985; Hirschmann, 1992; Sylvester, 1992).

Hobbes' story of gender knowledge and place in politics echoes Machiavelli's concerns and effectively evacuates "women" to sites in civil society that are nonpolitical and private. This means that conquering "men" are left inhabiting the governed places of Leviathans, and then the more democratically organized states. Viewed against this backdrop, *l'état c'est moi* is more than a monarch's statement of personal arrogance. It is a theory-sanctioned gender conflation that comes to assume proportions of considerable importance in western political culture. It metamorphoses under liberal theory to a state that is the sum total of its citizens. And yet even as "women" are admitted to a greater fullness of citizenship – through the franchise or the right to bear arms – their rarity in public office, their unequal status to men in the economy, and their assignment to the private sphere mean that citizens with the fullest entry to recognized politics remain "men." One might say that "citizensandstates" conflate into one gendered entity.

International politics is the IR-invented other site to national politics. Jean Bethke Elshtain (1992:143) tells us that in that space, sovereignty must be recognized or it could be violated. "War is the means to attain recognition." Since sovereignty is tied to a gendered place of politics, men fight for their territories as "the definitive test of political manhood" (p. 143). The process of declaring sovereignty and fighting for it recreates the Hobbesian state of nature beyond civilized governance; but it does so with a twist. Hobbes' original state of nature was peopled by evocations of "men" and "women." The IR state of nature remembered evokes only "men" – citizensandstates and their politics. This must mean, as Cynthia Enloe (1990) leads us to see, that womenandchildren are equally conflated entities in the lexicon of international relations. They are reliably ensconced inside the private homes that support public citizensandstates. With this sequestering, IR becomes a realm of politics removed from all births and all deaths, except those that memorialize the soldier forever as part of the state.

In these foundational stories, "women" are mythologically outside all politics-constituting knowledge of nation-states and international relations. Indeed, they are assigned jobs that free "men" to be "in the know" politically. Yet the renderings mask the way the discourses depend on evocations of "women" doing key tasks in order for politics to exist at all – in any place – and they mask the power that theorists attribute to "women" as strong and cunning ones who do not seem to know contracts and sovereignties.

In more contemporary renderings of IR, these patterns of gender politics reappear in and around the bananas marketed for international consumption, the beaches of our (western) contentment, and the bases of realist defense (Enloe, 1989). In these and other places international, "women's" identities and activities are denied salience in theory and practice. Yet here there are diplomatic wives, confidantes, secretaries, and companions, tourists, combat-denied female soldiers, and "nimble-fingered" Asian textile workers. Here are all those people who do not count in IR because their bodies are inscribed with conquest rather than with autonomy, agency, and authority (which also means that their minds do not produce quotable knowledge). Here are mothersandchildren as against the citizensandstates that own all sites of politics and therefore can craft international relations and the politics of IR with the aplomb of self-evident entitlement.

Consider instances of entitlement in the contemporary field. Realist progenitor Hans Morgenthau (quoted in Thompson, 1960b:17) denounced the early philosophical stories of politics, virtue, and place as "alien to theory" in IR. He accepted without comment, however, the gender implications rife in stories told by supposedly unsystematic thinkers such as Hobbes. Anyone acquainted with Morgenthau's (1965) principles of political realism knows that his sixth principle sets apart realist statesmen and scholars from the contaminating effects of "other standards." Morgenthau mentions a few of the standards that must be avoided – those of the lawyer or the economist, for instance. There are many more private standards assigned to "women" – homemaking and childcare for two – that do not merit even a dismissive mention. Apparently, there are some standards one should isolate from realism and there are other standards realists need not think about.

Later, crafting realism into neorealism, Kenneth Waltz (1979) endeavored to shift the level of usual realist analysis from states and statesmen to system interactions. There was a subtle gender politics in his move. Given a pre-existing tradition of citizensandstates, there could not be a relegation of "men" to homelessness in any of the locations and levels of politics they created and inhabited. Even as neorealism strove for objectivity through a minimization of human agency, it abstractly rehearsed an old gender story of masculine entitlement – this time, to pronounce on system mechanisms. Postmodernist Richard Ashley (1989) recognized some gender reductionism in IR and argued that state-craft, at least, had always been mancraft. But he did not notice what feminist Rebecca Grant (1991:18) could easily mark – that "the exclusion of women is a necessary part of the unproblematic figure of 'sovereign man.'"

To get through and around intended and unintended repetitions of "men's" place and knowledge, so as to reach more inclusive spaces of relations international, seems to require more than critique and point/counterpoint debate. It requires a vehicle of disturbance that can go beyond the limitations of any given theory, beyond debates that never quite see what is missing, and beyond awkward insertions of "women" into epistemologies that deny them certain places. We need methods that disturb all our places in theory (including the homeless sites some of us occupy), unsettling them and causing these slippages or mobilities in knowledge that prepare the way for cooperative reinterpretations of the field. This concern takes us to the method of empathetic cooperation and to feminist theories that sustain it.

Empathetic cooperation and feminism

Feminist constructions of politics reveal and defy the ban on "women." They deconstruct and interpret the conventions of sovereign citizens and states that routinely put people called women in apolitical places *vis-à-vis* the sacralized realms reserved for liberal "individuals." They interpret from the other side – the side of women and children – or conduct genealogical tracings of the social construction of gender-occluding political power in unsighted and, therefore, uncited realms of the international.

Sometimes they simply and eloquently evoke possibilities for theorizing that are currently foreclosed by our guiding premises of human and international behavior. Trinh Minh-ha (1989:1), for example, matter-of-factly inserts "women" into a hypothetical village meeting in an unnamed Third World country, showing us how a variety of standards of gender can be present in the politics of village life: "A mother continues to bathe her child amidst the group; two men go on playing a game they have started; a woman finishes braiding another woman's hair. These activities do not inhibit listening or intervening when necessary." That is, "women" need not put aside their usual activities in order to be public and political. Elshtain, by contrast, serves up "women" as the experienced postmoderns of contemporary western politics, the ones who cannot go on braiding each other's hair as in the past while listening in on the usual patriotic business of modern statecraft. She says: The chastened patriot – chastened in the sense of stripped of the excesses of nationalism – has "learned from the past. Rejecting counsels of cynicism, they modulate the rhetoric of high patriotic purpose by keeping alive the distancing voice of ironic remembrance and recognition of the way patriotism can shade into the excesses of nationalism" (1987:252–253).

In these renderings, there is a sense of urgency about bringing real women into view and into village meetings everywhere, finally valorizing women's experiences of knowing and being as alternatives to exclusionary citations. There is also evidence of skepticism about the very boundaries of gender identity that we chant like a mantra, wear like birthday suits, and turn into articles of ideological faith – or high patriotic purpose. Judith Butler (1993:188) puts the issue at stake as "the apparent need to formulate a politics which assumes the category of 'women' with the demand, often politically articulated, to problematize the category, interrogate its incoherence, its internal dissonance, its constitutive exclusions." The urgencies of the debate have often played out as a seeming struggle for feminist hegemony, something Elshtain (1993:100) decries:

> Of course, there are feminisms that push for hegemony, some all-encompassing narrative, theory, or model – I call them "narratives of closure" because they leave no room for ambiguity; instead, they aspire to hard and fast truths on the grand scale and eliminate complexity, irony and paradox as corrosive of totalized ideological commitment ... I ... criticize any and all such theories, whether feminist, nonfeminist, antifeminist, political economy, rational choice, realist, neorealist – I don't care.

There are other struggles at the fulcrum of feminist insights, however, that are nonhegemonic in style. What happens, asks Kathy Ferguson (1993:3), when "we simultaneously put women at the center and de-center everything including women?" What happens when we ride the hyphens of feminisms that accord women agency as knowers and that are radically skeptical of women? Is it possible to arrive at some location of commensurability or must one feminism be hegemonic?

Feminist standpoint epistemology researches and interprets the life experiences of women in order to bring them to bear on knowledge.

Much as classical Marxism valorized the experiences of proletarians in places dominated by bourgeois practice, standpoint feminism offers women as a locus both of knowledge and of the agency necessary to correct patriarchal practices (once those knowledges are freed from distortions brought on by life under patriarchy) (Hartsock, 1985).[7] Women are the mothers, household food preparers, agriculturalists, and caretakers of the world. Their activities sustain the species and provide fertile ground for developing particular knowledges about human relations, relations with "nature," about struggles for voice, recognition, and status as autonomous beings, and about the intricate ways that societies dominated by people with other assignments can block those knowledges. Says Ferguson (1993:6) of standpoint thinking, if we "interpret appearances properly in order to uncover an underlying meaning, [we find] a reality distorted but not destroyed by the power of those able to construct the appearances in the first place." Through feminist struggles for truth, respect, and dignity, women's ways of knowing can develop into epistemological and political standpoints that are less distorted than the canons shoring up and reproducing the standpointed knowledge of sovereign privilege – the world according to those who create and win wars.

In contrast to the interpretive approach of standpoint feminism, feminist postmodernism is genealogical. It traces the constituted nature of women's life experiences to dominant patterns of knowledge and power that foreclose a vast array of alternative identities. It "takes up a posture of subversion toward fixed meaning claims" (Ferguson, 1993:6) and reveals how men and women, as well as the divisions of labor we associate with them, are constructed as stable statuses. It investigates the social processes that order disorderly currents by asking how power is manifested in the gender stories that conventional society rehearses, and in the substitute stories standpointers spin. It asks how accidents of life are disciplined to fit a sense of preordination. It makes of the modern subject "data to be accounted for rather than . . . a source of privileged accounts of the world" (Ferguson, 1991:328). Its tool of analysis, deconstruction,

---

[7] Sandra Harding (1991:123) makes this point about the importance of mediating women's experiences rather than using the raw data as a source of alternative knowledge: "it cannot be that women's experiences in themselves or the things women say provide reliable grounds for knowledge claims about nature and social relations. After all, experience itself is shaped by social relations . . . Moreover, women (feminists included) say all kinds of things – misogynist remarks and illogical arguments; misleading statements about an only partially understood situation; racist, class-biased, and heterosexist claims – that are scientifically inadequate."

pulls apart gender in ways that, to use a hackneyed expression, "open spaces" for new and heretofore ignored identities, ontologies, and epistemologies to emerge. In other words, through this research methodology, women are revealed as subjects tied to subject statuses, and this very revelation enables a multiplication of options.[8]

Standpoint-based research has been accused of seeking alternative perspectives on truth that bubble forth from the experiences of unproblematized women. And yet we do not have to look too far to notice that, rather than discovering something called "a woman's way of knowing," standpoint feminist research has uncovered so many different experiences of so many different types of people called women that the essentialism implied by a standpoint has often gone by the wayside (e.g., Anzaldúa, 1990; Mohanty et al. 1991). Indeed, feminist standpoint research has helped to identify many identity communities among people called women, and many standpoints in feminism – African, lesbian, Jewish, peace, womanist, socialist, radical, and so on. By definition, postmodernist research in feminism has done something similar: it has revealed the power and politics laden in local acts of resistance to universalizing narratives. It has noted the places people carve out for themselves as they endeavor to decide their identities and knowledges rather than fit themselves to received wisdom (Bower, 1991; Butler, 1993; Elshtain, 1987; Jones, 1991; Sylvester, 1991a, 1993d).

A fulcrum of the two feminisms, therefore, eases into view. Elshtain (1993:101–102) sees it: "I would insist that to cease and desist from grand narratives of closure, to move instead toward perspectives and positions that, more modestly and surefootedly, give us insight, even inconsistencies robustly defended and drawing upon strong but various evidence – I'm not anti-empirical – is by far the better way to go as scholars and citizens." At this fulcrum of perspectives and positions (in the deliberate plural), there are efforts made to reveal the long histories of inherited statuses that bind women (a genealogical concern), and quests to make alternative readings of those statuses possible (says Ferguson (1993:27), "interpretation of various kinds is *all there is*"). At this fulcrum, "genealogy keeps interpretation honest, and interpretation gives genealogy direction" (1991:337). Here there are acts of resistance, insight, and insistency.

---

[8] Butler (1993:30) argues that "[t]o call a presupposition into question is not the same as doing away with it; rather, it is to free it from its metaphysical lodgings in order to understand what political interests were secured in and by that metaphysical placing, and thereby to permit the term to occupy and to serve very different political aims."

At this fulcrum, we the researchers can stand limbs akimbo to suspect and inspect the confining baggage that people called women are routinely meant to carry (e.g., motherhood, peace-lovingness, care). We know that a subject status – a bag carefully labeled – does not necessarily summarize the contents or the subject holding the bag. But we also know to look inside before discarding those burdens. Therein lie treasure troves of experience that have not been tapped for social theory. Therein are indications that the bags have traveled so widely and traversed so many terrains that their contents are liminal:

> He blinks twice
> and I realize there is much
> red arid brownness
> in the "whites" of his eyes.
> (Zook, 1990:87)

Liminality suggests borderlands that defy fixed homeplaces in feminist epistemology, places of mobility around policed boundaries, places where one's bag disappears and reappears before moving on. Feminist standpoint and postmodernist epistemologies are borders to each other, but they also ooze and leak. The different faces of feminism simply emphasize different subjectivities, different traveling experiences, which we can think of as mobile rather than fixed, criss-crossing borderlands rather than staying at home. Mobile subjectivities, says Ferguson (1993:154):

> are temporal, moving across and along axes of power (which are themselves in motion) without fully residing in them. They are relational, produced through shifting yet enduring encounters and connections, never fully captured by them. They are ambiguous: messy and multiple, unstable but persevering. They are ironic, attentive to the manyness of things. They respect the local, tend toward the specific, but without eliminating the cosmopolitan. They are politically difficult in their refusal to stick consistently to one stable identity claim; yet they are politically advantageous because they are less pressed to police their own boundaries, more able to negotiate respectfully with contentious others.

Ferguson's orchestration of a moving fulcrum of feminisms is fascinating. But it also poses methodological challenges for those who would try to forge a movement within mobilities or isolate a melody from the potential cacophony. I offer empathetic cooperation as a navigational method for politics at borderlands.

Empathy taps the ability and willingness to enter into the feeling or spirit of something and appreciate it fully in a subjectivity-moving way. It is to take on board the struggles of others by listening to what they have to say in a conversational style that does not push, direct, or break through to "a linear progression which gives the comforting illusion that one knows where one goes" (Trinh, 1989:1).[9] It is an ability and willingness to investigate questions of "women" (and other misdeeds in IR) in ways that open us up to the stories, identities, and sites that have been by-passed in "our" field. Along the way, our subjectivities travel to accommodate the new empathies. That is, they shift ranks or parameters of meaning as we listen. We then cooperate when we "negotiate respectfully with contentious others" (Ferguson, 1993:154) around the mobilities that empathy has revealed. Put differently, we jointly probe meaning and action in the face of homelessness within canons that have themselves been made to slip their moorings through empathetic readings, modes of listening, and ways of sighting. Together, empathy and cooperation enable "different 'worlds' and ourselves within them" (Lugones, 1990:396), as we engage in politically difficult negotiations at borderlands of knowledge, experience, differences, and subjectivities.

Interestingly, Ferguson (1993:33) explicitly rejects the idea that feminist standpoint and postmodernist differences can travel together via empathy. Following Donna Haraway (1989), she argues that approaches to reconciliation that rest on appeals to empathy can go astray: "empathy can readily be recruited into a gesture of appropriation (as in 'I know just what you mean' when I really don't know at all)." I sympathize with Ferguson's concerns, but that is precisely the point: "I"ness is a sign of sympathy and not empathy. Sympathy is a self-centered sentiment that allows for little if any slippage, mobility, and hyphenation of subjectivity and identity on the occasion of listening to someone else's tales. Says Butler (1993:118), "sympathy involves a substitution of oneself for another that may well be a colonization of the other's position *as* one's own." Empathy is something rather different. If one "hears" the different voices of IR empathetically, because one's own identities are less fixed than one thinks and because one is listening respectfully with many ears, new field-multiplying identities become possible in the face of shared alienations from master texts (and the homeless wanderings

---

[9] I would agree with Trinh and disagree with Elshtain that the feminist release from grand narratives of closure leaves us, as Elshtain (1993:101–102) says, "surefooted." Mobile subjectivities suggest that our many tracks prevent the emergence of hegemony.

they impose on "women"). This alienation renders a cooperative negoti-ation of knowledge both necessary and desirable as many subjectivities, in effect, interparticulate.

Exercises in cooperative knowledge generation call into question the cooperations that mainstream IR literatures define. Neorealism, for in-stance, tells us that cooperation is something that can afflict states but is less prevalent than self-help, owing to constraints imposed by anar-chic system structure (Waltz, 1979). Neoliberal institutionalism presents cooperation as a condition that states submit to in order to avoid subop-timal outcomes of self-help decision making, while keeping defection as an option (Keohane, 1989b). In the idealist tradition, cooperation is a natural human characteristic that can be exported to international relations (Suganami, 1989). Cooperation, in the sense in which I am us-ing it, is a process of negotiation that (real) theorists join because they have taken on board (rather than strategically calculated) enough of the texture of marginalized identities that their self-identity with canoni-cal knowledge is disturbed and must be renegotiated by enlarging the social scope of interpretation.

IR theorists need not, in Elshtain's (1993:106) words of caution, "col-lapse into empathy – you know, some thoroughgoing identification with 'oppressed people everywhere' . . . [in some] rather patronizing [sense that] . . . does not permit the necessary critical distance and analytic acuity." If our subjectivities are mobile and hyphenated, then no self-sacrifice takes place, no thoroughgoing identity take-over is possible. What is possible is a negotiation that heightens awareness of difference *and* enables us to appreciate that theory can be a range of coopera-tively decided or contending positions. Each of these positions can then be tested against demanding standards of empathy to create a "robust rather than an anemic dialogue" (p. 106).

Lest the charge of relativism be leveled at this approach, one can only say that relativism seems to be a refusal of cooperation among needed incompatibles in favor of an uninvolved position of "who am I to say?" Relativism is not a position from which one can engage in negotiation. It barricades spaces of difference as off-limits, beyond one's depth. It "otherizes" in the name of tolerance, denying that the invented other to whom one gives space could possibly have anything in common with one's (fixed sense of) Self.[10] It denies mobilities, transversals, and

---

[10] Uma Narayan (1989) warns us against assuming that in order to valorize difference we must stand apart and deny the possibility of any commonality.

commonalities in order to avoid the charge of colonialism; but then it ends up creating exotic and quaint ones that we visit, bomb, or cluck our tongues about. Overcoming relativism entails becoming more comfortable with chronic borderland statuses in ourselves that can tap empathetically into what only seems to be an experience or identity foreign to one-Self. We do not evacuate some subjectivities in a repetition of what happened to "women" in political theory, or throw away all previous knowledge so that the "collapse into empathy" can be achieved as a standpoint. Rather, all of us achieve a chastened place in theory-building by recognizing that none of us can appeal to a Self-evident reason for our endeavors. This is another way of saying that awareness of the identity borderlands we ourselves routinely transverse helps us to focus on relations international as a phenomenon that has eluded IR theory.

Hands-on empathetic cooperation in IR

Along with being a method for direct negotiation among theorists of seemingly incommensurable schools of thought, researchers aware of the possibilities of empathetic cooperation can use that knowledge to identify empirical instances of respectful negotiation and identity slippages in IR. I outline three such instances below. One is a case of a scholar hosting an empathetically cooperative conversation among two seemingly incommensurable identities – "soldier" and "mother." The second case telescopes a situation in which "women" cooperate empathetically to negotiate themselves into the practice of realist politics. The third is a negotiation, forbidden to usual studies of international political economy, which leads to an entangling of Zimbabwean producer cooperatives – far from even the margins of IR concerns – with international donors.

Good mothers and good soldiers

Elshtain's discussion of *Women and War* illuminates subtextual conversations occurring at the juncture of war/peace discourses. Elshtain analyzes how commonplace images of Beautiful Souls, who are socially assigned the domain of peace, and Just Warriors, who are necessary to war stories, ignore the in-between sites of identity that connect apparent opposites. Her entire book can be thought of as a hosted conversation about these caricatured knowledges of "men's" and "women's" proper places in war and peace. One section, however, is particularly exemplary of the identity mobility and slippage I associate with empathetically co-operative practice.

Elshtain maintains that two subidentities of Beautiful Soul and Just Warrior not normally theorized in IR literatures have important common ground that we should investigate. They are "mothers" and "soldiers." A good soldier is like a good mother. Both do their duty but "both are racked by guilt at not having done it right or of having done wrong as they did what they thought was right . . . One might have acted differently and a buddy been saved. One might have lived up to this ideal and a child spared that trauma or this distress" (Elshtain, 1987:222). Both are terribly concerned with bodily harm and with keeping sane: "The war lover on a killing binge [i]s someone who ha[s] 'lost it' just as the defensive mother who batters her child has lost it, having gone from protector to attacker" (p. 224). Many a warrior is sickened by the gung-ho attitudes displayed by noncombatants, just as a mother resents the advice of those who are removed from the daily requirements of children. "Men conceive of war as a freedom 'from' and find themselves pinned down, constrained; women see mothering as the ticket to adulthood and find themselves enmeshed in a dense fabric of responsibility that constrains even as it enables" (p. 225).

Elshtain uncovers a mutuality in difference that exposes commonplace understandings of "men in war" and "women in motherhood" as overwrought. That mutuality renders masculine soldiers and feminine mothers homeless in assigned places inside and outside IR respectively. But it does more than that. A simple but profound identity hyphenation of this sort has implications for IR theory. If the definitive test of political manhood has been war, and the definitive test of apolitical womanhood has been mothering, but both sites, identities, and knowledges exist in one person, a good citizenandstate is more a mix of gender-ruled assigned traits – more the motherandchild – than IR and much of its inherited political theory has acknowledged. An unspoken "other standard" that realists, in particular, have been admonished to avoid, becomes a mobile position inside rather than outside the realm of state identity and analysis. Lingering Machiavellian nightmares of states ruined on account of "women" can be turned around to reveal the many ways citizenandstate relations international actually model some of the "private" mothering activities of "women." Where are we then in our studies of international statecraft? Which soldierly and motherly intersections combine to form what types of states seeking what kinds of security? These questions require considerable cooperative conversation to resolve.

Walking "home"

In the early 1980s, a small group of mostly "women" left household places in Cardiff, Wales to walk 120 miles to a US air force base in Berkshire, England, where ninety-six cruise missiles were scheduled for deployment. The "women" had little intent to be radical. Once they brought pressure to bear on the Thatcher government to submit the deployment decision to parliamentary debate, these "walkers" planned to return home. Indeed, they initially seemed to be safeguarding the myth of Beautiful Souls, for they called their action "Women for Life on Earth." When the media ignored them, however – perhaps because there is no knowledge of "women" in international relations – they gradually became homeless in their identities as walkers and as Beautiful Souls for Life. They camped on Greenham Common, just outside the US base fences, and determined to maintain a presence there – a politics of resistance – until the missiles were stopped (Cook and Kirk, 1983; Harford and Hopkins, 1984; Liddington, 1989).

Greenham Common highlights the ways that subjectivities usually refused place in IR can become the basis of empathetically negotiated actions that strike at IR's core – realist defense. It also shows that homeless refusers of the protecter/protected *raison d'être* of security can develop a politics of empathetic cooperation that translates into organizational practices unknown to IR. These "women" eschewed usual political conventions, such as voting, designating leaders, and organizing committees, and operated well within anarchy. They enlarged the social base of knowledge around each problem that arose, each strategy that was contemplated. Sometimes consensus was reached on the shape of Greenham political actions and sometimes groups of "women" acted in ways that vented "local" or subgroup concerns. For example, some campers put implements of domesticity (potatoes) up exhaust pipes of trucks ferrying nuclear armor around England. Others defied gender place by pinning tea sets, diapers, and recipes to the base fence. In most cases, the usual Greenham style of deciding built empathy for difference through exercises that encouraged participants to listen to each other and cooperate, at minimum, by refusing to interrupt or to force conformity on others in the name of "the" cause.

Over time, existence on a damp English common turned into a borderland condition between actual physical homelessness and refused

homelessness in IR's security scripts. That is, facing daily eviction notices – the irony of insisting the "women" vacate homelessness in international politics for proper apolitical place at home – the campers
periodically cut down the perimeter fence and surged on to the military
base. The point they made was that the security of the homebase was
chimerical: soldiers are no more secure behind fences of defense than
the women are in protected English homes, so all might as well commingle on the common. Mutual homelessness around these fences raised
the prospect of respectful negotiation as an alternative to life on either
side. Moreover, daily negotiations at the fence were usually respectful. Rather than denounce or curse the soldiers or women on the other
side, each often engaged in "normal" banter with the other about family, weather, and mutual conditions of security. Defenses came down.
Common scripts were (potentially) revealed.

The insubordinations of Greenham Common Women's Peace Camp
fit what Pauline Rosenau (1992) refers to as an affirmative postmodern
movement. As is often the case in such politics, the myriad forms of
negotiation at the fences of defense, and within the group of Greenham
campers, neither succeeded nor failed. That is, neither did missiles leave
because of the women nor were they secured by the soldiers. Instead,
the peace camp became the bustling point of energy for a good anarchic system where, in the absence of rule-governed expectations, there
was room to change what and where one was properly supposed to be
through actions at the fences of assigned place. Constructivist Alexander
Wendt (1992) claims that "Anarchy is What States Make of It." Anarchy
is also what a variety of yet-to-be-heard people of international relations,
and their "strange" politics and conversations and empathies, make of
it. Rather than think of anarchy as a false projection of that cooperative
autonomy from "women" that disturbs so many feminist analysts, we
might rehabilitate "anarchy" to think about the ways contemporary relations international scramble and refuse IR standards of identity and
place.

Good families get international funding?

Through regular trips to Zimbabwe I have learned that a good producer
cooperative can be like a good family in the minds of "women" cooperators who work them, and in the eyes of some international donors.
In 1988 I conducted field research for a study on "women," "production," and "progress" in two provinces of Mashonaland, and came into
extended contact with a pair of all-"women" cooperatives in the process

of petitioning the then named European Community (EC) Microprojects Fund for Z$200,000 to improve their operations. The sponsors of the co-operatives were two locally resident Greek "women" who had imported silkworms and weaving machines from Greece and were teaching ap-proximately forty African "women" to tend the worms properly and to spin silk thread.

On several occasions while I was present, the EC team visited the coop-eratives and interrogated their business practices, asking about market-ing and pricing procedures, bookkeeping methods, and possibilities for export trade. The team told me they were seeking to ascertain whether these cooperatives maintained viable business standards. In each case, the Greek patrons answered all the questions, as though perpetuating yet another case of donor-directed development, of western knowledge steamrollering Third World "women," silencing them in the name of standards of business, turning them into spectators in their own lives. What I learned in contrast to this impression was that the women co-operators and the EC were developing the rudiments of an empatheti-cally cooperative conversation that would lead to unusual hyphenations and, especially, to renegotiated donor standards of appropriate projects to aid.

The members of the cooperatives were the ones who suggested to me that a good cooperative is like a good family. They said that both families and cooperatives teach skills to members and nourish dreams. Our dream, they said, is to turn these cooperatives into one big extended family – a factory that makes silk and other related products. For now they claimed to be asking the EC for money to buy mulberry trees, because silkworms thrive on mulberry leaves. They also needed fencing materials and transportation. From there, they said, we plan to expand into making mulberry jam and selling berries while doing silk. "The Europeans speak to each other about the funding, but we cooperators think our own thoughts."

The conflation of "families" with "cooperatives" and "factories" blurred the boundaries of identity and place, while the emphasis on "own thoughts" left some subjectivities open to further negotiation. As the private became public, domestic dreams mingled with international donor agendas, and "women's" agency was softly proclaimed. I then talked to the EC Microprojects team and found, quite unexpectedly, that they too were slipping boundaries of their organizational identity. They told me they knew full well that it was risky to fund cooperatives in Zimbabwe, because members frequently used the money for other than grant-designated things. They expressed annoyance at instances of local refusals of the rules. But the EC gave these two cooperatives the money anyway. Why? I was told that the cooperatives had been visited so often that they were now "like family."

The presence of Greek women may account for the conflation of "cooperatives" with "family." But the EC is not supposed to be funding families, only businesses. Moreover, unlike in parts of West Africa, "women" are outside business circles in Zimbabwe in ways analogous to being outside politics in the West. This means that the EC donors had to cross borderlands of usual professional identity in order to fund "families" on the advice of Greek "women."

The case of a business-minded intergovernmental organization negotiating in tacit empathy with local "women," who see themselves as sitting on the fence of "enterprises" and "families," prompts me to ask what other cooperative slippages may be occurring "out there" "beyond standards." Where else are the lines smudged between household places and international political economies in ways that reconstitute identities and redistribute resources? Where should we be looking, in other words, for relations of international political economy, and what transversals of place and knowledge might we find there?

Getting going

In this location in IR time and space, there is considerable discomfiture with an inherited stable of knowledge. Rob Walker (1993:5) goes so far as to claim that

> theories of international relations . . . are interesting less for the substantive explanations they offer about political conditions in the modern world than as expressions of the limits of the contemporary political imagination when confronted with persistent claims about and evidence of fundamental historical and structural transformation . . . attempts to think otherwise about political possibilities are constrained by categories and assumptions that contemporary political analysis is encouraged to take for granted.

These are sage words. Arguably there has been a profound failure of political imagination in IR, and this essay contends that one failure relates to longstanding conventions, explicitly argued in early political philosophy, that mark out all politics as "men's" places of knowledge. And yet Walker's words are ripe with irony, since efforts to encourage greater imagination can themselves fail to give proper time and space to the persistent claims of feminist analysts. Andrew Linklater (1992:78), for example, tells us that we are at a moment in IR when critical social theory, postmodernism, and feminism will have left an indelible impression on the field. In the course of his article he cites the names of postmodernists and critical theorists, but does not cite one feminist contributor to the indelible impression. Can indelibility be achieved by ghosts with no names, or is it not the case that we have no names because we are still out of sight and site when we are in politics (and theory)?

The politic thing to do these days may be to tip one's hat in the direction of feminist scholarship in IR. But a long history of staked-out turf prevents even critics of the mainstream from going the full distance to reapportionments of place. Thus the impetus for expanded political imagination is thrown back on to the feminist analysts ourselves. We are the ones who must get going and reach beyond debates to host a variety of conversations with the conventionals of IR, the critics, and those with persistent claims of other types. The goal is not to persuade one side to embrace the other, but to facilitate a process that has each side appreciating that the claims and accounts others present are important to a field of social knowledge. The process imparts a modicum of homelessness in all our inherited positions, which inspires cooperative ways of reaching across subjectivities, locations, and skepticisms. Analysts of IR would be wise to emulate instances of empathetic cooperation occurring in places remote from usual research gazes – where "women" make themselves homeless in IR's canon and walk from that position into a politics that in-secures the fences of security, where soldiers and mothers blend stories and assignments in ways that jostle our sense of statecraft, and where local cooperatives teach international donors to aid families that produce. Theorizing from such places throws up to us evidence of IR-"strange" empirical standpoints. These are the sites to visit and the methods to model as the many who are dissatisfied with the current state of IR knowledge endeavor to loosen its old-fashioned corsets.

Part IV
Citings

13 Feminist arts of International Relations

We reach a resting point in ongoing feminist IR/IR feminist journeying, a moment for summary looks around and off to horizons. The two chapters that compose a theme of citations appraise where feminists engaged with IR have been, where we are scuttling around to, where sticking points remain at the fulcrum of IR and feminist "nations" of scholarship, and how feminists/IR might work with our differences.

I have three concerns as we rest here. One is to recognize, insist on, herald, and caution those who have contributed to a cacophonous and multivectored journey. Some may think we are not as far ahead as we should be and others may wish to celebrate all gains made. Wherever we are is due to efforts, visions, and even the myopias of those who have been patiently drawing women and gender into and around the landscapes of IR and IR into feminism for nearly twenty years. Where "we" go next is no more preordained than the spaces already traversed; and, of course, there is no arrival point.

A second concern is that we expand our citational repertoire by bringing to feminist IR/IR feminism the worlds that appear in visual arts and fiction. I raised this issue in Part II and return to it here with an emphasis on visual arts in "Feminist Arts of International Relations" and on fiction in "Internations of Feminism and International Relations." To find, let alone meaningfully characterize, relations international that IR has been ill-equipped to detect, we need sharper acuities that spy unexpected locations and dramas of gender power. Fiction and art jog canon-bound brains by posing different representations of the places, figures, and activities we think of as international relations and by introducing us to new locations of our field.

The third concern is to present world-traveling as a feminist-inspired and fiction- and art-based methodology for navigating the many relations of the international. I wish to find ways of avoiding universalist thinking as we journey and yet not become so particularistic that we cannot engage in any activity that smacks of "representing the other." Even more so than previous essays in this volume, "Feminist Arts" and "Internations" elaborate and extend the world-traveling methods that Maria Lugones pioneered at the fulcrum of feminist and postcolonial analysis. My concern is to pose narrative and visual methods for seeing hybrid worlds, reading ourselves into them, and referencing the contributions of diverse others – all without making them into us.

"Feminist Arts," the first of the two essays in this part, gives meaning to neat but empty phrases we banter about in IR – "the art of politics," "the art of diplomacy," "the art of war." Each quickly evokes something other than anarchy, rationality, regimes, and decisions in international relations – but something that is never fully specified. It seems we like the way the word "art" sounds in our mouths or looks on paper. We are not prepared, however, to use the term as a marker for the art in international relations, any more than we reference the Surrealist movement when we routinely call bizarre events around us "surreal" (Sylvester, 1999a). Yet, is it not possible that art metaphors slipped past vigilant analytic blockades indicate submerged locations of the international and its colorful relations? In the search for visual acuity I take art seriously and world-travel through feminist looking-glasses to the arts of international relations. IR feminists already move interstitially with other disciplines (e.g., Cochran, 1999; Huntley, 1997; Saco, 1997). May I suggest doing so in the future with a world-traveling eye on the art and fictional "data" that most IR lacks?

To indicate how we might proceed, "Feminist Arts" highlights two visually based feminist methods. One outlines women's shapes in international relations and the other inlines the gender that radiates out through compositions that seemingly have no IR gender subject matter. Both approaches are avant-garde, indicating ways we can touch up or repaint aspects of IR, as Helen Brocklehurst (1999) is poised to do, and/or drip IR into feminism to yield a new school of thinking about international relations. As I noted in chapter 6, "avant-garde" signals a forerunning movement, which is certainly the story of feminist IR/IR feminism; but the term also harbors attachment to a hero-driven teleology that world-traveling would see as a misguide to the sights. Our methods should be innovative and also nonself-celebratory.

The canvas for "Feminist Arts" is large, with many figures set in European landscapes. If there is a spotlight in this piece, it is on the

Nordic states, geospaces I have returned to regularly since 1996, when a brilliant conference on gender and international relations, held at Lund University, produced a large installation of IR feminists from eastern Europe, Austria, Germany, Denmark, Greenland, Finland, Sweden, the UK, Canada. As I embark on yet another major professional move through the international – to the Institute of Social Studies in The (art-filled) Hague – I celebrate expeditionary Europeans who fill out IR or invite IR into worldly pictures of feminism.

* * *

Feminist International Relations is avant-garde. Along with postmodernism and critical theory, it breaks with tradition, seeks innovation, and shocks by portraying locations and agents of international relations that formalist IR has not imprimatured. It cites authorities unrecognized by gazers at states, military strategies and hardware, statesmen, presidents, tyrants, soldiers, decision-makers, World Bankers, United Nations diplomacy, war and a little peace. It shines lights into the corners of international tableaux, showing up, thereby, usual depictions of the world and its relations as the realm of the *fauve*. It adds clutter to neat pictures, filling right up to the edge, not out of some medieval *horror vacui* revisited, but from an ethical-aesthetic concern to fit in the figures, the shapes, and all the worldly colors usually left to places beyond the frame.

It is the research posture of standing in many locations, illuminating important relations and practices darkened by the long shadows of official IR, of painting international relations differently, that I wish to highlight here. Feminism has types and shifting forms. It is nonuniform, nonconsensual; it is a complex matter with many internal debates. To unravel feminism's contributions to the study of international relations, it is useful to consider how feminists approach their art, glimpsing along the way the netherworlds of significant action that feminist IR/IR feminist aesthetics reveal in and around the hero-worlds of IR.

The avant-garde and progress

To speak of feminist IR/IR feminism as an avant-garde pushing the boundaries of knowledge and technique is to position it as a cousin of progress. This is a compelling yet troubling thought (Shohat and Stam, 1998; Sylvester, 1999b). We noted earlier (chapter 6) that an avant-garde, a term associated with modern art movements, sees itself leading, advancing, moving forward, first at the rails, setting the trend, out in front, ahead of the pack, successful and nonconforming. Art critic Clement Greenberg (cited in Kuspit, 1993:2) once described the avant-garde as "uniquely authentic in an inauthentic society" of kitschy lawn ornaments sold as art. Not only could the avant-garde do something innovative and original (Krauss, 1985), Greenberg believed it would save art from lowbrow frivolity and moral disaster (Greenberg, 1985). (Think of feminism saving rooftop Santas from leading irradiated reindeer into realist wars.) Yet, the fact that an avant-garde reaches toward a travelog of the future means it operates with a belief in progress that feeds a need for ever newer signs of progress; and so we search the horizon for avants who are ahead of proliferating styles and new "inauthenticities." It all happens in those fifteen minutes Andy Warhol told us about: if an avant-garde does not make its mark quickly, it risks going unseen, being incorporated into lowbrow trends, or competing with – and possibly losing against – other attention-seekers.

To take this all back to feminism and IR, there are gains in being first and also losses at stake as avant-garde feminisms compete with other cults of progress. The Australian cultural studies writer John Docker (1994:21) warns us that most avant-gardes historically scorn "mass culture as female, as indeed a kind of bewitching succubus, overwhelming the masculine concentration and nerve that is necessary for true discrimination if the historical crisis [which spawns an avant-garde] is to be faced and thought through." This may explain some of IR's other avants' trouble with feminism: it is so, er, "mass." Yet the cults comprising women's studies can apparently have trouble with us too. Regard a range of feminist surveys and notice how rarely they cite work by known scholars of feminist IR (e.g., Caine and Pringle, 1995; Jackson and Pearson, 1998; Kaplan et al. 1999; Mohanty et al. 1991; Visvanathan et al. 1997; Weedon, 1999). How avant-garde can an avant-garde be without recognition of its avantness? And what of outcomes in which everyone copies aspects of everyone else in a canonical repudiation of avant-garde power and originality?

While avants jostle for position, progress urges on strivings, thrusts, movements, sorrows, make-believes, virtualities, compromises, cults, and cynicisms. Progress advances arrogantly and presumptuously, with cement, glass, and theory. It also stands us still in the wait for it, inviting nostalgia or holding out hope on an IMF platter. Once celebrated in the International Style of architecture, in Abstract Expressionist paintings, in Socialist Realist art, and in post-Cold War foreign policy, progress today is in tatters in some quarters (think of Angola, Bosnia, Cambodia,

Zimbabwe, Fiji). Yet even tattered progress is full of the talk of progress as process, rhythm, and change, the unfolding of potential and intent, simultaneous destruction and renewal. Look elsewhere: American novelist Toni Morrison (cited in Forbes, 1999:23) draws Bill Clinton as the first Black president of the USA. *Très avant*. Now we are getting somewhere?

Life is ever in progress. Whether it progresses in avant-garde or other ways, when, where, and how – and what is its style? – is an enormous question for development, international relations, art, and feminism. There are cautions, pits into which to fall, crocs to elude. In and amongst the temptations of visibility and ambition, and the dangers of elitist avant-gardist double edges, are all those canvases to paint, installations to assemble, clay to mold.

Feminists prime canvases

If feminist IR/IR feminism is avant-garde, which means it at least implicitly strives for higher form, subject matter, symbolism, design, and function than usual IR can deliver, what is the theory behind it? Avant-gardes always have a guiding theory (Danto, 1981) and yet Judith Butler and Joan Scott (1992:xiii) maintain that theory is a contested notion among feminists:

> what qualifies as "theory"? Who is the author of "theory"? Is it singular? Is it defined in opposition to something which is atheoretical, pretheoretical, or posttheoretical? What are the political implications of using "theory" for feminist analysis, considering that some of what appears under the sign of "theory" has marked masculinist and Eurocentric roots? Is "theory" distinct from politics? Is "theory" an insidious form of politics?

Iterated questioning about the nature of theorizing, particularly about the relationship between theory and politics, informs the entire feminist enterprise, wherever located. It marks a kind of avant-gardist self-consciousness about what one is doing and where one is placed in doing it. It refuses inherited notions of proper theory for trickier ontological and epistemological discussions about who puts what sorts of knowledge into what kinds of language and pictures. The very questioning of theory is a step along the progress path to something more just, something that does not foreground certain people, experiences, and texts while evacuating others from the history of ideas and actions.

Feminists have argued that "traditional epistemologies, whether intentionally or unintentionally, systematically exclude the possibility that women could be 'knowers' or *agents of knowledge* ... history is written from only the point of view of men (of the dominant class and race)" (Harding, 1986:3). In the thrust forward, many feminists have come to recognize that the portraits they painted in the 1970s of women's oppression and emancipation – under the titles of liberal, Marxist, radical, and socialist feminisms – naïvely relied on epistemologies with checkered records of gender awareness. Hammered by feminists who could not see themselves in the tidy pictures of women's liberation then being painted, and affected by claims of Eurocentrism and disregard for difference, feminist theorists turned in the 1980s to querying what it means to know, who may know, where knowers are located, and what the differences among them mean for pictures of women and gender. There was increasing concern to avoid tyrannizing some people while providing emancipatory tools for others, noticing and announcing and analyzing some activities relevant to international relations and failing to consider the salience of others. Feminists, long concerned with the politics of their theories, now brought the politics of theorizing women and men and the power of gender to the pictorial foreground. And they did so in more nebulous ways than the prescribed norms of the social sciences allowed. Specifically, they have probed (Sylvester, 1996b) inherited theories for the marks of sex and gender and their intersections with race, imperialism, and class issues, all of which reveal distortions, biases, exclusions, inequalities, and analytic denials; genealogies of gendered and sexed theories and methods that seem neutral, universal, and natural; and experiences, narratives, and images that deepen our knowledge of gender and its locations, which means that we now look in funny places for bodies, subjectivities, stories, or other "data" to fill out or rewrite what we think we know.

When feminist theorizing takes on the cumulative knowledge in IR, it locates gender-gaping holes in arguments, sights women, gender, and sex in places no one in IR suspected, and adds avant-garde citations to the roster of notables the field rehearses. Feminists find sex in nuclear weapons design and security discourse (Cohn, 1987). They find gender in the Foreign Service of the USA and other countries (McGlen and Sarkees, 1993; Miller, 1991). They look at Israeli-Palestinian relations and notice that women are made into occupied territories in relentless masculine plays of power (Jacoby 1999; Sharoni, 1993); similar constructions become evident in other conflicts (Duffy, 2000; Sharoni,

1998). Feminists see hypermasculinized behaviors in the New World Order (Niva, 1998) as well as in the capitalist developmental state in East Asia (Han and Ling, 1998). They spot gender in Thai export processing zones (Pearson and Theobald, 1998), in Kuwaiti restructuring programs (Tetreault, 1999), in the rationalist market so enamored of neoliberals (Plumwood, 1998), and at the cusp of international relations and feminist postcolonial thinking (Spivak, 1998). Citations to the situated knowledges of many people spring up everywhere. Progress is proclaimed.

It takes an eye for sex and gender to see the art of it all. Even then it is difficult. Surrounded by enchanted positivism, which promises progress in knowledge – yes, this is the way! – only a long learning curve has brought some of us to the point of X-raying and carbon-dating the facts presented as timeless tendencies, as "objective" IR. If we do not journey along the learning curve, we end up trying to draw without looking, observing, and reckoning with life. The Danish scholar, Hans Mouritzen (1997), for example, opens a paper on Denmark's spheres of action in the post-Cold War era with a promising aphorism from Alfred Whitehead: "Seek simplicity and distrust it." Feminists nod; we know about skepticism toward the seemingly simple. We feel encouraged. Mouritzen, however, does not seem to distrust his own analytic categories enough to wonder about gender as a salient action sphere or component of the spheres he cites. Mired in IR, Mouritzen is not skeptical enough to edge his work in an avant-garde direction, in which gender would be salient to Danish foreign policy.[1] He and other IR stalwarts do not see women in the Cuban missile crisis, at the gates of military fences at Greenham, washing the dishes in the embassy. Ole Waever (1996) writes about the interparadigm debate in IR. He too does so without sighting and citing the contributions to and around that debate made by feminists. He does not have awareness, it seems, of all the important "inters" that exist in the interstices of canonical disagreements. In both cases, a certain learned visuality is missing.

There are other myopias. The neorealist pronouncement of the international as a realm of anarchic politics belies the central governing

[1] Mouritzen (1997) presents spheres of action in which Denmark seeks to promote and safeguard its most important values and interests: the international power sphere, the coalition sphere with the EU, the parallel action sphere, and Denmark's special sphere of influence. Arguably, a masculine gender sphere of action shapes interactions in each of these spheres. Mouritzen does not see this. As well, the author poses egalitarianism as an important national value that refers to reducing "cleavages between rich and poor, both domestically and internationally" (p. 34). Gender may be an important element of poverty in many countries and yet may not be seen by foreign policy analysts.

function of those making the pronouncement. Men are never black-boxed in structures and systems or any other theory of international relations. They are never absent from any of the named levels of analysis, even though they appear explicitly in only one – man (the state and war).[2] Where is the IR discussion of features of the state that, says Wendy Brown (1995:167), "signify, enact, sustain, and represent masculine power as a form of dominance?" The international relations that IR creates can look normal because all the dutiful daily housekeeping tasks, which belie the neorealist claim that the international is a place of anarchy,[3] go unmentioned.

Along with exposing the seemingly neutral world of IR as not-so, along with tracing marks of gender strewn about, feminist theorizing also poses experiences, narratives, and images that counter or deepen our knowledge of gender and its locations. Often this leads us into ever more avant-garde ways of registering the world and its trends. Globalization's big presence these days offers few citations to gender movements and travels, an oversight that is being corrected by feminists (Eschle, 2001; Kofman and Youngs, 1996; Marchand and Runyan, 2000; Meyer and Prugl, 1999; Watson, 2000). We hear much in the corridors of academic IR of dispersals of international capital and production, but we also hear now about those whose labor bears the weight of such movements – women in Third World export industries (e.g., Boris and Prugl, 1996; Pearson and Theobald, 1998; Salzinger, 1997; Ward, 1990). Feminists notice the international trade around men as sex seekers and women as sex providers (e.g., Moon, 1997; Pettman, 1996b; Richey, 2001; Truong, 1990); they notice the world's many exile locations for "women" (Heitlinger, 1997); they even notice that the progressive states of Denmark and Sweden stand behind gendered security and development programs (Kronsell and Svedberg, 2001; Petersen, 2001). Feminist theorizing as avant-garde world-traveling puts us in worlds of art museums, novels, poetry, inside households, in and around EU law, on the the labels of soup cans (Bleiker, 1999, 2000b; Enloe, 2000a; Flynn, 1997; Lundstrom, 1997; Sylvester, 1997, 1998a, 1999a; *Women's Studies International Forum*, 1996). We find international relations lower than any low politics the field could imagine, in places where everyday people stuff the heroics and become the masses, with our kitschy nappies, tampons,

---

[2] Thus Andrew Linklater genders *Men and Citizens in the Theory of International Relations* (1980).
[3] I refer to the power of neorealist belief in anarchic system structure and its progenitor, Kenneth Waltz (1979).

and tea sets on the fences of war. Feminists are simultaneously out in front and back with the commoners who make pink flamingo lawn ornaments for export. Our avant-garde theorizing is different.

There are many ways to name the theorizing feminists do and bring to IR. Sandra Harding (1986) is keen on empiricist, standpoint, and postmodernist classifications. Kathy Ferguson (1993) presents a typology of praxis, cosmic, and linguistic feminisms. These categories of activity have certainly entered into my thinking many times. But when we talk about feminist IR/IR feminism as avant-garde, we need a frame that enables us to highlight the visual aspects of our work, as well as the elements that put us simultaneously out ahead and in an *atelier* surrounded by the detritus removed from a cult world of states and WTO. My addition to offerings meant to sort and order feminist thinking is the schema of "outlining" and "inlining."

Feminist outlinings

Feminist outlinings of gendered international relations work through the metaphor of a pristine landscape repainted with clutter added. Think of the busy skating parties and raucous drinkers depicted with consummate detail in Dutch and Flemish paintings of the early Westphalian era. Such genre works present, and thereby forever memorialize, anonymous everyday people of northern European life (Hecht, 1994).[4] Instead of aristocrats preening before an artist, instead of emergent middle-class merchants and ladies flaunting their riches, genre paintings of the likes of Jan Steen draw attention to the little people and the transgressive things they do. These are the people whose hard labor made commercial fortunes for the classes that could then look upon genre depictions as mere festive comedies or as "communal village pleasures" depicting loose moral values (Westermann, 1996:68).[5] Still, there they are, the unheroic people prancingly painted into the canons of *haut art* – though they were not deemed grand enough to be painted into the *longue durée* of international relations.

Feminist outlining in IR is akin to genre painting. It adds disorder and clutter to tidy pictures of international battles, to cabinet portraits, and

---

[4] Hecht (1994) is responding to arguments that seventeenth-century art was meant to be read symbolically rather than as representations of actual life at that time, of "the ever-increasing possibilities of its miraculously life-like art" (p. 163).
[5] Susan Alpers (1975–1976) uses the term "festive comedy" to describe the purposes of genre painting in the eyes of some elite viewers.

to all those UN declarations framed on the walls. The detail comes from inserting women and their usual activities into the architectures of war, decision, and symbolic force (into, say, Casimir Malevich's politically evocative *Red Square*, which is literally a square painted red). Think of feminist outliners putting the hands of a woman into sumptuous still lifes of the past, showing her laying the fruit into those bowls, pouring wine into pewter goblets, arranging the peonies and roses that are then painted as if they had emerged out of thin air. The added strokes enable certain people and details to be seen where either no women were pictured or no people were present at all.

Feminist outlining also alters scenes showing women lying around boudoirs in various odalisque poses – naked at home or in some bucolic setting with nothing to do but tempt or pleasure men. I think of this outlining activity as "correcting Matisse," as adding fully clothed women to Edouard Manet's *Luncheon on the Grass*, or as analyzing the sex work that hides behind the image of the beautiful naked body presented as art for art's sake. Feminists also re-picture messy, vomity, dog-urinating, bowl-crashing-to-the-floor households of wayward peasant or *nouveau-riche* Dutch genre women. Mariet Westermann (1996:12) tells us that "[a] popular Dutch proverb still describes messy homes as 'households of Jan Steen,' but did seventeenth-century homes really look that way?" Probably not, she concludes. Feminist outliners add to representation by painting new images into the old. Very importantly, they also seek local women from the sites once misrepresented to roil the oils.

Getting into the landscapes

Cynthia Enloe is IR feminism's consummate outliner. When she finds average women in diplomatic offices, vacationing on beaches abroad, working in textile home industries for Benetton, or making a living as sex workers around military bases, she is engaged in an important outlining project (Enloe, 1989, 1993, 2000a). She is finding and fitting women in – and in the process changing – the usual landscapes that depict a womanless international and its relations. I think of her rich but undramatic renderings of women in international relations as nicely counterpoised to the heroic, grim, Anselm Kiefer-like landscapes produced by neorealists and by romantic Gericaultian men battling for liberty and justice in the tradition of idealism. In those scenes, women are either out of sight altogether or they appear bigger than life as victims of men – screaming and beseeching as Benvenuto Cellini's slaves to the masculine city-state or as Eugene von Guerard's Sabine rapees. Enloe refuses such erasures and subjugations. Her counter is Carmen Miranda in the international political economy of exotic fruit exports, or a Native American princess facilitating early US relations with Britain. These women are sighted, sited, and cited in international relations with agency, centrality, and finesse.

Enloe's (1989:201) antidotal theorizing of international relations is marvelously prosaic: "We don't need to wait for a 'feminist Henry Kissinger' before we can start articulating a fresh, more realistic approach to international politics. Every time a woman explains how her government is trying to control her fears, her hopes and her labour such a theory is being made." She said recently that IR cannot hear a woman explaining her relationship with politics because the field "presumes *a priori* that margins, silences and bottom rungs are so naturally marginal, silent and far from power that exactly how they are *kept* there could not possibly be of interest to the reasoning, reasonable explainer" (Enloe, 1996:188). Enloe turns it all around, reverses the rungs, and recomposes the world as a question mark in the study of women.

Enloe-esque avant-gardism invites Jacqueline True (1997) to recount an episode of women doing international politics despite being told, in so many words, that they have no place and right there. Members of the Prague Center for Gender Studies, a unit made possible by changing relations of eastern and western Europe, set about doing something very mundane: opening an account for the organization. But the mundane turns otherworldly: "The teller asked if the organization these ladies were representing were a brothel" (p. 56). A trivial question? A *faux pas*? Unlikely. The ways in which even minor, bottom-rung dabblers in international politics are able to keep the idea going that women are only there – anywhere – to service men is a point that urges on women outlining measures.

Where to find and put the women in international landscapes? Enloe, an inveterate feminist world-traveler, wanders about wondering, as an implicit methodology: where are women in a world that keeps thrusting patriarchy to the fore? She looks everywhere. Anne Sisson Runyan (1996) considers gendered regimes of international political economy that paint the world, or various regions in it, as home spaces for men. She finds resistance springing from cross-border organizing activities, such as the Mujer a Mujer's Global Strategies School, a tri-national conference that was held on women, free trade, and economic integration, which put women into the North American Free Trade Area (NAFTA). Others find girl children in national and international wars (Nordstrom, 1997) or in racial zones of nations and inter-nations (Yuval-Davis, 1993). Nuket Kardam (1991) finds women and their issues variously displayed in international development programs. In each case, outlining answers back to evacuations of relevant subject sites and matter from well-known canvases. Its art suggests that we fool ourselves when we think there is no everyday to what seems a majestic field of men's wars, treaties, walls.

Equipped with the new feminist outlining efforts, the field should become better able to recognize the romanticizations of the international and its relations that lie behind so much IR – those end-of-history murals by Francis Fukuyama (1989), the gigantic clashing civilizations sketched by Samuel Huntington (1996). Such sweeping but garishly painted scenes portray struggles to conquer differences from the West; or they throw up suspicious, alien activities to be watched vigilantly for danger – activities of "Arabs." Out of the picture are relations that revolve around women organizing or serving or sewing or banking or trading or telling their international stories. In feminist IR outlining, in they go to IR's own Ned Kelly series of men fighting men and horses falling off cliffs and women screaming. Who watches from behind a headpiece of armor?

Feminist outlining puts women into a pregiven picture or rearranges the postures of those already present or repaints IR with people other than statesmen, soldiers, and businessmen in the scenes. In go women and men and transsexuals and queers and texts and terrorism and children, along with resisters, laborers, oozers, seepers, and lackers of phallic access. Periodically there is a featured woman, perhaps an Al(l)-bright. As these forbidden people enter the picture, they provincialize IR, to borrow and extend a thought from Dipesh Chakrabarty (1992, 2000). That is, under the influence of feminist outlining, IR must move a bit to the background by virtue of having to share a foreground.

Feminist inlining

Inlining is abstraction devoid of recognizable subjects doing recognizable things. The canvas is all colors, drips, swirls on top of swirls, strokes, scrapes, impastos defying flat surfaces; the sculptures are not naturalistic. Such works are often untitled. They are not about something, not narratives to read, not figures to judge. Yet look again and we think we see figures lurking in the history of a painting, if not on its surfaces. Look once more. There is no one fixedly and recognizably and reportedly there. Inlining offers a shadowy, muted, equivocal, and fragile sense of the real.

Jackson Pollock's *Blue Poles* is emblematic of inlining. Hung with pride in the National Gallery of Australia, though painted in New York State in the early days of the Cold War, and retrospected in London in 1999, *Blue Poles* has covered some territory. Art historians describe its genre of Abstract Expressionism as devoid of figuration but bursting with masculine sweep, size, and drama (Leja, 1993). Yet this particular painting came to life while a hypermasculine man danced around the canvas squirting domestic paints at it from kitchen spatulas. It is gender-slipped in its components. It is confused in the instruments of its messy Cold War-era making. The heroic man and his kitschy kitchen methods skid out and into relations international by becoming the controversial, Vietnam-era centerpiece of international art in a major Australian collection. Do we notice the relations international around it? How do we describe the world it has created, inhabited, traveled through?

Blurring the lines

Inliners notice and are troubled by the logic of gender identity that informs the feminist outlining project. Can we know women so easily? Can we be certain that women exist anywhere coherently? If we paint them into, or rearrange them within, inherited landscapes, do we do so at the expense of blurred identities or at the expense of people who refuse to stand still as models? Do we paint at the expense of those for whom gender is an arena of transgression?

We often think we know women. They are the ones who get pregnant and nurse babies, the ones who tie the shoelaces and stir the stews and carry the wood, water, and weapons to the bush – to the just as obvious men. Men, we know, go to the moon or try to keep the space stations up there. Women stay home. We know this. But what do we know? Consider this story by Chenjerai Shire (1994:158), a Zimbabwean:

> I came from school one day – I must have been about 14 – so excited about the news that the Americans had landed on the moon that I blurted it out to my grandmother in "Shona." Her response was swift. She grabbed me by the ear and started to beat me until I retracted my words. I had used a language permitted only in women's spaces; the phrase *kuenda kumwedzi* ('to go to the moon') is used to talk about menstruation. Later, as I sat, still sobbing, she turned on the radio and heard the news. She turned to me and said:

> I heard that Americans have gone to the moon. If they are men, how could they? And if they *have* gone to the moon – so what? Women have gone to the moon every month – so it is nothing new.

Reality, says Jim George (1994:1), "is not what it used to be in International Relations." Who goes to the moon? What is that moon? Where is it?

It seems no longer productive, say some, to tie the feminist colors to the star of women or even of gender, when it is possible that "women" and "gender" are mobile and undecidable locations of subjectivity and/or performance. Butler (1993) refers to the performativity of biological sex and social gender as a ritualized repetition of norms, as regulatory ideals that are as often walked through as walked straight. Try to paint a portrait of Margaret Thatcher and end up with *Man With Beehive Hairdo*. Not that Thatcher is a man; rather, she is an unrepresentable figure when she performs outside the regulatory ideal of women without power. Try to paint a portrait of a lesbian. Is she a woman? Not necessarily, suggests Monique Wittig (1989). Is she unrepresentable too, an ambiguous relation to the categories of women and men (Calhoun, 1995)? Try to paint women in war and along comes Vivienne Jabri (1998) painting women as (uni)form war's abject. Try to paint Mexican-Americans and you come up with people whose psyches, says Gloria Anzaldúa (1987), resemble bordertowns – Chicano, American, Indian, Mexicano, immigrant Latino. There are, Norma Alarcón (1990) tells us, multiple registers of existence. These multiplicities are not easy to outline.

I have tried to study "women" in cooperatives in Zimbabwe and find them moving in between domestic and international cooperations in some subterranean netherworld of identity, some place forbidden to academic IR. They have one foot in a world of competition and markets, another in households, and a hand in the till of development regimes. Are they women? Are their relations properly international? Elshtain (1987) goes looking for women and war and ends up following war stories as narratives of what people called men and women may legitimately do, recount, and remember about war. Who wars? Who says we in IR should study whose versions of which wars, of which international political economy?

Where are the boundaries, then? Who is a woman and who is a man and where are our places? Marianne Marchand (1994) notes that there were surprisingly few new ideas about international development put forth between the mid-1980s and the mid-1990s, despite growing recognition that it was difficult to differentiate between domestic and international forces impinging on people and states. There have been feminists, however, on the borderlands of identities and geospaces diligently reconfiguring "domestic" and "international" and what it takes to inhabit and develop within "them." Rudo Gaidzanwa (1993) tells of regular crossings of Zimbabwean women into South Africa, into and out of an import–export world, as they become itinerant traders who refuse usual class, occupational, and gender pictures of business. Can one be a woman in Zimbabwe and also develop the export trade that is assigned male businessmen there? Officially, it seems, the answer is no. The paints, however, drip trails of "women" moving where they are not drawn to be.

I have observed the dangers of failing to problematize the category "women" when experts on development bring their projects to the world (Sylvester, 1995b, 2000a; Sylvester and Bleiker, 1997). Whereas social scientists have long queried the meaning of development, albeit perhaps not very creatively, those who paint women into the landscapes of development (Women in Development), those who say women are already inlined in such landscapes (Women and Development), and even those who get at the "inters" of outlining and inlining gender (Gender and Development), fail to take the same care in defining the women they ultimately seek to develop. The result can be that programs designed to bring progress to women may fail, because the women they are designed for may not be the women that experts outline. Those borderlines of identity are not just academic; they matter.

Inlining entails ignoring heavily drawn outlines for the shadows and boundary areas that exist around the lines. It calls for vision to see and locate ourselves in many worlds without lionizing any one of them, without finding some true way to world the world (Loomba, 1993) into an order that IR can recognize. The point also is that if we cannot always be certain that we are sighting a woman when we cite someone who looks like our notions of one, how can we outline confidently?

In(out)lining

Outlining and inlining can overlap as they do in many portraits by Rembrandt, where backgrounds and fleshily identifiable figures become each other. Women at Greenham Common defied the lines that keep women out of international politics and walked from their homes in Wales into visibility at an international missile base in the UK. Initially they persisted in outlining themselves in international relations by artistically arranging household items on military fences, thereby refusing the usual public/private split that underlies IR's concern with diplomacy, nuclear weapons, and war. They then slid into inlining when they developed a difficult-to-model politics of decision at the fences of western defense. A close reading of accounts of the camp indicate high levels of cooperation without chairs and notetakers, consensus, voting, or committees. The participants did not follow rational, organizational, or bureaucratic decision-making models, did not engage in satisficing and other approaches students of IR think that decisions in international relations reveal (Harford and Hopkins, 1984; Liddington, 1989). Greenham's own decision making emerged in the shadows, one might say, of the official story of how things are done in international relations. It was inlined there by women whose outlines were fitted into the landscapes of international security by avant-garde painters working against convention.

Though overlapping, I want to argue that inlining has the edge at this moment of feminist world-travel around international relations. Inlining is IR brought home to a mobile and moving feminist enterprise that is out ahead of the conventional field. It is an enterprise that pictures progress, to the degree that it does, as curvilinear, n-dimensional, circular, not-there/there, unfolding. Inlining rarely works from IR frameworks or systematically critiques IR for its oversights, and therefore the questions of international relations it brings to feminism have an IR-provincializing outcome that is even more profound, perhaps, than outlining. Indeed it operates on the premise that outlines are optical illusions, compositional techniques to add balance and symmetry, lies that recreate other lies. Instead of painting a more crowded field, inlining has bodies rolling around on a paint surface until the writing fingers merge with the colors produced by nimble sewing fingers. What is the result? This branch of the feminist avant-garde refuses the authentic for a humble embrace of "bewitching succubus."

Traveling to feminist arts

The challenge ahead is to develop the visual acuity necessary to appreciate feminist avant-garde arts of international relations. We must develop tools to see the pillars, the ballasts, the shadows and the lighting of worlds we usually study and worlds we have not yet seen. One way forward is via a visual and locational travel method that takes us, colorfully and empathetically, into the possibility of "being in different worlds and ourselves within them" (Lugones, 1990:396). I suggest, as I have before, the method of world-traveling.

Travel, like most things in this late-modern era, is double- and triple-edged. It can be a dash for simple relief from daily life, via the cruises to nowhere or to the sand, surf, and "girlies" of adult theme parks of the world. It can take us to the Louvre and the Hermitage, to the MOMA and Beaubourg, into cool concrete and glass buildings that escape boisterous scenes outside them. It can take us to World Trade Centers in New York, Hong Kong, and Helsinki – clutching our business-class plane tickets, our laptops, our pocket organizers. It can take us on a grand cruise around IR and it can "open" large tracts of (seemingly empty) space for settlement by people bringing in the West, a place that, in W.J.T. Mitchell's (1992:15) words, "never designates where it is, but only where it hopes to go, its 'prospects' and frontiers": its art is manifest destiny, its canvases overlarge.

World-traveling is a form of more humble mobile visuality. It is about traveling to difference and recognizing it, living with its lessons, its aesthetics. World-traveling is not the turf of pith-helmeted colonials. Indeed, instead of painting cultural or racial difference as dangerous or as something that is (thankfully) tamed by watchful men, world-traveling art goes to Gauguin's only seemingly unidimensional Tahitian women and explores their contexts and watercolors. It marches to Asian markets and sweatshops to see another politics of multiplicity. It has us entering submerged identities in our own range of mobile subjectivities too, so that we can draw scenes that we would usually divorce from our professional work. Wherever we go, we do "not expect the world to be neatly packaged, ruly" (Lugones, 1990:400); nor do we expect the world to be "out there" and fully apart from "us." Once on the go, we remember the spirit of early Westphalian-era carnivals in Europe, when everyday people could don identities usually forbidden them and parade in front of deities and high priests in a comedy of altered expectations. Carnival gave permission to travel one's identity repertoire to another social self that could be recognized, performed, and made to be at home with the more usual public "I." This ironic form of travel allowed contending identities to be out and about openly, to reverse their usual meanings, to confuse gender and who had what aspects of it. Taboos lifted momentarily under the influence of mirth. We could see there was only a shadow between ourselves and the costumed other within us.

To world-travel, though, is not to mimic the other. "Rather," says Maria Lugones (p. 396, emphasis in original), "one *is* someone who has that personality or character or uses space and language in that particular way." World-travel gives us some agility in moving "inter" the very low and common, where IR would rather not go, and the high and mighty realms of war and peace conferences, European currency negotiations, diplomatic visits, strategic thinking. We enter the worlds of Hieronymus Bosch and add our demon wings and long snouts and skirts to the *mise-en-scène*. Peace conferences purporting to end wars where rape has been a fighting strategy can be appliquéd with women in the line-up of diplomats. Our easels set up in St. Petersburg, we can record the end of historic Communism as the carnival of investments and potholes filling and emptying of IMF jewels. Sketches: women of Russia sit one by one at the side of the road near the Finnish border, each with a jar of berries set in front of her, each trying to sell that one jar of berries to a Finn roaring by in carnivalesque mood, each failing in her export efforts and, therefore, unable to costume herself for the big ball. Women in Greenland prepare export skins and fish; and on their faces we can read indigenous challenges to pristine Norden. The ironies are exquisitely colorful, and they journey with us/are us.

On to novels and poetry we go. In rich-languaged territories we encounter fictions that glimpse the forbidden facts of international relations. Peter Hoeg's *Smilla* (1993) reveals complicated Danish–Greenland relations for the whole world to read easily now and contemplate. Near to Denmark's shores, at an ancient part of it, we encounter Jostein Gaarder (1994:15) warning his daughter in *Sophie's World* that "the world itself becomes a habit in no time at all ... as if in the process of growing up we lose the ability to wonder about the world." World-travel is wonder through wander into spaces and pictures we have not thought to think about before. The texts and scenery reach out to us and pull us wondrously into panoramas uncontemplated. There is travel method to reading/doing the arts of international relations.

Representations

I end with two tableaux of the feminist avant-garde at work. One illustrates a feminist outlining effort around IR and the other inlines gender powers that become visible only though feminist world-traveling.

Outlining the power

We are standing at a painting, oil on board, framed. It is a portrait of three women cleaning the corridors of a modern office building. They are bent over, faces averted, mops pushed ahead of them on the soapy floor. One is reaching a hand out to pick up what looks to be a white, business-sized envelope that someone has dropped. There are names on the office doors behind the women. One name is Kofi Annan.

An X-ray of the painting indicates that the artist's first inclination was to sketch figures of men holding papers and briefcases, striding purposively towards the viewer. The final scene of three women is a re-placement for that one. It is done in the style of late-1960s Jeffrey Smart, the Australian painter currently living in Italy, whose realist urban land-scapes both monumentalize and dwarf the people in them around lines that are sweeping and free of extraneous detail. The content of the re-vised painting, though, is not Smart; it is more like Mierle Laderman Ukeles at work. Feminist art critic Lucy Lippard (1995:258) describes Ukeles as "the preeminent 'garbage girl,'" who realized early in her career that in order to do art and also accomplish her domestic du-ties, she would have to rename her domestic duties "art." Her perfor-mances range from "donning and doffing snowsuits, changing diapers, and picking up toys, to scrubbing a museum floor … and finally to becoming the 'official artist in residence of the New York City Depart-ment of Sanitation,' where she has found her niche" (p. 259). Ukeles is opposed to what she sees as "the reigning principle of the avant-garde ('to follow one's own path to the death – do your own thing, dynamic change'). She thereby airs the real problem, what she calls 'the sour ball of every revolution: after the revolution, who's going to pick up the garbage on Monday morning?'" (p. 65). In outlining women garbage-pickers, Ukeles is ahead of all those who stride purposively down the halls of IR thinking they have all revolutions under control.

A mermaidenly moment

An IR question in feminism comes into view as a woman's bare back barely visible among the rocks. "She" is bent away from industrial and military installations set across the water, turned against Statoil tanks and glass-topped ferries that bring international visitors to take a look. An electric train hums in the background. She does not hum back. She does not look at us looking, does not appear to hear the din or to record the significance of herself. Yet she pulls us toward her as though she knows us and our sounds. She is tiny and young and dignified and odd and not-modern and a study in postmodern nostalgia. Her eyes down-cast, her body pawed at, leaned against, photo-opped, she nevertheless evades docility. Indeed, she commands the harbor. She is what people come to see as Copenhagen, no matter that local art critics and some feminists decry her old-fashioned style, her image of womanhood, her vulgar popularity. Gentle she is and unwavering, even with her head chopped off now and then. She is there winter after summer in unheroic pose yet monumental leadership. She, the creature, has achieved a divorce from her outliners. She was made, but now she makes herself and those around her.

They say she once wanted a soul. That is why she was made to sit there with her smooth body in the land of man. A nice sailor would marry her and thereby give her a soul. That would be progress in a story that has it that soul is a man's to give and that it makes a girl a true human. But she does not marry. She is there long after men pass by, or drool over her, or dress like her, or whatever it is they do there. She is now the one passing soul around. We travel to her and she travels to us with her soulful secret, known to feminist theorist Dorothy Dinnerstein (1976:2):

> Myth-images of half-human beasts like the mermaid...express an old, fundamental, very slowly clarifying communal insight: that our species' nature is internally inconsistent; that our continuities with, and our differences from, the earth's other animals are mysterious and profound; and that in these continuities, and these differences, lie both our sense of strangeness on earth and the possible key to a way of feeling at home here.

It's a carnival out there! And mermaid is dressed for it in glossy fish tail – the spectacle of beasts. Is she a woman, a fetish, a kitsch, a feminist, a set of hyphenations stretching beyond her tail? Her wonder is her strength and inspiration for those who wander near her arts. Ask her feminist questions and she – and others like her, as in the harbor of Pusan Korea – will return interpretations that their formal outlines defy. She is an international relations of ours.[6]

Life is ever in progress, and the serious question we must ask is this: what does it mean to talk the talk of avant-garde progress when talking about feminism in IR and IR in feminism? Mind the easy answers! Beware any temptation to take short-cuts to the wisdom of an Elshtain, Enloe, or Tickner, a cleaning woman, or a mermaid, all of whose dues pile as high as their credits. Outline the women, yes. But also inline the gender power that outlines can mark over. At the fulcrum of the two are the signifying arts of feminism in and around international relations.

[6] For another evocation of the mermaid, See Hansen (2001).

14 Internations of feminism and International Relations

"Internations" characterizes the fulcrum/impasse/fulcrum of IR and feminism and suggests literary ways to world-travel in and around it. Ann Tickner (1997:611–612) claims that "[w]hile feminist scholars, as well as a few IR theorists, have called for conversations and dialogue across paradigms ... few conversations or debates have occurred." To her, good communication stumbles around the different ontologies and epistemologies driving the two fields and mires around gaps in the power to set dominant discourse. This concluding essay offers another spin on the issue: the two fields talk past each other because they are so very similar, and powerfully so.

IR and feminism, it can be said, are variants of the imagined nations that Benedict Anderson (1991) describes. They are nations of knowledge, identity, and practice that endeavor to incorporate a great deal of territory and to embrace all eligible members. Each "nation," however, fails to persuade some constituencies that they are part of the enterprise and should throw in their lot with it. Feminism can be off-putting to Third World women (and postcolonial analysts such as Ien Ang (1995)), who suspect that their issues and identities will always languish in a nation that is western at its core. IR is supposedly about the vast international and its many relations but tends to leave a fair bit of both out of its nation, including feminists, all those "bottom-rung" types of whom Enloe speaks, and relations of the international that do not center on Great Power concerns.

Feminism is eager to offer all women in the world a home, eager to be accepted as well as part of the home-spaces of IR. IR is reluctant, stand-offish, snobbish, and exclusionary in general, despite its encompassing portfolio. One "nation" overreaches and the other puts up walls, but both are ambitious and prone to immodesty. Can they interact with each other productively without manifesting national perspectives that are at once ambitious and self-limited? Can each avoid invading or colonizing the other in order to appreciate – indeed thrive on – creative elements of their internations?

A "nation" problematic gave rise to IR and feminism to begin with. Both camp followers had experienced a certain homelessness or invisibility in fields that made universalizing claims but had, in fact, left them out. The swallowing-up entities around incipient IR were the fields of political science and diplomatic history. Feminist-minded scholars felt eviscerated within every academic story that used "he" or "mankind" to embrace the world. Today, the nation problematic continues, with postcolonial studies and feminism accusing IR of neglecting a range of global relations and gay and lesbian studies (as well as postcolonial scholars) needling feminism about problems with difference. Yet internations appear at points where aspects of IR nation cannot help but be part of cacophonous feminist nation and vice versa.

Having cited the heuristic potential of visual method in chapter 13, I return here in spirit to the third chapter of this volume ("Handmaids' Tales") and present a literary method to travel feminist/IR internations. That is to say, an unfinished journey continues by entering realms of difference that we in IR and we in feminism have trouble seeing when we stick to the usual data preferred by each field. Of course, feminism already incorporates literary approaches in its canons – so this exercise can be seen as yet another way of bringing IR questions onto feminist turf. Yet, judging by the arguments of postcolonial feminists, feminism has a great deal of reading left to do before it can cite the diversity of the world convincingly. Leaning on the literary assists both fields to develop in-sights and siting skills needed to cite the salient people, activities, movements, and odd relations of the world without commanding, ordering, appropriating, clashing with, or subsuming "them."

As we world-travel complex passages through literature, we learn to follow events, in an echo of Elshtain's early concerns, rather than impose so much on them. (How fresh such ideas sound still.) And, as the two IR plaintiffs from chapter 1 urged, we also learn to tolerate "the effrontery of others messing about in *our* intellectual territory" (Ferguson and Mansbach, 1991:38, emphasis in original). After all, claims Etienne Balibar (1995), who figures prominently in this piece, we are minorities in the worlds we think we shape and dominate. The results should be less nationally insistent but more encompassing, modest and more creatively bold; and they should make us more aware of how international relations and feminism intersect all the time whether we notice or not.

*   *   *

Three feminists go on a journey. One selects unfamiliar sites and wanders quietly, so as to avoid disturbing local culture. She talks to those around her but not about difficult or sensitive topics. Back home she decides against writing up what she has learned because to do so could distort and perhaps orientalize the "other." A second feminist visits places of difference too and does not keep a low profile once arriving. She seeks to bring international feminist standpoints to bear on what she sees, hears, and does – all as part of the effort to help disadvantaged women and their nations. She talks to locals but is also a bit remote, set apart – albeit being eager to record and report injustices. A third feminist monitors herself as both similar to and different than those she encounters through her various travels. Seeking out conversations, she asks others questions, lets herself be queried by locals, and queries herself – all in a context of slowly increasing comfort with situations that defy her control.

Three IR theorists are *en voyage*. One travels uneasily, preoccupied with water-borne diseases and the possible theft of personal items. Everything looms as a difference, and in that difference is a potential threat or conflict. This traveler is so distracted that he does not take much notice of feminists – or anyone else – he meets along the way. The second IR traveler is having a ball "out there." Wherever he goes he sees similarity: parents worry about their kids and heads of state bustle off to international meetings. It's like home, albeit colors, styles, and foods signal elseness. The feminists he runs into are proof to him that common norms can be found everywhere these days. For the third traveler from IR, the world is what he makes of it, as he analyzes how different countries respond to globalization's homogenizing cum difference-creating forces. He runs into the first feminist, talks with her for a while, finds many of her observations intriguing, and notes ways he can strengthen his own constructions by inserting some of her concerns into his frameworks.

Drawing on Benedict Anderson's (1991) imagined communities, Etienne Balibar's (1995) work on nations and universality, and Ien Ang's (1995) sense of feminism as constituting a nation, this essay offers a feminist/IR travelog. It ranges over the characteristics of feminism and IR as would-be universal nations and notes the ambiguities that diminish their solidity and force. It then takes both fields to what Dipesh

Chakrabarty (2000:254) calls "an alternative location for 'reason'" in and around three novel imaginaries that seemingly have nothing to do with the issues at hand. We find at that location the feminist and IR travelers noted above serendipitously converged at the edge of a rural town. Disengaging from backpacks, trunks lowered to the ground, each sits in his or her own space and reads in silence. Time passes; they are still there, first ignoring one another and then reading passages to fellow travelers and local passers-by, laughing, arguing, showing books around, telling and listening to stories. The travelers forget IR (Bleiker, 1997), and feminisms, and themselves as local *griots* and *n'angas* provide more tales to contemplate. Having become sociable, the travelers find themselves unpreoccupied with the next place to go, the self, the professional mission, the "strange other." Books and minds and national experiences open to the internations on view.

"Nations" of feminism and International Relations

The three feminist travelers seem different to each other. The first avoids speaking for "the other," knowing that her western-subject-centered "I" may block the sounds of another speaking (Spivak, 1988). The development feminist is willing to represent the other in order to help her (Parpart, 1995; Sylvester, 2000a). The third feminist listens and engages; she finds one or two nodes of common identity across difference and builds a learning experience around them with those she meets.

Different approaches, yes? In fact, Ien Ang (1995) argues, feminism is one nation that expands to incorporate as many women as possible. That nation is not marked by a common lingua franca, demarcated territory, or clear ethnic boundaries (although there may be some body boundaries). It is not a homogeneous nation either, but, rather, constructs its far-flung members in a spirit of contention and contingency. None the less, Ang (p. 57) thinks feminism is a western-identified effort to pose a "'natural' political destination for all women, no matter how multicultural." It is the motherlode, the culture point where differences compress into a tolerance-oriented, culturally white, western, feminist world. The amalgamation occurs – despite recognition that "women" is an unstable category cross-cut by statuses of class, race, ethnicity, nationality, age, and so on, despite travels that prove difference is indeed diverse. That two of the three feminist travelers strike out into the world from western locations would probably not surprise Ang. She thinks

feminist nation pledges allegiance to western feminist interest in di-
aloging with difference in order, ultimately, to overcome it, as the second
feminist traveler does (the first is immobilized by her sense of immutable
identities and cannot engage at all). Put differently, difference is to be respectfully inserted into a firmly established prior tradition that absorbs
the ambiguity of such sentiments as: "I'm a feminist but . . ."

To be fair, feminist nation knows that some women eschew feminism
and others accept aspects of it reluctantly, or with postcolonial anger.
Yet Anderson's (1991:6) words about nations as imagined communities
ring through this feminist land: nations are "imagined as both inherently limited and sovereign." A nation, he claims, takes shape from the
characteristic "style in which [it is] imagined" (p. 6), and Ang (1995:59)
is able to identify of what that style consists for western feminism writ
global: "an overconfident faith in the power and possibility of open and
honest communication to 'overcome' or 'settle' differences, of a power-
free speech situation without interference by entrenched presumptions,
sensitivities and preconceived ideas." All women can bring their differences to feminist nation, but communication within the national home
"confines itself to repairing the friction between white women and 'other
women'" (p. 61).

Ang overstates her case as a way of relaying postmodern skepticism
about modernist confidence in multicultural dialog. Her sense of the nation of feminism, though, teases us metaphorically and serves as a cautionary tale in which women are meant to inhabit two sites of the world
with empowering ease – a material living place and a special place of
women's politics and dreams. Terry Eagleton (cited in Wallace, 2000:39)
suggests the downside of this vision by asserting that people like to sit-
uate themselves and that so many cannot help but do so: "It's OK for
high-flying (literally) intellectuals to talk about mixing and mingling
identities [in a global world]; they can do it. Most people have to live
where they are. People live in a particular place in time. Most of them
can't afford to travel at all" (p. 39). Feminist Amy Kaminsky (1994:8)
also cautions that "[t]he ease with which so many North Americans can
cross most geographical borders too easily deceives us into thinking
that we are able to cross all borders – linguistic, cultural, historical –
with similar ease." That is, it is technologically possible for those with
money, careers, and the luxury of time and speech to travel the world
and to imagine, while doing so, that "in the minds of each lives the image of their communion" (Anderson, 1991:6). Western feminists become
the "I" single eye of imagined community, while dissidents to feminist

nation, such as Ang, Kaminsky, and Norma Alarcón (1990) – the latter warns us to be patient to tears to avoid disrupting ongoing dialogs we come upon – raise alarms about limitations of sovereign practice and desire.

Arguably, a parallel nation of global reach orbits near feminist nation. This is the academically imagined "nation" of International Relations (IR), the community that takes the relations of the world as its unique professional portfolio, its oyster. Through at least eighty years a small and elite nation has imagined the international and cited its imaginings as real: international relations have become what an IR clique makes them. The world it has imagined has been potentially vast – everywhere; but in fact the field narrowed early to something called, in cartoon language, Great Powers and their (important) relations. IR's small nation of like-minded thinkers (and their states) then took up places, often conflictually, under a shared umbrella; the majority of potential members (and their states) were on the outside getting wet. Instead of opening to all locations of international relations over time, IR persists in preferring those who can converse about impersonal, power-seeking, and functionally equivalent nation-states, an international society of states bound by common (mostly western) norms, patterns of international political economy emanating from or concerning the West (such as globalization), and decision-makers who enjoy playing games. With the western "I" stretched across only some parts of the planet, yet determining the international to be studied and the ways to do so, IR developed its own universality illusion. Whereas feminist nation has wanted every woman to feel comfortable within it, IR nation mostly wants to avoid uncomfortable journeys "out there" and associate more with its own kind. Thus, the first IR traveler is uneasy with difference and the second is ebullient because he sees himself wherever he goes.

Dissidents in IR fuss about this strange land, just as do dissidents from/in feminism; indeed, some feminists are inter-nationally positioned.[1] There is also sparring within the mainstream of the field, which gives the impression that IR nation welcomes controversy (now constructivists and rationalists are having their day). Yet dissidents find that the controversies they generate can be ignored or summarily dismissed by other national members;[2] or their ideas can be

---

[1] The term "dissident" is used by Ashley and Walker (1990a).
[2] Fred Halliday (1994:40) describes work from the poststructuralist-postmodern wing of dissidence as "pretentious, derivative and vacuous, an Anglo-Saxon mimesis of what was already, in its Parisian form, a confused and second-rate debate."

appropriated with the political guts removed first, *à la* IR's third traveler (Weber, 1999). As for feminist dissidents in IR, they tell of eerie spaces of masculinity they slide into when crossing from places where women are in the majority of feminist nation to homeless statuses in IR (Elshtain, 1987; Sylvester, 1994a; Tickner, 1992). Historically always-men secretaries-general of the UN have the "good offices" in international relations while unnoted secretaries keep their dinners warm. Wars emulate those violent software games (Shapiro, 1990) that are also known to target women. And diplomacy, in James Der Derian's (1987:199) words, is "the mediation of men estranged from an infinite yet abstracted power which they themselves have constructed." Periodically left out of even the good critiques, or included through arch representations by men (Ashley and Walker, 1990a), feminists crossing over to IR often sit apart reading each other's stories, like the IR dissidents do.

There is a nation of IR, imply critics of the field, which erects walls and evacuates many places, texts, people, and concerns from the small land of mainstream significance – all while proclaiming itself portfolio holder for the international and its relations. There is a nation of feminism, suggest dissident feminists, which shows the opposite tendency to immodest inclusiveness; concerns of those who do not necessarily seek to merge with feminism-plus-difference, or with feminism-helping-difference, are brought in anyway – for everyone's good. Members of the respective nations stage lively internal debates and yet the center tendencies basically hold.

Boundaries and "nations"

But wait. Can IR construct feminism as an alien nation? Can women who are assigned feminist nation be forced into homelessness in IR (Sylvester, 1998b) – "stuck," so to speak, inside feminist nation looking out at the rest of the world? Although analysts have taken up questions related to the exclusion or marginalization of feminism within IR (e.g., Stancich, 1998; Tickner, 1997), I wish to scrutinize the boundaries and ask whether feminism and IR *can* be universal in claims, memberships, and representations. Are there feminist places in nonfeminist IR and IR places in the proclaimed feminist homeplace of only-women? Are there internations of feminism and IR? In tackling these questions, I draw on an article by Etienne Balibar that has become a classic of left-leaning globalization literature.

Balibar (1995) addresses several universalizing tendencies and the ways they fail to capture the ambiguities of the time. He refers to nations as instances of fictitious universalism. Their sweep can be achieved only by deconstructing particularistic, primary identities of would-be members in order to reconstruct a common representation of "'what it means to be a person,' to 'be oneself,' or to be a 'subject'" (p. 56). IR and feminism fit this category if we bear in mind Anderson's argument that a national community need be no less false for being imagined. Feminism, for Ang (1995:73), represents the subjects "women," wherever they live and whether or not, as she puts it, other "identifications are sometimes more important and politically pressing than, or even incompatible with, those related to their being women." IR has deconstructed generations of student identifications in order to reconstruct canonical parameters for "what it means to be a person" who "does" IR. There is an obvious constructivist ring to fictive nation. "Material resources," to use Alexander Wendt's (1995:73) words, "only acquire meaning for human action through the structure of shared knowledge in which they are embedded." Or as Richard Price and Christian Reus-Smit (1998:266) put it, "institutionalized meaning systems are thought to define the social identities of actors, and . . . social identities are said to constitute actors' interests and shape their actions."

Where "things become of course more ambiguous" (Balibar, 1995:63), is in the processes by which an individual becomes a normal member of the nation:

> For normality is not the simple fact of adopting customs and obeying rules or laws: it means internalizing representations of the "human type" or the "human subject" (not exactly an essence, but a norm and a standard behavior) in order to be recognized as a person in its full right, to become *presentable* (fit to be seen) in order to be represented. To become *responsible* (fit to be answered) in order to be respected.
>
> (p. 63, emphasis in original)

These normalization practices conjure a situation in which the only way nonmembers can be represented and respected at all is if they can be seen to be the women that feminism embraces, the political entities and regions that count in IR.

And yet "nation" is not fully entrapping either, because nations are not power points of consensus. Within imagined communities are those who resist institutionally accepted ways "of being a person" and attend to contradictions in the rules of personhood. Balibar (1995:62) maintains that "[t]o confront the hegemonic structure by denouncing the gap or contradiction between its official values and the actual practice – with greater or lesser success – is the most effective way to enforce its universality." For Ang to struggle against feminist encompassings of all women, for critics in IR to denounce a field that does not account for all of the international nor study many relations, can be a badge of membership in the imagined communities of feminism and IR. Fighting words enforce the universalist claims of nations by keeping attention on the importance of normal community debates about "what it means to be a subject." One might say then that challengers *escape* aspects of national fictions when they reveal the social processes that construct the usual norms; but at the same time, they *maintain* national myths by drawing attention to the gap between national aspirations and the current moment of national reality. Ang is a feminist but . . . she both argues with feminism, beseeching the nation to countenance partiality, and reveals the flawed logic of the normal in feminism (that only seemingly universal category "women").

Critics of IR are often analogously placed in ambiguity, although with a different argument to make: at once many claim the field is narrow and exclusive, suggesting that it could take on more, and that the very epistemological foundations of the field are flawed, which leave it unable to take on more. Richard Ashley and R.B.J. Walker (1990b:376) express this doubleness:

> Whether one speaks of the "discipline of international studies," the "discipline of international relations," the "discipline of international politics," or the "discipline of world politics," the words manifestly fail, even as they promise, to discipline meaning. The words but broadly connote (they cannot denote) a boundless nontime and nonplace – a deterritorialized, extraterritorial zone of discourse – where the work of producing the subjects, the objects, and the interpretations of an institutional order and its limits visibly eludes the certain control of that order's supposedly reigning categories.

Ambiguity multiplies as one places the fictitious nation within a larger context of universality that Balibar (1995:49) calls a "real" universality of interdependencies between institutions, groups, individuals and processes that involve them, processes we think of as globalization. The reality of profound interdependencies means that, for the first time and in a very direct way, the extensive spatiality of the globe, "reach[es] *the individual himself/herself"* (p. 49, emphasis in original). The effects are intensive: "more aspects of the life of the constitutive units are dependent on what other units have been doing in the past, or are currently doing" (p. 49).

One might expect of real universality a unification of the world around identities and values made common. In fact, there is a backfire effect on the very processes of world-system expansion that, on some levels, brought humankind together. Centers are unable to incorporate as much as they once could. Instead, elements of peripheries appear in and influence old center sites. Transnational migrations, for example, generate "'minorities' everywhere, be they of ancient or recent origin, not only of local descent, but virtually coming from all over the world" (p. 53). Peripheries then become increasingly difficult to classify over time, because patterns emerge of "marrying partners from different 'cultures' and 'races,' living across the fictitious boundaries of communities, experiencing a divided or multiple 'self,' practicing different languages and memberships according to the private and public circumstances" (p. 54; also Appadurai, 1993a). With so many people in unclassifiable statuses, Balibar (1995:54) concludes that "what minority means becomes rather obscure," that *"the distinction between 'minorities' and 'majorities' becomes blurred"* (p. 53, emphasis in original). We can even face situations, as in the emerging political entity of Europe, of *"minorities without stable or unquestionable majorities"* (p. 55, emphasis in original), let alone speak of minorities created as refugees or human cargo.

Minorities proliferate in an era of mass global communications and so do real possibilities for contact across minority identities. In some cases, the contact enables prior conflict to diminish. In other cases, "global communication networks provide every individual with a distorted image or a stereotype of all the others, either as 'kin' or as 'aliens,' thus raising gigantic obstacles before any dialogue" (p. 56). Far from bringing global community together in a way that ends particularistic conflicts, real universality "coincides with a generalized pattern of conflicts, hierarchies, and exclusions . . . '[i]dentities' are less isolated *and* more compatible, less univocal *and* more antagonistic" (p. 56). And the prospect for a global social contract, which would end these Hobbesian wars or conflicts of difference, seems utterly utopian.

Caught in the ambiguous outcomes of intersecting universalizing tendencies, feminist and IR nations may seem to loom large before our eyes but, in fact, they cannot convincingly determine "what it means to be a person, a subject." National membership is increasingly porous and open, despite our best efforts to hold on to old membership rituals. Ang's warning about a nation of feminism at odds with the views of some it seeks to bring home illustrates this dynamic. Her concerns reflect the communication with/in western feminism that elements of real universality make possible. At the same time, those forces open feminist nation to contradictions of difference it cannot contain. Mainstream IR, wherever located, finds itself unable to stage a "debate" these days that it can absolutely win against all the minorities undermining national control. Internations of feminism and IR are not just possible, it is an era of internations. Nations exceed their moorings in a world instantaneously bombarded by interdependencies, disjunctures, assimilations and insurgencies, virtualities, fictions and more fictions.

"Nations" of IR and feminism struggle to be

Events suggest that IR cannot wrap up the world in the bosom of Great Power concerns and consign everything else – small states, working-class people, women, children, wives of diplomats, Zimbabwean co-operatives, Tongan chiefs, novels, and art museums – to near oblivion. Feminism cannot easily assimilate the challenges of minorities either, because the very existence of minorities disperses and diversifies the majority. The national ambitions of both – one to keep interlopers out and the other to assimilate all conceivable members – are impossible to realize. Events rapidly exceed national discourses of control.

IR exceeded

IR's world is exceeded by the world that complicates it – the world of simultaneous homogenizing forces around market capitalism, information technology, and global consumerism, and the world that begs the question Bruce Robbins (1995:167) asks: is "there . . . a single system . . . or perhaps only the *appearance* of a single system?" What of eastern Europe, where ethnic nations seeking states cause disintegrations around themselves and the build-up of particularistic nationalisms too? What of Africa's general expulsion from high-technology globalization, and other uneven, perhaps Satanic, geographies (Smith, 1997)? What of the Taliban wars on all ideas, practices, and art deemed non-Islamic? Balibar's discussion of the equivocity of universality supports the sense that we can be connected globally while, at the same time, connections spawn fictions, conflicts, and dis/connections.

IR is connected to feminism through the minority problematic that infiltrates it. Yet the field has not connected well with feminist scholarship in the sense of examining the gender concerns its own work raises. IR has not studied gender relations as relations of international power. It has never studied power as the ability of nations and professional academic fields to block "women" and their internationally relevant activities from scholarly significance (Enloe, 1989). IR is exceeded, therefore, by a dissident minority that its masculine performing "nation" has either tried to pull into normality (ignoring feminist queries about "what it means to be a person" in IR), ignored, or failed to capture or to quiet. It is exceeded by el(l)e-phants who paint the landscapes of IR differently, or who paint abstract shadowlands of gender that defy the normal outlines of a field.[3]

Closer to IR's national core, its realist narratives of transhistorical conflict can even be exceeded by claims that the end of the Cold War ushered in the end of world historical conflict. The Fukuyama (1989) thesis projects a future where proliferating and conflictual minorities are captured by the global system of democracy and capitalism. Third World states may still be mired in history and subject to conflicts, says Fukuyama, but the liberal capitalist idea and future cannot be extinguished. And liberal democracies, Michael Doyle (1986) tells us in a feel-good Kantian echo, do not fight each other. Opposite in end result to what Marx predicted, the proclaimed moment of universalism is one that Chakrabarty (2000:3) flays by pointing out that no historian of weight has publicly accepted it. In IR the Fukuyama thesis is still discussed. In the mid-1990s, Fred Halliday (1994:217) wrote that it provides "only one set of answers now acceptable on a world scale." Zaidi Laidi (1998) more recently calls markets and democracy our world time.

None the less, Fukuyama's unambiguous endism is ironically ambiguous when juxtaposed with Balibar's thinking. Balibar (1995:58) suggests that market liberalism is "opposed to 'totalitarian' worldviews, where all individuals are supposed to adopt one and the same system of beliefs . . ." Yet if liberal triumphs were truly to end history, then liberalism would become a totalizing universality, in which it could be said that "all individuals are supposed to adopt one and the same system of beliefs or follow compulsory rules, for the sake of salvation and identification with some common essence" (p. 58). Fukuyama tries to leap

---

[3] For a discussion of elephants who paint, and thereby turn topsy our notion of what elephant is, and el(l)e-phants who similarly step out of IR's shadows to paint relations international (where no such phantoms were supposed to exist), see Sylvester (1994a).

over this irony by making democracy and the market the victors of large historical trends rather than achievements by force. Yet the market is an impersonal and homeless space that binds all to it *and* touts minoritarian voluntarism. The democratic state is similarly a contradiction: it embraces market-model mechanisms *and* mires in market-fettering minority politics. We are meant to escape to the international – the global market – while maintaining nation-states as everyone's democratic center.

In Fukuyama's scheme, minority action sums to majority trends in a certain ideal-typical way, with the West carrying its promises around the world. Peripheries do not move into centers; centers continue, instead, to move into peripheries. That is the logic of endist universality. But as Ang notes with respect to feminism, end of history engirthings cannot actually handle important contingencies. What can endist thinking do, for example, with rape as a war fighting strategy in recent European wars? What about women slashing soybeans in Zimbabwe for the proper export market while the ZANU PF state dismantles the market? And do we want to say that the political economy of western sex tourism to Thailand is part of an international triumph of capitalism? In Fukuyama's homogenizing future, difference eventually calms itself or is normalized into the large "nation" of liberal market democracy. The universal fiction is tolerant and pluralistic, even as a center-out logic denies real and rich minority stories, except as troublesome reminders of some assigned past.

Meanwhile, a leftist pessimism about globalized endism has worried about what Halliday (1994:224) calls "the marginalisation of organised dissent and of radical criticism within the developed and underdeveloped world . . . [about] whether the wealth of richer countries can, given constraints historical and new, be diffused in any reasonable way to the rest of humanity." Such concerns have flagged liberal capitalism as encouraging dissent and disruption (Latham, 1993; Mansfield and Snyder, 1995). But can that dissent be heard? Balibar defuses this worry theoretically through his discussion of real universal links of communication; and it practically dissolves when a spate of protests against global capitalist diffusions and their impoverishing effects in Third World countries start up in 1999. We are still left, though, with enormous distributional skews in the world, despite the Asian Tiger phenomenon, despite foreign aid, despite the march of global capitalism and the marches against it. Relative poverty exceeds all of this and spills out beyond nations, markets, and endist prophecies.

While leftists have questioned the epistemological underpinnings of endism and related disorders (George, 1994), realists-in-spirit have warned about other pitfalls of the order everyone is supposedly embracing. We face clashing civilizations – the West against the Chinese and Islamic civilizations (Huntington, 1993) – and the prospect of threats from the international business civilization, religious movements, the European Union, and various domestic groups (Gaddis, 1991; Hoffman, 1990; Mearsheimer, 1990; Strange, 1990). These critiques of triumphalism recognize that transnational processes create multiple identity centers as markers of real universality. In such an environment, liberal democracies and peace will not necessarily go together to heaven (Brown, 1992b). Focused on forms of resistance to western majoritarianism carried out by other cultural monoliths, these worriers cannot bear to sit and read the world at all. Too many dangers impede victory (and should keep us on our toes).

John Gaddis (1991:121, 122) has urged a "middle course, while avoiding the rocks and shoals that lie on either side." His admonition, in effect, is to travel between contending points of view in IR. But travels of this sort can still by-pass some important sites and relations of the international (which, it must be noted, Balibar does not sight clearly either). When we think of the crumbling of the German Democratic Republic in 1989, for instance, we of IR rarely linger on women as a *force majeure* – the ones pushing baby carriages through the boundary and into internation. Yet that moment of wall-breaching people power was not absent women's agency, even if it was absent the heroics IR often studies (Bleiker, 2000a). One wonders what course might have emerged had western states not traveled so quickly to fill in all eastern spaces for the ordinary agents of that time and place in international relations. This is not, however, a standard IR wonder. Perhaps if it were, the ten-year anniversary of unification in 2000 might have been a less sober occasion in eastern places such as Halle, where an employment rate of 17 percent has turned many people into migrants seeking to elude the new (and fictitious) nation that IR studies (DVPW Kongress, 2000).

Gaddis would stand us between points in an effort to find a pragmatic place for IR nation to steady itself. That in-between can be insufficiently inter-nation in orientation. It can miss places where conflict and cooperation become mutually supportive of national ambitions and stand down the agency of minorities to rewrite the international and its relations from hybrid standpoints. To move such blockages requires not a position in between market optimism and leftist pessimism, say, but, at the least, that IR move to exceed its limitations by considering the many stories of relations international it has assigned to some other minority discipline to read.

Feminism exceeded

Feminism simultaneously is one of the minority groups created by the real universality of international relations and is itself beset by minorities everywhere and conflicts within. Its early association with a women's movement gave feminism the cast of what Balibar calls an ideal universality as insurrection against the many institutions of fictitious universality that excluded people called women. Balibar (1995:64) writes of insurgents "who collectively rebel against domination in the name of freedom and equality." Their very existence reflects "history as a general process of emancipation, a realization of the idea of man (or the human essence, or the classless society, etc.)" (p. 65). In the case of feminism, ideal universality is the realization of the idea of woman, but . . . Ang and other dissidents charge that the white, western, heterosexual woman became the model for all. This is not what Balibar (p. 72) means when he speaks of ideal universality as transindividual and, multiple "in the sense of being always already beyond any simple or 'absolute' unity, therefore a source of conflicts forever."

Herein is the feminist rub. In order to make the claim that feminism is a difference-tolerant univocality, dissidents to feminism have to make the assumption that white western culture is immune from periphery to center international migrations and conflicts – just as endists do in IR. Yet the minority position that dissidents to feminist nation believe they occupy in feminism (or at the edges of it) coexists with so much cross-migration – (just through UN conferences alone) that feminism is now, arguably, an ensemble of "minorities without stable or unquestionable majorities." It is not seen this way by those who believe that feminism continues to have the majoritarian components that were amply visible during days of debate between liberal, Marxist, radical, and socialist wings.[4] Although written and practiced earnestly, with good

[4] Liberal feminism sought to make liberal western rights of men applicable to women without querying what the men had built and bequeathed and would still manage for women as a group. The feminist development approach WID (women in development) is its descendant. Marxist feminist theorizing put biological women where social relations of production would activate a worker consciousness, without dealing with patriarchy in the workplace and women (and men) who, for various reasons, work at home. Radical feminism lambasted patriarchy and then reified its notions of women by lumping all such

intentions and some good results, these feminisms had a certain disregard for countervailing experiences. In the end, the feminist/women's movement fragmented into the various postmodern and postcolonial elements we see today. We should bear in mind, though, that mainstream feminism was always made up of contentious minorities, who disallowed one another from reaching hegemony or from writing what Jean Elshtain (1993) calls "a" narrative of closure. That is to say, the nation of feminist truth was always exceeded.

Ang argues that despite such permutations, what always seems to remain in feminism is a center, a majority imposition of western concern with women or gender over race and ethnicity.[5] She is not alone in her sense that feminism is inadequately penetrated by peripheries, or, more precisely, the peripheries are not always sighted and cited in ways that blur minorities and majorities. Jackie Huggins (1993) argues that "white women often fail to recognize the racism that attaches to their privileges in dominant culture." Evelynn Hammonds (1994:127) adds that "while it has been acknowledged that race is not simply additive to, or derivative of sexual difference, few white feminists have attempted to move beyond simply stating this point to describe the powerful effect that race has on the construction and representation of gender and sexuality." Around these quickly evoked critiques is the point that dissident minorities circle the nation of feminism and debates of all sorts rage within. The thrusts and parries do not let white women endism rest; indeed, they signal worry about "the marginalization of dissent" and actually urge a certain "clash of civilizations."

Minorities *vis-à-vis* feminism proliferate when they can hear feminism instantiating a center experience through the pipelines of "real" universal forces in the world. They can respond now nearly simultaneously, from many locations of many worlds. In other words, the fictions of imagined nation can engender the "normal" challenges to feminism that those eschewing secession offer; but the assaults, plural and ambiguous,

---

biologically determined people together as keepers of mysterious submerged wisdom or culture. WAD (women and development) has no pretensions toward mysticism, but does advocate a separatist work position for biological women in Third World societies. Socialist feminism sought to assault capitalism and patriarchy through progressive cross-cultural alliances; but, as with radical feminism, says Judith Grant (1993:45), "a universal female experience was necessary in order to ground [it]."

[5] It should be noted that English distinguishes between sex and gender, but other languages, such as German, do not do so. Thus, Braidotti (1994:37) says "the notion of 'gender' is a vicissitude of the English language."

land on a minoritarian "nation." Though seeking in some feminist quarters to achieve what Elshtain (1993:106) identifies as a "thoroughgoing identification with 'oppressed peoples everywhere,'" the point is that those peoples are themselves ambiguously located and on the move. To appreciate the mobilities requires that we bare the fictions, realities, and idealities that exceed big F Feminism, and that we do this as a minoritarian "national" strategy.

World-traveling the universals

IR has not found a method to accommodate the contradictions around it. It simply breaks into schools of thought and shouts across divides. Some feminism has success with IR when it speaks the language of that nation and takes on recognizable and delimited IR puzzles. It has less success when it brings IR to the language and concerns of minoritarian feminism, to the IR questions there. Recently, however, some feminists have considered ways to move across centers and peripheries instead of encouraging one-way travel to a (fictitiously) fixed nation of identity, from whence one tries to overcome difference (Gwin, 1996; Sylvester, 1994a, 1995a). We can therefore consider how to be in the world without reinforcing or instantiating nations of belief.

Maria Lugones (1990:396) is one progenitor of this expanding concern within feminist circles. Her form of travel takes us, empathetically and nonintegratively, on to moving terrains of identity and meaning and into the possibility of "being in different 'worlds' and ourselves within them." As noted in chapter 13, travel comes in many forms. It can relieve the routines of daily life and simultaneously add work for those who labor at the sites we visit (Enloe, 1989). Travel can more perniciously bring Filipina women to Saudi Arabia and other locations – not on vacation, not with much idea at all of where one goes when travel is to starkly exploitative conditions of work as "aliens" (Pickup, 1998; Tadiar, 1998). Travel can also "open" tracts of (seemingly empty) space for national settlement by people bringing in the West's myths and desires (Grewal, 1999; Kaplan, 1999; Mitchell, 1992). Two of the traveling feminists, and the three travelers from IR, are westerners physically traveling the world. World-travel is not like that; it is not even a physical experience necessarily. Rather it is a form of mobile identity that moves with equivocity to the point where one can have "memory of oneself as different without an underlying 'I'" (Lugones, 1990:396). It is travel as constant insurrection from a Self that has been constructed by fictitious universalisms to be a person who does X or Y. In and of worlds rather than recruiters to one supposed world or nation has us "not expect[ing] the world to be neatly packaged, ruly" (p. 400). Ye, we do not expect "the" world at all nor seek to know it through the usual forms of travel.

World-traveling disturbs the "nations" of feminism and IR by enabling the universality illusion to become obvious. As we world-travel, we watch our selves proliferate in response to information that unravels what it means to be a person who does feminism and/or IR – or who rehearses any other national creed. We enter the worlds, the relations, of minority discourse and identity that, to quote Homi Bhabha (1994:157), contest "genealogies of 'origin' that lead to claims for cultural supremacy and historical priority." The process takes us, in other words, beyond any simple or "absolute" unity and into a realm that diversifies majoritarian thinking, design, and in-house debate. Thus, world-traveling is not another normalizing practice of fictitious universalism – a crisis of minorities emerging in the nation of feminism or IR, which a coterie of "I" will resolve for everyone's good. It is not a "'metalanguage,' as the ultimate trope of difference, arbitrarily contrived to produce and maintain relations of power and subordination" (Hammonds, 1994:127).[6]

Still, it behoves us to world-travel cautiously because two errors *are* very possible. Ang raises one potential problem when she criticizes the advice Ann Russo (1991) gives to western feminists seeking to connect better with difference. That advice is to search our own lives for incidences of oppression. Ang (1995:61) responds this way:

> the white woman can become a "politically correct" anti-racist by disavowing the specificity of the experience of being a racialised "other", reducing it to an instance of an oppression essentially the same as her own, gender-based oppression. This form of appropriation only reinforces the security of the white point of view as the point of reference from which the other is made same, a symbolic annihilation of otherness which is all the more pernicious precisely because it occurs in the context of a claimed solidarity with the other.

The second error appears in Rosi Braidotti's (1994) otherwise useful discussion of nomadic subjects. Braidotti defines nomadism as "the kind of critical consciousness that resists settling into socially coded modes of thought and behavior" (p. 5). She tells us about her Italian

---

[6] Hammonds is referring not to world-travel but to race, and quoting, in part, Evelyn Brooks Higginbotham (1992:255).

heritage and her upbringing in Australia, where she learns to identify and appreciate her difference as a continental Europeanness in British Australia. A promising exploration of hyphenated, traveling identity then veers when Braidotti extols the virtues of her polyglot existence and generalizes it on to others she encounters in her physical travels. She says:

> Over the years, I have developed a relationship of great fascination toward monolingual people: those who were born to the symbolic system in the one language that was to remain theirs for the rest of their life. Come to think of it, I do not know many people like that, but I can easily imagine them: people comfortably established in the illusion of familiarity "their mother tongue" gives them. (p. 11)

Does the polyglot sees polyglotism everywhere and "disavow the specificity of existence" in her eagerness to get around the world?[7] The point is not to world everyone to polyglotism because one has had the opportunity to travel to polyglotism. Difference cannot accommodate easily to a Self that sights it and yet is not resited by it.

Being different in another world and oneself in it entails a constant struggle against both of these solipsisms. Yet world-traveling, as opposed to physical travel, is something westerners generally do not do well. We go as the gaping "I." Despite what Eagleton says, many less privileged people *must* world-travel, says Lugones (1990:390), in order to have "flexibility in shifting from the mainstream construction of life to other constructions of life where they must become more or less 'at home.'" Mexican–American borders of identity, for instance, require that some people world-travel daily to and from Anglo-Latina/o constructions of life, crossing uneven terrains of meaning, identity, language, culture, and expectations – just to make a living, just to get through a normal day. Meanwhile, the privileged traveler jets in, walks around, appraises projects, perhaps, and then drinks those travels down by the evening

---

[7] Braidotti (1994:11 emphasis in original) surprises me when she asserts: "Paradoxically, the average American – if we except the WASPs – is an immigrant who speaks *at least* one other language on top of their own brand of ado/apted English." She is right that the USA is a place of immigrants, but that does not mean "the average American" is an immigrant today, nor does it justify claiming – without any empirical evidence – that something called "the average American" exists and that s/he speaks *at least* one language other than various versions of English. Indeed, Anderson (1991:38) takes a different view entirely. Discussing the origins of national consciousness in language and writing, he supposes that "[i]n the sixteenth century, the proportion of bilinguals within the total population of Europe was quite small; very likely no larger than the proportion in the world's population today, and – proletarian internationalism notwithstanding – in the centuries to come. Then and now the bulk of mankind is monoglot."

fire. We often world the worlds we encounter "out there," discovering them and bringing them back home as photomontages of tourist exquisita. Some can say (as the second feminist and IR travelers might): "I have learned to sympathize with oppression." "I have learned that I am similar to her." "We can talk." ("I can find ways to make IR listen").

If world-traveling is the purview of the "other," it must be the case – we come around to the argument of fictions again – that the western assertion of feminist "we" cannot capture and harness those to whom we travel. The erstwhile nation of feminism Ang speaks of may be annoyingly engirthing in its presumed inclusivity, but its nationalism is easily walked through in the inter-national relations of world-traveling by those whose skills at living with minority status are better developed than ours. For them, world-traveling is compulsive and "in some sense against our wills" (Lugones, 1990:390). It is a process that fits Ruth Behar's (1993:320) concern that we "take our borders with us" into writing, speaking, telling. Then representation becomes less worrisome because it is less able to be practiced as a majoritarian pretense.

IR too, for all its apparent ease in corraling the world into a hieratic space infused with the icons of the West, does not convince us that it carries "the story" in its pouches. The world exceeds IR. The field travels (some of) the world, but in a time of mobility, world-traveling is not IR's talent. Interesting inter-nations are lost to it, to say nothing of the many questions of human values that the loss prevents IR from grasping. World-traveling is the talent of those formed in the crucible of contemporary internations that mainstream IR is too busy corraling to see and cite. To enter this space, those in the field must in some sense move against national illusions.

Bhabha (1994:141, emphasis in original) argues that "[i]f, in our travelling theory we are alive to the *metaphoricity* of the peoples of imagined communities – migrant or *metropolitan* – then we shall find that the space of the modern nation-people is never simply horizontal. Their metaphoric movement requires ... a temporality of representation that moves between cultural formations and social processes without a 'centred' causal logic.'" World-traveling confronts us with that metaphoricity. It helps us see, in Balibar's (1995:72) words, the "non-existence of any spontaneous or 'natural' front of the heterogeneous 'minorities' against the dominant universality, or the 'system' as such." It is a form of travel in which it is difficult for colonial forces of "I" to gain a foothold. It moves us nonhorizontally to Alarcón's (1990:366) awareness of multiple registers of existence which can be "lived in resistance to competing notions for one's allegiance or self-identification." It is a capacity to be in different worlds – our proliferating selves within them – through a minority epistemology/ontology that refuses control, assimilation, and the boundaries both assume.

World-traveling to internations through fiction

How to begin journeys that no amount of what Ang (1995:59) calls "recognition," or "unity in diversity" or "sisterhood" or even of "faith in our (limitless?) capacity not only to speak, but, more importantly, to listen and hear" can "resolve" into nation? I pose two propositions.

First, communication and engagement are essential to world-traveling; however, owing to issues of power surrounding most communicative acts, the engagement associated with world-traveling is not likely to take the form of direct speech – at least not initially. We may find that it more closely resembles the type of activity our six travelers find themselves doing when they sit and read. That is, we may lose our bearings and our national Self (what we are taught it means to be a person who does IR or feminism) by reading and listening to, reciting and discussing, stories we have not sighted, sited, or considered citationally relevant to our national knowledges.

The selection of good reading material is central to the process of world-traveling, and I argue that reading fiction – imaginative literature – enables us to sharpen our sense of the range of minority characters, plots, events, dilemmas, styles, and even tempos that produce and occupy internations. Moreover, fiction is part of who we are as national members; and it is part of the states of international relations that we occupy. Indeed, Michael Shapiro (1994:485–486) talks about the national stories nations construct to legitimate the state's boundaries of inclusion and exclusion: "Because this strategy is, first and foremost, a literary strategy involved in maintaining an unambiguous space that coincides with state borders; struggles against this strategy . . . also exist in the nation's literatures." Anderson too builds arguments about nations as imagined communities by citing literature from *The Travels of Marco Polo* (thirteenth century) to Mas Marco Kartodikromo's *Serarang Hitam* (1924). Both show, and Anderson (1991:36) says, that "fiction seeps quietly and continuously in anonymity which is the hallmark of modern nation."

To Chakrabarty (2000:254), that quiet seep leads to a realm of alternative reason that helps us get at the larger picture of "now." In his view, even if some stories are "not true ... [they] speak of possible thought practices in which the future that 'will be' never completely swamps the futures that already 'are.'" Fiction quietly seeps the news that boundaries and even presentness are not as they seem. Thus my second proposition is that we who are encumbered by feminist and IR national trappings should add "reading fiction" to our methodological tools.

Which fiction? James Der Derian (1987) has treated spy novels as the true source of IR writings on diplomacy. Others in the postmodernist genre have turned to science fiction, ancient Greek tales, and contemporary computer simulations (Constantinou, 1996; Shapiro, 1990; Weldes, 1999) as the IR national literature. Those at the fulcrum of IR and postcolonial studies argue for reading novels and poetry in/to a postcolonial IR (Darby, 1998; Sylvester, 2000b). As for feminism, the origins of many women's studies programs lie in the humanities, particularly in the study of English or comparative literature. That aficionados of the IR question in feminism and the feminist question in IR do not themselves call much upon imaginative literatures for their work is puzzling in light of this history.

Feminism sets forth theories of reading that are instructive for all of us. Minrose Gwin (1996), for one, argues that when feminists who are women read women writers of narrative prose, and stories of women's lives, two points of mobility intersect: the reader enters through the text into another's space, imaginatively and in ways that enhance identification; and the text travels to the reader as the spaces read reposition the characters and connect the reader to them in new ways. She calls this "space-travel." It is a method of world-traveling via national (feminist) literature reading as a communal, national activity:

> When "I-reader" travels the spaces occupied by "she-writer" or the "she-character" and those spaces reposition her within them, there is an opening perspective and hence a potential for the shifting of identity, a production of self somewhere in the interstices between "she" and "I." What permits this production of identity in the in-between spaces of the text is not a colonization/consumption of text by reader but, rather, a spatial overlap between the world of the reader and the world of the text. In this sense, both reader and text are mutually engaged in travel. (Gwin, 1996:879)

Text has power and reader has power but neither has the sort of power that can impose meaning or insist on dialog.

IR, by contrast, does not offer a theory of reading at all, notwithstanding postmodernist claims about the field as a set of stories. Perhaps, though, the Gwin theory has extended relevance. It surely seems that there is considerable empathy among white, western, professional men, who write most of IR, for experiences of others like themselves, who see the world similarly (Smith, 1998). That is, as masculine IR reads texts written by men, the texts travel to them in an analogously reinforcing pattern to the one Gwin identifies among feminists reading narratives by women.

If we are seeking internations, though, it might be wise to look in places other than those that exemplify the nations that already blind us. We would put aside tales that explicitly revolve around typical IR events (wars, spying, statesmanship) or feminist themes (motherhood, violence against women, women buddies) and turn to novels that seem irrelevant to our respective national agendas. Internations are oddly located, which is why Enloe endlessly world-travels to unexpected places and delights us with their sudden relevance to our concerns. To find "the production of self somewhere in the interstices," we can read nonobvious texts that implicate IR even though (perhaps because) they do not feature the usual cast of stalking men and Mata Hari women doing cloak-and-dagger things in some "dangerous" about-to-be-postcolonial location. Novels written by women and by men that are not obviously feminist tales may also reveal more internations than those that tip the scales in favor of feminist expectations.[8] To illustrate this point, let us consider three stories that our hypothetical feminist and IR readers shared at the beginning of this tale. Each is by a British author and each is patently "irrelevant" to the topics at hand here.

Hallucinating Foucault

Patricia Duncker draws us into the intricate relationship between writer and reader, displaying a sensitivity that provides clues to the intricacies of world-travel and its destinations in between the familiar and the new. In *Hallucinating Foucault* (1996), she imagines a meeting-up of a Cambridge graduate student, who studies the life of a mad and violent French writer, with that writer himself. The encounters take place through a series of compelling journeys. The student reader travels mentally to the texts of the writer. He then travels geospatially to archival

---

[8] For readings that seek relief in postcolonial fiction and poetry from the international relations of development, see Sylvester (2000a, 2000b).

sources in a Parisian library, and on to find and rescue the writer from a mental institution. The story is full of travel – to the south of France and across frontiers of sexuality and memory. The question is which of the travels brings the reader closer to the writer and which represents movement in circles that land the reader someplace other than where he had planned to go?

At every turn, scholar-reader confronts humility and self-limits. Finding odd and unknown texts of his writer-subject in the Parisian library, he raises his pen triumphantly, turns the pages. But what is this? "There was no typed index, no list of contents and no accompanying summaries. I had his writing before me, unmediated, raw, obscure. I shook my head carefully and tried to read. I could understand nothing" (p. 59). Reader traveled with the wrong tools for understanding and now circles about in *faux* engagement with writer. Reader moves on, determined not to be tripped up by secondary sources. The mental institution where writer now lives is the place where words, conversation, dialog will bring understanding. Reader finds writer cooperative and yet evasive. He seems to be there . . . but. As though listening in on Elshtain (1987:xii), reader becomes involved in an increasingly "complex tracking of the shifting construction" – reader's construction of writer and writer's construction of reader, and the moving and following that take each on to the turf of the other.

Writer now takes the wheel and begins to guide the journey. That reader and writer are now in the same small space of a car should clear everything up. But the writer "clearly loved travelling" (Duncker, 1996:138), and so there is much movement forward and backwards in 35° Celsius weather to beach houses and other attempted bases for more wanderings. Reader is intent on making his writer well, but the power to do so is not his, and it is subtly resisted. Reader and writer engage sexually, with reader smitten and writer knowing that "[t]he love between a writer and a reader is never celebrated" (p. 154). There is a storm. A demise. Reader's girlfriend, referred to throughout as The Germanist, and seemingly left behind as the travel to the author deepens, reappears. She has crafted part of the travel story that reader and we are reading. We are all surprised, even though reader told us early on that she "didn't quite add up" (p. 13).

Everyone is hidden from everyone else and everyone is a little revealed too. At one point, writer describes to reader-in-pursuit "the loneliness of seeing a different world from that of the people around you . . .

That's why I always lived in the bars – les lieux de drague – simply to be among the others who were like me" (p. 113). *Les lieux de drague* is a site where lessons in reading difference and sameness reside in tension and empathy. As events proceed, the reader is himself read into such places – against and with and against his will. Near the end, we come to "a painting I can never enter, a scene whose meaning remains unreachable, obscure" (p. 177). Reader is chastened by then by his shift from travel to the world-travels that bring empathy, understanding, pain, and the reach across one's steady stock of knowledge into another's moving and disruptive reality.

And what does all of this mean for internations of feminism and IR? Nothing directly and much in a roundabout way. World-travel is difficult and not always heart-warming. It relies on a shift in one's sense of correctness – of method and of facts – without an easy standard of replacement. It can take one away from certain preoccupations, as though they were never fully right, never nailed down, never free from mutuality. Imagine: I thought it was all there in the library, but there was no index and I went traveling and found readers passing texts through holes in (national) defenses. It was not as it seemed. And yet what one finds was there all along to be sighted and cited around "the" mission.

Behind the scenes at the museum

Kate Atkinson (1995) offers a tale of tense travels back and forth across the times and geospaces of an average Yorkshire family, reconstructed through the eyes of young Ruby. She and her parents live above the pet shop they run, in a "self-contained, seething kingdom with its own primitive rules" (p. 10). Pain issues from this enclosed family of the 1950s, an institution of foot soldiers patrolling nastiness and dark secrets so they do not ooze into public view. Mind the fences.

Ruby is a daughter of this family . . . but. She is skeptical of its claims on her history, or rather of its version of her history – in which she figures as a problem for everyone. She tries to sort it out by going back to the time when distant family members fought in World War I, her recountings see the mindless losses of that war and the abusive mundanities of postwar wars above the pet shop, amidst official peace all around. There are serious traumas that Ruby would like to trace and understand. Her naïve reading of her own unhappiness and our reading of her repositions all of us as characters who can pick up only a few clues to life at a time.

For most of the novel, Ruby does not know why she is deemed "bad." At the end, while tanks enter Prague, she is brought back to the moment of a twin sister: "I had no recollection of this sister, could bring no image to mind" (p. 328). Amnesia. Forgetting. Forget the sister/forget the self. To bring her back inclusively, to cite her as part of herself, Ruby realizes, she will have to remember lost bits, fragments, sites, and events where history went off the rails. She will also have to forget the parts that got it all wrong but that insist on being the only story. She will probably have to rework the twin. The whole process is uncomfortable, shocking, irreal: "'It's always *my* fault, isn't it?'" (p. 329). The question moved, Ruby now knows that "I have caught the slow train that stops everywhere ..." (p. 382). She, and the world she knows, comes to all spots in between the narratives of closure that envelop her and that simultaneously leave her out. This train is one feminists and IR need to ride into and out of their mean moments and bordered amnesias about each other. We are all part of the story ... but do not figure into it in the ways the main recounters think. Ponder unrevealed twins whose lives hold clues to the half-characters we have constructed – those states or those women we believe in – despite the sense we have that something is missing.

The Information

Martin Amis is a bad boy of contemporary British fiction, seemingly misogynist, arrogant, and self-absorbed. His *The Information* (1995) tells of another bad boy as a tipsy and spiteful writer suffering a sagging literary career. Richard Tull started promisingly but has not written anything more substantial than book reviews in years. Directing his considerable energies now to ruining a more successful writer friend, Tull is unable for most of the story to see all the information around that he could hitch up to his authorial talents.

The good material eludes him – always eludes him. At a dinner party, Tull leads himself into this conversational maze about the characteristics of fiction readers:

> Richard said, "Has anyone ever really established whether men prefer to read men? Whether women prefer to read women?"
> "Oh please. What is this?" said the female columnist. "We're not talking about motorbikes or knitting patterns. We're talking about *literature* for God's sake."
> ...He said, "Is this without interest? Nabokov said he was frankly homosexual in his literary tastes. I don't think men and women write and read in exactly the same way. They go at it differently."

"And I suppose," she said, "that there are *racial* differences too? . . . I can't believe I'm hearing this. I thought we came here today to talk about *art*. What's the matter with you? Are you drunk?"   (p. 29)

Too busy excluding Tull to hear him, the columnist insists on literature as a universal that transcends such "national" practices as gendered readership. Tull is so busy making technical and typological points – and being contemptuous and insecure – that he cannot see in this conversation the outlines of an ironic tale about a man offering a feminist-resonating line about difference to a woman who disavows any identification with feminist nation. Meanwhile, reader wonders where s/he stands on the issues.

Tull is the victim here and we empathize with him, to some degree, as a literary believer . . . but. He sees minority difference in the glitter of an imagined literary nation of equal men and women readers. He is the ghost of feminist tales unwritten owing to bullies about/he is his own ghost writer/he is Ang's (1995:61) suspect learner eyeing an "instance of an oppression essentially the same as her own . . ." We leave him here for a moment, contemplating his put-down, as we look over the shoulder of the person next to us, who is reading . . .

What does it mean?

The Passion: Jeanette Winterson (1987) fictionalizes Bonaparte's war travels in Europe by creating several companions who engage in ambiguous, bumptious, and bizarre repositionings of selves, as the reader reads on compulsively and mutually. The travels are tense, the characters both more and less so. The places they gather read oddly:

> The roulette table. The gaming table. The fortune tellers. The fabulous three-breasted woman. The singing ape. The double-speed dominoes and the tarot.
> She was not there.
> She was nowhere.   (p. 60)

But she is somewhere. Ambiguity does not mean (again Duncker [1996:177]), that "I stumble on towards him and I never come closer." It is not an exercise in relativist reading, detached while the purveyor of words "does her thing" without our condemnation or appropriation of her or the thing. Relativism barricades spaces of difference as off-limits, beyond one's depth. In the name of tolerance, it denies that the invented other to whom one gives space could possibly have anything in common with one's (fixed sense of) Self. Reading as a method of world-traveling helps identify and produce palpable identity where it has not been noticed before. There can be odd feminist bodies – "the fabulous three-breasted woman" and, as antidote to IR's once-were Cold War concerns about falling countries, those "double-speed dominoes." If nation is fictitious unity, and relativism is the assumption that in order to valorize difference we must stand apart and deny the possibility of common readings, then world-travel makes evident the fictions, the real, and ideal without requiring that any of it be banished to the nowhere.

And so the once-were separate feminist and IR travelers shake themselves off and make ready to journey on. Only something seems different. The certainty has departed. No one is able to articulate exactly where he or she is going next. Moorings have slipped, bearings are misplaced, the maps seem archaic. "Are we lost?" someone softly asks. Silence. The world-traveling feminist grins broadly. She chortles, now belly laughs, drops her bag, hugs her knees with glee. The others stare at her in unspoken embarrassment. One by one, though, they too sit down – the first IR traveler inspecting the ground carefully for spiders. Sheepish smiles creep on to professional faces. There is new information to process.

Tull too, after nearly 500 pages of Hobbesian/Disneyesque/Sad Sack swashbuckle, reprocesses his own information about himself and asks: "Who was he? Who had he been throughout? Who would he always be?"(Amis, 1995:494) He seems to crawl out from the last page of Elshtain's *Women and War* (1989:258) as the chastened patriot who "deflates fantasies of control" by admitting that he had been like "Abel Janszoon Tasman (1603–59): the Dutch explorer who discovered Tasmania without noticing Australia..." (Amis, 1995:494). Traveling without noticing the surrounds. How inappropriate, Tull latterly thinks. We the readers are not sure we like this bad boy defeat transformed by Tull's improved reading skills. We might prefer him taken down by his own insipid mean-making. Instead, we see engagement through extensions of identity and the hint of a future that is both now and full of equivocity.

The story ends ambiguously. We see Tull, his estranged wife, his son, and other characters as uncertain and on the move, their worlds less bounded than at the start. We read about Tull, taking him in, spitting him out, and we think about difficult connections that implicate but extend beyond any national "I" and its colonial efforts to inform all of us of where to take our proper places. We enter intersections, where there is more than one "I" with which to empathize and be empathized with, many memories of transitoriness to wake up to, many forms of responsibility to contemplate, and much information to read.[9]

Are we lost? Bhabha (1994:157) refers to "gathering points of political solidarity" in minority discourse. Feminism is one of them. It is a point of potential empathy – I prefer this formulation to the lines-drawn image of solidarity – with ambiguities of a project that is more "minor" writing than it may seem. IR too can be a gathering point of empathy if it takes up space-world-traveling to ambiguous minorities everywhere located in defiance of a national logic. For gathering points of minority empathies, says Bhabha (p. 157), do not "celebrate the monumentality of historicist memory, the sociological totality of society, or the homogeneity of cultural experience." The social journey is too endless for that, too equivocal and so "minor" it cannot find the monument to celebrate.

And so our ambiguous ending. William Connolly (1991:463) claims that IR is nostalgic for a time "when a coherent politics of 'place' could be imagined as a real possibility for the future." Some will try to resurrect that time and place through triumphalist thinking about Great Powers winning epochal battles. Others will remind us that the struggle for power is still the *modus operandi* of the international and its relations, irrespective of whether we speak of struggling nation-states or struggling civilizations. Still others will go reading and reconstructing and seeking to make the world a better place. But in all this, there can be nostalgia for a Wo(e)begon(e) gender politics, where the women are good-looking and hidden and men are strong and rational and in charge, if not always astute.[10]

Feminism is a real possibility for the future that, with good intentions and some good and some alienating results, tries to "save, expand, improve or enrich . . . a political home which would ideally represent all women" (Ang, 1995:72). It tries to build a sturdy yet porous nation which, unlike IR, strives for a visible inclusivity of great and small, western and nonwestern, visible and hidden women: the more inclusive, the

---

[9] In discussing "empathy" in my work, Molloy (1997) misses these key points.

[10] The Wo(e)begon(e) reference recalls the imagined small town of Lake Wobegon, Minnesota, where Garrison Keillor (1987), its creator-narrator and spinner of ironic tales, has us read that all the *women* are strong and all the *men* are good-looking and everyone is, in the long run, basically happy.

more tolerant of difference, the stronger, the wiser the nation of feminism. Its politics too can be nostalgic.

Reading fiction, ostensibly so modest an activity, can be a method to reach points of tangent IR and feminism. Both exist in a postnational time, when nations and analysts exceed their spaces and their imaginations, traveling out from themselves. As the arguments of this essay suggest, and as Arjun Appadurai (1993b:411) tells us pointedly, "[w]e need to think ourselves beyond the nation. This is not to suggest that thought alone will carry us beyond the nation . . ." We might pose the challenge as not just travel beyond but world-travel in, through, and around nations, minorities, fictions, ideals, worlds. That is the international relations of/with/in a feminism that is itself unmoored by dis/connections. It is open to surprise, because it journeys with the contradictions of fictions and ideals, interdependencies and places that globalizing trends have dropped from view.

So travel with that "curious man; a shrug of the shoulders and a wink and that's him. He's never thought it odd that his daughter cross-dresses for a living and sells second-hand purses on the side. But then, he's never thought it odd that his daughter was born with webbed feet. 'There are stranger things,' he said. And I suppose there are" (Winterson, 1987:61). Strange disconnected and webbed relations remain to be sighted, sited, read, and cited in places of information stuffed with the ambiguity Lugones (1990:398) calls "survival-rich." Join the rich and reinvigorating journeys through minority gathering points, alternative reason, and curious internations of IR/feminism. The trip will be ironic and curious . . . but. It will stick us into contexts around "national" politics, where those who embarked with certainty learn what it means to be without stable majoritarian aspirations as a person of feminism/IR today.

References

Aggestam, Karin, Astrid Hedin, Annica Kronsell, and Erika Svedberg, eds. (1997), "A World in Transition: Feminist Perspectives on International Relations," special issue of *Statsvetenskaplig Tidskrift*, 100

Alarcón, Norma (1990), "The Theoretical Subject(s) of *This Bridge Called My Back* and Anglo-American Feminism," in Gloria Anzaldúa, ed., *Making Face, Making Soul: Haciendo Caras: Creative and Critical Perspectives by Women of Color* (San Francisco: Aunt Lute):356–369

Alker, Hayward (1992), "The Humanistic Moment in International Studies: Reflections on Machiavelli and las Casas," *International Studies Quarterly*, 36, 4:347–371

Allison, Graham (1969), "Conceptual Models and the Cuban Missile Crisis," *American Political Science Review*, 63, 3:689–718
 (1971), *Essence of Decision: Explaining the Cuban Missile Crisis* (Boston: Little, Brown)

Alpers, Susan (1975–1976), "Realism as a Comic Mode: Low-Life Painting Seen Through Bredero's Eyes," *Simiolus*, 8:115–144

Amis, Martin (1995), *The Information* (London: HarperCollins)

Anderson, Benedict (1991), *Imagined Communities: Reflections on the Origins and Spread of Nationalism* (London: Verso)

Ang, Ien (1995), "'I'm a Feminist But . . .' Other Women and Postnational Feminism," in Barbara Caine and Rosemary Pringle, eds., *Transitions: New Australian Feminisms* (Sydney: Allen & Unwin):57–73

Anzaldúa, Gloria (1987), *Borderlands/La Frontera* (San Francisco: Spinsters / Aunt Lute) ed. (1990), *Making Face, Making Soul: Haciendo Caras: Creative and Critical Perspectives by Women of Color* (San Francisco: Aunt Lute)

Appadurai, Arjun (1993a), "Disjuncture and Difference in the Global Cultural Economy," in Patrick Williams and Laura Chrisman, eds., *Colonial Discourse and Post-Colonial Theory: A Reader* (London: Harvester Wheatsheaf):324–339
 (1993b), "Patriotism and Its Futures," *Public Culture*, 5, 3:411–429

Arndt, Heinz (1987), *Economic Development: The History of an Idea* (Chicago: University of Chicago Press)

References

Ashley, Richard (1981), "Political Realism and Human Interests," *International Studies Quarterly*, 25, 2:204–36

(1984), "The Poverty of Neorealism," *International Organization*, 38, 2:225–286

(1986), "The Poverty of Neorealism," in Robert Keohane, ed., *Neorealism and Its Critics* (New York: Columbia University Press):255–300

(1989), "Living on Border Lines: Man, Poststructuralism, and War," in James Der Derian and Michael Shapiro, eds., *International/Intertextual Relations: Postmodern Readings of World Politics* (Lexington: Lexington Books):259–321

Ashley, Richard and R.B.J. Walker (1990a), "Speaking the Language of Exile: Dissident Thought in International Studies," *International Studies Quarterly*, 34, 3:259–268

(1990b), "Reading Dissidence/Writing the Discipline: Crisis and the Question of Sovereignty in International Relations Theory," *International Studies Quarterly*, 34, 3:367–416

Ashworth, Georgina (1988), "An Elf Among the Gnomes: A Feminist in North–South Relations," *Millennium: A Journal of International Studies*, 17, 3:497–506

Atkinson, Kate (1995), *Behind the Scenes at the Museum* (London: Black Swan)

Atwood, Margaret (1985), *The Handmaid's Tale* (New York: Fawcett)

Australian Department of Defence (1994), *Defending Australia: Defence White Paper 1994* (Canberra: Australian Government Publishing Service)

Axelrod, Robert (1981), "The Emergence of Cooperation Among Egoists," *American Political Science Review*, 25:306–318

(1984), *The Evolution of Cooperation* (New York: Basic Books)

Axelrod, Robert and Robert Keohane (1985), "Achieving Cooperation Under Anarchy," *World Politics*, 38, 1:226–254

Balibar, Etienne (1995), "Ambiguous Universality," *Differences: Journal of Feminist Cultural Studies*, 7, 1:48–74

Banks, Michael (1985), "The Inter-Paradigm Debate," in Margot Light and John Groom, eds., *International Relations: A Handbook of Current Theory* (London: Pinter):7–26

Barber, Benjamin (1989), "Liberal Democracy and the Costs of Consent," in Nancy Rosenblum, ed., *Liberalism and the Moral Life* (Ithaca: Cornell University Press):54–68

Barrett, Lindsay (2001), *The Prime Minister's Christmas Card: 'Blue Poles' and Cultural Politics in the Whitlam Era* (Sydney: Power Publications).

Baylis, John and N.J. Rengger, eds. (1992), "Introduction: Theories, Methods, and Dilemmas in World Politics," in John Baylis and N.J. Rengger, eds., *Dilemmas of World Politics: International Issues in a Changing World* (Oxford: Oxford University Press):1–25

Behar, Ruth (1993), *Translated Woman: Crossing the Border with Esperanza's Story* (Boston: Beacon)

Bender, Jonathon and Thomas Hammond (1992), "Rethinking Allison's Models," *American Political Science Review*, 86, 2:301–322

Bernstein, Michael Andre (1992), *Bitter Carnival: Ressentiment and the Abject Hero* (Princeton: Princeton University Press)

Bhabha, Homi (1994), "Dissemination," in *The Location of Culture* (New York: Routledge):139–170

    (1994), "Introduction: Locations of Culture," in *The Location of Culture* (New York: Routledge):1–18.

Biersteker, Thomas (1989), "Critical Reflections on Post-Positivism in International Relations," *International Studies Quarterly*, 33, 3:263–267

Bleiker, Roland (1997), "Forget IR Theory," *Alternatives: Social Transformation and Humane Governance*, 22, 2:57–85

    (1999), " 'Give it the Shade': Paul Celan and the Politics of Apolitical Theory," *Political Studies*, 47, 4:661–676

    (2000a), *Popular Dissent, Human Agency and Global Politics* (Cambridge: Cambridge University Press)

    (2000b), " 'Stroll Through the Wall': Everyday Poetics of Cold War Politics," *Alternatives: Social Transformation and Humane Governance*, 25, 3: 391–408

    (2000c), "We Don't Need Another Hero: Women and the Collapse of the Berlin Wall," *International Feminist Journal of Politics*, 2, 1:1–28

Boltanski, Luc (1999), *Distant Suffering: Morality, Media and Politics*, trans. Graham Burchell (Cambridge: Cambridge University Press)

Bordo, Susan (1986), "The Cartesian Masculinization of Thought," *Signs: Journal of Women in Society and Culture*, 11, 3:439–456

    (1993), *Unbearable Weight: Feminism, Western Culture, and the Body* (Berkeley: University of California Press)

Boris, Eileen and Elisabeth Prugl, eds. (1996), *Homeworkers in Global Perspective* (New York: Routledge)

Botting, Fred (1995), "Culture, Subjectivity and the Real: Or, Psychoanalysis Reading Postmodernity," in Barbara Adam and Stuart Allen, eds., *Theorizing Cuture: An Interdisciplinary Critique After Postmodernism* (New York: New York University Press):87–99

Bower, Lisa (1991), " 'Mother' in Law: Conceptions of Mother and the Maternal in Feminism and Feminist Legal Theory," *Differences: A Journal of Feminist Cultural Studies*, 3, 1:20–38

Bradlee, Benjamin (1975), *Conversations with Kennedy* (New York: W.W. Norton)

Braidotti, Rosi (1989), "The Politics of Ontological Difference," in Teresa Brennan, ed., *Between Feminism and Psychoanalysis* (London: Routledge): 89–105

    (1994), *Nomadic Subjects: Embodiment and Sexual Difference in Contemporary Feminist Theory* (New York: Columbia University Press)

Braidotti, Rosi with Judith Butler (1994), "Feminism by Any Other Name," *Differences: A Journal of Feminist Cultural Studies*, 6, 2+3:27–61

Bretherton, Charlotte (1998), "Global Environmental Politics: Putting Gender on the Agenda?" *Review of International Studies*, 24, 1:85–100

Brocklehurst, Helen (1999), "Painting International Relations," *International Feminist Journal of Politics*, 1, 2:214–323

Brock-Utne, Birgit (1985), *Educating for Peace: A Feminist Perspective* (New York: Pergamon Press)

Brown, Chris (1992a), *International Relations Theory: New Normative Approaches* (New York: Columbia University Press)

(1992b), "Really Existing Liberalism and International Order," *Millennium: Journal of International Studies*, 21, 3:313–328

(1994), "Turtles All the Way Down: Anti-Foundationalism, Critical Theory, and International Relations," *Millennium: Journal of International Studies*, 23, 2:213–235

Brown, Sarah (1988), "Feminism, International Theory, and International Relations of Gender Inequality," *Millennium: Journal of International Studies*, 17, 3:461–476

Brown, Seymour (1974), *New Forces in World Politics* (Washington, DC: Brookings Institution Press)

Brown, Wendy (1991), "Feminist Hesitations, Postmodern Exposures," *Differences: A Journal of Feminist Cultural Studies*, 3, 1:63–84

(1995), *States of Injury: Power and Freedom in Late Modernity* (Princeton: Princeton University Press)

Bull, Hedley (1969), "International Theory: The Case for a Classical Approach," in Klaus Knorr and James N. Rosenau, eds., *Contending Approaches to International Politics* (Princeton: Princeton University Press): 20–38

(1977), *The Anarchical Society: A Study of Order in World Politics* (New York: Columbia University Press)

Bull, Hedley and Adam Watson, eds. (1986), *The Expansion of International Society* (Oxford: Clarendon Press)

Buck, Lori, Nicole Gallant and Kim Richard Nossal (1998), "Sanctions as Gendered Instrument of Statecraft: The Case of Iraq," *Review of International Studies*, 24, 1:69–84

Burch, Kurt and Robert A. Denemark, eds. (1997), *Constituting International Political Economy*, International Political Economy Yearbook, Volume 10 (Boulder: Lynne Rienner)

Burke, Anthony (2000), "Poetry Outside Security," *Alternatives: Social Transformation and Humane Governance*, 25, 3:307–322

Butler, Judith (1990), *Gender Trouble: Feminism and the Subversion of Identity* (New York: Routledge)

(1993), *Bodies That Matter: On the Discursive Limits of "Sex"* (New York: Routledge)

(1994), "Against Proper Objects," *Differences: A Journal of Feminist Cultural Studies*, 6, 2+3:1–26

(2001), "The End of Sexual Difference?" in Elisabeth Bronfer and Misha Kavka, eds., *Feminist Consequences: Theory for the New Century* (New York: Columbia University Press):414–434

Butler, Judith and Joan Scott, eds. (1992), *Feminists Theorize the Political* (New York: Routledge)

Buzan, Barry (1991), "New Patterns of Global Security in the Twenty-First Century," *International Affairs*, 67, 3:431–451

Caine, Barbara and Rosemary Pringle (1995), *Transitions: New Australian Feminism* (St. Leonards: Allen & Unwin)

Calhoun, Cheshire (1995), "The Gender Closet: Lesbian Disappearance Under the Sign 'Women,'" *Feminist Studies*, 21, 1:7–34

Campbell, David (1996), "Political Prosaics, Transversal Politics, and the Anarchical World," in Michael Shapiro and Hayward Alker, eds., *Challenging Boundaries: Global Flows, Territorial Identities* (Minneapolis: University of Minnesota Press):7–32

Caporaso, James (1993), "International Relations Theory and Multilateralism: The Search for Foundations," in John Ruggie, ed., *Multilateralism Matters: The Theory and Praxis of an Institutional Form* (New York: Columbia University Press):51–90

Carlsnaes, Walter (1992), "The Agency-Structure Problem in Foreign Policy Analysis," *International Studies Quarterly*, 36, 3:245–270

Carr, E.H. (1962), *The Twenty Years Crisis: An Introduction to the Study of International Relations* (London: Macmillan)

Carroll, Susan (1985), *Women as Candidates in American Politics* (Bloomington: Indiana University Press)

Carver, Terrell, Molly Cochran, and Judith Squires (1998), "Gendering Jones: Feminisms, IRs, and Masculinities," *Review of International Studies*, 24, 2:283–297

Chadwick, Whitney (1990), *Women, Art, and Society* (London: Thames & Hudson)

Chakrabarty, Dipesh (1992), "Postcoloniality and the Artifice of History: Who Speaks for 'Indian' Pasts?" *Representations*, 37 (Winter):1–26

(2000), *Provincializing Europe* (Princeton: Princeton University Press)

Chan, Stephen (1993), "Cultural and Linguistic Reductionisms and a New Historical Sociology for International Relations," *Millennium: Journal of International Studies*, 22, 3:423–442

Chapkis, Wendy and Cynthia Enloe, eds. (1983), *Of Common Cloth: Women in the Global Textile Industry* (Washington, DC: Transnational Institute)

Chase-Dunn, Christopher and Richard Robinson (1977), "Toward a Structural Perspective on the World-System," *Politics and Society*, 7, 4:453–476

Chay, Jogsuk, ed. (1990), *Culture and International Relations* (New York: Praeger)

Chin, Christine (1998), *In Service and Servitude: Foreign Female Domestic Workers and the Malaysian "Modernity" Project* (New York: Columbia University Press)

Chipp, Herschel B. (1968), *Theories of Modern Art: A Source Book by Artists and Critics* (Berkeley: University of California Press)

Chodorow, Nancy (1978), *The Reproduction of Mothering* (Berkeley: University of California Press)

Cixous, Hélène (1980), *Illa* (Paris: Editions des Femmes)

References

Clausewitz, Karl von (1984), *On War*, ed. and trans. Michael Howard and Peter Paret (Princeton: Princeton University Press)

Cochran, Molly (1999), *Normative Theory in International Relations* (Cambridge: Cambridge University Press)

Cockcroft, Eva (1985), "Abstract Expressionism, Weapon of the Cold War," in Francis Frascina, ed., *Pollock and After: The Critical Debate* (London: Harper & Row):125–133

Cohn, Carol (1987), "Sex and Death in the Rational World of Defense Intellectuals," *Signs: Journal of Women in Culture and Society*, 14, 4:687–718

Coker, Christopher (1990), "Women and International Relations," *Salisbury Review*, June:23–27

Connolly, Clara (1993), "Culture or Citizenship," *Feminist Review*, 44:104–111

Connolly, William (1991), "Democracy and Territoriality," *Millennium: Journal of International Studies*, 20, 3:463–484

Constantinou, Costas (1996), *On the Way to Diplomacy* (Minneapolis: University of Minnesota Press)

(2000), "Poetics of Security," *Alternatives: Social Transformation and Humane Governance*, 25, 3:287–306

Conway, Jill Kerr (1993), *True North: A Memoir* (London: Hutchinson)

Cook, Alice and Gwyn Kirk (1983), *Greenham Women Everywhere: Dreams, Ideas and Actions from the Women's Peace Movement* (London: Pluto Press)

Coombes, Annie (1994), *Reinventing Africa: Museums, Material Culture and Popular Imagination* (New Haven: Yale University Press)

Cox, Annette (1982), *Art-as-Politics: The Abstract Expressionist Avant Garde and Society* (Epping: Bowker)

Cox, Robert (1981), "Social Forces, States, and World Orders: Beyond International Relations Theory," *Millennium: Journal of International Studies*, 10, 2:126–155

(1986), "Social Forces, States and World Orders: Beyond International Relations Theory," in Robert Keohane, ed., *Neorealism and Its Critics* (New York: Columbia University Press):204–254

"Culture in International Relations" (1993), special issue of *Millennium: Journal of International Studies*, 22, 2

Curthoys, Ann (1993), "Feminism, Citizenship, and National Identity," *Feminist Review*, 44:19–38

Daly, Mary (1978), *Gyn/Ecology: The Metaethics of Radical Feminism* (Boston: Beacon Press)

(1984), *Pure Lust: Elemental Feminist Philosophy* (Boston: Beacon Press)

Danto, Arthur (1981), *The Transformation of the Commonplace* (Cambridge: Cambridge University Press)

Darby, Phillip (1997), *At the Edge of International Relations: Postcolonialism, Gender and Dependency* (London: Pinter)

(1998), *The Fiction of Imperialism: Reading Between International Relations and Postcolonialism* (London: Cassell)

De Beauvoir, Simone (1952), *The Second Sex*, trans. H.M. Parshley (New York: Vintage Books)

De Goede, Marieke (2000), "Mastering 'Lady Credit': Discourses of Financial Credit in Historical Perspective," *International Feminist Journal of Politics*, 2, 1:58–81

Der Derian, James (1987), *On Diplomacy* (Oxford: Basil Blackwell)
    (1993), "Fathers (and Sons), Mother Courage (and Her Children), and the Dog, the Cave, and the Beef," in James Rosenau, ed., *Global Voices: Dialogues in International Relations* (Boulder: Westview Press): 83–96

Der Derian, James and Michael Shapiro (1989), *International/Intertextual Relations: Postmodern Readings of World Politics* (Lexington: Lexington Books)

Derrida, Jacques (1993), *Memoirs of the Blind: The Self-Portrait and Other Ruins*, trans. Pascale-Anne Brault and Michael Naas (Chicago: University of Chicago Press)

Dessler, David (1989), "What's at Stake in the Agent-Structure Debate?" *International Organization*, 43, 3:441–473

Dinnerstein, Dorothy (1976), *The Mermaid and the Minotaur: Sexual Arrangements and Human Malaise* (New York: Harper & Row)

Dirlik, Arif (1994), "The Postcolonial Aura: Criticism in the Age of Global Capitalism," *Critical Inquiry*, 20, 2:328–356

Di Stefano, Christine (1983) "Masculinity as Ideology in Political Thought: Hobbesian Man Considered," *Women's Studies International Forum*, 6, 6: 633–644

Di Stefano, Christine (1986), "Dilemmas of Rationality: A Feminist Survey," paper presented at the Northwest Women's Studies Association Conference, Washington, DC
    (1990), "Rethinking Autonomy," paper presented at the annual meeting of the American Political Science Association, San Francisco

Docker, John (1994), *Postmodernism and Popular Culture: A Cultural History* (Cambridge: Cambridge University Press)

Doty, Roxanne (1996), *Imperial Encounters* (Minneapolis: University of Minnesota Press)

Dougherty, James and Robert Pfaltzgraff (1990), *Contending Theories of International Relations: A Comprehensive Survey*, 3rd edn., (New York: Harper and Row)

Doyle, Michael (1986), "Liberalism and World Politics," *American Political Science Review*, 80, 4:115–169

Drew, Philip (1994), *The Coast Dwellers: A Radical Reappraisal of Australian Identity* (Ringwood: Penguin Books Australia)

Duffy, Diane (2000), "Social Identity and its Influence on Women's Roles in East-Central Europe," *International Feminist Journal of Politics*, 2, 2: 214–243

Duncan, Carol (1973), "Virility and Domination in Early 20th-Century Vanguard Painting," *Artforum*, 12, 4:30–39

Duncker, Patricia (1996), *Hallucinating Foucault* (London: Serpent's Tail)

Dunne, Timothy (1995), "The Social Construction of International Society," *European Journal of International Relations*, 1, 3:376–389

(1998), *Inventing International Society: A History of the English School* (London: Macmillan)

DVWP Kongress (Deutschen Vereinigung für Politische Wissenschaft) (2000), Politik in einer entgrenzten Wet, Kongress, 1–5 October, Halle

Dyer, Hugh (1993), "EcoCultures: Global Culture in an Age of Ecology," *Millennium: Journal of International Studies*, 22, 2:483–504

Eagleton, Terry (1990), *The Ideology of the Aesthetic* (London: Basil Blackwell)

Eisenstein, Zillah (1981), *The Radical Future of Liberal Feminism* (New York: Longman)

Elshtain, Jean Bethke (1981), *Public Man, Private Woman: Women in Social and Political Thought* (Princeton: Princeton University Press)

ed. (1982), *The Family in Political Thought* (Amherst: University of Massachusetts Press)

(1985), "Reflections on War and Political Discourse," *Political Theory*, 13, 1: 39–57

(1986), *Meditations on Modern Political Thought: Masculine/Feminine Themes From Luther to Arendt* (New York: Praeger)

(1987), *Women and War* (New York: Basic Books)

(1990), *Power Trips and Other Journeys: Essays in Feminism as Civic Discourse* (Madison: University of Wisconsin Press)

(1992), "Sovereignty, Identity, Sacrifice," in V. Spike Peterson, ed., *Gendered States: Feminist (Re)Visions of International Relations Theory* (Boulder: Lynne Rienner):141–154

(1993), "Bringing It All Back Home, Again," in James Rosenau, ed., *Global Voices: Dialogues in International Relations* (Boulder: Westview Press):97–116

(1995), "Feminist Themes and International Relations," in James Der Derian, ed., *International Theory: Critical Investigations* (New York: New York University Press):340–360

(1997), *Real Politics: At the Center of Everyday Life* (Baltimore: The Johns Hopkins University Press)

(1998a), "*Women and War*: Ten Years On," *Review of International Studies*, 24, 4:447–460

(1998b), *New Wine and Old Bottles: International Politics and Ethical Discourse* (Notre Dame, IN: University of Notre Dame Press)

Enloe, Cynthia (1970), *Multi-Ethnic Politics: The Case of Malaysia* (Berkeley: University of California Press)

(1973), *Ethnic Confict and Political Development* (Boston: Little, Brown)

(1975), *The Politics of Pollution in Comparative Perspective* (New York: David McKay)

(1980a), *Ethnic Soldiers: State Security in a Divided Society* (New York: Penguin Books)

(1980b), *Police, Military and Ethnicity: Foundations of State Power* (New Brunswick: Transaction Books)

(1981), *Ethnicity and the Military in Asia* (New Brunswick: Transaction Books)

(1983), *Does Khaki Become You? The Militarization of Women's Lives* (London: Pandora)

(1989), *Bananas, Beaches, and Bases: Making Feminist Sense of International Relations* (London: Pandora Press)

(1990), " 'Women and children': Making Feminist Sense of the Persian Gulf Crisis," *Village Voice*, 25 September:29–32

(1993), *The Morning After: Sexual Politics at the End of the Cold War* (Berkeley: University of California Press)

(1996), "Margins, Silences and Bottom Rungs: How to Overcome the Underestimation of Power in the Study of International Relations," in Steve Smith, Ken Booth, and Marysia Zalewski, eds., *International Theory: Beyond Positivism* (Cambridge: Cambridge University Press):186–202

(2000a), *Maneuvers: The International Politics of Militarizing Women's Lives* (Berkeley: University of California Press)

(2000b), "The Surprised Feminist," *Signs: Journal of Women in Culture and Society*, 25, 4:1023–1026

Eschle, Catherine (2001), *Feminism, Social Movements, and the Globalization of Democracy* (Boulder: Westview Press)

Esteva, Gustavo (1992), "Development," in Wolfgang Sachs, ed., *The Development Dictionary* (London: Zed Books):6–25

Fay, Paul B. Jr. (1966), *The Pleasure of His Company* (New York: Harper and Row)

Femina Politica: Zeitschrift für feministische Politik-Wissenschaft (2000), special issue on Feministische Ansatze in den Internationalen Beziehungen, 1

Ferguson, Kathy (1984), *The Feminist Case Against Bureaucracy* (Philadelphia: Temple University Press)

(1991), "Interpretation and Genealogy in Feminism," *Signs: Journal of Women in Culture and Society*, 16, 2:322–339

(1993), *The Man Question: Visions of Subjectivity in Feminist Theory* (Berkeley: University of California Press)

Ferguson, Yale and Richard Mansbach (1988), *The Elusive Quest: Theory and International Politics* (Columbia, SC: University of South Carolina Press)

(1991), "Between Celebration and Despair: Constructive Suggestions for Future International Theory," *International Studies Quarterly*, 35, 4:363–386

Fergusson, Harvey (1936), *Modern Man: His Belief and Behavior* (New York: Alfred Knopf)

Fierke, K.M. (1999), "Besting the West: Russia's Machiavella Strategy," *International Feminist Journal of Politics*, 1, 3:403–434

Finnemore, Martha (1996), *National Interest in International Society* (Ithaca: Cornell University Press)

Flax, Jane (1987), "Postmodernism and Gender Relations in Feminist Theory," *Signs: Journal of Women in Society and Culture*, 12, 4:621–643

(1990), *Thinking Fragments: Psychoanalysis, Feminism, and Postmodernism in the Contemporary West* (Berkeley: University of California Press)

References

Flynn, Leo (1997), "Marketing the Union: Some Feminist Perspectives," *Statsvetenskaplig Tidskrift*, 100, 1:67–73

Forbes, Cameron (1999), "Soul Brother to Some," *The Weekend Australian*, 7–8 November:23

Forum on *Social Theory of International Politics* (by Alexander Wendt) (2000), *Review of International Studies*, 26, 1:123–180

Foucault, Michel (1973), *The Order of Things: An Archaeology of the Human Sciences* (New York: Random House)

Frascina, Francis, ed. (1985), *Pollock and After: The Critical Debate* (London: Paul Chapman)

French, Marilyn (1985), *Beyond Power: On Men, Women, and Morals* (New York: Summit Books)

Friday, Nancy (1977), *My Mother, My Self* (New York: Dell)

Friedan, Betty (1963), *The Feminine Mystique* (New York: W.W. Norton)

Frye, Marilyn (1983), "In and Out of Harm's Way," in *The Politics of Reality: Essays in Feminist Theory* (Trumansburg, NY: Crossing Press):52–83

Fukuyama, Francis (1989), "The End of History?" *National Interest*, 16 (September):3–18

Gaarder, Jostein (1994), *Sophie's World: A Novel About the History of Philosophy*, trans. Pauline Moller (London: Phoenix House)

Gaddis, John (1991), "Toward the Post-Cold War World," *Foreign Affairs*, 70, 2:102–122

Gaidzanwa, Rudo (1993), "Citizenship, Nationality, Gender and Class in Southern Africa," *Alternatives: Social Transformation and Humane Governance*, 18, 1:39–59

Galbraith, John Kenneth (1969), *Ambassador's Journal: A Personal Account of the Kennedy Years* (Boston: Houghton Mifflin)

Gatens, Moira (1996), *Imaginary Bodies: Ethics, Power and Corporeality* (London: Routledge)

Geldzahler, Henry (1973), Letter to James Mollison, June 22, Archives of the National Gallery of Australia

George, Jim (1994), *Discourses of Global Politics: A Critical (Re)Introduction to International Relations* (Boulder: Lynne Rienner)

Gilligan, Carol (1982), *In a Different Voice: Psychological Theory and Women's Development* (Cambridge, MA: Harvard University Press)

Gilpin, Robert (1981), *War and Change in International Relations* (New York: Cambridge University Press)

(1986), "The Richness of the Tradition of Political Realism," in Robert Keohane, ed., *Neorealism and its Critics* (New York: Columbia University Press):301–321

(1987), *The Political Economy of International Relations* (Princeton: Princeton University Press)

Goldstein, Joshua (1994), *International Relations* (New York: HarperCollins)

Goldstein, Judith and Robert Keohane (1993), *Ideas and Foreign Policy: Beliefs, Institutions, and Political Change* (Ithaca: Cornell University Press)

Gowa, Joanne (1986), "Anarchy, Egoism and Third Images: The Evolution of Cooperation and International Relations," *International Organization*, 40, 1:167–186

Gramsci, Antonio (1971), *Selections from Prison Notebooks*, ed. and trans. Quinton Hoare and Geoffrey Newell Smith (London: Lawrence & Wishart)

Grant, Judith (1993), *Foundational Feminism: Contesting the Core Concepts of Feminist Theory* (New York: Routledge)

Grant, Rebecca (1991), "The Sources of Gender Bias in International Relations Theory," in Rebecca Grant and Kathleen Newland, eds., *Gender and International Relations* (Bloomington: Indiana University Press):8–26

Grant, Rebecca and Kathleen Newland, eds. (1991) *Gender and International Relations* (Bloomington: Indiana University Press)

Greenberg, Clement (1961), *Art and Culture* (Boston: Beacon)
  (1985), "Avant-Garde and Kitsch," in Francis Frascina, ed., *Pollock and After: The Critical Debate* (London: Paul Chapman):21–33

Grewal, Inderpal (1996), *"Home" and Harem: Nationalism, Imperialism, and Women's Culture in Nineteenth Century England* (Durham, NC: Duke University Press)
  (1999), "The British Museum and its Guidebooks," in Lisa Bloom, ed., *With Other Eyes: Looking at Race and Gender in Visual Culture* (Minneapolis: University of Minnesota Press):44–57

Grieco, Joseph (1990), *Cooperation Among Nations: Europe, America, and Non-Tariff Barriers to Trade* (Ithaca: Cornell University Press)

Griswold, A.B. (1961), *King Mongkut of Siam* (New York: Asia Society)

Gronemeyer, Marianne (1992), "Helping," in Wolfgang Sachs, ed., *The Development Dictionary: A Guide to Knowledge as Power* (London: Zed Books):53–69

Grosz, Elizabeth (1994), *Volatile Bodies: Toward a Corporeal Feminism* (Bloomington: Indiana University Press)

Guilbaut, Serge (1983), *How New York Stole the Idea of Modern Art: Abstract Expressionism, Freedom, and the Cold War*, trans. Arthur Goldhammer (Chicago: University of Chicago Press)

Gunning, Isabella (1991–1992), "Arrogant Perception, World-Travelling and Multicultural Feminism: A Case of Female Genital Surgeries," *Columbia Human Rights Law Review*, 23, 3:189–248

Gwin, Minrose (1996), "Space Travel: The Connective Politics of Feminist Readings," *Signs: Journal of Women in Culture and Society*, 21, 4:870–905

Haas, Ernst (1975), "Is There a Hole in the Whole? Knowledge, Technology, Interdependence, and the Construction of International Regimes," *International Organization*, 29, 3:827–876

Haas, Ernst, M.P. Williams, D. Babai (1977), *Scientists and World Order* (Berkeley: University of California Press)

Hackett, Pat, ed. (1989), *The Andy Warhol Diaries* (New York: Warner Brothers)

Halliday, Fred (1988), "Hidden From International Relations: Women and the International Arena," *Millennium: Journal of International Studies*, 17, 3: 419–428

References

(1994), *Rethinking International Relations* (Vancouver: University of British Columbia Press)

Hammonds, Evelynn (1994), "Black (W)holes and the Geometry of Black Female Sexuality," *Differences: A Journal of Feminist Cultural Studies*, 6, 2+3: 126–145

Han, Jongwoo and L.H.M. Ling (1998), "Authoritarianism in the Hypermasculinized State: Hybridity, Patriarchy, and Capitalism," *International Studies Quarterly*, 42, 1:53–78

Hansen, Lene (2001), "The Little Mermaid's Silent Security Dilemma and the Absence of Gender in the Copenhagen School," *Millennium: Journal of International Studies*, 29, 2:285–306

Haraway, Donna (1985), "A Manifesto for Cyborgs: Science, Technology, and Socialist Feminism in the 1980s," *Socialist Review*, 15 (March–April):65–108

(1989), *Primate Visions: Gender, Race, and Nature in the World of Modern Science* (New York: Routledge)

(1991), "The Biopolitics of Postmodern Bodies: Constitutions of Self in Immune System Discourse," in Donna Haraway, ed., *Simians, Cyborgs, and Women: The Reinvention of Nature* (New York: Routledge):203–230

Harding, Sandra (1986), *The Science Question in Feminism* (Ithaca: Cornell University Press)

(1987), "Introduction: is There a Feminist Method? in *Feminism and Methodology: Social Science Issues* (Milton Keynes: Open University Press):1–14.

(1991), *Whose Science? Whose Knowledge? Thinking From Women's Lives* (Ithaca: Cornell University Press)

(1998), *Is Science Multicultural? Postcolonialism, Feminisms, and Epistemologies* (Bloomington: Indiana University Press)

Harford, Barbara and Sarah Hopkins, eds. (1984), *Greenham Common: Women at the Wire* (London: Women's Press)

Harris, Clay (1997), "Modern Woman of Universal Appeal," *Financial Times*, September 1

Hartsock, Nancy (1982), "The Barracks Community in Western Political Thought: Prolegomena to a Feminist Critique of War and Politics," *Women's Studies International Forum*, 5:3–4

(1983), *Money, Sex and Power: Toward a Feminist Historical Materialism* (New York: Longman; 2nd edn., 1985, Boston: Northeastern University Press)

Hauptman, William (1973), "The Suppression of Art in the McCarthy Decade," *Artforum*, 12, 2:48

Hecht, Peter (1994), "Dutch Seventeenth Century Genre Painting: A Reassessment of Some Current Hypotheses," in Willem Melching and Wyger Velema, eds., *Main Trends in Cultural History: Ten Essays* (Amsterdam: Rodopi):150–163

Heitlinger, Alena (1997), "Emigré Perspectives on Feminisms in Europe – East and West," *Statsvetenskaplig Tidskrift*, 100, 1:42–46

Hersh, Seymour (1998), *The Dark Side of Camelot* (London: HarperCollins)

Herwitz, David (1993), *Making Theory/Constructing Art: On the Authority of the Avant-Garde* (Chicago: University of Chicago Press)

Herz, John (1951), *Political Realism and Political Idealism* (Chicago: University of Chicago Press)

Hickey, Dave, (1997), "Andy's Enterprise: Nothing Special," in José Mugrabin, ed., *Andy Warhol: Exhibition Catalogue* (Helsinki: Taidehalli):24–29

Higginbotham, Evelyn Brooks (1992), "African-American Women's History and the Metalanguage of Race," *Signs: Journal of Women in Culture and Society*, 17, 2:251–274

Hilsman, Roger (1996), *The Cuban Missile Crisis: The Struggle Over Policy* (Westport: Praeger)

Hirschmann, Nancy (1989), "Freedom, Recognition, and Obligation: A Feminist Approach to Political Theory," *American Political Science Review*, 83: 1227–1244

(1992), *Rethinking Obligation: A Feminist Method for Political Theory* (Ithaca: Cornell University Press)

Hobbes, Thomas (1966), *Philosophical Rudiments Concerning Government and Society, in The English Works of Thomas Hobbes of Malmesbury*, vol. II (Scientia Verlag Aalen)

Hoeg, Peter (1993), *Smilla's Sense of Snow*, trans. Tina Nunnally (New York: Delta)

Hoffmann, Mark (1987), "Critical Theory and the Inter-Paradigm Debate," *Millennium: Journal of International Studies*, 16, 2:231–251

Hoffman, Stanley (1990), "A New World and Its Troubles," in Nicholas Rizopoulous, ed., *Sea Changes: American Foreign Policy in a World Transformed* (New York: Council on Foreign Relations Press):274–292.

Hollist, W. Ladd (1981), "Anticipating World System Theory Synthesis," in W. Ladd Hollist and James Rosenau, eds., *World System Structure: Continuity and Change* (Beverly Hills: Sage):289–300

Hollist, W. Ladd and James Rosenau, eds. (1981), *World System Structure: Continuity and Change* (Beverly Hills: Sage)

Holsti, K.J. (1985), *The Dividing Discipline: Hegemony and Diversity in International Theory* (Boston: Unwin Hyman)

Hooper, Charlotte (2001), *Manly States: Masculinities, International Relations and Gender Politics* (New York: Columbia University Press)

Huggins, Jackie (1993), "A Contemporary View of Aboriginal Women's Relationship to the White Women's Movement," in Norma Grieve and Ailsa Burns, eds., *Australian Women: Contemporary Feminist Thought* (Melbourne: Oxford University Press):70–79

Huntington, Samuel (1993), "The Clash of Civilizations," *Foreign Affairs*, 73, 3:22–49

(1996), *The Clash of Civilizations and the Remaking of World Order* (New York: Simon & Schuster)

Huntley, L. Wade (1997), "An Unlikely Match? Kant and Feminism in IR Theory," *Millennium: Journal of International Studies*, 26, 2:279–320

Irigaray, Luce (1984), *Ethique de la différence sexuelle* (Paris: Editions de Minuit)

Jabri, Vivienne (1998), "(Uni)form Instrumentalities and War's Abject," *Millennium: Journal of International Studies*, 27, 4:885–902

Jackson, Cecile and Ruth Pearson, eds. (1998), *Feminist Visions of Development* (London: Routledge)

Jacoby, Tami Amanda (1999), "Gendered Nation: A History of the Interface of Women's Protest and Jewish Nationalism in Israel," *International Feminist Journal of Politics*, 1, 2:382–402

Jaggar, Alison (1983), *Feminist Politics and Human Nature* (Totowa, NJ: Rowan & Allenheld)

Jaggar, Alison and Paula Rothenberg (1984), *Feminist Frameworks: Alternative Theoretical Accounts of the Relations Between Women and Men* (New York: McGraw-Hill)

James, Oliver (1997), "Diana on the Couch – and her mother-in-law, too," *Sunday Times*, August 10, section 4:1

Jameson, Fredric (1991), *Postmodernism: Or, the Cultural Logic of Late Capitalism* (London: Verso)

Jaquette, Jane (1982), "Women and Modernization Theory: A Decade of Feminist Criticism," *World Politics*, 34, 2:267–284

Jephson, P.D. (2000), *Shadows of a Princess: Diana Princess of Wales 1987–1996* (London: HarperCollins)

Jervis, Robert (1978), "Cooperation Under the Security Dilemma," *World Politics*, 30:167–214

Jolly, Margaret and Kalpana Ram (1998), *Maternities and Modernities: Colonial and Postcolonial Experiences in Asia and the Pacific* (Cambridge: Cambridge University Press)

Jones, Kathleen (1990), "Citzenship in a Women-Friendly Polity," *Signs: Journal of Women in Culture and Society*, 15, 4:781–812

(1991), "The Trouble with Authority," *Differences: A Journal of Feminist Cultural Studies*, 3, 1:104–127

(1993), *Compassionate Authority: Democracy and the Representation of Women* (New York: Routledge)

Kaminsky, Amy (1994), "Gender, Race, *Raza*," *Feminist Studies*, 20, 1:7–31

Kaplan, Caren (1995), " 'Getting to Know You': Travel, Gender, and the Politics of Representation in *Anna and the King of Siam* and *The King and I*," in Roman de la Campa, E. Ann Kaplan, and Michael Sprinker, eds., *Late Imperial Culture* (London: Verso):33–52

(1999), "The Body Shop's Trans/National Geographics," in Lisa Bloom, ed., *With Other Eyes: Looking at Race and Gender in Visual Culture* (Minneapolis: University of Minnesota Press):139–156

Kaplan, Caren, Norma Alarcón, and Minoo Moallem, eds. (1999), *Between Woman and Nation: Nationalism, Transnational Feminisms, and the State* (Durham, NC: Duke University Press)

Kaplan, Morton (1969), "The New Great Debate: Traditionalism vs. Science in International Relations," in Klaus Knorr and James N. Rosenau, eds.,

Contending Approaches to International Politics (Princeton: Princeton University Press):39–61

Kardam, Nuket (1991), *Bringing Women In: Women's Issues in International Development Programs* (Boulder: Lynne Rienner)

Keeley, James (1990), "Toward a Foucauldian Analysis of International Regimes," *International Organization*, 44, 1:83–105

Keillor, Garrison (1987), *Leaving Home* (New York: Viking)

Keller, Evelyn Fox (1985), *Reflections on Gender and Science* (New York: Yale University Press)

Keohane, Robert (1984), *After Hegemony: Cooperation and Discord in the World Political Economy* (Princeton: Princeton University Press)

  ed. (1986), *Neorealism and its Critics* (New York: Columbia University Press)

  (1989a), "International Relations Theory: Contributions of a Feminist Standpoint," *Millennium: Journal of International Studies*, 18, 2:245–254

  (1989b), *International Institutions and State Power: Essays in International Relations Theory* (Boulder: Westview Press)

  (1998), "Beyond Dichotomy: Conversations Between International Relations and Feminist Theory," *International Studies Quarterly*, 42, 1:193–197

Keohane, Robert and Joseph Nye (1977), *Power and Interdependence* (Boston: Little, Brown)

Kindleberger, Charles (1973), *The World in Depression, 1929-1939* (Berkeley: University of California Press)

Kirk, Gwyn (1989a), "Our Greenham Common: Feminism and Nonviolence," in Adrienne Harris and Ynestra King, eds., *Rocking the Ship of State: Toward a Feminist Peace Politics* (Boulder: Westview Press):115–130

  (1989b), "Our Greenham Common: Not Just a Place but a Movement," in Adrienne Harris and Ynestra King, eds., *Rocking the Ship of State: Toward a Feminist Peace Politics* (Boulder: Westview Press):263–280

Klein, Bradley (1987), *Strategic Discourse* (New York: CUNY, the John Jay College of Criminal Justice)

  (1988), "After Strategy: The Search for a Post-Modern Politics of Peace," *Alternatives: Social Transformation and Humane Governance*, 13, 3:293–318

  (1989), "Textual Strategies of Military Strategy: Or, Have You Read Any Good Defense Manuals Lately?" in James Der Derian and Michael Shapiro, eds., *International/Intertextual Relations* (Lexington, MA: Lexington Books): 97–112

  (1994), *Strategic Studies and World Order: The Global Politics of Deterence* (Cambridge: Cambridge University Press)

Klein, Naomi (1999), *No Logo: Taking Aim at the Brand Bullies* (New York: St. Martin's Press)

Klotz, Audie (1995), "Reconstituting National Interests," *International Organization*, 49, 3:451–478

Kofman, Eleanor and Gillian Youngs, eds. (1996), *Globalization: Theory and Practice* (London: Pinter)

Kothari, Rajni (1988), *Transformation and Survival: In Search of a Humane World Order* (New Delhi: Ajanta)

Kozloff, Max (1973), "American Painting During the Cold War," *Artforum*, 11, 9:43–54

Krasner, Stephen (1976), "State Power and the Structure of International Trade," *World Politics*, 28, 3:317–347

(1982), "Structural Causes and Regime Consequences: Regimes as Intervening Variables," *International Organization*, 36:185–206

Kratochwil, Friedrich (1993), "Norms Vesus Numbers: Multilateralism and the Rationalist and Reflexivist Approaches to Institutions – a Unilateral Plea for Communicative Rationality," in John Ruggie, ed., *Multilateralism Matters: The Theory and Praxis of an Institutional Form* (New York: Columbia University Press):443–474

Kratochwil, Friedrich and John Ruggie (1986), "International Organization: A State of the Art on the Art of the State," *International Organization*, 40:753–776

Krauss, Rosalind (1985), *The Originality of the Avant-Garde and Other Modernist Myths* (Cambridge, MA: MIT Press)

Kreisky, Eva and Birgit Sauer, eds. (1997), "Geschlechterverhaltnisse im Kontext Politischer Transformation," special issue of *Politische Vierteljahresschrift*, 28

Kriger, Norma (1992), *Zimbabwe's Guerrilla War: Peasant Voices* (Cambridge: Cambridge University Press)

Kristeva, Julia (1982), *Powers of Horror: An Essay on Abjection*, trans. Leon S. Roudiez (New York: Columbia University Press)

Kronsell, Annica and Erika Svedberg (2001), "The Duty to Protect: Gender in the Swedish Practice of Consumption," *Cooperation and Conflict*, 36, 2:153–176

Kuspit, Donald (1993), *The Cult of the Avant-Garde Artist* (Cambridge: Cambridge University Press)

Lacan, Jacques (1977), *The Four Fundamental Concepts of Psychoanalysis*, trans. A. Sheridan (London: Penguin Books)

Laclau, Ernest and Chantel Mouffe (1985), *Hegemony and Socialist Strategy* (Norfolk: Thetford Press)

Laidi, Zaki (1998), *A World Without Meaning: The Crisis of Meaning in International Politics*, trans. June Burnham and Jenny Coulon (London: Zed Books)

Lapchick, R. and Stephanie Urdang (1982), *Oppression and Resistance* (Westport, CT: Greenwood Press)

Lapid, Yosef (1989), "The Third Debate: On the Prospects of International Theory in a Post-Positivist Era," *International Studies Quarterly*, 33, 3:235–254

Lapid, Yosef and Friedrich Kratochwil, eds. (1996), *Return of Culture and Identity in International Relations Theory* (Boulder: Lynne Rienner)

Lasch, Christopher (1970), *The Agony of the American Left* (London: André Deutsch)

Latham, Robert (1993), "Democracy and War Making: Locating the International Liberal Context," *Millennium: Journal of International Studies*, 22, 2:139–164

Law, Lisa (2000), *Sex Work in Southeast Asia: The Place of Desire in a Time of AIDS* (London: Routledge)

Lebow, Richard Ned and Janice Gross Stein (1994), *We All Lost the Cold War* (Princeton: Princeton University Press)

Leja, Michael (1993), *Reframing Abstract Expressionism: Subjectivity and Painting in the 1940s* (New Haven: Yale University Press)

Leonowens, Anna (1953), *Siamese Harem Life* (New York: E.P. Dutton & Company)

(1954), *The English Governess at the Siamese Court* (London: Arthur Baker)

Lerner, Gerda (1986), *The Creation of Patriarchy* (New York: Oxford University Press)

Levy, Jack (1992), "Prospect Theory and International Relations: Theoretical Applications and Analytical Problems," *Political Psychology*, 13, 2:283–310

Leys, Colin (1996), *The Rise and Fall of Development Theory* (London: James Currey)

Liddington, Jill (1989), *The Road to Greenham Common: Feminism and Anti-Militarism in Britain Since 1820* (Syracuse: Syracuse University Press)

Ling, Lily (2001), *Postcolonial International Relations: Conquest and Desire Between Asia and the West* (London: Palgrave)

Link, Andrew (1989), "Reflections on Paradigmatic Complementarity in the Study of International Relations," in Ernst-Otto Czempiel and James Rosenau, eds., *Global Changes and Theoretical Challenges: Approaches to World Politics of the 1990s* (Lexington: Lexington Books):99–116

Linklater, Andrew (1980), *Men and Citizens in the Theory of International Relations* (London: Macmillan)

(1990), *Beyond Realism and Marxism* (London: Macmillan)

(1992), "The Question of the Next Stage in International Relations Theory: A Critical-Theoretical Point of View," *Millennium: Journal of International Studies* 21, 1:77–100

(1998), *The Transformation of Political Community* (Cambridge: Polity Press)

Linton, Rhoda (1989), "Seneca Women's Peace Camp: Shapes of Things to Come," in Adrienne Harris and Ynestra King, eds., *Rocking the Ship of State: Toward a Peace Politics* (Boulder: Westview Press):239–262

Lippard, Lucy R. (1995), *The Pink Glass Swan: Selected Feminist Essays on Art* (New York: The New Press)

Lippmann, Walter (1946), "La Destinée Americaine," *Les Etudes Americaines*, 1 (April–May)

Lloyd, Michael and Michael Desmond (1991), *European and American Paintings and Sculptures 1870–1970 in the Australian National Gallery* (Canberra: Australian National Gallery)

Loomba, Ania (1993), "Overworlding the 'Third World,'" in Patrick Williams and Laura Chrisman, eds., *Colonial Discourse and Post-Colonial Theory: A Reader* (New York: Harvester Wheatsheaf):305–323

Lugones, Maria (1990), "Playfulness, World-Travelling, and Loving Perception," in Gloria Anzaldúa, ed., *Making Face, Making Soul: Haciendo Caras: Creative and Critical Perspectives by Women of Color* (San Francisco: Aunt Lute):390–402

References

Luke, Timothy (1991), "Prepositional Phases: The Political Effects of Art on Audience," *International Political Science Review*, 12, 1:67–86

Lundstrom, Karin (1997), "Women Caught in a Logical Trap in EC Law: An Analysis of the Use of Quotas in the Case of Kalanke," *Statsvetenskaplig Tidskrift*, 100, 1:74–86

Lyotard, Jean-François (1991), *The Inhuman: Reflections on Time*, trans. Geoffrey Bennington and Rachel Bowlby (Stanford: Stanford University Press)

McClintock, Anne (1993), "The Angel of Progress: Pitfalls of the Term 'Post-Colonialism,'" in Patrick Williams and Laura Chrisman, eds., *Colonial Discourse and Post-Colonial Theory: A Reader* (London: Harvester Wheatsheaf): 291–304

McGlen, Nancy and Meredith Sarkees (1993), *Women in Foreign Policy. The Insiders* (New York: Routledge)

Machel, Samora (1974), *Mozambique: Sowing the Seeds of Revolution* (London: CFMAG)

Mackie, Alwynne (1989), *Art/Talk: Theory and Practice in Abstract Expressionism* (New York: Columbia University Press)

Mansbach, Richard and John Vasquez (1981), *In Search of Theory* (New York: Columbia University Press)

Mansfield, E.D. and J. Snyder (1995), "Democratization and War," *Foreign Affairs*, 74, 3:79–98

Maoz, Zeev (1989), "Power, Capabilities, and Paradoxical Conflict Outcomes," *World Politics*, 41:239–266

Marchand, Marianne (1994), "Gender and New Regionalism in Latin America: Inclusion/Exclusion," *Third World Quarterly*, 15, 1:63–76

Marchand, Marianne, Julian Reid, and Boukje Berents (1998), "Migration, (Im)mobility, and Modernity: Toward a Feminist Understanding of the 'Global' Prostitution Scene in Amsterdam," *Millennium: Journal of International Studies*, 27, 4:955–982

Marchand, Marianne and Ann Sisson Runyan, eds. (2000), *Gender and Global Restructuring: Sightings, Sites and Resistances* (Boulder: Lynne Rienner)

Matthews, Jessica Tuchman, ed. (1991), *Greenhouse Warming: Negotiating a Global Regime* (Washington, DC: World Resources Institute)

Mbilinyi, Marjorie (1992), "Research Methodologies in Gender Issues," in Ruth Meena, ed., *Gender in Southern Africa: Conceptual and Theoretical Issues* (Harare: Sapes Books):31–70

Mearsheimer, John (1990), "Back to the Future: Stability in Europe After the Cold War," *International Security*, 15, 1:5–56

Meyer, M.K. and E. Prugl, eds. (1999), *Gender Politics in Global Governance* (Lanham, MD: Rawman & Littlefield)

Mies, Maria (1986), *Patriarchy and Accumulation on a World Scale: Women in the International Division of Labour* (London: Zed Books)

Millennium: Journal of International Studies (1988), special issue on "Women and International Relations," 17, 3

(1992), special issue on "Beyond International Society", 21, 3

Miller, Carol (1991), "Women in International Relations? The Debate in Inter-War Britain," in Rebecca Grant and Kathleen Newland, eds., *Gender and International Relations* (Bloomington: Indiana University Press): 64–82

Miller, Dorothy (1946), *Fourteen Americans* (New York: MOMA)

Millman, Marcia and Rosabeth Moss Kanter, eds. (1975), *Another Voice: Feminist Perspectives on Social Life and Social Science* (New York: Anchor Books)

Mitchell, W.J.T. (1992), "Postcolonial Culture, Postimperial Criticism," *Transition*, 56:11–19

Mohanty, Chandra, Ann Russo, and Lourdes Torres, eds. (1991), *Third World Women and the Politics of Feminism* (Bloomington: Indiana University Press)

Mollison, James (1989), "The Making of the Australian," part II, interviewed by Rosalie Gascoigne, David McNeill and Peter Townsend, *Art Monthly*, 24 (September):3

Molloy, Patricia (1997), "Face to Face with the Dead Man: Ethical Responsibility, State-Sanctioned Killing, and Empathetic Impossibility," *Alternatives: Social Transformation and Humane Governance*, 22, 4:467–492

Moon, Katherine (1997), *Sex among Allies: Military Prostitution in US–Korea Relations* (New York: Columbia University Press)

Moore, Jane (1995), "Theorizing the Body's Fictions," in Barbara Adams and Stuart Allen, eds., *Theorizing Culture: An Interdisciplinary Critique After Postmodernism* (New York: New York University Press):70–86

Morgan, Robin (1989), *The Demon Lover: On the Sexuality of Terrorism* (London: Methuen Press)

Morgenthau, Hans J. (1965), *Politics among Nations: The Struggle for Power and Peace* (New York: Alfred Knopf)

Mouritzen, Hans (1997), *Denmark in the Post-Cold War Era: The Salient Action Spheres* (Copenhagen: Danish Institute of International Affairs)

Mugrabin, José, ed. (1997), *Andy Warhol: Exhibition Catalogue* (Helsinki: Taidehalli)

Naifeh, Steven and Gregory White Smith (1992), *Jackson Pollock: An American Saga* (London: Pimlico)

Narayan, Uma (1989), "The Project of Feminist Epistemolgy: Perspectives from a Nonwestern Feminist," in Alison Jaggar and Susan Bordo, eds., *Gender/Body/Knowledge: Feminist Reconstructions of Being and Knowing* (New Brunswick: Rutgers University Press):256–269

Neale, Palena (1998), "The Bodies of Christ as International Bodies: The Holy See, Wom(b)an, and the Cairo Conference," *Review of International Studies*, 24, 1:101–118

Neufeld, Mark (1995), *The Restructuring of International Relations Theory* (Cambridge: Cambridge University Press)

Nietzsche, Friedrich (1969), *On the Genealogy of Morals and Ecce Homo*, trans. Walter Kaufmann (New York: Vintage Books)

Nilsson, Peter (1997), "Nuoruuteni Andyn kanssa," in José Mugrabin, ed., *Andy Warhol: Exhibition Catalogue* (Helsinki: Taidehalli):30–33

Niva, Steve (1998), "Tough and Tender: New World Order Masculinity and the Gulf War," in Marysia Zalewski and Jane Parpart, eds., *The "Man" Question in International Relations* (Boulder: Westview Press):109–128

Nordstrom, Carolyn (1997), *Girls and Warzones: Troubling Questions* (Uppsala: Life and Peace Institute)

Northrup, Terrell (1989), "The Dynamic of Identity in Personal and Social Conflict," in Louis Kriesberg, Terrell Northrup, and Stuart Thorson, eds., *Intractable Conflicts and Their Transformation* (Syracuse: Syracuse University Press):55–82

Onuf, Nicholas (1989), *World of Our Making: Rules and Rule in Social Theory and International Relations* (Columbia, SC: University of South Carolina Press)

Parker, Richard B. (1993), *The Politics of Miscalculation in the Middle East* (Bloomington: Indiana University Press)

Parmet, Herbert S. (1984), *JFK: The Presidency of John F. Kennedy* (New York: Penguin Books)

Parpart, Jane (1995), "Deconstructing the Development 'Expert': Gender, Development and the 'Vulnerable Groups,'" in Marianne Marchand and Jane Parpart, eds., *Feminism/Postmodernism/Development* (London: Routledge): 221–243

Pateman, Carole (1988), *The Sexual Contract* (Stanford: Stanford University Press)

Pauker, Guy, Frank Golay, and Cynthia Enloe (1977), *Diversity and Development in Southeast Asia: The Coming Decade* (New York: McGraw-Hill)

Pearson, Ruth and Sally Theobald (1998), "From Export Processing to Erogenous Zones: International Discourses on Women's Work in Thailand," *Millennium: Journal of International Studies*, 27, 4:983–994

Peterson, Karen Lund (2001), "Trafficking in Women: The Danish Construction of Baltic Prostitution," *Cooperation and Conflict*, 36, 2:213–238

Peterson, V. Spike (1990), "Whose Rights?" *Alternatives: Social Transformation and Humane Governance*, 15, 3:303–344

ed. (1992), *Gendered States: Feminist (Re)Visions of International Relations Theory* (Boulder: Lynne Rienner Press)

Peterson, V. Spike and Ann Sisson Runyan (1993), *Global Gender Issues* (Boulder: Westview Press)

Pettman, Jan Jindy (1996a), *Worlding Women: A Feminist International Relations* (St. Leonards: Allen & Unwin)

(1996b), "An International Political Economy of Sex?" in Eleanor Kofman and Gillian Youngs, eds., *Globalization: Theory and Practice* (London: Pinter):191–208

Pickup, Francine (1998), "Deconstructing Trafficking in Women: The Example of Russia," *Millennium: Journal of International Studies*, 27, 4:995–1022

Pieterse, Jan Nederveen (1998), "My Paradigm or Yours: Alternative Development, Post-Development, Reflexive Development," in *Development and Change*, 29:343–373

Pirages, Dennis (1978), *Global Ecopolitics* (North Scituate, MA: Duxbury Press)
(1990), "Technology, Ecology and Transformations in the Global Political Economy," in Dennis Pirages and Christine Sylvester, eds., *Transformations in the Global Political Economy* (London: Macmillan):1–21
Plumwood, Val (1998), "The Crisis of Reason, the Rationalist Market and Global Ecology," *Millennium: Journal of International Studies*, 27, 4:903–926
Polcari, Stephen (1993), *Abstract Expressionism and the Modern Experience* (Cambridge: Cambridge University Press)
"Politics of Art" (1991), special issue of *International Political Science Review*, 12, 1
Price, Richard and Christian Reus-Smit (1998), "Dangerous Liaisons? Critical International Theory and Constructivism," *European Journal of International Relations*, 4, 3:259–294
Probyn, Elspeth (1990), "Travels in the Postmodern: Making Sense of the Local," in Linda Nicholson, ed., *Feminism/Postmodernism* (New York: Routledge):176–189
Rapley, John (1996), *Understanding Development: Theory and Practice in the Third World* (Boulder: Lynne Rienner)
Reardon, Betty (1985), *Sexism and the War System* (New York: Teacher's College, Columbia University)
Reeves, Richard (1993), *President Kennedy: Profile of Power* (New York: Simon & Schuster)
Rengger, Nicholas (1988), "Going Critical? A Response to Hoffman," *Millennium: Journal of International Studies*, 17, 1:81–89
Resnick, Stephen, John Sinisi and Richard Wolff (1985), "Class Analysis of International Relations," in W. Ladd Hollist and F. LaMond Tullis, eds., *International Political Economy Yearbook*, vol. 1 (Boulder: Westview Press):87–123
Rich, Adrienne (1976), *Of Women Born* (New York: Norton)
Richey, Lisa Ann (2001), "In Search of Feminist Foreign Policy: Gender, Development, and Danish State Identity," *Cooperation and Conflict*, 36, 2: 177–212
Riding, Laura Jackson (1980), "How Blind and Bright," in *The Poems of Laura Riding* (Manchester: Carcanet New Press):24
Riley, Denise (1988), *Am I That Name? Feminism and the Category of "Women" in History* (Minneapolis: University of Minnesota Press)
Robbins, Bruce (1995), "The Weird Heights: On Cosmopolitanism, Feeling, and Power," *Differences: A Journal of Feminist Cultural Studies*, 7, 1:165–187
Robertson, Bryan (1961), *Jackson Pollock* (New York: Abrams)
(1973), Letter of June 26, to Max Hutchison, Archives of the National Gallery of Australia
Robinson, James Harvey (1921), *The Mind in the Making* (New York: Harper & Brothers)
Rosenau, James (1981), "Interpreting Aggregative Processes in the International Political Economy: Third World Demands as Empirical Data," in W. Ladd Hollist and James Rosenau, eds., *World System Structure: Continuity and Change* (Beverly Hills: Sage):262–288

(1990), *Turbulence in World Politics: A Theory of Change and Continuity* (Princeton: Princeton University Press)

Rosenau, Pauline (1992), *Postmodernism and the Social Sciences: Insights, Inroads and Intrusions* (Princeton: Princeton University Press)

Rosenblum, Nancy (1987), *Another Liberalism: Romanticism and the Reconstruction of Liberal Thought* (Cambridge, MA: Harvard University Press)

Ruddick, Sara (1983), "Pacifying the Forces: Drafting Women in the Interests of Peace," *Signs: Journal of Women in Society and Culture*, 8, 3:471–489

Ruggie, John (1983), "Continuity and Transformation in the World Polity: Toward a Neorealist Synthesis," *World Politics*, 35, 2:261–285

(1986), "Continuity and Transformation in the World Polity," in Robert Keohane, ed., *Neorealism and Its Critics* (New York: Columbia University Press):131–157

ed.(1993), *Multilateralism Matters: The Theory and Praxis of an Institutional Form* (New York: Columbia University Press)

Runyan, Anne Sisson (1996), "The Places of Women in Trading Places: Gendered Global/Regional Regimes and Inter-nationalized Feminist Resistance," in Eleanor Kofman and Gillian Youngs, eds., *Globalization: Theory and Practice* (London: Pinter):238–252

Runyan, Anne and V. Spike Peterson (1991), "The Radical Future of Realism: Feminist Subversions of IR Theory," *Alternatives: Social Transformation and Humane Governance*, 16 (Winter):67–106

Rushing, W. Jackson (1995), *Native American Art and the New York Avant-Garde: A History of Cultural Primitivism* (Austin: University of Texas Press)

Russett, Bruce (1985), "The Mysterious case of Vanishing Hegemony: Or, Is Mark Twain Really Dead?" *International Organization*, 39, 1:208–231.

Russo, Ann (1991), "We Cannot Live Without Our Lives: White Women, Antiracism and Feminism," in Chandra Mohanty, Ann Russo, and Lourdes Torres, eds., *Third World Women and the Politics of Feminism* (Bloomington: Indiana University Press):297–313

Saco, Diane (1997), "Gendering Sovereignty: Marriage and International Relations in Elisabethan Times," *European Journal of International Relations*, 3, 3:291–318

Said, Edward (1993), "Orientalism," in Patrick Williams and Laura Chrisman, eds., *Colonial Discourse and Post-Colonial Theory: A Reader* (London: Harvester Wheatsheaf):132–149

Salzinger, Leslie (1997), "From High Heels to Swathed Bodies: Gendered Meanings under Production in Mexico's Export-Processing Industry," *Feminist Studies*, 23, 3:549–575

Schlesinger, Arthur (1965), *A Thousand Days: John F. Kennedy in the White House* (Boston: Houghton Mifflin)

Schmidt, Brian (1998), *The Political Discourse of Anarchy: A Disciplinary History of International Relations* (Albany: State University of New York Press)

Scholte, Jan Aart (2000), "Cautionary Reflections of Seattle," *Millennium: Journal of International Studies*, 29, 2:115–121

Schwartz-Shea, Peregrine and Debra Burrington (1990), "Free Riding, Alternative Organization, and Cultural Feminism: The Case of Seneca Women's Peace Camp," *Women and Politics*, 10:1–37

Scott, James (1990), *Domination and the Arts of Resistance: Hidden Transcripts* (New Haven: Yale University Press)

Shapiro, David and Cecile (1985), "Abstract Expressionism: The Politics of Apolitical Painting," in Francis Frascina, ed., *Pollock and After: The Critical Debate* (London: Paul Chapman):135–151

Shapiro, Michael (1990), "Stategic Discourse/Discursive Strategy: The Representation of 'Security Policy' in the Video Age," *International Studies Quarterly*, 34, 3:327–340

(1994), "Moral Geographies and the Ethics of Post-Sovereignty," *Public Culture*, 6, 3:479–502

Sharoni, Simona (1993), "Middle East Politics Through Feminist Lenses: Toward Theorizing International Relations from Women's Struggles," *Alternatives: Social Transformation and Human Governance*, 18, 1:5–18

(1998), "Gendering Conflict and Peace in Israel/Palestine and the North of Ireland," *Millennium: Journal of International Studies*, 27, 4:1061–1090

Shaw, George Bernard (1957), *Pygmalion: A Romance in Five Acts* (London: Longmans, Green and Co.)

(1970), *Pygmalion: A Romance in Five Acts* (Harmondsworth: Penguin Books)

Sheth, D.L. (1987), "Alternative Development as Political Practice," *Alternatives: Social Transformation and Humane Governance*, 12, 2:155–171

Shire, Chenjerai (1994), "Men Don't Go to the Moon: Language, Space and Masculinities in Zimbabwe," in Andrea Cornwall and Nancy Lindisfarne, eds., *Dislocating Masculinity: Comparative Ethnographies* (London: Routledge):147–158

Shohat, Ella and Robert Stam (1998), "Narrativizing Visual Culture: Towards a Polycentric Aesthetics," in Nicholas Mirzoeff, eds., *The Visual Culture Reader* (London: Routledge):27–49

Simon, Herbert (1982), *Models of Bounded Rationality* (Cambridge, MA: MIT Press)

Smith, Dorothy (1990), *The Conceptual Practices of Power: A Feminist Sociology of Knowledge* (Boston: Northeastern University Press)

Smith, J., J. Collins, T. Hopkins, and H. Muhammad (1988), *Racism, Sexism, and the World-System* (New York: Greenwood Press)

Smith, Neil (1997), "The Satanic Geographies of Globalization: Uneven Development in the 1990s," *Public Culture*, 10, 1:169–189

Smith, Steve (1992), "The Forty Years Detour: The Resurgence of Normative Theory in International Relations," *Millennium: Journal of International Studies*, 21, 3:489–508

(1995), "The Self-Images of a Discipline: A Genealogy of International Relations Theory," in Ken Booth and Steve Smith, eds., *International Relations Theory Today* (University Park, PA: University of Pennsylvania Press):1–37

(1996), "Positivism and Beyond," in Steve Smith, Ken Booth, and Marysia Zalewski, eds., *International Theory: Positivism and Beyond* (Cambridge: Cambridge University Press):11–44

(1998), " 'Unacceptable Conclusions' and the 'Man' Question: Masculinity Gender, and International Relations," in Marysia Zalewski and Jane Parpart, eds., *The "Man" Question in International Relations* (Boulder: Westview Press):54–72

Snidal, Duncan (1985), "The Game Theory of International Politics," *World Politics*, 38, 1:25–57

Sorensen, Theodore (1966), *Kennedy* (New York: Bantam Books)

Spender, Stephen (1948), "We Can Win the Battle for the Mind of Europe," *New York Times Magazine*, April 25, 1948:33

Spiegel, Steven and Kenneth Waltz, eds. (1971), *Conflict in World Politics* (Cambridge, MA: Winthrop)

Spivak, Gayatri Chakravorty (1985), "The Rani of Sirmur: An Essay in Reading the Archives," *History and Theory*, 24, 3:247–269

(1988), "Can the Subaltern Speak?" in Cary Nelson and Lawrence Grossberg, eds., *Marxism and the Interpretation of Culture* (Urbana: University of Illinois Press):271–313

(1998), "Gender and International Studies," *Millennium: Journal of International Studies*, 27, 4:809–832

Stancich, Lara (1998), "Discovering Elephants and a Feminist Theory of International Relations," *Global Society*, 12, 1:125–140

Staniland, Martin (1985), *What is Political Economy: A Study of Social Theory and Underdevelopment* (New Haven: Yale University Press)

Staudt, Kathy (1987), "Women's Politics, the State, and Capitalist Tranformation in Africa," in Irving Leonard Markovitz, ed., *Studies in Power and Class in Africa* (Oxford: Oxford University Press):193–208

Steans, Jill (1997) *Gender and International Relations* (Cambridge: Polity Press)

Stein, Arthur (1984), "The Hegemon's Dilemma: Great Britain, the United States, and the International Economic Order," *International Organization*, 38, 2: 355–386

(1990), *Why Nations Cooperate: Circumstances and Choices in International Relations* (Ithaca: Cornell University Press)

Stiehm, Judith (1984) *Women's and Men's Wars* (Oxford: Pergamon Press)

Strange, Susan (1982), " 'Cave! Hic Dragones': A Critique of Regime Analysis," *International Organization*, 33:479–496

ed. (1984), *Paths to International Political Economy, 1959–1984* (London: George Allen & Unwin)

(1990), "The Name of the Game," in Nicholas Rizopoulos, ed., *Sea Changes: American Foreign Policy in a World Transformed* (New York: Council on Foreign Relations Press):238–273

Suganami, Hidemi (1989) *The Domestic Analogy and World Order Proposals* (Cambridge: Cambridge University Press)

Sylvester, Christine (1983), "An African Dilemma," *The Progressive*, January: 40–43

(1985), "Continuity and Discontinuity in Zimbabwe's Development History," *African Studies Review*, 28, 1:19–44

(1987), "Some Dangers in Merging Feminist and Peace Projects," *Alternatives: Social Transformation and Humane Governance*, 12, 4:493–509

(1989), "Patriarchy, Peace, and Women Warriors," in Linda Forcey, ed., *Peace: Meanings, Politics, Strategies* (New York: Praeger Press):97–112

(1990), "The Emperors' Theories and Transformations: Looking at the Field Through Feminist Lenses," in Dennis Pirages and Christine Sylvester, eds., *Transformations in the Global Political Economy* (London: Macmillan): 230–254

(1991a) "'Urban Women Cooperators,' 'Progress,' and 'African Feminism' in Zimbabwe," in *Differences: A Journal of Feminist Cultural Studies*, 3, 1: 39–62

(1991b), *Zimbabwe: The Terrain of Contradictory Development* (Boulder: Westview Press)

(1992), "Feminists and Realists Look at Autonomy and Obligation in International Relations," in V. Spike Peterson, ed., *Gendered States: Feminist (Re)Visions of International Relations Theory* (Boulder: Lynne Rienner Press): 259–306

ed. (1993a), "Feminists Write International Relations," special issue of *Alternatives: Social Transformation and Humane Governance*, 18, 1

(1993b), "Homeless in International Relations? 'Women's Place in Canonical Texts and in Feminist Reimaginings," in Marjorie Ringrose and Adam Lerner, eds., *Reimagining the Nation* (London: Open University Press): 76–97

(1993c), "Riding the Hyphens of Feminism, Peace, and Place in Four- (Or More) Part Cacophony," *Alternatives: Social Transformation and Humane Governance*, 18, 1:109–118

(1993d), "Reconstituting a Gender-Eclipsed Dialogue," in James Rosenau, ed., *Global Voices: Dialogues in International Relations* (Boulder: Westview Press):27–53

(1994a), *Feminist Theory and International Relations in a Postmodern Era* (Cambridge: Cambridge University Press)

(1994b), "Empathetic Cooperation: A Feminist Method for IR," *Millennium: Journal of International Studies*, 23, 2:315–336

(1995a), "African and Western Feminisms: World-Traveling the Tendencies and Possibilities," *Signs: Journal of Women in Culture and Society*, 20, 4:941–969

(1995b), "'Women' in Rural Producer Groups and the Diverse Politics of Truth in Zimbabwe," in Marianne Marchand and Jane Parpart, eds., *Feminism/Postmodernism/Development* (New York: Routledge):182–203

(1996a), "Picturing the Cold War: An Art Graft/Eye Graft," *Alternatives: Social Transformation and Humane Governance*, 21, 4:393–418

(1996b), "The Contributions of Feminist Theory to International Relations," in Steve Smith, Ken Booth, and Marysia Zalewski, eds., *International Theory: Positivism and Beyond* (Cambridge: Cambridge University Press):254–278

(1997), "A Woman's Place in Harare: Art Review," *Gallery Magazine* (Harare: Gallery Delta)

(1998a), "Handmaids' Tales of Washington Power: The Abject and the Real Kennedy White House," *Body and Society*, 4, 3:39–66

(1998b), "Homeless in International Relations? 'Women's Place in Canonical Texts and in Feminist Reimaginings," in Anne Phillips, ed., *Feminism and Politics* (New York: Oxford University Press):44–66

(1999a), "(Sur)Real Internationalism: Emigrés, Native Sons and Ethical War Creations," *Alternatives: Social Transformation and Humane Governance*, 24, 2:219–247

(1999b), " 'Progress' in Zimbabwe: Is 'It' a 'Woman?' " *International Feminist Journal of Politics*, 1, 1:89–118

(1999c), "Development Studies and Postcolonial Studies: Disparate Tales of the 'Third World,' " *Third World Quarterly*, 20, 4:703–721

(1999d), "In-Between and in Evasion of So Much: Third World Literatures, International Relations, and Postcolonial Analysis," *Postcolonial Studies*, 2, 2:249–263

(2000a), *Women and Progress in Zimbabwe: Narratives of Identity and Work from the 1980s* (Portsmouth, NH: Heinemann)

(2000b), "Development Poetics," *Alternatives: Social Transformation and Humane Governance*, 25, 3:335–351

(2000c), "Masculinity and Femininity in the Construction of a New Order of Peace: The Korean Case," in Hahnso Park, ed., *Word Order and Peace at the Millennium* (Seoul: Yonsei University Press):87–105

(2001), "Vacillations in Zimbabwe Around 'Women,' " in Staffan Darnolf and Liisa Laakso, eds., *Indigenization of a Polity: Zimbabwe's Twenty Years of Independence* (London: Macmillan)

Sylvester, Christine and Roland Bleiker (1997), " 'Meine Stimme ein Vogellaut': Sprachkritik, Empathie und Internationale Geschlechter-regime," *Politische Vierteljahresschrift*, 28:411–424

Tadiar, Neferti Zina M. (1998), "Prostituted Filipinas and the Crisis of Philippine Culture," *Millennium: Journal of International Studies*, 27, 4:927–954

Tetreault, Mary Ann (1999), "Sex and Violence: Social Reactions to Economic Restructuring in Kuwait," *International Feminist Journal of Politics*, 1, 2:237–255

Thiele, Beverly (1986), "Vanishing Acts in Social and Political Thought: Tricks of the Trade," in Carole Pateman and Elizabeth Grosz, eds., *Feminist Challenges: Social and Political Theory* (Boston: Northeastern University Press): 30–43

Thompson, Kenneth (1960a), *Political Realism and the Crises of World Politics* (Princeton: Princeton University Press)

(1960b), "Toward a Theory of International Politics," in Stanley Hoffmann, ed., *Contemporary Theory in International Relations* (Englewood Cliffs, NJ: Prentice-Hall):17–28

Thompson, Robert Smith (1992), *The Missiles of October: The Declassified Story of John F. Kennedy and the Cuban Missile Crisis* (New York: Simon & Schuster)

Tickner, J. Ann (1987), *Self-Reliance Versus Power Politics: The American and Indian Experiences in Building Nation-States* (New York: Columbia University Press)

(1988), "Hans Morgenthau's Principles of Political Realism: A Feminist Reformulation," *Millennium: Journal of International Studies*, 17, 3:429–440

(1992), *Gender in International Relations: Feminist Perspectives on Achieving Global Security* (New York: Columbia University Press)

(1996), "Identity in International Relations Theory: Feminist Perspectives," in Yosef Lapid and Friedrich Kratochwil, eds., *The Return of Culture and Identity in IR* (Boulder: Lynne Rienner):147–162

(1997), "You Just Don't Understand: Troubled Engagements Between Feminists and IR Theorists," *International Studies Quarterly* 41:611–633

(2001), *Gendering World Politics: Issues and Approaches in the Post-Cold War Era* (New York: Columbia University Press).

Tooby, John and Irven DeVore (1987), "The Reconstruction of Hominid Behavioral Evolution Through Strategic Modeling," in Warren Kinzey, ed., *The Evolution of Human Behavior: Primate Models* (Albany: State University of New York Press):183–237

Trinh Minh-ha (1989), *Women, Native, Other: Writing Postcoloniality and Feminism* (Bloomington: Indiana University Press)

Tronto, Joan (1987), "Beyond Gender Differences to a Theory of Care," *Signs: Journal of Women in Cuture and Society*, 1:644–663

Trotsky, Leon (1957), *Literature and Revolution* (New York: Russell & Russell)

True, Jacqueline (1997), "Victimization or Democratization? Czech Women's Organizing Potential in a Globalizing Political Economy," *Statsvetenskaplig Tidskrift*, 100, 1:47–62

Truong, Thanh-Dam (1990), *Sex, Money, and Morality: Prostitution and Tourism in South-East Asia* (London: Zed Books)

Tyrer, Bob (1997), "Dangerous Di," *Sunday Times*, August 10, 1997, section 4:1

Urdang, Stephanie (1979), *Fighting Two Colonialisms: Women in Guinea Bissau* (New York: Monthly Review Press)

Vesonder, Timothy (1977), "Eliza's Choice: Transformation Myth and the Ending of *Pygmalion*," in Rodell Weintraub, ed., *Fabian Feminist: Bernard Shaw and Woman* (University Park, PA: The Pennsylvania State University)

Viotti, Paul and Mark Kauppi (1987), *International Relations Theory: Realism, Pluralism, Globalism* (London: Collier Macmillan)

Visvanathan, Nalini, Lynn Duggan, Laurie Nisonoff, and Nan Wiegersma, eds. (1997), *The Women, Gender and Development Reader* (London: Zed Books)

Vitale, Robert (2000), "The Graceful and Generous Liberal Gesture: Making Racism *In* visible in American International Relations," *Millennium: Journal of International Studies*, 29, 2:331–356

Waever, Ole (1996), "The Rise and Fall of the Inter-Paradigm Debate," in Steve Smith, Ken Booth, and Marysia Zalewski, eds. *International Theory Positivism and Beyond* (Cambridge: Cambridge University Press):149–185

Walker, R.B.J. (1987), "Realism, Change, and International Political Theory," *International Studies Quarterly*, 31, 1:65–86

(1988), *One World, Many Worlds: Struggles for a Just World Peace* (Boulder: Lynne Rienner)

(1993), *Inside/Outside: International Relations as Political Theory* (Cambridge: Cambridge University Press)

Wallace, Jennifer (2000), "Ease in Rediscovery of Irish Roots," *The Australian*, January 12:39

Wallerstein, Immanuel (1974a), *The Modern World System I* (New York: Academic Press)

(1974b), "The Rise and Future Demise of the World Capitalist System: Concepts for Comparative Analysis," *Comparative Studies in Society and History*, 16:387–415

(1991), *Geopolitics and Geoculture: Essays on the Changing World-System* (Cambridge: Cambridge University Press)

Waltz, Kenneth (1959), *Man, the State, and War: A Theoretical Analysis* (New York: Columbia University Press)

(1970), "The Myth of National Interdependence," in Charles Kindleberger, ed., *The International Corporation* (Cambridge, MA: MIT Press):205–223

(1979), *Theory of International Politics* (Reading, MA: Addison-Wesley)

Waltzer, Michael (1970), *Obligations* (Cambridge, MA: Harvard University Press)

Ward, K. ed., (1990), *Women Workers and Global Restructuring* (Ithaca: ILR Press)

Watson, Peggy (2000), "Re-Thinking Transition: Globalism, Gender and Class," *International Feminist Journal of Politics*, 2, 2:185–213

Watson, Peter (1992), *From Manet to Manhattan: The Rise of the Modern Art Market* (London: Random House)

Weber, Cynthia (1999), "IR: The Resurrection or New Frontiers of Incorporation," *European Journal of International Relations*, 5, 4:435–450

Weedon, Chris (1999), *Feminism, Theory and the Politics of Difference* (Oxford: Basil Blackwell)

Weldes, Jutta (1999), "Going Cultural: *Star Trek*, State Action, and Popular Culture," *Millennium: Journal of International Studies*, 28, 1:117–134

Wendt Alexander (1987), "The Agent-Structure Problem in International Relations Theory," *International Organization*, 41, 2:391–425

(1992), "Anarchy is What States Make of It: The Social Construction of Power Politics," *International Organization*, 46, 2:391–425

(1995), "Constructing International Politics," *International Security*, 20, 1:71–81

(1999), *Social Theory of International Politics* (Cambridge: Cambridge University Press)

Wendt, Alexander and Raymond Duvall (1989) "Institutions and International Order," in Ernst-Otto Czempiel and James Rosenau, eds., *Global Changes and Theoretical Challenges: Approaches to World Politics of the 1990s* (Lexington: Lexington Books):51–73

Westermann, Mariet (1996), *A Wordly Art: The Dutch Republic 1585-1718* (New York: Harry N. Abrams)

White, Mark (1996), *The Cuban Missile Crisis* (Basingstoke: Macmillan)

Whitworth, Sandra (1994), *Feminism and International Relations: Towards a Political Economy of Gender in Interstate and Non-governmental Institutions* (London: Macmillan)

Wight, Martin, Hedley Bull, and Carsten Holbraad (1978), *Power Politics* (New York: Holmes & Meier)

Winterson, Jeanette (1987), *The Passion* (London: Penguin Books)

 (1995), *Art Objects: An Essay on Ecstasy and Effrontery* (London: Jonathon Cape)

Wittig, Monique (1989), "The Straight Mind," *Feminist Issues*, 1, 1:103–111

Women's Studies International Forum (1996), special issue on "Links across Difference: Gender, Ethnicity, and Nationalism"

Wylie, Philip (1941), *Generation of Vipers* (New York: Rinehart)

Young, Oran (1988), *International Cooperation: Building Regimes for Natural Resources and the Environment* (Ithaca: Cornell University Press)

Yuval-Davis, Nira (1993), "Gender and Nation," *Ethnic and Racial Studies*, 16, 4:623–632

Zalewski, Marysia (1995), "Well, What is the Feminist Perspective on Bosnia?" *International Affairs*, 71, 1:339–356

Zalewski, Marysia and Jane Parpart, eds., (1998) *The "Man" Question in International Relations* (Boulder: Westview Press)

Zimbabwe Women's Bureau (1981), *We Carry a Heavy Load* (Harare: Zimbabwe Women's Bureau)

 (1992), *We Carry a Heavy Load, Part II* (Harare: Zimbabwe Women's Bureau)

Zizek, S. (1989), *The Sublime Object of Ideology* (London: Verso)

Zook, Kristal Bent (1990), "What Does that Yellow Bitch Know About Being Black Anyway?" in Gloria Anzaldúa, ed., *Making Face, Making Soul: Haciendo Caras: Creative and Critical Perspectives by Women of Color* (San Francisco: Aunt Lute):86–87

Index

CAMBRIDGE STUDIES IN INTERNATIONAL RELATIONS